KT-434-965

Warwickshire College

* 0 0 5 1 0 3 2 6 *

Weed Control Handbook

Volume II

Weed Control Handbook

Volume II · Recommendations
including plant growth regulators

Issued by the
British Crop Protection
Council
and edited by
J. D. Fryer MA

*Director, Agricultural Research Council, Weed Research Organization;
Chairman, Recommendations Committee (Weeds)
of the British Crop Protection Council*

and R. J. Makepeace BSc

*Herbicides Liaison Officer, Agricultural Chemicals Approval Scheme,
Ministry of Agriculture, Fisheries and Food*

Editorial Assistant
J. H. Fearon

Agricultural Research Council, Weed Research Organization

Eighth edition
A Companion to Volume I, Sixth Edition

Blackwell Scientific Publications
OXFORD LONDON EDINBURGH MELBOURNE

Blackwell Scientific Publications,
Osney Mead, Oxford OX2 0EL
8 John Street, London WC1N 2ES
9 Forrest Road Edinburgh EH1 2QH
PO Box 9, North Balwyn, Victoria, Australia

First published 1958
Second edition 1960
Third edition 1963
Fourth edition 1965
Fifth edition 1968
Sixth edition 1970
Seventh edition 1972
Eighth edition 1978

British Library
Cataloguing in Publication Data

British Crop Protection Council
Weed control handbook.
Vol. 2: Recommendations including plant growth
regulators.—8th ed.
1. Weed control—Great Britain
I. Title   II. Fryer, John Denny   III. Makepeace,
Richard John
632'.58'0941   SB 613.G7

ISBN 0-632-00219-0

Printed by The Whitefriars Press Ltd, London and Tonbridge

Contents

Editorial and introductory notes

The *Weed Control Handbook* consists of two volumes. *Volume I* provides basic information and principles about weeds, weed control techniques and plant growth regulators, with special emphasis on chemical methods. *Volume II* consists of recommendations for the use of herbicides and plant growth regulators. The two volumes are designed to be complementary and should be read in conjunction with one another. Whilst every attempt has been made to provide sufficient information in Volume II to ensure satisfactory results the reader is advised to consult Volume I before a recommendation is put into practice, as well as the literature of the herbicide supplier.

The information provided in this edition covers the use of herbicides in Great Britain and Northern Ireland. They have been compiled by the Recommendations Committee (Weeds) of the British Crop Protection Council guided by an advisory group within this committee. Each chapter has been written by a team of specialists drawn from official organizations, industry and universities, headed by a leading expert in the topic of the chapter. Altogether the experience and knowledge of some sixty-six contributors, representing the forefront of expertise available in Britain on the use of herbicides and plant regulators, have been brought together to produce the information contained in this new edition. The text has been completely revised and much of it re-written. Many new recommendations have been added. The chapter on plant growth regulators continues the activities of the British Crop Protection Council in which the regulation of plant growth by synthetic chemicals is accepted within the field of crop protection science and technology.

With increasing costs of publication and the enormous demand on the time of contributors, it will no longer be feasible to publish another edition of the *Weed Control Handbook* in its present form. It is anticipated that the 8th edition will be replaced by a number of specialist crop-based publications.

The information and recommendations

When using Volume II it is important to distinguish between the recommendations and information paragraphs. Each recommendation has been cleared for safety to humans, domestic animals and wild life under the Pesticides Safety Precautions Scheme of the Ministry of Agriculture, Fisheries and Food. In addition the recommendations are approved by the Agricultural Chemicals Approval Scheme unless stated otherwise. These recommendations are printed in italics and followed by explanatory notes giving information on such matters as possible risks to following crops from soil residues, taint in crops for processing, varietal differences in response to the treatment etc. Paragraphs preceded by [**For information**] describe new treatments which show some promise and a few older treatments that have been superseded. Such treatments may not have been cleared by the Pesticides Safety Scheme or been fully tested for safety to the crop and for efficacy. They should not be used without first consulting the supplier, unless a firm recommendation has been made on the product label.

The information and recommendations are valid for crops grown in Great Britain. They have been examined by specialists in Scotland and Northern Ireland. Only where local conditions are considered to have modified required treatment is mention made of separate regional recommendations. Overseas readers should interpret all recommendations with caution.

Metrication

The metric system has been used throughout this edition in recognition of the trend towards metrication in the UK and elsewhere. The figures given in this volume have been obtained by conversion of the current Imperial units into their metric equivalents. This has been done with only a minor attempt to 'round-off' the figures thereby facilitating the re-conversion into Imperial units when required. Where manufacturers have published metric recommendations these have been used. A conversion table is provided in the Appendix.

Paragraph numbering

Following on from the system first introduced in the sixth edition, paragraph numbers have now been used throughout. This it is hoped will increase the speed with which information can be found in the book. The page numbers have been replaced by paragraph numbers and the tables and figures take the appropriate paragraph number indicating their position in the text. Distinction is made between text and table references in the index.

Nomenclature

For the nomenclature of chemicals BSI-approved common chemical names are used, as published in BS 1831. In the absence of a BSI-approved name, names approved by the Weed Science Society of America have been adopted. Recommendations for use are given in terms of active ingredient per unit area. Crops are referred to by their common names but weeds are given their botanical name followed by their common names where possible. The authority for the botanical name is the *Flora of the British Isles,* 2nd ed. 1962 by Clapham, Tutin and Warburg (Cambridge University Press) and the authority for the common name is *English Names of Wild Flowers,* 1974 by Dony, Rob and Perring (Butterworths).

Acknowledgments

The editors, on behalf of the British Crop Protection Council, would like to record their grateful appreciation of the tremendous amount of private time voluntarily given by the members of the Recommendations Committee (Weeds) and the members of the chapter sub-committees in the preparation of this book. We hope that it will be of great assistance to workers in the UK and overseas and, moreover, that it will be regarded as a testimony to the enthusiasm and dedication of those engaged in developing more efficient methods for the control of weeds.

Finally, we wish to thank the publishers, Messrs Blackwell Scientific Publications, Oxford, for their co-operation.

J. D. FRYER
R. J. MAKEPEACE
Editors

Every effort has been made to ensure that the recommendations and statements made in this handbook are correct but the British Crop Protection Council cannot accept responsibility for any loss, damage, or other accident arising from carrying out the methods advocated in the Handbook.

Contributors to the handbook
Volume II, Eighth edition

Members of the British Crop Protection Council
Recommendations Committee (Weeds)

J. D. Fryer*	(Chairman)
R. J. Makepeace*	(Secretary)
J. H. Fearon	(Assistant Secretary)
M. J. Allen	Shell Chemicals UK Ltd
P. J. Attwood	Agricultural Development and Advisory Service
R. M. Brown	Forestry Commission
A. D. Courtney	Ministry of Agriculture for Northern Ireland
J. G. Davidson	ARC Weed Research Organization
G. W. Cussans	ARC Weed Research Organization
J. G. Elliott	ARC Weed Research Organization
D. S. C. Erskine	The Edinburgh and East of Scotland College of Agriculture
A. W. Evans	National Institute of Agricultural Botany
S. A. Evans	Agricultural Development and Advisory Service
R. J. Haggar	ARC Weed Research Organization
J. Holroyd	ARC Weed Research Organization
J. E. Y. Hardcastle	ARC Weed Research Organization
K. Holly*	ARC Weed Research Organization
P. J. Jones	Agricultural Development and Advisory Service
M. G. O'Keeffe	Monsanto Ltd, Agricultural Division
D. Montgomery	Borax Consolidated Ltd
R. K. Pfeiffer*	Fisons Ltd, Agrochemical Division
D. Pycraft	Royal Horticultural Society
H. A. Roberts*	National Vegetable Research Station
T. O. Robson	ARC Weed Research Organization
G. R. Sagar	University College of North Wales
J. P. Shildrick	Sports Turf Research Institute
J. A. Silk	Plant Protection Ltd
G. Stell	Ministry of Agriculture, Fisheries and Food, Plant Pathology Laboratory
T. H. Thomas	National Vegetable Research Station
A. Walker	National Vegetable Research Station
M. Way	Monks Wood Research Station

* Member of the Planning Group of the Recommendations Committee (Weeds).

Contributors to the handbook

The Chapter Manager is the first name in the list of contributors for each chapter

Chapter 1   Cereals
P.J. Attwood	Agricultural Development and Advisory Service
R.W.E. Ball	The Boots Co. Ltd
C.J. Edwards	Fisons Ltd, Agrochemical Division
J.D. Forrest	Bayer UK Ltd, Agrochem Division
R.J. Makepeace	Agricultural Development and Advisory Service
T.G. Marks	Ciba-Geigy (UK) Ltd, Agrochemical Division
M.G. O'Keeffe	Monsanto Ltd, Agricultural Division
F.R. Stovell	Shell Chemicals UK Ltd
D.R. Tottman	ARC Weed Research Organization

Chapter 2   Annual crops other than cereals
M.G. O'Keeffe	Monsanto Ltd, Agricultural Division
P.D.W. Birch	37 Holmewood Ave, Cuffley, Herts
W.E. Bray	Norfolk Agricultural Research Station
A.G. Jones	Agricultural Development and Advisory Service
J.M. King	Processors and Growers Research Organization
R. Orpin	Farm Protection Ltd
J.B. Palmer	J.W. Chafer Ltd
J.M. Proctor	Agricultural Development and Advisory Service
H.A. Roberts	National Vegetable Research Institute

Chapter 3   Perennial, flower and glasshouse crops
J.G. Davison	ARC Weed Research Organization
A.R. Carter	Agricultural Development and Advisory Service
E. Gunn	Advisory Department, East Kent Packers Ltd
H.M. Hughes	Agricultural Development and Advisory Service
A.G. Jones	Agricultural Development and Advisory Service
H.M. Lawson	Scottish Horticultural Research Institute
P.D. Scott	Plant Protection Division, ICI Ltd
C.D. Walker	Agricultural Development and Advisory Service

Chapter 4   Crops grown for seed
A.W. Evans	National Institute of Agricultural Botany
W.E. Bray	Norfolk Agricultural Research Station
E.G. Budd	National Institute of Agricultural Botany

W.G. Gwynne   Agricultural Development and Advisory Service
P.C. Longden   Brooms Barn Experimental Station
H. Mead   Agricultural Development and Advisory Service

Chapter 5   Grassland and herbage legumes
R.J. Haggar   ARC Weed Research Organization
A.D. Courtney   Ministry of Agriculture for Northern Ireland
R.M. Deakin   Agricultural Development and Advisory Service
G.B. Lush   The Boots Co. Ltd
C.I. Mantle   Trumpington Farm Company
J. Page   Plant Protection Division, ICI Ltd
D. Soper   May and Baker Ltd

Chapter 6   Sports turf and lawns
J.P. Shildrick   Sports Turf Research Institute
D.G. Gooding   Synchemicals Ltd
C.J. Head   Chipman Ltd
G.B. Lush   The Boots Co. Ltd
R.L. Morris   Fisons Ltd, Agrochemical Division
R.W. Palin   Suttons Seeds Ltd
D. Soper   May and Baker Ltd
J. Stubbs   Plant Protection Division, ICI Ltd

Chapter 7   Control of herbaceous vegetation
J.M. Way   Institute of Terrestrial Ecology
C.J. Head   Chipman Ltd
V.F. Woodham   Burts and Harvey Ltd

Chapter 8   Forestry and scrub control
M.J. Allen   Shell Chemicals UK Ltd
J.R. Lang-Brown   Oliver and Lang-Brown, Bruton
G.J. Mayhead   Forestry Commission
W.J. McCavish   Forestry Commission

Chapter 9   Total weed control
R.J. Makepeace   Agricultural Development and Advisory Service
D. Hodkinson   Monsato Ltd, Agricultural Division
D. Montgomery*   Borax Consolidated Ltd

Chapter 10   Aquatic weeds
T.O. Robson   ARC Weed Research Organization
P.R.F. Barrett   ARC Weed Research Organization
M.C. Fowler   ARC Weed Research Organization
M. de Lara   Applied Horticulture Ltd
D.H. Spencer-Jones   Duphar-Midox Ltd
F.R. Stovell   Shell Chemicals UK Ltd

Chapter 11   Garden weed control
D. Pycraft   Royal Horticultural Society
R.J. Makepeace ·   Agricultural Development and Advisory Service
D.M. Moore   Agricultural Development and Advisory Service

Chapter 12   Individual weeds
G.W. Cussans   ARC Weed Research Organization
R.J. Chancellor   ARC Weed Research Organization
J.G. Davison   ARC Weed Research Organization
C.J. Head   Chipman Ltd
R.J. Makepeace   Agricultural Development and Advisory Service
R. Morris   Fisons Ltd, Agrochemical Division
R. Pink*   May and Baker Ltd
B.J. Wilson   ARC Weed Research Organization

Chapter 13   Plant growth regulators
T.H. Thomas   National Vegetable Research Station
J.J.B. Caldicott   Cyanamid of Great Britain Ltd
J.W. Dicks   University of Leeds
J.E. Jackson   Agricultural Development and Advisory Service

Chapter 14   Acts and regulations affecting herbicide use
P.J. Jones   Agricultural Development and Advisory Service
J.A.R. Bates   Agricultural Development and Advisory Service
M.J. Woodman   Institute of Terrestrial Ecology

---

* The deaths of D. Montgomery and R. Pink are recorded with deep sorrow.

List of tables

List of figures

Chapter 1
Recommendations for the control of annual weeds in cereal crops

Contents

Introduction

1.001 This chapter aims to provide practical recommendations for the control of annual broad-leaved and grass weeds in cereals. The control of perennial weeds, especially grasses, is dealt with elsewhere (Chapter 12). It is assumed that the annual weeds present have been correctly identified, and that the need to control them is justified (Vol. I).

Within each section recommendations are listed alphabetically using the common chemical name of the major constituent, or the one which determines the chief characteristic of a mixture.

Cereal growth stages and correct spray timing

1.002 The tolerance of cereals to most herbicide treatments varies with the stage of development of the cereal at the time of treatment. Accurate determination of growth stage is therefore essential before applying a post-emergence herbicide. Cereal growth stages are described in this volume in accordance with the scale devised by Zadoks, Chang and Konzak (Appendix VI). This is a decimal scale based on the developmental stages of the cereal plant. These are;

    0   Germination
    1   Seedling growth
    2   Tillering
    3   Stem elongation

4   Booting
5   Inflorescence emergence
6   Anthesis
7   Milk development
8   Dough development
9   Ripening

Great care has been taken to use correct terminology that will be understood internationally and for this reason some of the terms used may not exactly agree with those used hitherto in the United Kingdom. It is of utmost importance therefore that the stage-of-growth description is given prominence and that the stage number be used in parentheses. In this edition it will be prefixed with the letter ZCK.

1.003   Main stem leaf number is a good guide to the development of spring cereal varieties. Only those leaves arising from the main shoot should be counted and tillers or their leaves should not be included (1.005, 1.006). A leaf should be counted as a full leaf only when the tip of the succeeding leaf can be seen.

1.004   In winter cereals a good guide to spray timing is given by the length of the leaf sheaths. When the main stem leaf sheaths form 'pseudo-stems' approximately 50 mm tall (ZCK 30) the crop has reached what has hitherto been described as the 'fully-tillered' stage.

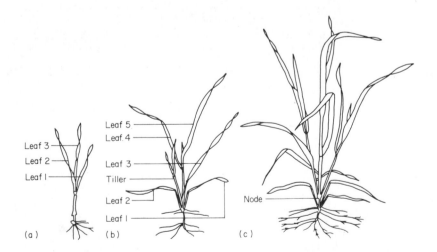

Fig. 1.005   Stages of growth of cereals: (a) two- to three-leaf stage; (b) 5-leaf stage; (c) start of 'shooting' or 'jointing'. All drawings × ¼. (Drawn by R. J. Chancellor from paintings of wheat plants by E. C. Large.)

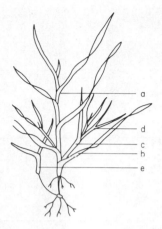

Fig. 1.006 Diagrammatic representation of the way tillers arise in young cereal plants. (a) main shoot; (b) first leaf on main shoot; (c) primary tiller arising in axil of first leaf of main shoot; (d) secondary tiller arising in axil of first leaf of primary tiller; (e) tiller arising from seed.

1.007 To avoid ear deformities such as those illustrated in 1.009 the phenoxy acetic acid herbicides (MCPA at full dose and 2,4-D) should not be applied before the five- to six-leaf stage of spring wheat or barley or before leaf sheath extension of winter crops.

1.008 Spraying after the first nodes are detectable on the stem involves a risk of producing sterile florets with shrivelled grain, a condition known as 'rat-tailing' (1.009). The thin ears are often quickly colonized by secondary infections of black sooty moulds.

1.009   Deformities of cereal ears caused by growth-regulator herbicides

1. Abnormal ears of wheat showing opposite and supernumerary spikelets.
2. Normal ears of wheat
3. 'Rat-tailed' wheat ears caused by benzoic acid herbicides
4. Abnormal ears of barley showing whorled spikelets and extended internodes of the rachis.
5. Abnormal ears of barley showing a tubular leaf trapping the emerging ear and kinking the stem, and aborted spikelets.

Control of annual broad-leaved weeds

1.010   **Benazolin** *at 0·19 kg/ac with up to 0·3 kg/ha* **MCPA** *and up to 1·7 kg/ha*
2,4-DB *in winter and spring wheat, barley and oats from pseudo-stem
erection (ZCK 30) in winter cereals and 5-leaf stage (ZCK 15) in spring
cereals, until jointing (ZCK 31).*

Benazolin mixtures are of particular use in cereals undersown with
clover (with or without grass) where *Stellaria media* (Common
Chickweed) and *Galium aparine* (Cleavers) are present. The small
amount of MCPA is added to control *Sinapsis arvensis* (Charlock) and
Raphnus raphinistrum (Wild Radish). 2,4-DB assists the control of
Polygonum spp.

For the additional control of *Galeopsis tetrahit* (Common Hempnettle)
MCPB at 1·10 kg/ha with further MCPA at 0·16 kg/ha should be added.
Benazolin is also used in mixture with dicamba (1.026).

1.011   **Bentazone** *at up to 1·3 kg/ha with* **dichlorprop** *at up to 1·7 kg/ha on
winter and spring wheat, barley and oats from tillering (ZCK 30) or 1-
leaf stage (ZCK 11) until the 2-node stage (ZCK 32).*

Bentazone alone can be used on cereals at all stages of growth. It is
particularly effective on *Chrysanthemum segetum* (Corn Marigold),
Tripleurospermum maritimum ssp. *inodorum* (Scentless Mayweed) and
Matricaria recutita (Scented Mayweed). In addition it will control
Galium aparine (Cleavers) and *Stellaria media* (Common Chickweed).

The addition of a small amount of dichlorprop to improve the control
of *Polygonum* spp. restricts the time of using the mixture but at the rate
used it has been found to be safe up to the 2-node stage (ZCK 32).

1.012   **Bromoxynil** *ester at up to 0·28 kg/ha with esters of* **MCPA** *on spring
cereals at all stages up to the start of jointing (ZCK 31).*

Bromoxynil is a contact herbicide. MCPA is added to control
Galeopsis spp. (Hempnettle).

1.013   **Bromoxynil** *and* **ioxynil** *esters at up to 0·84 kg/ha total on spring cereals
at all stages, also if undersown with clover, lucerne or grasses before
emergence of clover or lucerne.*

Bromoxynil and ioxynil are contact herbicides. Ioxynil gives good
control *Tripleurospermum, Matricaria* and *Anthemis* spp. (Mayweeds).
Bromoxynil is effective on these weeds and in addition *Polygonum* spp.
The mixture at the high dose is of particular value against
Chrysanthemum segetum (Corn Marigold).

Although primarily intended for use in spring cereals the mixture can
be used as an emergency treatment in winter cereals which have passed
the safe stage for applying growth regulator herbicides.

The lack of residual activity makes this mixture suitable for use in
cereals prior to undersowing with another crop.

1.014   **Bromoxynil** *ester at up to 0·21 kg/ha with* **ioxynil** *ester at up to 0·28 kg/ha plus* **dichlorprop** *ester with or without* **MCPA** *ester on spring cereals at all stages up to the start of jointing (ZCK 31).*

1.015   **Bromoxynil** *and* **ioxynil** *salts at up to 0·63 kg/ha total plus salts of* **dichlorprop** *and* **MCPA** *in winter cereals from 5-leaf stage (ZCK 15) to pseudo-stem erection (ZCK 30) and in spring cereals at all stages up to the start of jointing (ZCK 31).*

Bromoxynil and ioxynil are contact herbicides and the stage of application is restricted by the presence of growth regulator herbicides. Their addition gives control of shoots of perennial broad-leaved weed species. Dichlorprop also increases the effect on *Stellaria media* (Common Chickweed) and *Galium aparine* (Cleavers). The addition of MCPA gives better control of *Galeopsis* spp. (Hempnettle).

Ester formulations give more reliable weed control than salts under adverse climatic conditions.

1.016   **Bromofenoxim** *with* **terbuthylazine** *at 0·34 + 0·21 kg/ha or 0·51 + 0·32 kg/ha in spring sown crops of wheat, barley or oats from 1 leaf (ZCK 11) onwards.*

This mixture is a mainly contact herbicide and should be applied before the crop covers the inter-row space, but not later than the three- to four-leaf stage of the weeds.

At the lower dose the mixture controls a wide range of broad-leaved weeds, including *Tripleurospermum maritimum* ssp. *inodorum* (Scentless Mayweed), *Stellaria media* (Common Chickweed) and *Polygonum* spp.

When used at the higher dose the mixture will also control *Chrysanthemum segetum* (Corn Marigold).

1.017   **Cyanazine** *at up to 0·37 kg/ha with* **MCPA** *at up to 1·7 kg/ha on winter sown wheat, barley and oats from pseudo-stem erection (ZCK 30) until jointing; on spring sown wheat and barley from 4-leaf stage (ZCK 14) until jointing (ZCK 31) and on spring oats from 2-leaf stage (ZCK 12) until jointing (ZCK 31).*

Cyanazine has contact and soil activity but in the cereal crop the combination with MCPA has increased activity and the mixture is equally effective on soils with high or low organic content. Mecoprop at up to 1·3 kg/ha should be added to improve the control of *Galium aparine* (Cleavers) in winter sown crops. Cyanazine should not be used on cereals undersown with legumes.

1.018   **2,4-D-amine** *at 1·1 kg/ha on winter barley and oats and 1·4 kg/ha on winter wheat and rye from pseudo-stem erection (ZCK 30) to start of jointing (ZCK 31), 1·1 kg/ha on spring wheat and barley from 5 leaves (ZCK 15) to jointing (ZCK 31).*

2,4-D-amine is not recommended on spring oats.

1.019   **2,4-D-ester** *at 0·7 kg/ha on winter wheat and rye, 0·56 kg/ha on winter barley and 0·28 kg/ha on winter oats from pseudo-stem erection (ZCK 30) to start of jointing (ZCK 31), at 0·56 kg/ha on spring barley and wheat from 5 leaves (ZCK 15) to start of jointing (ZCK 31).*

2,4-D-ester is not recommended on spring oats.

1.020   **2,4-DB-salt** *at up to 2·2 kg/ha on winter wheat, barley and oats from pseudo-stem erection (ZCK 30) to start of jointing (ZCK 31), on spring oats and barley from the 1-leaf stage (ZCK 11) until the start of jointing (ZCK 31) and on spring wheat from the 3-leaf stage (ZCK 13) until the start of jointing (ZCK 31).*

2,4-DB is used primarily for weed control in forage legumes and undersown cereals. In cereals it is usually only used in mixtures with benazolin, 2,4-D or MCPA (1.010. 1.018 and 1.042).

On spring oats the recommended dose is restricted to 1·7 kg/ha.

Mixtures containing 2,4-D are not recommended on oats nor on spring wheat or barley before the 5-leaf stage (ZCK 15). Not more than 1·7 kg/ha of 2,4-DB is recommended on spring oats.

Mixtures of 2,4-DB with MCPA or MCPA and benazolin can be applied to cereals at the same stages as for 2,4-DB alone.

1.021   **2,4-DB** *salt at 2·2 kg/ha plus* **MCPA** *on winter wheat, barley and oats from pseudo-stem erection (ZCK 30) to start of jointing (ZCK 31), on spring wheat from 3-leaves (ZCK 13) until start of jointing (ZCK 31), and barley from 1-leaf (ZCK 11) until start of jointing (ZCK 31).*

Spring oats may be sprayed from 1-leaf stage (ZCK 11) until the start of jointing (ZCK 31) at up to 1·7 kg/ha.

1.022   **2,4-DB** *salt at 2·2 kg/ha plus* **2,4-D** *and* **MCPA** *on winter wheat, barley and oats from pseudo-stem erection (ZCK 30) to start of jointing (ZCK 31), on spring wheat and spring barley from 3-leaves (ZCK 13) until start of jointing (ZCK 31).*

1.023   **2,4-DB** *salt at 2·2 kg/ha alone or plus* **MCPA** *with or without* **2,4-D** *on cereals undersown with mixtures containing red or white clover, provided most of the clover seedlings have reached the first trifoliate leaf stage and the cereal the growth stage specified above.*

The mixtures are unsafe on lucerne and sainfoin but are safe on clover provided the ratio of total phenoxyacetic acid (MCPA and/or 2,4-D) to 2,4-DB does not exceed 1:6. The mixture with MCPA is unsafe on established clover. Small amounts of MCPA are added to improve the control of *Sinapsis arvensis* (Charlock) and *Raphanus raphinistrum* (Wild Radish) the addition of a little 2,4-D may give some control of *Polygonum* spp.

1.024   **2,4-DB** *at 2·2 kg/ha on cereals undersown with lucerne, provided most of* *the lucerne seedlings have reached the first trifoliate leaf stage and the cereal the growth stage specified above* (1.020).

1.025   **Dicamba** *at up to 0·1 kg/ha with* **dichlorprop, mecoprop** *or* **MCPA** *on winter cereals from pseudo-stem erection (ZCK 30) until just before the start of jointing (ZCK 31) and on spring cereals from 5-leaf stage (ZCK 15) until just before the start of jointing (ZCK 31).*

Due to the sensitivity of flower primordia it is important that dicamba is not applied to cereals at or after the onset of jointing (ZCK 31).

Dicamba is particularly useful against all common *Polygonum* spp., *Stellaria media* (Common Chickweed) and *Spergula arvensis* (Corn Spurrey).

1.026   **Dicamba** *at up to 0·14 kg/ha on winter cereals and 0·1 kg/ha on spring cereals; with* **benazolin** *at up to 0·21 kg/ha mixed with* **MCPA** *or* **dichlorprop.**

Dicamba and benazolin can be applied to winter cereals at any stage up to the start of jointing (ZCK 31). Spring cereals can be sprayed from the 1-leaf stage (ZCK 11) to start of jointing (ZCK 31). It is important that they are not sprayed beyond the start of jointing (ZCK 31) due to susceptibility of flower primordia. The earliest recommended stage of growth for spraying these mixtures is generally limited by the presence of MCPA.

Dicamba with benazolin is of particular use against *Tripleurospermum maritimum* ssp. *inodorum* (Scentless Mayweed), *Anthemis cotula* (Stinking Chamomile) *Matricaria recutita* (Chamomile/Scented Mayweed) and also *Matricaria matricarioides* (Pineappleweed).

1.027   **Dichlorprop-salt** *at 2·8 kg/ha on winter wheat, barley and oats from pseudo-stem erection (ZCK 30) to start of jointing (ZCK 31) and on spring wheat, barley and oats from 1-leaf (ZCK 11) to start of jointing (ZCK 31).*

A minimum volume of 225 l/ha should be used where foliage is dense or where *Galium aparine* (Cleavers) is to be controlled.

The use of dichlorprop on rye is not recommended.

1.028   **Dichlorprop-salt** *at up to 2·2 kg/ha plus* **2,4-D** *at up to 0·56 kg/ha on winter cereals from pseudo-stem erection (ZCK 30) to start of jointing (ZCK 31) and on spring wheat and spring barley from 5-leaves (ZCK 15) to start of jointing (ZCK 31).*

Dichlorprop is not recommended on rye and the mixture with 2,4-D is not recommended on spring oats. The addition of 2,4-D improves the control of *Polygonum* spp. and *Tripleurospermum maritimum* ssp. *inodorum* (Scentless Mayweed).

1.029   **Dichlorprop-salt** *at up to 2·8 kg/ha plus* **MCPA** *at up to 1·7 kg/ha on* *winter cereals from pseudo-stem erection (ZCK 30) to start of jointing (ZCK 31) and on spring cereals from 3-leaf stage (ZCK 13) to start of jointing (ZCK 31).*

Dichlorprop is not recommended on rye. MCPA can be applied to spring wheat and barley from the 3-leaf stage provided no more than 0·84 kg/ha is used but may cause deformities if used before the 5-leaf stage (ZCK 15). 1·7 kg/ha can be used on spring oats from the 1-leaf stage (ZCK 11). The addition of MCPA gives control of *Galeopsis* spp. (Hempnettle).

1.030   **Dichlorprop-salt** *plus* **mecoprop-salt** *at up to 3·6 kg/ha (total) on winter cereals from pseudo-stem erection (ZCK 30) to start of jointing (ZCK 31) and on spring cereals from 1-leaf stage (ZCK 11) to start of jointing (ZCK 31).*

Dichlorprop is not recommended on rye.

1.031   **Dinoseb-ammonium** *at 1·7 kg/ha on winter wheat, barley and rye or at 1·1 kg/ha on winter oats and at 1·7 kg/ha on spring wheat and barley or at 1·1 kg/ha on spring oats.*

1.032   **Dinoseb-amine** *at 2·2 kg/ha on winter wheat, barley and rye or at 1·4 kg/ha on winter oats and at 2·2 kg/ha on spring wheat and barley or at 1·7 kg/ha on spring oats.*

1.033   **Dinoseb-acetate** *at 2·8 kg/ha on winter cereals and spring cereals from 3 leaves (ZCK 13) to the start of jointing (ZCK 31).*

1.034   Winter wheat can be sprayed in the winter or spring, winter barley, oats and rye only in the spring, and spring cereals from 3 leaves (ZCK 13) to the start of jointing (ZCK 31).

1.035   Dinoseb-ammonium and dinoseb-amine can be applied to cereals undersown with clover or lucerne (and grass) either within a period of 3 days after drilling grass and clover or lucerne, or after the clover or lucerne has developed 2 trifoliate leaves, provided in each case that the cereal is at a suitable stage of growth. Dinoseb-acetate should be sprayed on undersown cereals only when the clover has 1–3 trifoliate leaves, and the crop is between the 3-leaf stage (ZCK 13) and the start of jointing (ZCK 31). Application volume should be at least 450 l/ha.

1.036   The dose of dinoseb-ammonium and dinoseb-amine must be adjusted according to the weather conditions. Decrease the dose by 20 per cent for all crops in warm moist weather and increase by 20 per cent (for all crops but oats) in cold dry weather in the spring; in winter reduce by 25 per cent because the risk of frost after spraying, although aiding weed control, may lead to the treatment causing serious damage to the wheat. Normally a period of 4 h freedom from rain following spraying is sufficient to give satisfactory weed control, but the period following spraying in the winter needs to be considerably longer. Weeds should be young when sprayed. The control of certain weeds, especially *Chrysanthemum segetum* (Corn Marigold) and perennial weeds, is improved by the addition of 0·21 to 0·28 kg/ha of MCPA to dinoseb. The herbicide manufacturer should be consulted before mixing products.

1.037   Dinoseb-amine and dinoseb-acetate can also be applied to mixtures of cereals and peas, beans and vetches provided that the dose is not higher than recommended for the most susceptible cereal in the mixture or for peas (2.292, 2.293) or for vetches.

1.038   The maximum dose for vetches and beans is 1·7 kg/ha. The treatment will scorch the crop and, as there is some risk of check to beans or vetches, mixtures containing these should normally be sprayed only if the legume has not grown too rapidly and is protected to some extent from the spray by the cereals and the weed.

1.039   **Ioxynil** *salt at up to 0·63 kg/ha plus either* **dichlorprop** *and* **MCPA** *or plus* **mecoprop** *in winter cereals from pseudo-stem erection (ZCK 30) until start of jointing (ZCK 31) and in spring cereals at all stages up to the start of jointing (ZCK 31).*

Ioxynil is a contact herbicide with a good effect on *Tripleurospermum, Matricaria* and *Anthemis* spp. (Mayweeds). The addition of growth regulator herbicides adds effect on shoots of perennial weeds. Both dichlorprop and mecoprop increase the effect on *Stellaria media* (Common Chickweed) and *Galium aparine* (Cleavers). The addition of MCPA gives better control of *Galeopsis* spp. (Hempnettle).

1.040   **Ioxynil** *and* **linuron** *at up to 0·42 kg/ha of each as equal mixed components on spring wheat and barley from 2 leaves (ZCK 12) until the start of tillering (ZCK 31).*

This type of mixture incorporates a soil-acting component and therefore gives residual weed control on weeds germinating after application. The contact effect will control most broad-leaved weeds including *Chrysanthemum segetum* (Corn Marigold) and *Polygonum aviculare* (Knotgrass). Some weeds germinating after application especially *Fumaria officinalis* (Common Fumitory) will not be fully controlled.

1.041   **Linuron** *at 0·7 to 0·84 kg/ha according to soil type in medium volume on spring cereals applied pre-emergence of the crop and weed.*

Linuron is not effective on heavy or organic soils. Some crop damage can occur on sand soils but on other soils there is little effect on the crop from treatment. This treatment is specially recommended for the control of *Chrysanthemum segetum* (Corn Marigold).

1.042 **MCPA-salt** *at up to 1·7 kg/ha on winter cereals from pseudo-stem erection (ZCK 30) to start of jointing (ZCK 31), on spring cereals from 1-leaf (ZCK 11) to start of jointing (ZCK 31).*

A maximum of 0·84 kg/ha is recommended on spring wheat and barley at the 3- to 5-leaf stage.

Sodium and potassium salt formulations are preferable to amine salts on oats before the 3-leaf stage. Spraying of spring oats with products containing surface active agents should be restricted to the 5-leaf stage (ZCK 15) to the start of jointing (ZCK 31).

MCPA is a common constituent of herbicide mixtures used in cereals.

1.043 **MCPB-salt** *at 2·2 kg/ha on undersown winter wheat, barley and oats at any time in the spring to the start of jointing (ZCK 31), on undersown spring cereals from 1-leaf (ZCK 11) to start of jointing (ZCK 31).*

1.044 **MCPB-salt** *at 2·2 kg/ha on cereals undersown with grass and clover mixtures containing red or white clover or sainfoin, provided most of the clovers have reached the trifoliate leaf stage.*

1.045 **MCPB-salt** *at 2·2 kg/ha on mixtures of cereals and peas when the peas have developed between 3 and 6 leaves.*

MCPB is principally used for weed control in legumes in cereals, usually with MCPA as above or benazolin (1.010).

The mixture with MCPA is not recommended on cereals with peas or sainfoin.

The mixture can be safely applied to cereals undersown with grass and clover mixtures containing red and white clover provided the ratio of MCPA to MCPB does not exceed 1:6.

The small amount of MCPA is added to improve the control of *Sinapis arvensis* (Charlock) and *Raphanus raphanistrum* (Wild Radish).

1.046 **MCPB** *ester at 0·33 kg/ha with* **mecoprop, dichlorprop** *and* **barban** *on certain varieties of spring barley from 2-leaf stage (ZCK 12) to the start of jointing (ZCK 31).*

The mixture is principally for controlling *Avena* spp. (Wild-oats) but will control many broad-leaved weeds notably *Polygonum* spp. and *Stellaria media* (Common Chickweed) in addition to *Avena* spp. (Wild-oats). Within the limits of crop stage the mixture is normally applied when the majority of wild-oats are at 1 to 2·5 leaves.

1.047 **Mecoprop salt** *at up to 2·8 kg/ha on winter wheat, barley and oats from pseudo-stem erection (ZCK 30) to start of jointing (ZCK 31) and on* *spring wheat, barley and oats from 1-leaf (ZCK 11) to start of jointing (ZCK 31).*

Winter wheat, barley and oats can be sprayed with 2·2 kg/ha before end of year to control *Stellaria media* (Common Chickweed). Treatment of late autumn-sown crops can be delayed to end of January. Beyond this time winter cereals become susceptible to mecoprop until the fully-tillered stage (ZCK 31) is reached.

A minimum volume of 225 l/ha should be used where foliage is dense or where *Galium aparine* (Cleavers) is to be controlled.

1.048 **Mecoprop** *with* **2,4-D** *at up to 2·8 kg/ha total ae on winter wheat, barley and oats from pseudo-stem erection (ZCK 30) to start of jointing (ZCK 31) and on spring wheat and barley from 5-leaves (ZCK 15) to start of jointing (ZCK 31).*

Mecoprop is not recommended on Rye. It is used particularly for the control of *Galium aparine* (Cleavers) and *Stellaria media* (Common Chickweed).

1.049 **Mecoprop** *at up to 2·8 kg/ha with* **fenoprop** *at up to 0·28 kg/ha on winter wheat, barley and oats from pseudo-stem erection (ZCK 30) to start of jointing (ZCK 31) and on spring wheat, barley and oats from 3-leaves (ZCK 13) to start of jointing (ZCK 31).*

Fenoprop is added to mecoprop to enhance the control of *Tripleurospermum maritimum* ssp. *inodorum* (Scentless Mayweed). 2,4-D is added to improve the control of *Polygonum* spp. To be effective on these weeds a full dose of the mixture must be sprayed when they are small and crop competition will assist subsequently.

1.050 **Methabenzthiazuron** *at 1·6 kg/ha pre-emergence (ZCK 06) of winter barley and oats and on winter wheat within 6 weeks of drilling (but before the end of November).*

Methabenzthiazuron controls *Poa annua* (Annual Meadow-grass) and *Poa trivialis* (Rough Meadow-grass) in addition to a range of broad-leaved weeds including *Stellaria media* (Common Chickweed) and *Matricaria* spp. (Mayweed).

It is not recommended on soils with more than 5 per cent organic matter or on crops to be undersown with clover mixtures.

Application should be made to a firm level seedbed, preferably rolled, in a minimum of 200 l/ha water when frost is not expected.

Manufacturers' literature should be consulted for successfully treated spring barley and oat varieties. All varieties of winter sown wheat, barley, oats and rye may be treated.

1.051 **2,3,6-TBA** *at 0·14 kg/ha plus* **dicamba** *at 0·1 kg/ha with* **mecoprop** *and* **MCPA** *on winter cereals from pseudo-stem erection (ZCK 30) until just* *before the start of jointing (ZCK 31) and spring cereals from 5-leaves (ZCK 15) until just before the start of jointing (ZCK 31).*

Due to the sensitivity of flower primordia it is important that neither 2,3,6-TBA nor dicamba are applied to cereals at or after the onset of jointing.

Straw from crops treated with herbicides containing 2,3,6-TBA may contain residues which, if introduced into glasshouses as either straw, manure or compost could damage some crops. Straw from 2,3,6-TBA treated crops should not be used in any form for crops grown under glass.

2,3,6-TBA gives control of *Galium aparine* (Cleavers), *Stellaria media* (Common Chickweed), *Tripleurospermum maritimum* ssp. *inodorum* (Scentless Mayweed), *Anthemis cotula* (Stinking Chamomile) and *Matricaria recutita* (Scented Mayweed).

1.052 **Terbutryne** *at 1·5 kg/ha on winter sown wheat and barley applied pre-emergence of the crop (ZCK 06).*

At the above dose terbutryne will control *Poa annua* (Annual Meadow-grass) and several broad-leaved weeds including *Stellaria media* (Common Chickweed) and *Tripleurospermum* and *Matricaria* spp. (Mayweeds). It should not be used on crops drilled after mid-November and is less satisfactory in mild, wet winters.

1.053 **(For information.)** 3,6-dichloropicolinic acid at 0.064–0.08 kg/ha with mecoprop at 2.1–2.8 kg/ha has given good control of annual broad-leaved weeds in winter cereals when applied from the 1 leaf stage (ZCK 11) to the beginning of jointing (ZCK 31).

It shows particular promise for the control of *Matricaria recutita* (Scented Mayweed), *Tripleurospermum maritimum* spp. *inodorum* (Scentless Mayweed), *Chrysanthemum segetum (Corn Marigold)* and *Polygonum* spp.

Straw from crops treated with 3,6-dichloropicotinic acid should not be used for composting or in glasshouses.

The susceptibility of annual broad-leaved weeds to herbicides used in cereals

1.054 Para. 1.054 indicates the response of annual weeds to individual herbicides at the two doses shown at the head of each column and which represent the upper and lower doses generally used in cereals. Mixtures of these herbicides are also available in commercial products. The table also refers to six herbicides which are not available individually but only in commercial mixtures with other herbicides shown in the table. These are benazolin, bentazone. cyanazine, dicamba, linuron and 2,3,6-TBA. The table indicates the weeds on which they are particularly useful and which they will effectively control if the other constituent of the mixture will not.

Fenoprop, not included in the table, is available in commercial mixtures with some growth-regulator herbicides which are the main constituents of the mixture. The table does not allow the user to predict accurately the effect of mixtures of herbicides. There are no known cases of a mixture giving poorer weed control than that obtained by its individual components and as a practical guide the potential value of a mixture can be surmised by combining the list of weeds susceptible to each constituent, except where the dose of a constituent is appreciably lower than the lower dose shown in the table. It is not possible to select the more appropriate mixture for weeds which are not classified as S or MS to the herbicides. The final choice must be made on the claims of the manufacturers and be confined to products approved under the Agricultural Chemicals Approval Scheme.

Four categories have been selected to indicate the degree of weed control obtained at either of two stages of growth of the weed by one or two stated doses of herbicide applied. The categories of susceptibility are defined as follows:

S—**Susceptible**	Complete or almost complete kill.
MS—**Moderately susceptible**	Effective suppression with or without mortality.
MR—**Moderately resistant**	Temporary suppression, the duration and degree depending on the vigour of the crop and the weather.
R—**Resistant**	No useful effect.

The stages of growth are defined as follows:

Sd—*Seedling stage*	Cotyledon up to 2 or 3 leaves.
Yp—*Young plant stage*	3 to 4 leaves to early flower-bud stage.

If there is insufficient information a single tentative category is given, indicating the general response to a dose within the given range.

Perennial weeds are dealt with individually in Chapter 12.

15

1.054 The susceptibility of annual broad-leaved weeds to herbicides used in cereals

Additives legend:
B = benazolin-salt
Be = bentazone
C = cyanazine
D = dicamba-salt
L = linuron
T = 2,3,6-TBA-salt

Weed		MCPA-salt 0.84 1.7	2,4-D-amine‡ 0.7 1.4	MCPB-salt 1.7 2.2	2,4-DB-salt 1.7 2.2	Mecoprop-salt 2.2 2.8	Dichlorprop-salt 2.2 2.80	Dinoseb	Bromoxynil plus Ioxynil	Additives
1. Aethusa cynapium (Fool's Parsley)	Sd	R	R	R	R	R	R	—	S	Be
	Yp								MS	
2. Amsinkia intermedia (Tar Weed)	Sd	—	—	R	R	—	—	—	S	
	Yp								MS	
3. Anagallis arvensis (Scarlet Pimpernel)	Sd	MR MS	MR MS	MR MS	MR MS	MR	MR	S	S	Be
	Yp	R MR	R MR	R R	R R	—	—	S	S	
4. Anthemis arvensis (Corn Chamomile)	Sd	R MR	R MR	R	R	MR MR	MR MR	S	S	B+D, T
	Yp	R R	R R			R MR	R MR	MR	MS	
5. Anthemis cotula (Stinking Chamomile)	Sd	R	R	R	R	R	R	MS	S	B+D, T
	Yp							MR	MS	
6. Aphanes arvensis (Parsley-piert)	Sd	R	R	R	R	R	R	S	MS	—
	Yp							MS	R	
7. Atriplex patula (Common Orache)	Sd	MS MS	MS	MR MS	MS MS	MS S	MS S	S	MS	—
	Yp	MR MS	MR MS	R MR	R MR	MR MS	MR MS	MR	R	
8. Brassica nigra (Black Mustard)	Sd	S*	S*	S	MS	S S	S S	S	S	
	Yp	S†	S†	MS	MR MS	S S	S S	S	S	

* S to 0.17 kg. † S to 0.35 kg.
‡ Weed response is similar with half the amount of 2,4-D-ester.

Additives legend:

B = benazolin-salt
Be = bentazone
C = cyanazine
D = dicamba-salt
L = linuron
T = 2,3,6-TBA-salt

Weed		MCPA-salt 0·84	1·68	2,4-D-amine‡ 0·70	1·40	MCPB-salt 1·68	2·24	2,4-DB-salt 1·68	2·24	Meco-prop-salt 2·24	2·80	Dichlor-prop-salt 2·24	2·80	Dinoseb	Bromoxynil plus Ioxynil	Additives
9. *Brassica rapa* ssp. *campestris* (Wild Turnip)	Sd	MS	S	MS	S	MR	MR	MS	S	MS	S	MS	S	S	—	—
	Yp	MR	MS	MR	MS	R	R	MR	MS	MR	MS	MR	MS	S		
10. *Capsella bursa-pastoris* (Shepherd's-purse)	Sd	S	S	S	S	S	S	S	S	S	S	S	S	S	S	L
	Yp	S	MS	S	MS	MR	MS	MR	MS	S	MS	S	MS	S	S	
11. *Cerastium holosteoides* (Common Mouse-ear)	Sd	MR	MS	MR	MS	R		R		MS		MS		MR	MR	B+D, T, B
	Yp	R	MR	R	MR									R	S	
12. *Chenopodium album* (Fat-hen)	Sd	S		S		S	S	S	S	S	S	S		S	S	B+D Be, L
	Yp	S		S		MS	S	MS	S	S	S	S		MS	S	
13. *Chrysanthemum segetum* (Corn Marigold)	Sd	R		R		R		R		R		R		MS	S	Be, L
	Yp													MR	MR	
14. *Descurainia sophia* (Flixweed)	Sd	—		—		MS		MS		—		—		—	S	—
	Yp					MR		MR							S	
15. *Echium vulgare* (Viper's-bugloss)	Sd	MR		MR		R		R		MR		MR		MS	MS	C
	Yp													MR	R	
16. *Erysimum cheiranthoides* (Treacle Mustard)	Sd	S	S	S	S	MS	S	MS	S	S	S	S	S	S	—	—
	Yp	S	S	S	S	MR	MS	MR	MS	S	MS	S	MS	S		

Chemical and dose in kg acid equivalent per ha

16

Values are given as Sd (seedling) / Yp (young plant). The final column lists other herbicides (letter codes).

Weed	1	2	3	4	5	6	7	8	9	Other herbicides
17. *Euphorbia helioscopia* (Sun Spurge)	MR	MR	—	—	—	—	—	MS / R	MR / R	—
18. *Fumaria officinalis* (Common Fumitory)	MS / MR	MR / R	MR / R	MS / R	MS / MR	MS / MR	S / MS	S / MS	S / MS	B + D, Be
19. *Galeopsis tetrahit* (Common Hemp-nettle)	MS / MR	MR / R	MR / R	MS / MR	MS / MR	MS / MR	S / S	S / S	MS / MR	—
20. *Galium aparine* (Cleavers)	R	R	R / MR	R	R	R	R / MR	S / MS	MR / R	B, Be, D, L, T
21. *Geranium molle* (Dove's-foot Crane's-bill)	MR	MR	MR	MS	MS	MS	MS	MS	MS / R	—
22. *Lamium* spp. (Dead-nettles)	R	R / MR	R	R	R	R	R	—	MS / MR	L
23. *Lapsana communis* (Nipplewort)	R	R	R	R / MR	R / MR	R / MR	S	S	S / MS	D, T
24. *Lithospermum arvense* (Field Gromwell)	MR / R	MR / R	MS / MR	R / MR	R / MR	R / MR	R / MR	S / MS	MS / MR	Br
25. *Lycopsis arvensis* (Bugloss)	MR	MR	MR	—	MR	MR	MR	MS	S / S	C, T
26. *Matricaria matricarioides* (Pineappleweed)	R	R	R	R	R	R	R	S / MR	S / S	Be, B + D, T, L
27. *Matricaria recutita* (Scented Mayweed)	R	R	R	R	R	R	R	S / MR	S / S	Be, B + D, T, L
28. *Myosotis arvensis* (Field Forget-me-not)	MS	MS	MR	R	R	R	R	S / MS	S / MS	Be

* S to 0·17 kg. † S to 0·35 kg.

‡ Weed response is similar with half the amount of 2,4-D-ester.

17

Weed		MCPA-salt 0·84	1·68	2,4-D-amine‡ 0·70	1·40	MCPB-salt 1·68	2·24	2,4-DB-salt 1·68	2·24	Meco-prop-salt 2·24	2·80	Dichlor-prop-salt 2·24	2·80	Dinoseb	Bromoxynil plus Ioxynil	Additives
29. *Papaver rhoeas* (Common Poppy)	Sd	MS	S	MS	S	MS	S	MS	S	MR	MS	R	MS	S	S	Be, L
	Yp	MR	MS	MR	MS	R	MR	R	MR	R	MR	R	MR	MR	S	B+D
30. *Polygonum aviculare* (Knotgrass)	Sd	R	MR	MR	MS	MR	MR	MS	MS	R	MR	R	MS-MR	S	S	D, T, L
	Yp	R	R	R	MR	R	R	R	MR	R	R	R	MR	MR	S	
31. *Polygonum convolvulus* (Black-bindweed)	Sd	R	MR	MR	MS	R	MR	MR	MS	R	MR	MS	S	S	S	D, L, T
	Yp	R	R	R	MR	R	R	R	MR	R	MR	MR	S	MR	S	
32. *Polygonum lapathifolium* (Pale Persicaria)	Sd	R	MR	MR	MS	R	MR	MS	S	MR	MR	S	MS	S	S	D, L, T
	Yp	R	R	R	MR	R	R	MR	MS	R	R	MS	S	R	S	
33. *Polygonum persicaria* (Redshank)	Sd	R	MR	MR	MS	R	MR	MS	S	MR	MR	MS	S	S	S	D, L, T
	Yp	R	R	R	MR	R	R	MR	MS	R	R	MS	S	MR	S	
34. *Ranunculus arvensis* (Corn Buttercup)	Sd	S	S	S	S	S	S	S	S	S	S	S	S	S	MS	—
	Yp	S	MS	S	MS	S	MS	S	S	MS	MS	MR	MS	R	MR	
35. *Raphanus raphanistrum* (Wild Radish)	Sd	S	S	S	S	R		R		S	S	S	S	S	S	Be
	Yp	S	MS	S	MS					S	S	S	S	MS	S	
36. *Scandix pecten-veneris* (Shepherd's-needle)	Sd	MR	MS	MR	MS	R		R		—		MR		S	—	—
	Yp	R	R	R	R					—		MR		MR		

Chemical and dose in kg acid equivalent per ha

Additives:
B = benazolin-salt
Be = bentazone
C = cyanazine
D = dicamba-salt
L = linuron
T = 2,3,6-TBA-salt

#	Weed	Stage	1	2	3	4	5	6	7	8	9	10	11	12	13	
37	*Senecio vulgaris* (Groundsel)	Sd	MR	MR	MR	R	MR	MS	R	MR	MS	MR	MS	S	S	Be, L
		Yp	R	R	R	R	MR	R	R	MR	MR	MR	MR	MR	S	
38	*Sinapis alba* (White Mustard)	Sd	S	S	S	MS	MR	MS	MS	S	S	S	S	S	MS	—
		Yp	S	S	S	MR	R	MR	MR	MS	MS	S	S	S	MR	
39	*Sinapis arvensis* (Charlock)	Sd	S*	S*	S*	MS	MS	S	S	MR	S	S	S	S	S	Be, L
		Yp	S†	S‡	S†	MS	MR	MS	MS	MS	MS	S	MS	S	S	
40	*Solanum nigrum* (Black Nightshade)	Sd	MR	MR	MR	R	R	MR	MR	MR	MR	MR	MR	R	MS	—
		Yp	R	R	R	R	R	R	R	R	MR	R	R		MR	
41	*Sonchus asper* (Prickly Sowthistle)	Sd	MS	MS	MS	MS	S	MS	MS	MS	MS	MR		S	S	—
		Yp	MR	MS	MR	MS	MS	MR	MS	MS	MR			MR	MS	
42	*Sonchus oleraceus* (Smooth Sowthistle)	Sd	MS	MS	MS	MS	S	MS	MR	MR	MS	MR	MR	S	S	Be, D. L
		Yp	MR	MS	MR	MS	MS	MR	MR	R	MR	R	R	MR	S	
43	*Spergula arvensis* (Corn Spurrey)	Sd	MR	MR	MR	R	R	R	R	MR	MR	MS	MS	MS	MR	Be, B+D, D, L, T
		Yp	R	R	R	R	R			R	R	MR	MR	MR	R	
44	*Stellaria media* (Common Chickweed)	Sd	MR	MR	MR	R	R	R	R	MS	MS	S	S	S	S	Be, B, C, D, L, T
		Yp	R	R	R	R	R			MR	MR	S	S	S	MS	
45	*Thlaspi arvense* (Field Penny-cress)	Sd	S	S	S	S	S	S	S	S	S	S	MS	S	S	—
		Yp	S	S	S	MS	MS	MS	MS	MS	MS	MS	MS	S	S	
46	*Tripleurospermum maritimum* ssp. *inodorum* (Scentless Mayweed)	Sd	R	R	R	R	R		R	MR	MS	R	R MS-MR	S	S	Be, B, D T
		Yp	R	R	R	R	R			R	MR	R	R	MR	S	
47	*Urtica urens* (Small Nettle)	Sd	MS	S	S	S	MS	MS	MS	S	S	S	S	S	S	B+D, Be, L
		Yp	MR	MS	MS	MS	MR	MS	MS	MS	S	S	S	MR	S	

* S to 0.17 kg.   † S to 0.35 kg.

‡ Weed response is similar with half the amount of 2,4-D-ester.

19

Weed		MCPA-salt 0.85 1.68	2,4-D-amine‡ 0.70 1.40	MCPB-salt 1.68 2.24	2,4-DB-salt 1.68 2.24	Meco-prop-salt 2.24 2.80	Dichlor-prop-salt 2.24 2.80	Dinoseb	Bromoxynil plus Ioxynil	Additives B = benazolin-salt Be = bentazone C = cyanazine D = dicamba-salt L = linuron T = 2,3,6-TBA-salt
48. *Veronica agrestis* (Green Field speedwell)	Sd	MR MR	MR MR	R	R	R	—	S	S	—
	Yp	R R	R R					MR	MS	
49. *Veronica arvensis* (Wall Speedwell)	Sd	MR	MR	—	—	MR	— MR	S	S	—
	Yp						— —	MR	MS	
50. *Veronica hederifolia* (Ivy-leaved Speedwell)	Sd	MR MS	MR MS	R	R	MR	—	S	S	L
	Yp	R R	R R					MS	MR	
51. *Veronica persica* (Common Field-speedwell)	Sd	MR MR	MR MS	MR MS	R MR	MR MS	MR	S	S	C, L
	Yp	R R	R R	R R	R R	R MR	—	MR	MS	
52. *Vicia hirsuta* (Hairy Tare)	Sd	S	S	—	—	MS	—	MR	—	—
	Yp									
53. *Viola* spp. (Field Pansy)	Sd	R	R MR	R	R	MR MR	MR MR	MS	MS	—
	Yp	R R	R R			R R	R R	MR	MS	

Chemical and dose in kg acid equivalent per ha

* S to 0.17 kg.   † S to 0.35 kg.
‡ Weed response is similar with half the amount of 2,4-D-ester.

Control of annual grass weeds

1.055   **Barban** *at 0·31–0·35 kg/ha to control* Avena *spp.* (Wild-oats) *from 1 to 2·5 (ZCK 11–12) leaves and to* Alopecurus myosuroides *(Blackgrass) which has at least 2 leaves (ZCK 12) in wheat and barley.*

Winter cereals should not be treated from mid-January to the end of February. Treatments applied from the end of February until early April may cause a temporary check, but recovery is generally complete. Some varieties may respond differently under these circumstances.

Barban can be applied safely to many varieties of spring cereals, but spring wheat Maris Butler and several spring barley varieties including Impala, Maris Badger, Mazurka and Proctor are susceptible and may be severely damaged.

With the exception of the sensitive varieties and conditions above, spring wheat or barley mixed with peas, beans or vetches can be treated with barban, and also cereals may be undersown with clover and grass 3 days after the application of barban. MCPB and barban may be applied together but other herbicides should not be used within 3 days of using barban.

The effect of barban diminishes when wild-oats are beyond the 2·5 leaf stage. Volume of application is critical and should not be more than 225 l water/ha. Timing is made difficult as the emergence of wild-oats is generally uneven.

A more active formulation of barban is now also available for post-emergence wild-oat control. Its use is restricted to those spring barley varieties mentioned above.

1.056   **Barban** *at 0·35 kg/ha with* **MCPB, mecoprop** *and* **dichlorprop** *esters on certain varieties of spring barley only from 2 fully-expanded leaves (ZCK 12) and before the onset of jointing (ZCK 31) when wild oats are between 1 and 2·5 leaves (ZCK 11–12).*

The mixture also controls some broad-leaved weeds (1.046).

1.057   **Benzoylprop-ethyl** *at 1·1 kg/ha in medium volume in winter and spring sown wheat to control* Avena *spp.* (Wild-oats).

Best results are obtained when spraying is delayed until the wild oats have tillered (ZCK 25), provided that the wheeling damage to the crop is acceptable. This also ensures control of later flushes of weed. Benzoylprop-ethyl should not be used within 10 days of applying growth regulator herbicides.

1.058   **Chlorfenprop-methyl** *at 4·8 kg/ha to control* Avena fatua *(Wild-oat) in wheat, barley and some spring oat varieties (also if undersown with grasses and clover).*

Application should be made when wild-oats have between 2 and 3 leaves (ZCK 12–13) but before tillering commences (ZCK 20).

Crops may be treated at any stage of growth. Some varieties of spring barley are susceptible to scorch which can be accentuated by mixing with growth regulator herbicides. Symptoms are normally rapidly outgrown. A transitory scorch of emerged clovers may occur.

Adequate spray cover is essential. The use of fan jets, a volume of 250 l/ha (up to 400 l/ha in dense crops), a minimum pressure of 3 bars, and a forward speed of no more than 5 km/h are recommended. *Avena ludoviciana* (Winter Wild-oat) is not controlled.

Manufacturers' literature should be consulted for varieties of spring oats which may be treated.

1.059   **Chlortoluron** *at 3·6 kg/ha pre-emergence within 7 days of drilling, at 3·1 kg/ha post-emergence before the end of December when the crop has 1–4 leaves (ZCK 11–14), or at 2·7 kg/ha post-emergence in the spring between the 3-leaf and tillering stage (ZCK 13–25) of the crop on certain winter wheat and barley varieties drilled before December to control* Alopercurus myosuroides *(Blackgrass) and* Avena fatua *(Wild-oat).*

Alopecurus myosuroides (Blackgrass) will be controlled up to the 5-leaf stage (ZCK 15), together with other seedling grasses. Most annual broad-leaved weeds are also controlled, but *Galium aparine* (Cleavers) and *Veronica* spp. (Speedwells) are resistant.

Avena fatua (Wild-oat) will be controlled by pre-emergence treatment. Applications made up to the 2-leaf stage (ZCK 12) of the wild-oat are less effective. With very heavy infestations it may be necessary to treat with an approved wild-oat herbicide in the following spring.

Certain cereal varieties are susceptible to Chlortoluron and the manufacturers' literature should be consulted for further information.

1.060   **Difenzoquat** *at 1·0 kg/ha in 225 l/ha on winter and spring barley, most varieties of winter wheat and spring wheat to control* Avena fatua *(Wild-oats) when wild-oats are between 2·5 leaves (ZCK 12) and the end of tillering (ZCK 30).*

The cereal growth stage is not critical but spraying is recommended when the cereals are at the tillering stage (ZCK 21–25). Some transitory yellowing of the crop may occur about one week after spraying, which may be more severe in cold weather.

The use of fan jets is preferred and a pressure of 2–3 bars. The volume is critical due to the need to maintain the concentration of wetter when diluting the current formulations. The use of an anti-foam agent is recommended.

The product should not be mixed with other herbicides.

1.061   **Flamprop isopropyl** *at 0·98 kg/ha in medium volume on winter and spring barley to control* Avena spp. *(Wild-oats).*

Application is recommended between late tillering (ZCK 25) and first-node formation of the crop (ZCK 31) when both the crop and the wild-oats are growing vigorously.

The use of fan jets is preferred and a pressure of 2·8 bars. A volume of 225–450 l/ha is recommended, the higher amount in dense crops.

Flamprop isopropyl must not be sprayed on barley within 10 days of any other herbicide.

1.062 **Flamprop methyl** *at 0·52 kg/ha in medium volume on winter and spring wheat, including undersown crops, from pseudo-stem erection (ZCK 30) to first node detectable (ZCK 31) for the control of* Avena spp. *(Wild-oats).*

The stage of growth of wild-oats is less important than the stage of growth of the crop. Good growing conditions and a vigorous crop are however necessary for good results.

Other herbicides should not be mixed with flamprop methyl or applied to the same crop within 10 days.

1.063 **Isoproturon** *at 2·5 kg/ha pre-emergence within 7 days of drilling or 2·1 kg/ha post-emergence in the spring when the crop has more than 2 leaves (ZCK 12) in medium volume to winter wheat or barley drilled before December.*

Isoproturon may also be applied early post-emergence from the 2 leaf stage (ZCK 12) of the crop up to the end of December at 2·5 kg/ha.

Alopecurus myosuroides (Blackgrass) and other seedling grasses will be controlled by pre- or post-emergence applications up to the early tillering stage of the weeds (ZCK 21). In addition, autumn or early spring applications may give useful control of *Avena fatua* (Wild-oats).

Under wet soil conditions in autumn and winter early spring post-emergence applications are likely to give better weed control than pre-emergence applications. Several annual broad-leaved weeds are also controlled (1.074).

1.064 **Methabenzthiazuron** *at 1·6 kg/ha pre-emergence (ZCK 06) in winter wheat, barley and oats, also post-emergence within 6 weeks of drilling but before the end of November on winter wheat to control* Poa annua *(Annual Meadow-grass) and* Poa trivialis *(Rough Meadow-grass).*

Some broad-leaved weeds are also controlled (1.074). The application should be made on a firm level seedbed, rolled prior to spraying if possible.

The treatment is unsuitable for soils with more than 5 per cent organic matter or when frost is expected.

All varieties of winter wheat, barley, oats or rye may be treated.

1.065 **Methabenzthiazuron** *at 3·2 kg/ha pre-emergence (ZCK 06) in winter wheat, barley and oats, also post-emergence within 6 weeks of drilling but* *before the end of November on winter wheat to control* Alopecurus myosuroides *(Blackgrass).*

Many autumn germinating broad-leaved weeds are also controlled (1.074) together with annual grasses.

Applications after blackgrass has more than 2 leaves (ZCK 12) will be less effective. Other precautions are given above (1.064).

1.066   **Methoprotryne + Simazine**   *at   0·91 + 0·21 kg/ha   post-emergence   in medium volume to winter wheat crops sown after mid-November to suppress* Alopecurus myosuroides *(Blackgrass).*

Applied between mid-February and the end of March, when the crop has at least 4 leaves (ZCK 14), the mixture gives a useful suppression of *Alopecurus myosuroides* (Blackgrass) plants which have not reached the 6-leaf stage (ZCK 16). Several annual broad-leaved weeds are also controlled.

This treatment has given variable results on crops drilled before mid-November, since the blackgrass in such crops is often too far advanced at the time of spraying.

1.067   **Metoxuron** *at up to 4·5 kg/ha post-emergence on winter barley and some varieties of winter wheat from the 2-leaf stage (ZCK 12) until fully tillered (ZCK 25) to control* Alopecurus myosuroides *(Blackgrass) at 1-leaf (ZCK 11) to commencement of tillering (ZCK 21).*

Many annual broad-leaved weeds are also controlled (1.074). Other grasses controlled include *Poa* spp. (Meadow-grasses) and *Lolium* spp. (Rye-grasses) at the seedling stage. *Avena* spp. (Wild-oats) present at the time of spraying are sometimes controlled.

A dose of 4·5 kg/ha is recommended when the blackgrass is in the seedling stage (ZCK 11–13) increasing to 5·6 kg/ha when the blackgrass is between 3 leaves (ZCK 13) and start of tillering (ZCK 21).

On light sandy soils the dose must be restricted to 4·5 kg/ha. The efficiency of the treatment is reduced on soils with high organic matter content, and on all soils under very dry conditions or if continuous periods of frost occur.

Manufacturers' literature should be consulted for the list of tolerant cereals varieties that may be treated.

1.068   **Metoxuron** *at 3·4 kg/ha plus* **simazine** *at 0·21 kg/ha on winter barley and wheat from the 3-leaf stage (ZCK 13) until fully tillered (ZCK 25) for the control of* Alopecurus myosuroides *(Blackgrass).*

Some cereal varieties are sensitive to metoxuron. Blackgrass is controlled up to and including the 5-leaf stage (ZCK 15). This generally coincides with the commencement of tillering. Control will be reduced by continuous periods of frost and by organic soil.

1.069   **Nitrofen** *at 2·1 kg/ha pre-emergence of winter wheat on mineral soils to control* Alopecurus mysuroides *(Blackgrass).*

Poa annua (Annual Meadow-grass) and some broad-leaved weeds are also controlled (1.074).

Applications should be made in medium volume to a reasonably fine seedbed within 7 days after drilling (or within 3 days if wheat germination is likely to be rapid). Nitrofen is not recommended on poorly-drained sites. Under very dry or cloddy conditions high volume (1000 l/ha) should be used.

1.070 **Terbutryne** *at 2·8 kg/ha pre-emergence in medium volume within 7 days after drilling winter wheat and barley drilled before mid-November to control* Alopecurus myosuroides *(Blackgrass).*

Terbutryne remains active in the soil for two to three months and controls successive autumn germinations of weeds. Control of blackgrass is not reliable in crops drilled after mid-November, since a higher proportion of the seedlings will emerge in spring after terbutryne residues have disappeared. It also controls *Poa annua* (Annual Meadow-grass) and several annual broad-leaved weeds (1.074).

1.071 **Tri-allate** *as an emulsifiable concentrate at 1·4–2·2 kg/ha pre-sowing or pre-emergence on winter or spring wheat or barley for the control of germinating* Avena spp. *(Wild-oats) and* Alopecurus myosuroides *(Blackgrass).*

As an emulsifiable concentrate tri-allate must be mixed with the soil immediately after application. It will control both species of wild-oats provided they have not germinated at the time of application.

The mixing of the tri-allate with the soil should ideally distribute it uniformly in the upper 25 mm. This can only be achieved when the soil is in a good workable condition. In heavy and cloddy soils an even distribution is difficult to achieve. Seedbeds should be adequately consolidated before drilling takes place. Farm implements are not designed basically to mix herbicides with the soil. Suitable distribution can be attained by straight-toothed or spring-tined harrows set to penetrate to a depth of 75–100 mm, if the tine-tracks are not more than 100 mm apart. Two passes with the implement are made at a wide angle to one another.

The cereal seeds should be drilled at about 40 mm deep so that they are separated from the tri-allate by a layer of untreated soil. Farm drills usually place seeds at variable depths and some thinning of the crop stand, particularly wheat, may occur.

1.072 Winter barley or wheat can be treated with 1·7 kg/ha tri-allate, spring barley with 1·4–1·7 kg/ha (1·4 kg/ha on light sandy soils) either before (up to 21 days) or after drilling but before the wild-oats germinate.

Spring wheat can be treated with 1·4 kg/ha tri-allate either before (2–21 days) or fairly soon after drilling but before the wild-oats germinate.

Crops should not be undersown with grasses after tri-allate has been used, but mixtures of cereals with peas, beans and vetches can be treated with doses relevant to the particular cereal crop.

On organic soils considerably higher doses of tri-allate will be required. In general pre-drilling treatments are more effective than post-drilling.

1.073   **Tri-allate** *as a granular formulation at 1·7 kg/ha pre-emergence or 2·2 kg/ha post-emergence on winter or spring wheat or barley.*

Winter wheat or barley and spring wheat must be treated post-drilling but spring barley can be treated either pre- or post-drilling, provided the wild-oats have not germinated.

The granular formulation of tri-allate is applied to the soil surface and does not need to be mixed into the soil. The granules must be distributed as evenly as possible and excessively cloddy soils should be rolled before treatment.

Applications made before the wild-oats have emerged are the most effective but good control of wild-oats with up to 2·5 leaves (ZCK 12) can be obtained.

Treatments applied to organic soils are relatively ineffective.

Tri-allate granules are not effective on emerged blackgrass.

1.074 The susceptibility of annual weeds to herbicides applied for the control of annual grass weeds

This table indicates the susceptibility of annual weeds to herbicides applied principally for the control of annual grass weeds. The categories of susceptibility are defined as follows:

S–Susceptible Complete or almost complete kill.   MS–Moderately Susceptible Effective suppression or variable amounts of kill.
MR–Moderately Resistant Variable suppression depending on the weather and vigour of the crop.   R–Resistant No useful effect.

Weed	Chlortoluron 2·7–3·6 kg/ha	Iso-proturon 2·1–2·5 kg/ha	Methoprotryne/simazine 0·91+0·21 kg/ha	Metoxuron 4·5–5·6 kg/ha	Metoxuron/simazine 3·4–0·21 kg/ha	Methabenzthiazuron 1·6–3·2 kg/ha	Nitrofen 2·1 kg/ha	Terbutryne 1·1–2·8 kg/ha
1. *Aragallis arvensis* (Scarlet Pimpernel)	—	—	—	—	—	S	—	—
2. *Aphanes arvensis* (Parsley-piert)	—	—	—	—	—	S	—	—
3. *Capsella bursa-pastoris* (Shepherd's-purse)	—	S	—	—	—	—	R	—
4. *Cerastium holosteoides* (Common Mouse-ear)	—	—	—	—	—	S	—	—
5. *Chenopodium album* (Fat-hen)	S*	S	—	S	S	—	S	—
6. *Fumaria officinalis* (Common Fumitory)	—	—	—	—	MS	—	MR	—
7. *Galium aparine* (Cleavers)	R	R	R	MS	MS	R	R	R
8. *Lamium purpureum* (Red Dead-nettle)	—	—	—	—	—	MS	—	—
9. *Lolium* spp. (Rye-grasses)	S*	S*	—	S*	—	—	—	—
10. *Matricaria recutita* (Scented Mayweed)	S*	S	S	S	S	S	R	S
11. *Myosotis arvensis* (Field Forget-me-not)	—	S	—	—	—	—	—	—

27

Weed	Chlortoluron 2·7–3·6 kg/ha	Iso-proturon 2·1–2·5 kg/ha	Methoprotryne/simazine 0·91+0·21 kg/ha	Metoxuron 4·5–5·6 kg/ha	Metoxuron/simazine 3·4–0·21 kg/ha	Methabenzthiazuron 1·6–3·2 kg/ha	Nitrofen 2·1 kg/ha	Terbutryne 1·1–2·8 kg/ha
12. *Papaver rhoeas* (Common Poppy)	S*	S	S*	S	S	S	MR	S
13. *Poa annua* (Annual Meadow-grass)	S*	S	S	S*	S	S	S	S
14. *Poa trivialis* (Rough Meadow-grass)	S*	S	MS	S*	S	S	—	R
15. *Polygonum aviculare* (Knotgrass)	—	MR	MR	—	R	—	S	—
16. *Polygonum convolvulus* (Black-bindweed)	S*	MS	MS	S	S	—	S	R
17. *Polygonum persicaria* (Redshank)	—	MS	MS	S	S	—	S	R
18. *Raphanus raphanistrum* (Wild Radish)	—	—	—	—	—	—	R	—
19. *Senecio vulgaris* (Groundsel)	—	S	—	MS	—	—	R	—
20. *Sinapis arvensis* (Charlock)	S*	S	—	S	S	S	R	S
21. *Stellaria media* (Common Chickweed)	S*	S	S	S	S	S	R	S
22. *Tripleurospermum maritimum* ssp. *inodorum* (Scentless Mayweed)	S*	S	S	S	S	S	R	S
23. *Veronica* spp. (Speedwells)	R	R	MR	S	R	S	MS	R
24. *Viola arvensis* (Field Pansy)	—	—	—	—	—	R	—	—

* Susceptible post-emergence at the seedling stage only.

28

Recommendations for weed control in undersown cereals

Cereals undersown with grasses

1.075 All the materials recommended for the control of annual broad-leaved weeds in cereals can theoretically be safely applied to crops undersown with pure grass mixtures. The exceptions are methabenzthiazuron and terbutryne when recommended for the control of annual weeds rather than *Alopecurus myosuroides* (Blackgrass) (1.050, 1.052). Not all the materials are however recommended for this use by manufacturers and some herbicides in this category, notably dichlorprop, are not recommended at all for this use. For guidance on the correct stages at which to treat the grass safely see Chapter 4.

Cereals undersown with grasses and clovers, lucerne or sainfoin

1.076 The following herbicides are recommended for this use:

Barban (1.055)
Benazolin (1.010)*
Benzoylprop-ethyl (1.057)
Bromoxynil + ioxynil (1.015)
Chlorfenprop-methyl (1.058)
2,4, DB (1.020)
Dinoseb (1.035)
Flamprop methyl—clover only (1.062)
MCPB (1.044)*

* These herbicides or any of the above which also contain 2,3-D or MCPA should not be used on cereals undersown with lucerne.

Cereals undersown with peas, beans or vetches

1.077 The following herbicides are recommended for this use:

Barban (1.055)
Bromoxynil + ioxynil (1.015)
Dinoseb (1.035)
MCPB—peas only (1.044)
Tri-allate (1.073)

Chapter 2
Recommendations for the use of herbicides in annual crops other than cereals

General information

2.001 Before using any of the recommendations given in this chapter on crops likely to be used for manufacturing purposes the processing company should be consulted for information about any restriction on the use of herbicides which might cause taint.

CONTACT HERBICIDE TREATMENTS COMMON TO MOST CROPS

The following herbicides may be used as contact treatments, pre-sowing or pre-emergence, or as directed sprays for inter-row weed control.

2.002 **Dimexan** *9·3 kg/ha in medium to high volume to control emerged seedling weeds and young annual weeds.*

Dimexan is volatile and does not persist in soil, but the vapour phase may penetrate into the surface layer of the soil immediately after application and kill some shallow-germinating weeds which have not yet emerged. It should be applied when the weed foliage is dry. Crops should be drilled at least 6 mm deep if dimexan is to be used after sowing. Use nozzles recommended for 110 litres/ha at 4 bars.

2.003 **Paraquat** *formulated with a wetter at 0·3–1·1 kg/ha in medium volume to control emerged seedling weeds and young annual weeds.*

The higher dose should be used when weeds have more than 3 true leaves. On light sandy soils and highly organic soils the spray should not be applied later than 3 days before the crop is expected to emerge.

Galium aparine (Cleavers) is relatively tolerant and best results are obtained when 2 whorls of true leaves are present; the control of *Fumaria officinalis* (Common Fumitory) and *Polygonum aviculare* (Knotgrass) is also better when the first true leaves have formed than it is at the cotyledon stage. For effective control of *Avena* spp. (Wild-oats) at least 2 leaves should be present at the time of spraying.

2.004 **Sulphuric acid** *as a 12 per cent v/v solution at 1120 litres/ha (i.e.*

130 litres of 100 per cent acid in 990 litres water or 170 litres B.O.V. in
950 litres water) to control emerged seedling weeds and most emerged
annual broad-leaved weeds.

A wetting agent of the sulphonated oil type should be added at the rate
of 0·56 litres/1000 litres spray. When diluting sulphuric acid always add
it slowly to the water and never vice versa. Special acid-resistant spraying
equipment is needed. *Poa annua* (Annual Meadow-grass) is not usually
killed by this treatment.

Recommendations

BEAN (broad and field)

PRE-SOWING TREATMENTS

2.005 **TCA** *17·0 kg/ha in medium or high volume to suppress* Agropyron
repens *(Common Couch) and control* Avena fatua *(Wild-oat).*

An interval of 6 weeks should be allowed between application of the
chemical and drilling. The herbicide should be incorporated into the soil.
Control of Wild-oats is variable and depends on the depth of germination
and rainfall.

2.006 **Tri-allate** *1·7 kg/ha in medium to high volume applied and immediately*
incorporated into the soil to control germinating Avena *spp. (Wild-oats)*
and Alopecurus myosuroides *(Black-grass).*

This treatment may also be applied and incorporated soon after drilling
but this tends to be less efficient than pre-sowing treatments, particularly
against *Alopecurus myosuroides* (Black-grass).

2.007 **Trifluralin** *1·1 kg/ha in medium volume incorporated into the seedbed to*
control annual weeds (2.122) on mineral soils. For incorporation details
see 2.103.

Beans should be planted at least 75 mm deep.

Trifluralin is not recommended for sands or soils containing 10 per cent
or more of organic matter. Only recommended crops should be drilled or
planted within 5 months of treatment.

Soil should be thoroughly cultivated to a depth of at least 150 mm
before drilling or planting succeeding crops other than recommended
crops. After an autumn application of trifluralin cereal and grass crops
should not be sown until the following autumn.

PRE-EMERGENCE CONTACT TREATMENTS

2.008 *Contact pre-emergence sprays to kill seedling weeds that emerge before*
*the crops (*2.002).

Where beans are sown in the winter or early spring little weed growth can be expected before emergence of the crop.

PRE-EMERGENCE RESIDUAL TREATMENTS

2.009   **Carbetamide** *2·1 kg/ha in medium volume for pre-emergence control of mainly grass weeds including* Alopecurus myosuroides *(Black-grass),* Poa *spp. (Meadow-grasses),* Avena *spp. (Wild-oats) and self-sown cereals.*

To be used on winter-sown field beans only. Broadcast beans may be slightly checked at emergence.

2.010   **Chlorpropham** *1·1 kg/ha plus* **fenuron** *0·3 kg/ha or* **diuron** *0·2 to 0·4 kg/ha in medium volume within a few days of sowing and before crop emergence to control annual broad-leaved weeds in spring-sown broad and field beans.*

To prevent crop damage the beans must be sown 50–80 mm deep. Heavy rain, following application on very sandy or gravelly soils or silts deficient in clay or organic matter, may cause distortion or stunting of bean plants leading to yield losses.

2.011   **Propyzamide** *0·84 kg/ha in medium volume for the control of annual weeds.*

Apply within 7 days of drilling to winter-sown beans between 1st October and 31st December.

2.012   **Simazine** *0·56 kg/ha on very light soils, 0·84 kg/ha on light soils or up to 1·1 kg/ha on medium and heavy soils in medium to high volume to control annual weeds.*

The seedbed should have a fine even tilth and the crop should be sown so that there is at least 75 mm of settled soil over the seed. On autumn-sown beans the spray can be applied up to the end of February, but the control of emerged weeds may not be complete from a post-emergence application; emerged bean plants will be unharmed. With spring-sown beans the spray should be applied before the weeds emerge. Where heavy rain follows spraying or the beans are planted too shallow, blackening of the leaf margins may occur and some plants may succumb to the treatment. At least 7 months should elapse after spraying and the soil should be inverted by ploughing before cereals or other susceptible crops are sown.

2.013   **Tri-allate** *1·7 kg/ha in medium to high volume or as granules applied and immediately incorporated into the soil to control germinating* Avena *spp. (Wild-oats) and* Alopecurus myosuroides *(Black-grass).*

Winter-sown field beans may be treated immediately after drilling and harrowing the crop or after the seed has been ploughed in.

If *Avena* spp. (Wild-oats) have emerged and for post-emergence application of granules to winter-sown field beans the higher dose of 2·0 kg/ha should be used.

Spring-sown crops of field beans may only be treated before or immediately after drilling and the granules should be incorporated with straight-toothed harrows.

2.014 **Trietazine** *0·66–1·1 kg/ha plus* **simazine** *0·09–0·16 kg/ha according to soil types as for peas* (2.291) *for the control of annual weeds.*

Field beans should be treated pre-emergence and the seeds should be covered by at least 30 mm of soil.

POST-EMERGENCE TREATMENTS

2.015 **Barban** *0·53–0·70 kg/ha to control* Avena *spp. (Wild-oats) at the 1- to 2·5-leaf stage in both autumn- and spring-sown crops.*

Control will depend on crop competition and crops sown in narrow rows will generally provide the best smother to achieve a good control particularly at the lower dose. Where an autumn spray is possible it will also control *Alopecurus myosuroides* (Black-grass) in winter beans. No varietal susceptibility of field or broad beans to barban has been observed. A pre-emergence application of simazine does not appear to make beans any more sensitive to barban, but enables the use of the lower dose for *Avena* spp. (Wild-oat) control.

2.016 **Benzoylprop-ethyl** *1·1 kg/ha in medium volume to control* Avena *spp. (Wild-oats).*

Apply when field beans are growing vigorously in May or early June and wild oats are fully tillered.

2.017 **Carbetamide** *2·1 kg/ha in medium volume for control of mainly grass weeds including* Alopecurus myosuroides *(Black-grass),* Poa *spp. (Meadow-grasses),* Avena *spp. (Wild-oats) and self-sown cereals.*

Do not treat after the end of February or after the crop begins to grow away in spring. May be used after pre-emergence use of simazine. Some broad-leaved weeds are also controlled.

2.018 **Dinoseb-acetate** *2·8 kg/ha in medium volume to control seedling broad-leaved weeds.*

The dose should be reduced to 2·1 kg/ha if the land has been previously treated with sodium trichloroacetate. In cool weather or if the weeds have passed the seedling stage a dose of 3·5 kg/ha may be used. The crop may be sprayed from just after emergence up to first flower providing the weeds are at a suitable growth stage. Crops which have been damaged in any way by weather or pests should not be sprayed. There is some evidence that high humidity at the time of spraying can increase crop scorch.

2.019   **Dinoseb-amine** *1·7 kg/ha in high volume as a contact post-emergence spray in winter-sown field beans in early spring when they are about 75 mm high and while growth is still hard, i.e. before rapid growth starts to control broad-leaved weeds.*

PRE-HARVEST DESICCATION

2.020   **Diquat** *0·4—0·6 kg/ha in medium volume on beans to be harvested dry.*
The treatment will not hasten ripening, but is of value to ease harvesting of unevenly ripening or weedy crops. The treatment should not be applied until the majority of the pods are mature.

2.021   **Sulphuric acid** *7 litres/ha undiluted B.O.V.*
Either of these treatments is suitable for desiccating the leaves and succulent stems of field beans and broad beans grown for seed to facilitate harvesting. The pods must be mature when sprayed. Unripe pods will be damaged: the treatments will not hasten ripening.

BEAN (dwarf, dried or navy)

PRE-SOWING TREATMENTS

2.022   **Tri-allate** *1·7 kg/ha in medium to high volume applied and immediately incorporated into the soil to control germinating* Avena *spp. (Wild-oats) and* Alopecurus myosuroides *(Black-grass).*
Details as for dwarf green beans (2.029).

2.023   **Trifluralin** *0·84 kg/ha in medium volume incorporated for residual control of annual weeds.*
The spray can be applied during soil preparation at any time from 14 days before until immediately before planting, but must be mechanically incorporated into the top 50 mm of soil within 30 min after application. For details of incorporation see 2.103. Trifluralin is not recommended on sands or on soils with 10 per cent or more of organic matter.

2.024   [**For information.**] EPTC 4·5 kg/ha applied on the soil in medium volume and immediately incorporated by rotary cultivation or cross-discing has given promising control of annual and perennial grasses. The crop should not be drilled until 2 weeks after treatment.

PRE-EMERGENCE CONTACT TREATMENTS

2.025   *Contact pre-emergence sprays to kill seedling weeds that emerge before the crop (2.000—2.003).*

34

2.026   **Dinoseb-amine** *3·4—4·5 kg/ha or dinoseb in oil 2·5 kg/ha in medium to high volume for contact and some residual control of annual weeds (2.336).*

The seedbed should be left with a fine even tilth and there should be not less than 25 mm of soil above the crop seed after consolidation. The spray can be applied at any time after sowing until about 3 days before crop emergence. By delaying spraying until this time, the effective period of residual weed control is lengthened.

2.027   **Dinoseb-acetate** *up to 2·5 kg/ha plus* **monolinuron** *up to 0·84 kg/ha in medium to high volume for contact and residual control of annual weeds (2.336).*

The dose is varied with soil type, lower doses being used on lighter soils and those with low organic content. On early sown crops application should be made while the weeds are in the seedling stage, not later than 5 days before crop emergence. When the crop is expected to emerge rapidly application should be made immediately after drilling. Very heavy rain after application may result in some crop damage.

2.028   **Bentazone** *1·4 kg/ha in medium volume to control annual broad-leaved weeds (2.353).*

The application should not be made until after the crop has developed 1—2 trifoliate leaves. Some scorch may occur but will be outgrown. Do not apply if the air temperature is above 21°C. Bentazone is normally used following the pre-sowing applications of trifluralin or pre-emergence herbicides, provided the crop is undamaged. Weed control obtained will depend on the combination of the first herbicide with bentazone.

BEAN (dwarf green)

2.029   **Tri-allate** *1·7 kg/ha in medium to high volume applied and immediately incorporated into the soil to control germinating* Avena *spp. (Wild-oats) and* Alopecurus myosuroides *(Black-grass).*

This treatment may also be applied and incorporated soon after drilling but this tends to be less efficient than pre-sowing treatments particularly against *Alopecurus myosuroides* (Black-grass). Incorporation 1.071. Field experience indicates that these treatments will not interfere with other soil-applied herbicides used for broad-leaved weed control.

2.030   **Trifluralin** *0·84 kg/ha in medium volume incorporated into the seedbed to control annual weeds (2.122) on mineral soils. For incorporation details see* 2.103.

Beans should be planted at least 75 mm deep.

A follow up treatment with another herbicide either pre- or post-emergence is recommended where resistant weeds are present.

Trifluralin is not recommended for sands or soils containing 10 per cent or more of organic matter. Only recommended crops should be drilled or planted within 5 months of treatment.

Soil should be thoroughly cultivated to a depth of at least 150 mm before drilling or planting succeeding crops other than those recommended.

2.031   [**For information.**] EPTC 4·5 kg/ha applied to the soil in medium volume and immediately incorporated by rotary cultivation or cross-discing has given promising control of annual and perennial grasses. The crop should not be drilled until 3 weeks after treatment.

PRE-EMERGENCE CONTACT TREATMENTS

2.032   *Contact pre-emergence sprays to kill seedling weeds that emerge before the crop (2.002–2.003).*

PRE-EMERGENCE RESIDUAL TREATMENTS

2.033   **Dinoseb-amine** *3·4–4·5 kg/ha or dinoseb in oil 2·5 kg/ha in medium to high volume for contact and some residual control of annual weeds (2.336).*

The seedbed should be left with a fine even tilth and there should be not less than 25 mm of soil above the crop seed after consolidation. The spray can be applied at any time after sowing until about 3 days before crop emergence. By delaying spraying until this time, the effective period of residual weed control is lengthened.

2.034   **Dinoseb-acetate** *up to 2·5 kg/ha plus* **monolinuron** *up to 0·84 kg/ha in medium to high volume for contact and residual control of annual weeds (2.336).*

The dose is varied with soil type, lower doses being used on lighter soils and those with low organic content. On early sown crops application should be made while the weeds are in the seedling stage, not later than 5 days before crop emergence. When the crop is expected to emerge rapidly application should be made immediately after drilling. Very heavy rain after application may result in some crop damage. Some varieties are sensitive to monolinuron and the manufacturers should be consulted on the suitability of the treatment for specific varieties.

2.035   **Paraquat** *up to 0·7 kg/ha plus* **monolinuron** *up to 0·98 kg/ha in medium to high volume for contact and residual control of annual weeds* (2.336).

The dose is varied with soil type, lower doses being used on lighter soils and those with low organic content. Some varieties are sensitive and the manufacturers should be consulted on the suitability of the treatment for specific varieties.

2.036   **Bentazone** *1·4 kg/ha in medium volume to control seedling annual broad-leaved weeds (2.353).*

The crop should not be treated until it has developed at least 2 trifoliate leaves. Later applications, up to the flowering stage, may be made if late germination of weeds occurs, but the crop may then be checked. Do not apply if the air temperature is above 21°C.

Bentazone may be used following the pre-sowing applications of tri-allate and trifluralin or pre-emergence herbicides, provided the crop is undamaged.

BEAN (runner)

2.037   **Tri-allate** *1·7 kg/ha in medium to high volume applied and immediately incorporated into the soil to control germinating* Avena *spp. (Wild-oats) and* Alopercurus myosuroides *(Black-grass).*

This treatment may also be applied and incorporated soon after drilling but this tends to be less efficient than pre-sowing treatments particularly against *Alopecurus myosuroides* (Black-grass). Incorporation 1.071.

2.038   **Trifluralin** *0·84 kg/ha in medium volume incorporated into the seedbed to control annual weeds (2.122) on mineral soils. For incorporation details see 2.103.*

Beans should be planted at least 75 mm deep.

A follow up treatment with another herbicide either pre- or post-emergence is recommended where resistant weeds are present.

Trifluralin is not recommended for sands or soils containing 10 per cent or more of organic matter.

Only recommended crops should be drilled or planted within 5 months of treatment.

Soil should be thoroughly cultivated to a depth of at least 150 mm before drilling or planting succeeding crops other than recommended crops.

2.039   [**For information.**] Dinitramine 0·25–0·45 kg/ha in 110–170 litres water incorporated has shown promise for residual control of annual weeds in runner beans.

Spray overall, within 14 days before drilling, onto a weed and clod free seed-bed. Thoroughly incorporate into the top 50 mm of soil within 24 h of spraying.

PRE-EMERGENCE TREATMENTS

2.040   *Contact pre-emergence sprays to kill seedling weeds that emerge before the crop (2.002–2.003).*

PRE-EMERGENCE RESIDUAL TREATMENTS

2.041   **Diphenamid** *3·4–4·5 kg/ha in medium volume for residual control of annual weeds.*

The dose used should be varied with soil type, the lower amount being used on light soils. Application should be made as soon as possible after sowing on freshly prepared seedbeds. Under dry conditions shallow incorporation will improve control.

2.042   **Dinoseb-amine** *3·4–4·5 kg/ha or* **dinoseb in oil** *2·5 kg/ha in medium to high volume for contact and some residual control of annual weeds (2.336).*

The seedbed should be left with a fine even tilth and there should be not less than 25 mm of soil above the crop seed after consolidation. The spray can be applied at any time after sowing until about 3 days before crop emergence. By delaying spraying until this time, the effective period of residual weed control is lengthened.

2.043   [**For information.**] Dinoseb-acetate up to 2·1 kg/ha plus monolinuron up to 0·7 kg/ha in medium to high volume for contact and residual control of annual weeds. The dose used should be varied with soil type, lower amounts being used on light soils and those with low organic content. Runner beans are more sensitive to monolinuron than dwarf beans and some crop damage may occur if the beans are not drilled to a sufficient depth or if heavy rain follows application.

POST-EMERGENCE TREATMENT

2.044   **Bentazone** *1·4 kg/ha in medium volume to control seedling annual broad-leaved weeds (2.353).*

The application should not be made until after the crop has developed 1–2 trifoliate leaves. Some scorch may occur, but will be outgrown. Do not apply if the air temperature is above 21°C. Bentazone may be used following the pre-sowing applications of tri-allate and trifluralin or pre-emergence herbicides, provided the crop is undamaged.

BEAN (soya)

PRE-SOWING TREATMENT

2.045 [**For information.**] Trifluralin 0·56–1·1 kg/ha in medium volume as a pre-planting spray for control of annual weeds. Immediate and thorough incorporation is essential (2.103).

PRE-EMERGENCE TREATMENT

2.046 [**For information.**] Linuron 0·56–0·84 kg/ha in medium volume for control of annual weeds has given good results in limited usage. The lower dose would be used on the lighter soils.

POST-EMERGENCE TREATMENTS

2.047 [**For information.**] Chloroxuron 2·2 kg/ha in medium volume as an early post-emergence treatment before the weeds are more than 50 mm and after the crop has formed true leaves, is widely used in America and Europe to control annual broad-leaved weeds.

BEET (fodder and sugar) and mangel

PRE-SOWING TREATMENTS

2.048 **Cycloate** *2·0–4·0 kg/ha plus* **lenacil** *0·39–0·84 kg/ha in medium volume and immediately incorporated in mineral soils to control* Avena fatua *(Wild-oat),* Alopercurus myosuroides *(Black-grass) and annual broad-leaved weeds.*

Application should be made to an even seedbed and thoroughly mixed to a depth of 50 mm within 15 min of spraying. The combination is not recommended on loamy coarse sand, sands, gravelly or stony soils or those with more than 5 per cent organic matter.

2.049 **Di-allate** *1·1–1·7 kg/ha in medium or high volume applied and immediately incorporated into the soil to control germinating* Avena spp. *(Wild-oats) and* Alopecurus myosuroides *(Black-grass).*

Because di-allate is a volatile chemical it should be thoroughly incorporated into the soil preferably by two harrowings at right angles to each other with tines penetrating 75–100 mm. Efficacy is very dependent on adequate post-spraying cultivation. 1·4 or 1·7 kg/ha should be used where there is any doubt about the efficiency of incorporation and where a very high degree of control is required.

To control broad-leaved weeds as well as Wild-oat and Black-grass pyrazone may be applied in combination with di-allate.

2.050   **Lenacil** *1·8–2·7 kg/ha in medium volume incorporated into organic soils with 15 per cent or more organic matter, the dose increasing with increase in organic matter.*

Application should be made onto an even seedbed. The herbicide should be thoroughly mixed into the top 25–50 mm of soil on the day of application. Drilling into the treated layer should not be shallow and can take place any time after incorporation.

2.051   **Propham** *2·2–5·0 kg/ha in medium or high volume thoroughly incorporated into soil to control* Avena fatua *(Wild-oat) and certain other weeds (2.080).*

A dose of 3·4 kg/ha is normally recommended for medium and heavy loam soils but this dose can retard the crop on lighter, sandy soils where the dose should be reduced to 2·2 kg/ha. Conversely on some heavy clay soils and peats a dose of 5·0 kg/ha may be necessary to achieve satisfactory wild oat control. Spraying should preferably be on to an even seedbed rather than plough furrows, 1 to 5 days before drilling the crop. Propham is a volatile chemical and must be worked into the soil immediately after spraying. Incorporation can usually be done satisfactorily during the course of normal seedbed preparations. The crop may be slightly checked by the treatment, but this may pass unnoticed because it is normally quickly outgrown without detriment to the crop. As with TCA, only germinating wild oats are affected and the chemical should not be applied too far ahead of likely wild oat germination.

2.052   **Pyrazone** *at 1·4–4·0 kg/ha in medium to high volume incorporated into mineral soils to control annual weeds (2.080).*

Pyrazone is used as a pre-emergence residual treatment applied as a band or overall treatment. When overall applications are made, soil incorporation may be found more satisfactory under dry soil conditions. The dose is varied with soil type, the high amounts being used on heavier soils.

2.053   **Pyrazone** *1·8–3·2 kg/ha plus* **di-allate** *1·2 or 1·4 kg/ha in medium to high volume incorporated into the soil to control* Avena fatua *(Wild-oat) and other annual weeds.*

This treatment is not recommended for use on organic soils or soils with less than 1 per cent organic matter. The higher rate of di-allate gives maximum Wild-oat control but should only be used on medium and heavy soils that are heavily infested. The mixture should be applied and incorporated as outlined in 2.049.

2.054   **TCA** *7·8–16·0 kg/ha in medium or high volume to suppress* Agropyron repens *(Common Couch) and control* Avena fatua *(Wild-oat).*

There may be a slight check to the crop from applications close to drilling but this does not normally affect yield. Current commercial literature should be consulted for the interval that may be left between application and drilling. The lower dose should be used where wild-oat is the only problem. Control of Wild-oat is variable and depends on the depth of germination and rainfall. For couch grass suppression the higher dose can be used but this should be reduced to 11·0 kg/ha on light soils as with these higher doses there is some risk of seedling loss under adverse conditions and the seed spacing of the beet should be reduced accordingly.

The herbicide should be incorporated into the soil during seedbed preparation, preferably to a depth of 130–150 mm.

2.055   [**For information**]. Tri-allate at 1·9 kg/ha for control of Wild-oat and Black-grass has been used successfully. It should be incorporated as outlined for di-allate (2.049). The crop should be drilled between 2 and 21 days after spraying.

PRE-EMERGENCE CONTACT TREATMENTS

2.056   *Contact pre-emergence sprays (2.002–2.003) to kill seedling weeds that emerge before the crop.*

PRE-EMERGENCE RESIDUAL TREATMENTS

2.057   **Dimexan** *5·6 kg/ha plus* **chlorbufam** *0·21 kg/ha plus* **cycluron** *0·32 kg/ha in high volume 2 to 4 days before crop emergence to control annual weeds (2.080) on soils other than very light sandy soils and those with high organic matter content.*

The mixture is less efficient when applied to heavy soils than to medium soils. This treatment combines the contact action of dimexan to control weeds which have emerged, or are about to emerge, with the residual activity of chlorbufam and cycluron. The treatment will normally control weeds up to the time of singling.

2.058   **Ethofumesate** *1·0–2·0 kg/ha plus* **pyrazone** *1·4–2·7 kg/ha or* **lenacil** *0·45–0·78 kg/ha in medium volume to control annual weeds (2.080).*

The dose is dependent on soil type and the manufacturer should be consulted. The mixtures should give longer persistence than most other pre-emergence applied herbicides available for use in beet. Weeds which germinate and grow can be sensitized to a post-emergence spray of phenmedipham. A period of 5 months should elapse after application, the soil invert ploughed to a minimum depth of 150 mm, before any but a tolerant crop is grown.

2.059   Lenacil *0·9–2·2 kg/ha in medium volume applied within 7 days after drilling to control annual weeds.*
The dose is dependent on soil type and current commercial literature should be consulted.

This treatment is not recommended on any very stony or gravelly soils, nor on extremely light soils, including sands and loamy coarse sands, nor clays and clay loams, black fen or other highly organic soils. On organic soils an incorporated pre-sowing treatment is recommended (2.050).

Weeds which have emerged at the time of application will not be killed unless rainfall follows closely after spraying. A moist fine seedbed will aid the treatment and sufficient rainfall after application to carry the chemical into the root zone of the germinating weeds is necessary for maximum efficiency. Exceptionally heavy rainfall shortly after application may cause excess leaching and kill some beet plants. A 4-month period must elapse after application before any but a tolerant succeeding crop is grown. To control Wild-oat and Black-grass, lenacil is recommended for use with cycloate (2.048).

2.060   Lenacil *1·2–2·0 kg/ha plus* **propham** *0·24–0·41 kg/ha in medium volume to control annual weeds (2.080).*
The dose is dependent on soil type and manufacturers should be consulted. This mixture is not recommended on light sands, heavy clay soils and soils with high organic matter content. It has similar properties to lenacil.

2.061   Propham *2·2–5·0 kg/ha immediately after drilling in medium volume to control certain annual weeds (2.080).*
The use of propham alone has been largely superseded by other materials or by complementary applications that control a wider range of species of broad-leaved weeds.

2.062   Propham *0·77 to 2·2 kg/ha plus* **chlorpropham** *0·21 to 0·56 kg/ha plus* **fenuron** *0·14 to 0·42 kg/ha at the time of drilling on a wide range of soil types including organic soils but not very sandy soils to control annual weeds (2.080).*
Dose is dependent on soil type and manufacturers should be consulted. Results are influenced considerably by soil moisture so that the most satisfactory results are likely to follow applications made in early spring when occurrence of rain soon after spraying is probable. For this reason applications after mid-April are unlikely to prove very effective.

2.063   Pyrazone *1·4–4·0 kg/ha in medium to high volume at the time of drilling on a wide range of soil types except those rich in organic matter to control annual weeds (2.080).*
Dose is dependent on soil type and current commercial literature should be consulted. Results are influenced considerably by soil moisture

so that the most satisfactory results are likely to follow applications made in early spring when occurrence of rain soon after spraying is probable. For this reason applications after mid-April are unlikely to prove very effective. Should dry soil and/or dry climatic conditions prevail or be expected to occur before mid-April the herbicide should be applied and incorporated before sowing. Any susceptible weeds that have emerged at the time of application will be killed provided they have not developed beyond the seedling stage.

POST-EMERGENCE TREATMENTS

2.064 **Barban** *0·7 kg/ha in low volume to control seedling* Avena *spp. (Wild-oats) in sugar beet.*
The wild oats must be at the 1 to 2·5-leaf stage at the time of spraying. The control of *Avena fatua* (Wild-oat) will not be complete, because crop competition at the time of spraying will not be very vigorous, but treatment allows cultivations and singling of the crop to be carried out over a longer period without serious hindrance. This treatment should be regarded essentially as an emergency measure when more efficient pre-emergence treatments have not been adopted.

2.065 **Dalapon-sodium** *4·7 kg/ha in medium volume to check grass weeds.*
This is essentially an emergency measure to ease cultural means of grass control. The crop may be checked. Higher doses are not tolerated by the crop. Application should be made when the crop has 2—6 true leaves and when the air temperature is not greater than 16°C.

2.066 **Phenmedipham** *1·1 kg in 240 litres/ha water to control seedling broad-leaved weeds (2.080).*
The crop may be checked if the spray is applied when the temperature is 21°C or more, especially if this follows a cold period or if the crop is suffering from insect damage or manganese deficiency. Damage can be prevented by spraying late in the day or by a slight reduction in dose.
Improved broad-leaved weed control, particularly of *Polygonum* spp., may be obtained by using barban at 0·35 kg/ha with phenmedipham as recommended above. If Wild-oats are present, useful suppression can be achieved by increasing the barban dose to 0·7 kg/ha.

2.067 **Phenmedipham** *plus* **pyrazone** *or* **lenacil** *has given interesting results on annual weeds combining a predominantly contact action with some residual activity.*

2.068 **Phenmedipham** *0·8 or 1·1 kg/ha plus adjuvant oil 5·0 litres/ha in 160—240 litres/ha of water.*
The lower dose should be used in the low water rate when the weeds are at their most susceptible stage of growth and when the beet have 2—4

true leaves. The higher dose will control weeds at a later growth stage but the beet must have 4 or more true leaves. The crop may be checked if the application is made when the temperature is 21°C or more, especially if the crop is under any stress.

2.069   **Trifluralin** *1·1 kg/ha in medium volume for the control of late germinating annual weeds (2.122) on mineral soils when applied overall and immediately incorporated at the 4- to 6-leaf stage when sugar beet are at least 75 mm high.*

Incorporation is carried out between the beet rows using a spring-tined harrow of the Triple K type, set to a working depth of 100 mm and travelling at 8 kph with the tines set to throw some of the treated soil into the beet.

Trifluralin is not recommended for sands or soils containing 10 per cent or more of organic matter. Only recommended crops should be drilled or planted within 5 months of treatment.

Soil should be thoroughly cultivated to a depth of at least 150 mm before drilling or planting succeeding crops other than recommended crops.

2.070   [**For information.**] Ethofumesate 1·0 kg/ha plus phenmedipham 1·1 kg/ha in 240 litres/ha has given promising results on annual weeds following pre-emergence treatment with lenacil or pyrazone. Metamitron has also given promising results on annual weeds applied at weed emergence (3.353).

BEET (red)

PRE-SOWING TREATMENTS

2.071   **Cycloate** *2·0–4·0 kg/ha plus* **lenacil** *0·39–0·84 kg/ha in medium volume and immediately incorporated in mineral soils to control* Avena fatua *(Wild-oat),* Alopecurus myosuroides *(Black-grass) and annual broad-leaved weeds.*

Application should be made to an even seedbed and thoroughly mixed to a depth of 50 mm within 15 min of spraying. The combination is not recommended on loamy coarse sand, sands, gravelly or stony soils or those with more than 5 per cent organic water.

2.072   **Di-allate** *1·1–1·7 kg/ha in medium to high volume incorporated for control of germinating* Avena spp. *(Wild-oats) and* Alopecurus myosuroides *(Black-grass).*

Incorporation 2.049. Field experience indicates that this treatment will not interfere with other soil-applied herbicides used for broad-leaved weed control. 1·4–1·7 kg/ha should be used where there is any doubt about the

44

efficiency of incorporation and where a very high degree of control is required.

2.073 **Lenacil** *1·8–2·7 kg/ha incorporated into organic soils with 15 per cent or more organic matter, the dose increasing with increase in organic matter.*
Application should be made on to an even seedbed. The herbicide should be thoroughly mixed into the top 25–50 mm of soil on the day of application. Drilling into the treated layer should not be shallow and can take place any time after incorporation.

PRE-EMERGENCE CONTACT TREATMENTS

2.074 *Contact pre-emergence sprays (2.002–2.003) to kill seedling weeds that emerge before the crop.*

PRE-EMERGENCE RESIDUAL TREATMENTS

2.075 **Dimexan** *5·6 kg/ha plus* **chlorbufam** *0·21 kg/ha plus* **cycluron** *0·32 kg/ha in high volume 2–4 days before crop emergence to control annual weeds (2.080) on soils other than very light sandy soils and those with high organic matter content.*
The mixture is less effective on heavy than on medium soils. This treatment combines the contact action of dimexan to control weeds which have emerged, or are about to emerge, with the residual activity of chlorbufam and cycluron. For best results, rainfall or irrigation should follow application, and residual activity is reduced if there is warm weather after application to summer-drilled crops. Breakdown is sufficiently rapid for other crops to be drilled after harvest of early-drilled bunching beet.

2.076 **Lenacil** *0·9 kg/ha–2·2 kg/ha in medium volume applied immediately after drilling to control annual weeds (2.080).*
The dose is dependent on soil type. The seed should be sown at a uniform depth of not less than 12·5 mm, and the best results are obtained when applied immediately after drilling to a moist seedbed with a fine tilth. For effective weed control, rain during the period after spraying is necessary, but exceptionally heavy rain may cause some reduction in stand. Because adequate soil moisture is less likely at the time red beet are normally drilled, weed control results may be more variable than those obtained in sugar beet. To control *A. fatua* and *A. myosuroides*, lenacil is recommended for use with cycloate.

2.077 **Propham** *0·77–2·2 kg/ha plus* **chlorpropham** *0·21–0·56 kg/ha plus* **fenuron** *0·14–0·42 kg/ha at the time of drilling on a wide range of soil types including organic soils but not very sandy soils to control annual weeds (2.080).*

Dose is dependent on soil type and current commercial literature should be consulted. Results are influenced considerably by soil moisture so that the most satisfactory results are likely to follow applications made in early spring when occurrence of rain soon after spraying is probable. For this reason applications after mid-April are unlikely to prove very effective.

POST-EMERGENCE TREATMENTS

2.078 **Phenmedipham** *1·1 kg/ha in 240 litres/ha water to control seedling broad-leaved weeds (2.080).*

The crop may be checked if the spray is applied when the temperature is 21°C or higher, especially if this follows a cold period or if the crop is suffering from insect damage or manganese deficiency. Damage can be prevented by spraying late in the day or by a slight reduction in dose and the crop should always have fully expanded cotyledons before spraying.

Improved broad-leaved weed control, particularly of *Polygonum* spp., may be obtained by using barban at 0·35 kg/ha with phenmedipham as recommended above.

2.079 [**For information.**] Phenmedipham plus lenacil has given promising results on annual weeds, combining contact and some residual activity.

2.080 The susceptibility of annual weeds to herbicides used on beet

This table is intended to provide a general indication of the response of annual weeds to those herbicides used in beet and related crops in the range of doses given in the relevant paragraphs. The table is divided into response of weeds to soil-applied and foliage-applied treatments and the categories of response are defined below. The 'chlorbufam plus cycluron' colum refers to the soil-activity of the commercial mixture which also contains dimexan, in which the dimexan, a contact herbicide, controls emerged weeds.

Soil-applied treatments

S — **Susceptible** Complete or near complete kill.
MS — **Moderately susceptible** Good kill under favourable conditions.
MR — **Moderately resistant** Partial kill.
R — **Resistant** No useful effect.

Foliage-applied treatments

S — **Susceptible** Complete or near complete kill.
MS — **Moderately susceptible** Effective suppression with partial kill.
MR — **Moderately resistant** Temporary suppression, the duration depending on the environment.
R — **Resistant** No useful effect.

They refer to two stages of growth:
Sd — **Seedling stage** Cotyledon to 2 to 3 leaves.
Yp — **Young plant stage** 3 to 4 leaves to early flower-bud stage.

Weeds	Soil-applied							Foliage-applied		
	Chlor-bufam and cycluron	Cyclo-ate/ lenacil	Ethofum-esate/ pyrazone lenacil	Lenacil	Propham	Propham/ fenuron/ chlor-propham	Pyrazone	Stage of growth	Nitrate of soda	Phen-medipham
1. *Aethusa cynapium* (Fool's Parsley)	—	—	R	—	R	—	—	Sd / Yp	— / —	R / R
2. *Alopecurus myosuroides* (Black-grass)	S	S	S	—	S	S	—	Sd / Yp	— / —	R / R
3. *Anagallis arvensis* (Scarlet Pimpernel)	—	S	S	S	R	R	MS	Sd / Yd	S / MS	S / MR

47

Weeds	Soil-applied							Foliage-applied		
	Chlorbufam and cycluron	Cycloate/lenacil	Ethofumesate/pyrazone/lenacil	Lenacil	Propham	Propham/fenuron chlorpropham	Pyrazone	Stage of growth	Nitrate of soda	Phenmedipham
4. *Anthemis arvensis* (Corn Chamomile)	R	—	—	S	R	MS	S	Sd / Yp	MS / R	— / —
5. *Anthemis cotula* (Stinking Chamomile)	—	—	S	S	R	MS	S	Sd / Yd	MS / R	MR / MR
6. *Aphanes arvensis* (Parsley Piert)	—	—	—	—	—	—	—	Sd / Yp	S / MS	— / —
7. *Atriplex patula* (Common Orache)	MS / R	S	S	S	R	—	S	Sd / Yp	R / R	S / MS
8. *Avena fatua* (Wild-oat)	—	S	MS	MR	MS	MR	R	Sd / Yp	R / R	R / R
9. *Brassica nigra* (Black Mustard)	—	—	—	—	—	—	—	Sd / Yp	MS / MR	— / —
10. *Brassica rapa* ssp. *campestris* (Wild Turnip)	—	—	—	—	—	—	—	Sd / Yp	— / —	— / —
11. *Capsella bursa-pastoris* (Shepherd's-purse)	S	S	S	S	R	MR	S	Sd / Yp	S / MS	S / MR
12. *Cerastium holosteoides* (Common Mouse-ear)	—	S	—	—	S	—	—	Sd / Yp	— / —	— / —
13. *Chenopodium album* (Fat-hen)	S	S	S	S	R	S	S	Sd / Yp	MR / R	S / MS
14. *Chrysanthemum segetum* (Corn Marigold)	—	S	—	S	R	R	—	Sd / Yp	R / R	MS / R

Weed	C1	C2	C3	C4	C5	C6	C7	(Sd/Yp)	C8 (Sd/Yp)	C9 (Sd/Yp)
15. *Descurania sophia* (Flixweed)	—	S	—	—	—	—	—	Sd / Yp	— / —	— / —
16. *Echium vulgare* (Viper's-bugloss)	R	—	—	—	—	—	—	Sd / Yp	— / —	— / —
17. *Erysimum cheiranthoides* (Treacle Mustard)	—	—	—	—	R	—	—	Sd / Yp	— / —	— / —
18. *Euphorbia exigua* (Dwarf Spurge)	—	—	—	R	—	—	MR	Sd / Yp	MR / R	MR / R
19. *Euphorbia helioscopia* (Sun Spurge)	—	—	MS	R	—	—	MR	Sd / Yp	R / R	R / R
20. *Euphorbia peplus* (Petty Spurge)	—	—	—	R	R	—	MR	Sd / Yp	— / —	— / —
21. *Fumaria officinalis* (Common Fumitory)	S	S	S	S	R	MS	MS	Sd / Yp	S / MR	S / MS
22. *Galeopsis speciosa* (Large-flowered Hemp-nettle)	—	S	—	—	MS	—	—	Sd / Yp	MS / R	S / S
23. *Galeopsis tetrahit* (Common Hemp-nettle)	MS	S	MS	—	MS	MS*	S	Sd / Yp	MS / R	S / MS
24. *Galinsoga parviflora* (Gallant Soldier)	—	—	R	—	R	—	—	Sd / Yp	S / MS	— / —
25. *Galium aparine* (Cleavers)	R	MR	S	R	R	MR	MR	Sd / Yp	MR / MS	MR / —
26. *Geranium dissectum* (Cut-leaved Crane's-bill)	—	—	—	—	—	—	—	Sd / Yp	— / —	R / R
27. *Geranium pusillum* (Small-flowered Crane's-bill)	—	—	—	—	—	—	—	Sd / Yp	— / —	R / R
28. *Lamium amplexicaule* (Henbit Dead-nettle)	MR	S	R	MR	R	—	—	Sd / Yp	MS / R	— / —

	Soil-applied							Foliage-applied		
Weeds	Chlor-bufam and cycluron	Cyclo-ate/lenacil	Ethofum-esate/pyrazone lenacil	Lenacil	Propham	Propham/fenuron chlor-propham	Pyrazone	Stage of growth	Nitrate of soda	Phen-medipham
29. Lamium purpureum (Red Dead-nettle)	—	S	R	MR	R	MR	S	Sd / Yp	MS / R	S / MS
30. Lapsana communis (Nipplewort)	—	R	—	—	—	—	—	Sd / Yp	— / —	R / R
31. Lithospermum arvense (Field Gromwell)	—	—	—	—	—	—	—	Sd / Yp	— / —	R / R
32. Lycopsis arvensis (Bugloss)	—	—	—	MS	—	—	—	Sd / Yp	MS / R	S / MS
33. Matricaria matricarioides (Pineappleweed)	S	S	S	S	R	—	S	Sd / Yp	MS / R	MR / R
34. Matricaria recutita (Scented Mayweed)	S	—	S	S	R	—	S	Sd / Yp	MS / R	MR / R
35. Medicago lupulina (Black Medick)	—	—	—	—	—	—	—	Sd / Yp	— / —	— / —
36. Melandrium album (White Campion)	—	S	—	S	—	—.	—	Sd / Yp	— / —	— / —
37. Myosotis arvensis (Field Forget-me-not)	—	S	S	S	—	—	—	Sd / Yp	S / MS	MR / R
38. Papaver dubium (Long-headed Poppy)	—	S	—	S	S	S	—	Sd / Yp	S / MR	— / —
39. Papaver rhoeas (Common Poppy)	S	S	S	S	S	S	S	Sd / Yp	S / MR	S / MS

50

Weed	1	2	3	4	5	6	7	8	9	10	11	12	13
40. *Poa annua* (Annual Meadow-grass)	S	S	S	S	S	S	S	Sd	R	MR	R	R	—
41. *Polygonum aviculare* (Knotgrass)	MR	MS	S	S	S	S	S	Sd	Yp	S	MS	MS	MR
42. *Polygonum convolvulus* (Black Bindweed)	S	MS	S	S	S	S	S	Sd	Yp	S	MS	MS	MR
43. *Polygonum lapathifolium* (Pale Persicaria)	—	MS	S	S	S	S	—	Sd	Yp	S	MS	MS	MR
44. *Polygonum persicaria* (Redshank)	S	MS	S	S	S	S	S	Sd	Yp	S	MS	MS	MR
45. *Ranunculus arvensis* (Corn Buttercup)	MR	S	—	S	MS	—	—	Sd	Yp	—	—	—	—
46. *Raphanus raphanistrum* (Wild Radish)	S	S	S	S	R	MR	S	Sd	Yp	S	MR	S	MS
47. *Reseda lutea* (Wild Mignonette)	—	—	—	R	—	—	—	Sd	Yp	—	—	—	—
48. *Scandix pecten-veneris* (Shepherd's-needle)	—	—	—	—	—	—	—	Sd	Yp	—	—	—	—
49. *Senecio vulgaris* (Groundsel)	S	MS	MS	MS	R	MS	MS	Sd	Yp	S	MS	S	MR
50. *Sinapis alba* (White Mustard)	S	—	—	—	R	MS	—	Sd	Yp	S	MS	—	—
51. *Sinapis arvensis* (Charlock)	S	MS	S	S	R	MS	S	Sd	Yp	S	MS	S	MS
52. *Solanum nigrum* (Black Nightshade)	R	MS	MS	R	R	R	S	Sd	Yp	—	—	MR	R
53. *Sonchus asper* (Prickly Sow-thistle)	R	—	—	—	R	—	MS	Sd	Yp	MS	R	R	R

	Soil-applied							Foliage-applied		
Weeds	Chlor-bufam and cycluron	Cyclo-ate/ lenacil	Ethofum-esate/ pyrazone lenacil	Lenacil	Propham	Propham/ fenuron chlor-propham	Pyrazone	Stage of growth	Nitrate of soda	Phen-medipham
54. *Sonchus oleraceus* (Smooth Sow-thistle)	R	S	S	S	R	R	MR	Sd / Yp	MS / R	R / R
55. *Spergula arvensis* (Corn Spurry)	S	S	S	S	S	Sd	S	S / Yp	MR	MS
56. *Stellaria media* (Common Chickweed)	S	S	S	S	S	S	S	Sd / Yp	S / MR	S / MS
57. *Thlapsi arvense* (Field Pennycress)	S	MS	MS	S	R	S	S	Sd / Yp	MS / R	MS / MR
58. *Tripleurospermum maritimum* ssp. *inodorum* (Scentless Mayweed)	—	S	S	S	R	S	S	Sd / Yp	S / MR	MR / R
59. *Urtica urens* (Small Nettle)	S	MS	MS	MS*	S	S	S	Sd / Yp	S / MS	S / MS
60. *Veronica agrestis* (Green Field-speedwell)	S	—	—	—	MR	MS	S	Sd / Yp	— / —	— / —
61. *Veronica arvensis* (Wall Speedwell)	S	—	—	—	MR	MS	S	Sd / Yp	— / —	— / —
62. *Veronica hederifolia* (Ivy-leaved Speedwell)	MR	MS	R	MR	MS	S	Sd	S / Yp	S / MS	MS
63. *Veronica persica* (Common Field-speedwell)	S	S	S	MR	MR	MS	S	Sd / Yp	S / MS	S / MS
64. *Vicia hirsuta* (Hairy Tare)	—	—	—	—	R	—	MR	Sd / Yp	— / —	— / —

65. *Vicia sativa* (Common Vetch)	—	—	—	—	R	—	MR	Sd Yp	—	—
66. *Viola arvensis* (Field Pansy)	—	MS	MS	R	—	MR	MR	Sd Yp	S MS	S MS
67. *Viola tricolor* (Wild Pansy)	S	—	MS	—	MR	MR	—	Sd Yp	S MS	S MS

* MR on organic soils.

53

BROCCOLI—see CAULIFLOWER (2.147).

BRUSSELS SPROUT (drilled)

PRE-SOWING TREATMENTS

2.081   **Di-allate** *1·7 kg/ha in medium to high volume incorporated for control of germinating* Avena *spp. (Wild-oats) and* Alopecurus myosuroides *(Black-grass).*
    Incorporation 2.049. Field experience indicates that this treatment will not interfere with other soil-applied herbicides used for broad-leaved weed control.

2.082   **TCA** *11·0–17·0 kg/ha in medium to high volume incorporated for control of* Agropyron repens *(Common Couch) and other grasses* (12.019).
    An interval of at least 7 days must elapse between application and drilling.

2.083   **Trifluralin** *1·2 kg/ha in medium volume incorporated for residual control of annual weeds* (2.122).
    The spray can be applied during soil preparation at any time from 14 days before until immediately before drilling, but must be mechanically incorporated into the top 50 mm of soil within 30 min after application. For details of incorporation methods and following crops see 2.103. Trifluralin is not recommended on sands or on soils with 10 per cent or more of organic matter. Because of its persistence, it is not recommended for use on plant-raising beds.

PRE-EMERGENCE CONTACT TREATMENTS

2.084   *Contact pre-emergence sprays (2.002–2.003) to kill seedling weeds that emerge before the crop.*

PRE-EMERGENCE RESIDUAL TREATMENTS

2.085   **Nitrofen** *3·4 kg/ha in medium to high volume within 3 days after drilling for residual control of annual weeds* (2.122).
    Nitrofen is most effective when there is a fine surface tilth and the soil is moist at the time of weed emergence. Incorporation, whether mechanical or by irrigation, reduces the effectiveness. Heavy rainfall shortly after spraying may lead to some crop damage.

2.086   **Propachlor** *4·4 kg/ha on mineral soils or 6·5 kg/ha on organic soils in medium to high volume or as granules shortly after drilling for residual control of annual weeds (2.122).*

Best results are obtained when the seedbed has a fine even tilth and is free from clods. A temporary check to crop growth may occur, but recovery is normally complete and maturity is not affected.

2.087 **Sulfallate** *2·0 kg/ha plus* **chlorpropham** *0·28 kg/ha in high volume within 2 days after drilling for residual control of annual weeds (2.122).*

The seed should be drilled to an even depth and best results are obtained when the seedbed is moist and has a fine tilth. This treatment is not effective on black fen or other highly organic soils.

POST-EMERGENCE TREATMENTS

2.088 **Aziprotryne** *2·00 kg/ha in medium to high volume for contact and residual control of annual weeds (2.122).*

The spray should not be applied until the crop plants are 65 mm high and have 3 true leaves. Emerged weeds which have more than 2 true leaves are not effectively controlled and application should normally follow pre-emergence treatment with another herbicide. Only one application of aziprotryne should be made to any one crop.

2.089 **Desmetryne** *0·28–0·42 kg/ha in medium volume for contact kill of some seedling broad-leaved weeds (2.122).*

Spraying should not be attempted until the crop plants have developed 3 true leaves and are at least 125 mm high. Best results are obtained when the weeds are still small at this time and a fine spray is used.

2.090 **Propachlor** *4·4 kg/ha on mineral soils or 6·5 kg/ha on organic soils in medium to high volume or as granules when the crop has developed 3–4 true leaves for residual control of annual weeds (2.122).*

This treatment can be applied to clean crops which have received contact pre-emergence sprays, once the correct growth stage has been reached. Weeds that have passed the cotyledon stage will not be killed. Best results are obtained when the weeds are germinating and just beginning to emerge.

2.091 **Sodium monochloroacetate** *22 kg/ha in 220 litres/ha as a post-emergence spray when the crop plants have 3–4 true leaves for contact kill of some seedling broad-leaved weeds (2.122).*

Some scorch may occur, but this is not usually serious. Wetting agents must not be added, otherwise crop damage will result. A period of at least 12 hr of fine weather after spraying is essential for success.

BRUSSELS SPROUT (transplanted)

PRE-PLANTING TREATMENTS

2.092 **Di-allate** *1·7 kg/ha in medium to high volume incorporated for control of* *germinating* Avena *spp.* *(Wild-oats) and* Alopecurus myosuroides *(Black-grass).*

Incorporation 2.049. Field experience indicates that this treatment will not interfere with other soil-applied herbicides used for broad-leaved weed control.

2.093   **TCA** *11·0–17·0 kg/ha in medium to high volume incorporated for control of* Agropyron repens *(Common Couch) and other grasses* (12.019).

An interval of at least 7 days must elapse between application and planting.

2.094   **Trifluralin** *1·1 kg/ha in medium volume incorporated for residual control of annual weeds (2.122).*

The spray can be applied during soil preparation at any time from 14 days before until immediately before planting, but must be mechanically incorporated into the top 50 mm of soil within 30 min after application. For details of incorporation methods and following crops see 2.103. Trifluralin is not recommended on sands or on soils with 10 per cent or more of organic matter.

2.095   [**For information.**] Dinitramine has shown promise at 0·25–0·35 kg/ha in 110–170 litres water for residual control of annual weeds (2.122).

Spray overall within 14 days before transplanting onto a weed and clod free seedbed. Thoroughly incorporate into the top 50 mm of soil within 24 hr of spraying.

POST-PLANTING TREATMENTS

2.096   **Aziprotryne** *2·2 kg/ha in medium to high volume for contact and residual control of annual weeds (2.122).*

On very light soils with more than 85 per cent sand the dose should be reduced to 2·0 kg/ha. The spray should not be applied until the crop is established, usually about 2 weeks after planting, and best results are obtained when most of the weeds are just emerging.

2.097   **Desmetryne** *0·28–0·42 kg/ha in medium volume as a fine spray after the crop has become established, at least 2 weeks after planting and when a flush of seedling weeds has appeared, for contact kill of some seedling broad-leaved weeds (2.122).*

2.098   **Propachlor** *4·4 kg/ha on mineral soils or 6·5 kg/ha on organic soils in medium to high volume or as granules shortly after planting for residual control of annual weeds (2.122).*

Best results are obtained when application is made before the weeds have emerged and when the soil surface is even and free from clods.

2.099 **Sodium monochloroacetate** *22·0 kg/ha in 225 litres/ha after the crop has become established and a flush of seedling weeds has appeared, for contact kill of some seedling broad-leaved weeds (2.122).*

Some scorch may occur but this is not usually serious. Wetting agents must not be added, otherwise crop damage will result. A period of at least 12 hr of fine weather after spraying is essential for success.

2.100 [**For information**] Simazine 0·42 kg/ha in high volume as an overall spray shortly after transplanting has given satisfactory results for residual control of annual weeds on certain soils. The soil round the plants should be firm before the herbicide is applied. On light soils there is a risk of serious crop damage if heavy rain follows application.

CABBAGE (drilled)

PRE-SOWING TREATMENTS

2.101 **Di-allate** *1·7 kg/ha in medium to high volume incorporated for control of germinating* Avena *spp. (Wild-oats) and* Alopecurus myosuroides *(Black-grass).*

For incorporation details see 2.049. Field experience indicates that this treatment will not interfere with other soil-applied herbicides used for broad-leaved weed control.

2.102 **TCA** *11·0–17·0 kg/ha in medium to high volume incorporated for control of* Agropyron repens *(Common Couch) and other grasses (12.019).*

An interval of at least 7 days must elapse between application and drilling.

PRE-SOWING TREATMENTS

2.103 **Trifluralin** *1·1 kg/ha in medium volume incorporated into the seedbed for residual control of annual weeds (2.122) on loamy sands, sandy loams, loams and clay loams.*

The spray can be applied during soil preparation any time from 14 days before, until immediately before drilling, but must be mechanically incorporated within 30 min after application.

Thorough incorporation is important. The distribution of trifluralin must be uniform in the top 50 mm of the soil which can be achieved only when the soil is in a good workable condition.

A rotary cultivator set to a working depth of 50 mm with high rotor speed and slow forward travel (up to 6 kph) will give the desired distribution with one pass. Where spring-tined harrows, tandem disc harrows or power driven reciprocating harrows are used, these must be set to a working depth of 100 mm and travel at least at 8 kph and preferably faster. With spring-tined harrows, sufficient tines should be used so that the tine tracks are not more than 100 mm apart. Two passes at right angles are required with these three types of harrow.

No other type of implement is recommended for the incorporation of trifluralin.

Where farmyard manure or other bulky organic materials are to be used, these must be buried to a depth of 150 mm before applying trifluralin.

Because of its persistence trifluralin is not recommended for use on plant-raising beds.

Trifluralin is not recommended for sands or soils containing 10 per cent or more of organic matter.

Only recommended crops should be drilled or planted within 5 months of treatment.

Soil should be thoroughly cultivated to a depth of at least 150 mm before drilling or planting succeeding crops other than recommended crops.

After an autumn application of trifluralin, cereal and grass crops should not be sown until the following autumn.

PRE-EMERGENCE CONTACT TREATMENTS

2.104 *Contact pre-emergence sprays (2.002–2.003) to kill seedling weeds that emerge before the crop.*

PRE-EMERGENCE RESIDUAL TREATMENTS

2.105 **Nitrofen** *3·4 kg/ha in medium to high volume within 3 days after drilling for residual control of annual weeds (2.122).*

Nitrofen is most effective when there is a fine surface tilth and the soil is moist at the time of weed emergence. Incorporation, whether mechanical or by irrigation, reduces the effectiveness. Heavy rainfall shortly after spraying may lead to some crop damage.

2.106 **Propachlor** *4·4 kg/ha on mineral soils or 6·5 kg/ha on organic soils in medium to high volume or as granules shortly after drilling for residual control of annual weeds (2.122).*

Best results are obtained when the seedbed has a fine even tilth and is free from clods. A temporary check to crop growth may occur, but recovery is normally complete and maturity is not affected.

2.107 **Sulfallate** *2·0 kg/ha plus* **chlorpropham** *0·28 kg/ha in high volume within 2 days after drilling for residual control of annual weeds (2.122).*

The seed should be drilled to an even depth and best results are obtained when the seedbed is moist and has a fine tilth. This treatment is not effective on black fen or other highly organic soils.

2.108 **Aziprotryne** *2·0 kg/ha in medium to high volume for contact and residual control of annual weeds (2.122).*

The spray should not be applied until the crop plants are 65 mm high and have 3 true leaves. Emerged weeds which have more than 2 true leaves are not effectively controlled and application should normally follow pre-emergence treatment with another herbicide. Only one application of aziprotryne should be made to any one crop.

2.109 **Carbetamide** *2·1 kg/ha in medium volume on spring cabbage and spring greens after 4 true leaves have developed for control of mainly grass weeds, such as self-sown cereals and* Avena *spp. (Wild-oats).*

Application may be made from mid-autumn to late winter, normally mid-October to February, and should follow use of a standard pre- or early post-emergence herbicide.

2.110 **Desmetryne** *0·28–0·42 kg/ha in medium volume for contact kill of some seedling broad-leaved weeds (2.122).*

Spraying should not be attempted until the crop plants have developed 3 true leaves and are at least 125 mm high. Best results are obtained when the weeds are still small at this time and a fine spray is used.

2.111 **Propachlor** *4·4 kg/ha on mineral soils or 6·5 kg/ha on organic soils in medium to high volume or as granules when the crop has developed 3 to 4 true leaves for residual control of annual weeds (2.122).*

This treatment can be applied to clean crops which have received contact pre-emergence sprays, once the correct growth stage has been reached. Weeds that have passed the cotyledon stage will not be killed. Best results are obtained when the weeds are germinating and just beginning to emerge.

2.112 **Sodium monochloroacetate** *22 kg/ha in 225 litres/ha when the crop plants have 3–4 true leaves for contact kill of some seedling broad-leaved weeds (2.122).*

Some scorch may occur, but this is not usually serious. Wetting agents must not be added, otherwise crop damage will result. A period of at least 12 hr of fine weather after spraying is essential for success.

CABBAGE (transplanted)

2.113 **Di-allate** *1·7 kg/ha in medium to high volume incorporated for control of germinating* Avena *spp. (Wild-oats) and* Alopecurus myosuroides *(Black-grass).*

Incorporation 2.049. Field experience indicates that this treatment will not interfere with other soil-applied herbicides used for broad-leaved weed control.

2.114   **TCA** *11–17 kg/ha in medium to high volume incorporated for control of* Agropyron repens *(Common Couch) and other grasses* (12.019).

An interval of at least 7 days must elapse between application and planting.

2.115   **Trifluralin** *1·1 kg/ha in medium volume as a pre-planting spray for residual control of annual weeds (2.122) on loamy sands, sandy loams, loams and clay loams.*

The spray can be applied during soil preparation at any time from 14 days before up until immediately before planting, but must be mechanically incorporated into the top 50 mm of soil within 30 min of application. For incorporation details see 2.103.

Trifluralin is not recommended for soils containing 10 per cent or more of organic matter.

Only recommended crops should be drilled or planted within 5 months of treatment.

Soil should be thoroughly cultivated to a depth of at least 150 mm before drilling or planting succeeding crops other than recommended crops.

After an autumn application of trifluralin cereal and grass crops should not be sown until the following autumn.

POST-PLANTING TREATMENTS

2.116   **Aziprotryne** *2·2 kg/ha in medium to high volume for contact and residual control of annual weeds (2.122).*

On very light soils with more than 85 per cent sand the dose should be reduced to 2·0 kg/ha. The spray should not be applied until the crop is established, usually about 2 weeks after planting, and best results are obtained when most of the weeds are just emerging.

2.117   **Carbetamide** *2·1 kg/ha in medium volume on spring cabbage and spring greens after 4 true leaves have developed for control of mainly grass weeds, such as self-sown cereals and* Avena *spp. (Wild-oats).*

Application may be made from mid-autumn to late winter, normally mid-October to February, and should follow use of a standard herbicide for broad-leaved weed control.

2.118   **Desmetryne** *0·28–0·42 kg/ha in medium volume as a fine spray after the crop has become established, at least 2 weeks after planting and when a flush of seedling weeds has appeared, for contact kill of some seedling broad-leaved weeds (2.122).*

2.119   **Propachlor** *4·4 kg/ha on mineral soils or 6·5 kg/ha on organic soils in medium to high volume or as granules shortly after planting for residual control of annual weeds (2.122).*

Best results are obtained when application is made before the weeds have emerged and when the soil surface is even and free from clods.

2.120   **Sodium monochloroacetate** *22 kg/ha in 225 litres/ha after the crop has become established and a flush of seedling weeds has appeared, for contact kill of some seedling broad-leaved weeds (2.112).*

Some scorch may occur but this is not usually serious. Wetting agents must not be added, otherwise crop damage will result. A period of at least 12 hr of fine weather after spraying is essential for success.

2.121   [**For information.**] Simazine 0·42 kg/ha in high volume as an overall spray shortly after transplanting has given satisfactory results for residual control of annual weeds on certain soils. The soil round the plants should be firm before the herbicide is applied. On light soils there is a risk of serious crop damage if heavy rain follows application.

CALABRESE—see CAULIFLOWER (2.147).

2.122   The susceptibility of annual weeds to herbicides used in brassica crops

This table is intended to provide a general indication of the response of annual weeds to those herbicides used in brassica crops at the range of doses given in the relevant paragraphs. The table is divided into response of weeds to soil-applied and foliage-applied treatments and the categories of response are defined as follows:

Soil-applied treatments
S—**Susceptible**   Complete or near complete kill.
MS—**Moderately susceptible**   Good kill under favourable conditions.
MR—**Moderately resistant**   Partial kill.
R—**Resistant**   No useful effect.

Foliage-applied treatments
S—**Susceptible**   Complete or near complete kill.
MS—**Moderately susceptible**   Effective suppression with partial kill.
MR—**Moderately resistant**   Temporary suppression, the duration depending on the environment.
R—**Resistant**   No useful effect.

They refer to two stages of growth:
Sd—**Seedling stage**   Cotyledon to 2 to 3 leaves.
Yp—**Young plant stage**   3 to 4 leaves to early flower-bud stage.

Weeds	Soil-applied						Stage of growth	Foliage-applied		
	Azi-protryne	Dinitra-mine	Nitrofen	Propa-chlor	Sulfallate plus chlor-propham	Tri-fluralin		Azi-protryne	Des-metryne	Sodium mono-chloro-acetate
1. *Aethusa cynapium* (Fool's Parsley)	R	—	R	—	—	R	Sd	MR	—	—
							Yp	—	—	—
2. *Alopecurus myosuroides* (Black-grass)	MS	—	S	S	MS	S	Sd	—	R	R
							Yp	—	R	R
3. *Anagallis arvensis* (Scarlet Pimpernel)	S	—	S	S	—	S	Sd	S	S	S
							Yp	—	—	MS

Weed	1	2	3	4	5	Sd / Yp	6	7	8	9	10	11
4. *Anthemis arvensis* (Corn Chamomile)	R	R	S	—	—	Sd / Yp	R	R	—	R	—	—
5. *Anthemis cotula* (Stinking Chamomile)	R	R	S	R	—	Sd / Yp	R	R	—	R	—	—
6. *Aphanes arvensis* (Parsley-piert)	R	R	—	—	—	Sd / Yp	R	—	—	R	—	—
7. *Atriplex patula* (Common Orache)	R	R	S	MR	—	Sd / Yp	MS	MS	MR	S	—	—
8. *Avena fatua* (Wild-oat)	R	R	MR	—	MR	Sd / Yp	MS	R	—	MS	MS	—
9. *Brassica nigra* (Black Mustard)	—	·	MS	—	—	— / Yp	R	R	R	R	—	—
10. *Brassica rapa* ssp. *campestris* (Wild Turnip)	R	—	MR	—	MS	Sd / Yp	Sd	RZR	R	R	—	—
11. *Capsella bursa-pastoris* (Shepherd's-purse)	S	MS	MR	R	S	Sd / Yp	R	MR	S	R	MR	S
12. *Cerastium holosteoides* (Common Mouse-ear)	S	S	S	MR	—	Sd / Yp	S	MR	—	R	—	—
13. *Chenopodium album* (Fat-hen)	R	R	S	S	S	Sd / Yp	S	MR	MS	S	S	S
14. *Chrysanthemum segetum* (Corn Marigold)	R	R	—	—	—	Sd / Yp	R	—	S	R	—	—
15. *Erysimum cheiranthoides* (Treacle Mustard)	—	—	—	—	—	Sd / Yp	R	—	—	R	—	—
16. *Euphorbia exigua* (Dwarf Spurge)	—	—	R	R	—	Sd / Yp	MS	—	—	—	—	—
17. *Euphorbia helioscopia* (Sun Spurge)	S	—	R	R	—	Sd / Yp	MS	—	R	—	—	—

Weeds	Soil-applied						Stage of growth	Foliage-applied		
	Azi-protryne	Dinitra-mine	Nitrofen	Propa-chlor	Sulfallate plus chlor-propham	Tri-fluralin		Azi-protryne	Des-metryne	Sodium mono-chloro-acetate
18. *Euphorbia peplus* (Petty Spurge)	—	—	—	—	—	MS	Sd / Yp	— / —	R / R	S / —
19. *Fumaria officinalis* (Common Fumitory)	MS	MS	MR	R	R	MS	Sd / Yp	MS / —	S / MS	R / R
20. *Galeopsis speciosa* (Large-flowered Hemp-nettle)	—	S	—	—	—	—	Sd / Yp	S / —	S / MS	S / MS
21. *Galeopsis tetrahit* (Common Hemp-nettle)	—	S	S	S	—	S	Sd / Yp	S / —	S / MS	S / MS
22. *Galinsoga parviflora* (Gallant Soldier)	—	—	—	S	—	R	Sd / Yp	— / —	S / MS	— / —
23. *Galium aparine* (Cleavers)	R	R	R	S	R	R	Sd / Yp	R / —	MS / MR	MS / MS
24. *Geranium dissectum* (Cut-leaved Crane's-bill)	—	—	—	—	R	R	Sd / Yp	— / —	— / —	R / R
25. *Geranium pusillum* (Small-flowered Crane's-bill)	—	—	—	—	R	R	Sd / Yp	— / —	— / —	R / R
26. *Lamium amplexicaule* (Henbit Dead-nettle)	MS	—	S	MS	S	S	Sd / Yp	S / —	— / —	S / MS
27. *Lamium purpureum* (Red Dead-nettle)	R	—	S	S	MS	MS	Sd / Yp	S / —	R / R	S / MS
28. *Lapsana communis* (Nipplewort)	—	—	—	—	—	R	Sd / Yp	— / —	— / —	— / —

65

29. *Lithospermum arvense* (Field Gromwell)	—	—	—	—	—	—	Sd / Yp	— / —	— / —	R / R
30. *Lycopsis arvensis* (Bugloss)	—	—	MR	—	—	R	Sd / Yp	— / —	S / MS	S / —
31. *Matricaria matricarioides* (Pineappleweed)	S	MS	R	S	R	R	Sd / Yp	S / —	S / MS	MR / R
32. *Matricaria recutita* (Scented Mayweed)	S	MS	R	S	R	R	Sd / Yp	S / —	S / MS	MR / R
33. *Medicago lupulina* (Black Medick)	—	—	—	—	—	R	Sd / Yp	— / —	— / —	— / —
34. *Myosotis arvensis* (Field Forget-me-not)	—	—	—	—	—	R	Sd / Yp	— / —	— / —	— / —
35. *Papaver dubium* (Long-headed Poppy)	—	—	—	—	—	—	Sd / Yp	— / —	— / —	R / R
36. *Papaver rhoeas* (Common Poppy)	—	—	MR	—	—	MS	Sd / Yp	MS / —	S / MS	R / R
37. *Poa annua* (Annual Meadow-grass)	S	S	S	S	S	S	Sd / Yp	S / —	R / R	R / R
38. *Polygonum aviculare* (Knotgrass)	MS	S	S	MR	MS	S	Sd / Yp	S / —	MR / R	R / R
39. *Polygonum convolvulus* (Black-bindweed)	MS	S	S	MR	S	S	Sd / Yp	S / —	MS / R	S / S
40. *Polygonum lapathifolium* (Pale Persicaria)	—	—	S	—	S	S	Sd / Yp	— / —	S / MS	S / S
41. *Polygonum persicaria* (Redshank)	S	MS	S	MR	S	S	Sd / Yp	S / —	S / MS	S / S
42. *Ranunculus arvensis* (Corn Buttercup)	—	—	—	—	—	—	Sd / Yp	— / —	MR / —	MR / R

	Soil-applied							Foliage-applied		
Weeds	Azi-protryne	Dinitra-mine	Nitrofen	Propa-chlor	Sulfallate plus chlor-propham	Tri-fluralin	Stage of growth	Azi-protryne	Des-metryne	Sodium mono-chloro-acetate
43. *Raphanus raphanistrum* (Wild Radish)	R	—	R	R	R	R	Sd / Yp	R / —	MS / MR	MS / MR
44. *Scandix pecten-veneris* (Shepherd's-needle)	—	—	R	—	—	R	Sd / Yp	— / —	— / —	— / —
45. *Senecio vulgaris* (Groundsel)	S	R	R	S	R	R	Sd / Yp	S / —	MS / MR	MS / MS
46. *Sinapis alba* (White Mustard)	—	—	R	R	—	R	Sd / Yp	— / —	— / —	S / MS
47. *Sinapis arvensis* (Charlock)	MR	R	R	R	R	R	Sd / Yp	S / —	MS / MR	S / MS
48. *Solanum nigram* (Black Nightshade)	S	MS	S	MS	MR	R	Sd / Yp	S / —	S / MS	S / MR
49. *Sonchus asper* (Prickly Sow-thistle)	MS	—	R	MS	R	R	Sd / Yp	— / —	S / —	MS / R
50. *Sonchus oleraceus* (Smooth Sow-thistle)	MR	MS	R	MS	R	R	Sd / Yp	MS / —	S / —	MS / R
51. *Spergula arvensis* (Corn Spurrey)	—	MS	S	S	—	MS	Sd / Yp	MS / —	S / S	S / S
52. *Stellaria media* (Common Chickweed)	S	S	R	MS	S	S	Sd / Yp	S / —	S / MS	S / MR
53. *Thlaspi arvense* (Field Penny-cress)	R	—	R	R	R	R	Sd / Yp	MR / —	MS / R	S / MS

Weed							Sd / Yp					
54. *Tripleurospermum maritimum* ssp. *inodorum* (Scentless Mayweed)	S	MS	S	R	S	R	Sd / Yp	R	S	S	MS	S
55. *Urtica urens* (Small Nettle)	S	S	S	S	S	MS	Sd / Yp	MS	S	S	S	S
56. *Veronica agrestis* (Green Field-speedwell)	—	—	S	—	S	S	Sd / Yp	S	S	MR	—	—
57. *Veronica arvensis* (Wall Speedwell)	—	—	S	—	S	S	Sd / Yp	S	S	—	—	—
58. *Veronica hederifolia* (Ivy-leaved Speedwell)	MR	—	S	MS	S	S	Sd / Yp	S	S	MS	—	—
59. *Veronica persica* (Common Field-speedwell)	MS	S	S	MS	S	S	Sd / Yp	S	S	S	S	S
60. *Vicia hirsuta* (Hairy Tare)	—	—	—	—	—	R	Sd / Yp	R	—	—	S	S
61. *Vicia sativa* (Common Vetch)	—	—	—	—	—	R	Sd / Yp	R	—	—	MR	R
62. *Viola arvensis* (Field Pansy)	S	—	S	R	MR	S	Sd / Yp	S	R	S	S	S
63. *Viola tricolor* (Wild Pansy)	—	—	—	—	—	S	Sd / Yp	S	—	—	S	S

CARROT

2.123   **TCA** *17·0 kg/ha in medium or high volume to suppress Common Couch and control* Avena fatua *(Wild-oat).*
An interval of 6 weeks should be allowed between application of the chemical and drilling. The herbicide should be incorporated into the soil (2.054). Control of Wild-oats is variable and depends on the depth of germination and rainfall.

2.224   **Tri-allate** *1·7 kg/ha in medium to high volume applied and immediately incorporated into the soil to control germinating* Avena spp. *(Wild-oats) and* Alopecurus myosuroides *(Black-grass).*
Thorough incorporation is important (1.071). Field experience indicates that this treatment will not interfere with other soil-applied herbicides used for broad-leaved weed control.

2.125   **Trifluralin** *1·1 kg/ha in medium volume incorporated for residual control of annual weeds (2.122).*
The spray can be applied during soil preparation at any time from 14 days before until immediately before planting, but must be mechanically incorporated into the top 50 mm of soil within 30 min after application. For details of incorporation methods and following crops see 2.103. Trifluralin is not recommended on sands or on soils with 10 per cent or more of organic matter. Treatment with trifluralin should form part of a spray programme and be followed by a post-emergence spray.

2.126   *Contact pre-emergence sprays (2.002–2.003) to kill seedling weeds that emerge before the crop.*

2.127   **Chlorbromuron** *0·55 kg/ha–1·1 kg/ha in medium to high volume for contact and residual control of annual weeds (2.139) on mineral soils.*
Application made as the weeds are just emerging will give optimum control. For prolonged weed control this treatment should be followed by a post-emergence application. On peat and other high-organic soils the post-emergence application only is recommended.

2.128   **Chlorpropham** *1·1–1·7 kg/ha in medium to high volume for residual control of annual weeds (2.139).*
The carrot seed should be sown at an even depth of not less than 12 mm and the spray applied within 3 days after drilling. This treatment is

not effective on black fen or other highly organic soils and is not recommended on very open sandy soils with a low organic content because of the risk of crop damage if heavy rainfall should occur after application.

2.129 **Linuron** *0·55–1·1 kg/ha in medium to high volume for contact and residual control of annual weeds* (2.336).

The carrot seed should be sown at an even depth of not less than 10 mm and on mineral soils application should be made within 4 days of drilling. On peaty and peat soils, linuron may be applied at any time after drilling but preferably at weed emergence. The soil should be moist at the time of application. Good weed control depends upon sufficient rain falling after treatment to at least maintain soil moisture but on very open sandy soils with a low organic content there may be some risk of crop damage if heavy rain follows application. For maximum weed control pre-emergence treatment should be followed by a post-emergence application.

POST-EMERGENCE TREATMENTS

2.130 **Chlorbromuron** *0·55–1·7 kg/ha in medium to high volume for contact and residual control of annual weeds* (2.139).

The spray should not be applied until the crop has 2 true leaves. On mineral soils, application would normally follow a pre-emergence treatment. Where no pre-emergence treatment has been applied, a single post-emergence application of 1·1 kg/ha on light soils or 1·7 kg/ha on organic and other soils may be made when the crop has two true leaves. Carrots should not be sprayed when they are suffering from drought or in very hot sunshine.

2.131 **Dalapon-sodium** *at up to 7·6 kg/ha in medium volume once the carrots have reached the stage of 'pencil thickness' for the suppression of* Agropyron repens *(Common Couch) and other grasses.*

Application of 4·7 kg/ha followed by a further application of 4·7 kg/ha 2 weeks later has proved both safe and effective. The spray should be applied in a volume of 220–350 litres/ha and should thoroughly wet the grass foliage.

2.132 **Linuron** *0·55 kg/ha–1·1 kg/ha in medium to high volume for contact and residual control of annual weeds* (2.336).

Where a pre-emergence treatment has previously been made, this treatment should be applied when fresh weed germination occurs. If no pre-emergence treatment has been made it should be applied as soon as possible after the carrots have developed the first true leaf. The selectivity of linuron can be influenced by formulation and certain formulations may not be recommended for post-emergence use on carrots. Application during very hot weather is not advisable because of the risk of some crop scorch.

2.133   Metoxuron *2·7–4·0 kg/ha in medium volume as a fine spray to control* Matricaria *spp. and* Tripleurospermum maritimum *ssp.* inodorum *(Mayweeds).*
Carrots should be drilled at an even depth of not less than 15 mm and may be treated when they are beyond the 2 true leaf stage of growth. Application should not be made to carrots grown on sands or coarse sands or on any soil with less than 1 per cent organic matter.
Mayweeds will be controlled by the above doses at the pre-rosette to initiation of flowering shoot stages but if the weed exceeds the 8-leaf stage the doses should in each case be increased by 0·4 kg/ha. Other annual weeds will be controlled at the seedling stage. The treatment should not be applied when the shade temperature is above 25°C. Slight leaf scorch and chlorosis of the crop may occur but these symptoms quickly disappear. Metoxuron residues may affect subsequent crops drilled within 6 weeks of application.

2.134   Pentanochlor *2·2 kg/ha in high volume for contact kill of seedling annual weeds (2.139).*
Application should be made after the carrots have fully developed their cotyledons and the first true leaf is showing. The use of a coarse low-pressure spray is desirable. A second application may be made at a later stage of growth if further weeds emerge after treatment.

2.135   Pentanochlor *1·7 kg/ha plus* **chlorpropham** *0·84 kg/ha in high volume for contact and residual control of annual weeds.*
Application should be made after the carrots have fully developed their cotyledons and the first true leaf is showing. The use of a coarse low-pressure spray is desirable.

2.136   Prometryne *1·1 kg/ha in medium to high volume for contact and residual control of annual weeds (2.139).*
The spray should be applied after the carrots have developed 1 or more true leaves and best results are obtained when the weeds are small.

2.137   *Certain* mineral oils *for contact kill of seedling annual weeds (2.139).*
Proprietary selective mineral oils are approved by the Agricultural Chemicals Approval Scheme which requires that they shall have a distillation range of between 140 and 210°C and an aromatic content of not less than 15 per cent and not more than 25 per cent of the oil. There is less risk of crop scorch and taint with these selected grades of oil than with tractor vaporizing oils. The doses range from 450 to 900 litres/ha of ground sprayed and should be applied after the carrots have fully developed their cotyledons and while the weeds are still small. Spraying

should not be attempted after the carrots reach 'pencil thickness'. Frame-grown carrots can be similarly treated provided that adequate ventilation can be given during the period following treatment.

Most tractor vaporizing oils can be used in a similar manner on main-crop carrots, provided it is not intended to market the thinnings. These oils should not be applied before the carrots have 1 true leaf, and spraying during the heat of the day should be avoided. Because different brands and batches of vaporizing oils vary in their effects on plants, a test should be carried out first to verify that the particular oil is satisfactory. Late spraying should be avoided, so as not to incur a risk of tainting the crop, and vaporizing oils should not be used on carrots grown for bunching, either outdoors or in frames.

PRE-HARVEST TREATMENT

2.138 **Dimexan** *at 9·3 kg in 220–330 litres of water/ha applied when the ideal distribution of sizes within the crop has been reached, to maintain that situation or when splitting commences, to arrest further splitting.*

2.139   The susceptibility of annual weeds to herbicides used in umbelliferous crops

This table is intended to provide a general indication of the response of annual weeds to those herbicides used in carrots and other umbelliferous crops in the range of doses given in the relevant paragraphs. The table is divided into response of weeds to soil-applied and foliage-applied treatments and the categories of response are defined as follows:

Soil-applied treatments

S—**Susceptible**   Complete or near complete kill.
MS—**Moderately susceptible**   Good kill under favourable conditions.
MR—**Moderately resistant**   Partial kill.
R—**Resistant**   No useful effect.

Foliage-applied treatments

S—**Susceptible**   Complete or near complete kill.
MS—**Moderately susceptible**   Effective suppression with partial kill.
MR—**Moderately resistant**   Temporary suppression, the duration depending on the environment.
R—**Resistant**   No useful effect.

They refer to two stages of growth:

Sd—**Seedling stage**   Cotyledon to 2 to 3 leaves.
Yp—**Young plant stage**   3 to 4 leaves to early flower-bud stage.

When linuron or prometryne is used as a foliage-applied treatment, residual activity in the soil will also occur, the extent depending on soil-type and weather. The susceptibility of annual weeds to **chlorbromuron** is given in paragraph 2.336.

Weeds	Soil-applied				Stage of growth	Foliage-applied				
	Chlor-bro-muron	Chlor-propham	Linuron	Prometryne		Chlor bro-muron	Linuron	Mineral oil	Prometryne	Pentano-chlor
1. *Aethusa cynapium* (Fool's Parsley)	MS	R	R	—	Sd	MS	MS	R	—	R
					Yp		MR	t1R	—	R
2. *Alopecurus myosuroides* (Black-grass)	—	S	MR	—	Sd	—	R	—	MS	R
					Yp	—	R	—	—	R

Weed						Sd / Yp						
3. *Anagallis arvensis* (Scarlet Pimpernel)	S	S	S	R	S	Sd / Yp	S	S	MS	MS	MS	S
4. *Anthemis arvensis* (Corn Chamomile)	—	MS	MS	—	—	Sd / Yp	—	R	R	R	R	R
5. *Anthemis cotula* (Stinking Chamomile)	—	MS	MS	R	—	Sd / Yp	—	R	R	R	R	S
6. *Aphanes arvensis* (Parsley-piert)	—	MS	R	MS	—	Sd / Yp	—	MR	MR	R	R	—
7. *Atriplex patula* (Common Orache)	—	S	MS	S	R	Sd / Yp	—	S	S	MS	S	S
8. *Avena fatua* (Wild-oat)	R	R	MS	R	R	Sd / Yp	R	R	R	R	R	—
9. *Brassica nigra* (Black Mustard)	—	MS	—	—	—	Sd / Yp	—	S	S	S	MS	S
10. *Brassica rapa* ssp. *campestris* (Wild Turnip)	—	MS	MR	MS	—	Sd / Yp	—	MS	MR	R	R	S
11. *Capsella bursa-pastoris* (Shepherd's Purse)	S	S	MS	S	S	Sd / Yp	S	S	S	MS	S	S
12. *Cerastium holosteoides* (Common Mouse-ear)	S	S	S	S	—	Sd / Yp	S	S	S	S	MS	S
13. *Chenopodium album* (Fat-hen)	S	S	MS	S	S	Sd / Yp	S	S	MS	MS	S	S
14. *Chrysanthemum segetum* (Corn Marigold)	—	R	R	S	—	Sd / Yp	—	R	R	R	R	R
15. *Erysimum cheiranthoides* (Treacle Mustard)	—	—	MS	MS	—	Sd / Yp	—	—	—	—	—	S
16. *Euphorbia exigua* (Dwarf Spurge)	—	—	—	—	—	Sd / Yp	—	MS / MR	—	—	—	—

Weeds	Soil-applied				Stage of growth	Foliage-applied				
	Chlor-bro-muron	Chlor-propham	Linuron	Prometryne		Chlor-bro-muron	Linuron	Mineral oil	Prometryne	Pentano-chlor
17. *Euphorbia helioscopia* (Sun Spurge)	—	—	—	—	Sd	—	MS	—	MR	S
					Yp	—	MR	—	—	—
18. *Euphorbia peplus* (Petty Spurge)	—	—	—	—	Sd	—	MS	—	—	S
					Yp	—	MR	—	—	—
19. *Fumaria officinalis* (Common Fumitory)	R	MS	R	S	Sd	R	R	MS	S	S
					Yp	R	R	R	MR	S
20. *Galeopsis speciosa* (Large-flowered Hemp-nettle)	—	S	S	—	Sd	—	S	S	—	S
					Yp	—	MS	MR	—	—
21. *Galeopsis tetrahit* (Common Hemp-nettle)	—	S	S	S	Sd	—	S	S	S	S
					Yp	—	MS	MR	S	—
22. *Galinsoga parviflora* (Gallant Soldier)	—	R	S	—	Sd	—	S	S	S	S
					Yp	—	S	MS	—	—
23. *Galium aparine* (Cleavers)	MS	R	MR	R	Sd	MR	R	—	R	S
					Yp	R	R	—	R	S
24. *Geranium dissectum* (Cut-leaved Crane's-bill)	—	R	—	—	Sd	—	—	—	—	—
					Yp	—	—	—	—	—
25. *Geranium pusillum* (Small-flowered Crane's-bill)	—	—	—	—	Sd	—	—	—	—	MR
					Yp	—	—	—	—	R
26. *Lamium amplexicaule* (Henbit Dead-nettle)	MR	R	MR	—	Sd	MR	MR	S	—	S
					Yp	R	R	MS	—	MR
27. *Lamium purpureum* (Red Dead-nettle)	S	MR	MS	—	Sd	S	MS	S	—	S
					Yp	—	MR	MS	R	MR

28. *Lapsana communis* (Nipplewort)	—	R	S	—	Sd	—	—	—	—	—
					Yp	—	—	—	—	—
29. *Lithospermum arvense* (Field Gromwell)	—	—	S	—	Sd	—	—	—	—	—
					Yp	—	—	—	—	—
30. *Lycopsis arvensis* (Bugloss)	—	—	MS	—	Sd	—	—	—	S	—
					Yp	—	—	—	—	—
31. *Matricaria matricarioides* (Pineappleweed)	S	R	S	S	Sd	MS	R	MS	R	R
					Yp	MR	R	R	R	R
32. *Matricaria recutita* (Scented Mayweed)	S	R	S	S	Sd	MS	R	MS	R	R
					Yp	MR	R	R	R	R
33. *Medicago lupulina* (Black Medick)	—	R	MR	—	Sd	—	MS	—	—	—
					Yp	—	MR	—	—	R
34. *Myosotis arvensis* (Field Forget-me-not)	S	—	MS	—	Sd	MS	MS	—	—	—
					Yp	MR	MR	—	—	—
35. *Papaver dubium* (Long-headed Poppy)	—	S	S	—	Sd	—	S	S	—	—
					Yp	—	MR	MR	—	—
36. *Papaver rhoeas* (Common Poppy)	—	S	S	S	Sd	—	S	S	S	—
					Yp	—	MR	MR	MS	—
37. *Poa annua* (Annual Meadow-grass)	S	S	MS	S	Sd	MS	MR	S	R	MS
					Yp	R	R	S	R	MR
38. *Polygonum aviculare* (Knotgrass)	S	S	MS	S	Sd	MS	MS	S	R	S
					Yp	R	R	MR	R	MR
39. *Polygonum convolvulus* (Black-bindweed)	MS	S	S	S	Sd	MR	S	—	—	S
					Yp	R	MS	—	—	MS
40. *Polygonum lapathifolium* (Pale Persicaria)	S	S	S	—	Sd	S	S	S	S	S
					Yp	—	MR	MR	MS	S
41. *Polygonum persicaria* (Redshank)	S	S	S	S	Sd	S	S	S	S	S
					Yp	—	MR	MR	MS	S

Weeds	Stage of growth	Soil-applied Chlorbromuron	Chlorpropham	Linuron	Prometryne	Foliage-applied Chlorbromuron	Linuron	Mineral oil	Prometryne	Pentanochlor
42. *Ranunculus arvensis* (Corn Buttercup)	Sd	—	—	MR	—	—	—	—	MR	—
	Yp					—	—	—	—	—
43. *Raphanus raphanistrum* (Wild Radish)	Sd	—	MR	S	S	—	S	MS	MS	S
	Yp				MS	—	MS	MR	MR	S
44. *Scandix pecten-veneris* (Shepherd's-needle)	Sd	—	—	—	—	—	—	—	—	—
	Yp					—	—	—	—	—
45. *Senecio vulgaris* (Groundsel)	Sd	S	R	S	S	S	MS	MS	MS	MS
	Yp					—	R	R	R	R
46. *Sinapis alba* (White Mustard)	Sd	—	MR	MS	—	—	S	S	—	S
	Yp					—	MS	MS	—	—
47. *Sinapis arvensis* (Charlock)	Sd	S	MR	S	S	S	S	S	MS	S
	Yp				MS	—	MS	MS	MR	—
48. *Solanum nigrum* (Black Nightshade)	Sd	R	R	MS	S	R	MS	S	S	R
	Yp					R	MR	MR	MS	R
49. *Sonchus asper* (Prickly Sow-thistle)	Sd	—	R	S	—	—	S	MS	—	—
	Yp					—	MS	R	—	—
50. *Sonchus oleraceus* (Smooth Sow-thistle)	Sd	MS	R	S	S	MR	S	MS	—	S
	Yp					R	MS	R	—	S
51. *Spergula arvensis* (Corn Spurrey)	Sd	—	S	S	S	—	S	S	S	S
	Yp					—	S	MS	S	S
52. *Stellaria media* (Common Chickweed)	Sd	S	S	S	S	S	S	S	S	S
	Yp					—	S	S	S	S

Weed					Stage					
53. *Thlaspi arvense* (Field Penny-cress)	S	S	S	S	Sd / Yp	MR / R	S / MS	S / MS	S / MS	S / S
54. *Tripleurospermum maritimum* ssp. *inodorum* (Scentless Mayweed)	S	R	S	S	Sd / Yp	MR / R	R / R	MS / R	R / R	R / R
55. *Urtica urens* (Small Nettle)	S	S	S	S	Sd / Yp	S / —	S / MS	MS / MR	S / MR	S / MS
56. *Veronica agrestis* (Green Field-speedwell)	—	S	MR	S	Sd / Yp	— / —	MS / R	— / —	— / —	— / —
57. *Veronica arvensis* (Wall Speedwell)	—	S	MR	S	Sd / Yp	— / —	MS / R	S / MR	— / —	— / —
58. *Veronica hederifolia* (Ivy-leaved Speedwell)	MR	MS	MR	S	Sd / Yp	MR / R	MS / R	S / MR	S / —	— / —
59. *Veronica persica* (Common Field-speedwell)	MS	S	MR	S	Sd / Yp	MR / R	MS / R	S / MR	S / —	S / MS
60. *Vicia hirsuta* (Hairy Tare)	—	R	MR	—	Sd / Yp	— / —	MR / R	— / —	— / —	— / —
61. *Vicia sativa* (Common Vetch)	—	R	R	—	Sd / Yp	— / —	MR / R	— / —	— / —	— / —
62. *Viola arvensis* (Field Pansy)	S	R	S	—	Sd / Yp	MR / R	MS / MR	MS / R	S / —	S / —
63. *Viola tricolor* (Wild Pansy)	—	R	S	—	Sd / Yp	— / —	MS / R	MS / R	— / —	— / —

77

CAULIFLOWER (drilled)

2.140   **Di-allate** *1·7 kg/ha in medium to high volume incorporated for control of germinating* Avena spp. *(Wild-oats) and* Alopecurus myosuroides *(Black-grass).*

Incorporation details (2.049). Field experience indicates that this treatment will not interfere with other soil-applied herbicides used for broad-leaved weed control.

2.141   **Trifluralin** *1·1 kg/ha in medium volume incorporated into the soil to control annual weeds (2.122) on loamy sands, sandy loams, loams and clay loams.*

The treatment can be applied during soil preparation at any time from 14 days before, until immediately before drilling but must be mechanically incorporated within 30 min after application. For incorporation details see 2.103.

Because of its persistence trifluralin is not recommended for use on plant-raising beds.

Trifluralin is not recommended for sands or soils containing 10 per cent or more of organic matter.

Only recommended crops should be drilled or planted within 5 months of treatment.

Soil should be thoroughly cultivated to a depth of at least 150 mm before drilling or planting succeeding crops other than recommended crops.

After an autumn application of trifluralin cereal and grass crops should not be sown until the following autumn.

2.142   *Contact pre-emergence sprays (2.002–2.003) to kill seedling weeds that emerge before the crop.*

2.143   **Nitrofen** *3·4 kg/ha in medium to high volume within 3 days after drilling for residual control of annual weeds (2.122).*

Nitrofen is most effective when there is a fine surface tilth and the soil is moist at the time of weed emergence. Incorporation, whether mechanical or by irrigation, reduces the effectiveness. Heavy rainfall shortly after spraying may lead to some crop damage.

2.144   **Propachlor** *4·4 kg/ha on mineral soils or 6·5 kg/ha on organic soils in* *medium to high volume or as granules shortly after drilling for residual control of annual weeds (2.122).*

Best results are obtained when the seedbed has a fine even tilth and is free from clods. A temporary check to crop growth may occur, but recovery is normally complete and maturity is not affected.

2.145   **Sulfallate** *2·0 kg/ha plus* **chlorpropham** *0·28 kg/ha in high volume within 2 days after drilling for residual control of annual weeds (2.122).*

The seed should be drilled to an even depth and best results are obtained when the seedbed is moist and has a fine tilth. This treatment is not effective on black fen or other highly organic soils.

POST-EMERGENCE TREATMENT

2.146   **Propachlor** *4·4 kg/ha on mineral soils or 6·5 kg/ha on organic soils in medium to high volume or as granules when the crop has developed 3 to 4 true leaves for residual control of annual weeds (2.122).*

This treatment can be applied to clean crops which have received contact pre-emergence sprays, once the correct crop growth stage has been reached. Weeds that have passed the cotyledon stage will not be killed. Best results are obtained when the weeds are germinating and just beginning to emerge.

CAULIFLOWER (transplanted)

PRE-PLANTING TREATMENTS

2.147   **Di-allate** *1·7 kg/ha in medium to high volume incorporated for control of germinating* Avena *spp. (Wild-oats) and* Alopecurus myosuroides *(Black-grass).*

For incorporation details see 2.049. Field experience indicates that this treatment will not interfere with other soil-applied herbicides used for broad-leaved weed control.

2.148   **Trifluralin** *1·1 kg/ha in medium volume incorporated for residual control of annual weeds (2.122).*

The spray can be applied during soil preparation at any time from 14 days before until immediately before planting, but must be mechanically incorporated into the top 50 mm of soil within 30 min after application. For details of incorporation methods and following crops see 2.103. Trifluralin is not recommended on sands or on soils with 10 per cent or more of organic matter.

2.149   [**For information.**] Dinitramine has shown promise at 0·25–0·35 kg/ha in

110–170 litres water incorporated for residual control of annual weeds (2.122).

Spray overall within 14 days before transplanting onto a weed and clod free seedbed. Thoroughly incorporate into the top 50 mm of soil within 24 hr of spraying.

POST-PLANTING TREATMENT

2.150 **Propachlor** *4·4 kg/ha on mineral soils or 6·5 kg/ha on organic soils in medium to high volume or as granules shortly after planting for residual control of annual weeds (2.122).*

Best results are obtained when application is made before the weeds have emerged and when the soil surface is even and free from clods.

CELERY

PRE-EMERGENCE CONTACT TREATMENT

2.151 *Contact pre-emergence sprays (2.002–2.003) to kill seedling weeds that emerge before the crop.*

POST-EMERGENCE TREATMENTS

2.152 **Chlorbromuron** *0·55–1·7 kg/ha in medium to high volume for contact and residual control of annual weeds (2.336).*

Application may be made to drilled or transplanted crops when the crop is fully established or when direct seeded plants have at least 2 leaves. Slight yellowing of the foliage may sometimes occur but is soon outgrown.

2.153 **Linuron** *0·55–1·1 kg/ha in medium to high volume for contact and residual control of annual weeds (2.335).*

On plant beds and drilled crops, application should be made when the crop has developed the first true leaf. On transplanted crops application should be made once the plants have become established. The selectivity of linuron can be influenced by formulation and certain formulations may not be recommended for post-emergence use on celery. Application during very hot weather is not advisable because of the risk of some crop scorch.

2.154 **Pentanochlor** *2·2 kg/ha in high volume for contact kill of seedling annual weeds (2.139).*

Application should be made after the celery seedlings have fully developed their cotyledons and the first true leaf is showing. The use of a coarse, low-pressure spray is desirable. A second application may be made at a later stage of growth if further weeds emerge after treatment.

2.155 **Pentanochlor** *1·7 kg/ha plus* **chlorpropham** *0·84 kg/ha in high volume for contact and residual control of annual weeds (2.139).*
  Application should be made after the celery seedlings have fully developed their cotyledons and the first true leaf is showing. The use of a coarse, low pressure spray is desirable. A second application may be made at a later stage of growth if further weeds emerge after treatment. This treatment may be applied also to transplanted celery as soon as the seedling weeds have reached the cotyledon stage, normally 2–3 weeks after planting out.

2.156 **Prometryne** *1·1 kg/ha in medium to high volume on plant beds or drilled crops for contact and residual control of annual weeds (2.139).*
  Transplanted crops may be sprayed when established and drilled crops once the celery has at least 2 true leaves. If further seedlings appear, repeat applications may be made at intervals of 3 to 4 weeks provided that at least 6 weeks elapse between last spraying and harvesting of the crop.

2.157 **Certain mineral oils** *(2.137) at 550 litres/ha for contact kill of seedling weeds in seedbeds (2.139).*
  Applications may be made at any time from the cotyledon stage until the crop has 4–5 true leaves.

2.158 [**For information.**] Chlorpropham 1·1–2·2 kg/ha has given good results when applied as a medium or high volume post-planting spray on pricked-out celery, within a week after pricking-out.

CHICORY

PRE-EMERGENCE RESIDUAL TREATMENT

2.159 **Propyzamide** *1·1 kg/ha in medium volume to control annual weeds (3.156).*
  Apply after drilling but before crop emergence. Under dry conditions the dose should be increased to 1·4 kg/ha and control is improved by irrigation. Optimum weed control is obtained by spraying before weeds have more than 2 true leaves.

CORIANDER

2.160 Wide-scale field trials have not been carried out on this crop in the UK but the following information is based on limited experimental work and field usage.

PRE-SOWING TREATMENT

2.161   **[For information.**] Tri-allate 1·68 kg/ha in medium to high volume has given good results when applied and immediately incorporated to control germinating *Avena* spp. (Wild-oats) and *Alopecurus myosuroides* (Black-grass). Thorough incorporation is important (1.071).

PRE-EMERGENCE CONTACT TREATMENT

2.162   *Contact pre-emergence sprays (2.002–2.003) to kill seedling weeds that emerge before the crop.*

PRE-EMERGENCE RESIDUAL TREATMENTS

2.163   **[For information.**] Atrazine 1·1–1·7 kg/ha in medium to high volume has been satisfactorily used in trials to control annual weeds. Moist soil conditions are required and in dry areas application should be made soon after sowing.

2.164   **[For information]** Linuron 0·56–0·7 kg/ha in medium to high volume has proved satisfactory when used to control annual weeds. The treatment may be applied any time between drilling and crop emergence. Under dry conditions application to moist soil soon after drilling is likely to give the best weed control.

POST-EMERGENCE TREATMENTS

2.165   **[For information.**] Mineral oils and tractor vaporizing oil applied as for carrots (2.137 and 2.139) for the control of annual weeds.

2.166   **[For information.**] Prometryne 1·7 kg/ha when the crop is at the 2–4 leaf stage to control seedling broad-leaved annual weeds. Weeds which have grown beyond the cotyledon stage are unlikely to be controlled but some residual activity against germinating weeds is likely.

FIELD BEAN see BEAN (broad and field) (2.005)

KALE

PRE-SOWING TREATMENTS

2.167   **Aminotriazole** *4·48 kg/ha in medium volume to control* Agropyron repens *(Common Couch),* Rumex *spp. (Docks) and* Cirsium *spp. (Thistles).*

Spray between mid-March and the end of October when the actively growing foliage is 3–4 inches high in the autumn or at least 3 inches high in the spring. Plough 3–6 weeks later, completely inverting the soil.

The crop may be sown as soon as ploughing and cultivations are completed, but on very light soils and sands, an interval of 6 weeks must lapse between application and sowing. If drought occurs after spraying, planting should not take place until several days after reasonable rainfall.

2.168 **Di-allate** *1·7 kg/ha in medium or high volume incorporated for control of germinating* Avena *spp. (Wild-oats) and* Alopecurus myosuroides *(Black-grass).*

Thorough incorporation is important (2.049). Field experience indicates that this treatment will not interfere with herbicides used to control broad-leaved weeds.

2.169 **TCA** *33·0 kg/ha in medium or high volume at least 4 weeks before drilling to control perennial grass weeds* (12.019).

The chemical should be sprayed on to the soil surface and incorporated to a depth of 100 to 125 mm. Cultivations which also fragment the couch grass rhizomes will greatly improve control.

2.170 **TCA** *7·8–17·0 kg/ha in medium or high volume to suppress perennial grasses and control germinating* Avena fatua *(Wild-oat)* (12.019).

An interval of 5–7 days should be allowed between application of the chemical and drilling. The lower doses should be used where wild oat is the only problem. The herbicide should be incorporated into the soil during seedbed preparation. Control of *Avena fatua* (Wild-oat) is variable and depends on the depth of germination and rainfall.

2.171 **Trifluralin** *1·1 kg/ha in medium volume incorporated into the soil for residual control of annual weeds (2.122) on loamy sands, sandy loams, loams and clay loams.*

The treatment can be applied during soil preparation at any time from 14 days before until immediately before drilling but must be mechanically incorporated within 30 min of application. For incorporation details see 2.103.

Trifluralin is not recommended for sands or soils containing 10 per cent or more of organic matter.

Only recommended crops should be drilled or planted within 5 months of treatment.

Soil should be thoroughly cultivated to a depth of at least 150 mm before drilling or planting succeeding crops other than recommended crops.

After the autumn application of trifluralin cereal and grass crops should not be sown until the following autumn.

2.172 **[For information.]** Dinitramine has shown promise at 0·25–0·45 kg/ha in 110–170 litres water incorporated for residual control of annual weeds (2.000).

Spray overall, within 14 days before drilling, onto a weed and clod free seedbed. Thoroughly incorporated into the top 5 cm of soil within 24 hr of spraying.

PRE-EMERGENCE CONTACT TREATMENTS

2.173   *Contact pre-emergence sprays (2.002–2.003) to kill seedling weeds that emerge before the crop.*

These treatments are likely to prove more reliable in areas of moderate or high rainfall than in the drier regions of the country.

PRE-EMERGENCE RESIDUAL TREATMENTS

2.174   **Nitrofen** *3·4 kg/ha in medium to high volume within 3 days after drilling for residual control of annual weeds (2.122).*

Nitrofen is most effective when there is a fine surface tilth and the soil is moist at the time of weed emergence. Heavy rainfall shortly after spraying may lead to some crop damage. Add chlorpropham for control of *Stellaria media* (Common Chickweed).

2.175   **Propachlor** *4·4 kg/ha in medium to high volume or as granules shortly after drilling for the control of annual broad-leaved weeds (2.122).*

Best results are obtained where the seedbed has a fine even tilth and is free of clods. A temporary check to crop growth may occur but recovery is rapid under good growing conditions.

2.176   [**For information.**] Alachlor 1·7–2·1 kg/ha in medium volume shortly after drilling for the control of annual broad-leaved weeds. This treatment is not recommended for direct drilled crops.

POST-EMERGENCE TREATMENTS

2.177   **Aziprotryne** *at 2·0 kg/ha on all soil types when the crop is at least 65 mm high and has more than 3 true leaves on marrowstem and thousand-head types controls for the annual weeds (2.122).*

Weeds with more than 2 true leaves will not be controlled. The chemical is rainfast once the initial spray has dried.

2.178   **Desmetryne** *0·28–0·42 kg/ha as a medium volume fine spray, preferably at high pressure, for the control of annual weeds particularly* Chenopodium album *(Fat-hen) (2.122).*

The higher dose should normally be used in low rainfall areas or during drought conditions. The kale plants should have 3 true leaves and be at least 12 cm high before spraying. There may be some scorch on the edges of the leaves especially in thin crops and the leaf colour may become paler than normal but complete recovery takes place after a few weeks. Rain within 24 hr of spraying may lessen the amount of herbicide taken in by the weed foliage and so reduce the effectiveness of weed control. A minimum interval of 4 weeks following treatment should elapse before the crop is fed to livestock.

2.179   **Sodium monochloroacetate** *22·0 kg/ha in medium or high volume to control certain broad-leaved weeds (2.122) in marrowstem and thousand-head kale when the crop plants have 2–5 true leaves.*

The dose should be increased to 28 kg/ha applied in not less than 270 litres/ha of water when the weed growth is hard as often occurs following drought conditions. Damage to the crop increases markedly after the 5-leaf stage. Increasing the volume to 1100 litres/ha reduces the risk of crop damage but may also give poorer weed control.

2.180   [**For information.**] Aziprotryne 1 kg/ha in tank mixture with desmetryne 0·13–0·22 kg/ha for control of annual broad-leaved weeds.

Limited experience indicates that this mixture gives useful results when weeds are too big or not susceptible to either aziprotryne or desmetryne applied alone. Apply when the crop has at least 6 true leaves which have good wax cover. Not for use on hungry gap or rape kale.

LEEK (drilled)

PRE-EMERGENCE CONTACT TREATMENTS

2.181   *Contact pre-emergence sprays (2.002–2.003) to kill seedling weeds that emerge before the crop.*

PRE-EMERGENCE RESIDUAL TREATMENTS

2.182   **Chlorpropham** *1·1–2·2 kg/ha or* **Chlorpropham** *1·1 kg/ha plus* **fenuron** *0·28 kg/ha in medium to high volume for residual control of annual weeds (2.336).*

The seedbed should be left with a fine tilth and the crop seed drilled at an even depth. These treatments are not advised on very light sandy soils with a low organic content because of the risk of crop damage if heavy rain follows application. The risk of damage is least when the spray is applied just before crop emergence.

2.183   **Propachlor** *4·4 kg/ha in medium to high volume or as granules to control annual weeds (2.122).*

The spray may be applied at any time before or after crop emergence but best results are obtained when the weeds are germinating and just beginning to emerge, and when the seedbed has a fine even tilth, free from clods. On black fen soils the residual effect is shorter than on mineral soils; some improvement may be obtained on black fen by increasing the dose to 6·5 kg/ha. A second application can be made if necessary to control late-germinating weeds.

2.184   **Pyrazone** *0·84 kg/ha plus* **chlorbufam** *0·70 kg/ha on light and medium soils or* **pyrazone** *1·1 kg/ha plus* **chlorbufam** *0·91 kg/ha on heavy soils in medium to high volume for contact and residual control of annual weeds.*
Application on light sands or sandy loam soils is not recommended because of the risk of crop damage. On highly organic soils, the treatment is effective only against seedling weeds that have already emerged. Application may be made at any time after drilling until shortly before emergence, but the crop should not be sprayed during emergence. With leeks drilled early in the year it is an advantage to delay spraying until 2–3 weeks after drilling.

2.185   [**For information.**] Tank mixtures of paraquat with propachlor, plus chlorpropham where soil type allows, have given successful contact and residual control of annual weeds. The herbicide manufacturers should be consulted before mixing products.

POST-EMERGENCE TREATMENTS

2.186   **Aziprotryne** *2·0 kg/ha in medium to high volume for contact and residual control of annual weeds (2.122).*
The spray should not be applied until the crop has 3 true leaves. Emerged weeds which have more than 2 true leaves are not effectively controlled, and application should normally follow pre-emergence treatment with another herbicide.

2.187   **Ioxynil** *as the octanoate ester at 0·7 kg/ha in medium to high volume to control emerged annual broad-leaved weeds (2.353).*
The treatment should be applied after the 3-leaf stage of the crop, but not later than 7 days before harvest. Some leaf scorch and distortion may occur but this is transitory except on crops damaged by adverse growing conditions, which should not be sprayed.

2.188   **Ioxynil** *up to 0·56 kg/ha plus* **linuron** *up to 0·56 kg/ha in medium to high volume for the contact and residual control of annual broad-leaved weeds.*
The treatment should be applied between the 2·5-leaf stage of the crop and the unrolling of the leaves. Some slight leaf scorch may occur especially if the crop has been damaged in any way.

2.189   **Methazole** *1·7–2·1 kg/ha in low or medium volume for contact and residual control of annual broad-leaved weeds.*
The spray should not be applied until the crop has three true leaves.

Best results are obtained when weeds are in the seedling stage, but some weeds are controlled at the 6–8 leaf stage.

Certain leek varieties are susceptible to methazole but the following may be safely treated although a temporary check to growth may occur:

Artico, Elephant (Oliphant), Empire K7, Goliath, Hubertus, Inverno, Kilima, Lyon, Marble Pillar, Musselburgh, Odin, Rex, Regius, Siberia, Splendid, Titan, Winter Giant, Winter Reuzen.

2.190 **Monolinuron** *at 0·84 kg/ha in medium volume for contact and residual control of annual weeds (2.336).*

This treatment is recommended on all soil types using the higher volume where weed or crop density might restrict spray penetration. The treatments should not be applied until the plants are 170 mm high. The crop should normally be weed free at the time of application. Where a contact material has been applied allow 14 days before the application of monolinuron.

2.191 **Pyrazone** *1·1 kg/ha plus* **chlorbufam** *0·91 kg/ha in medium to high volume for contact and residual control of annual weeds (3.156).*

This treatment is not recommended on light sands or sandy loam soils because of the risk of crop damage. Application should be made after the crop has passed the crook stage and before the weeds present have more than 2 true leaves. Post-emergence application may follow a pre-emergence spray.

2.192 **Sodium monochloroacetate** *28·0 kg/ha in 280 litres/ha applied after the crook stage has been passed but before 4 true leaves have developed, for contact kill of some annual broad-leaved weeds (2.122).*

Wetting agents must not be added to the spray, otherwise crop damage will result. A period of at least 12 hr of fine weather after spraying is essential for success, and spraying should not be attempted if frost is imminent.

LEEK (transplanted)

POST-PLANTING TREATMENTS

2.193 **Aziprotryne** *2·0 kg/ha in medium to high volume for contact and residual control of annual weeds (2.122).*

The spray should not be applied until the crop is established, normally about 2 weeks after planting, and best results are obtained when most of the weeds are just emerging.

2.194 **Chlorpropham** *1·1–2·2 kg/ha or* **chlorpropham** *1·1 kg/ha plus* **fenuron**

0·28 kg/ha in medium to high volume for residual control of annual weeds (2.139).

These treatments should not be applied until the crop is established, normally about 2 weeks after planting. They are not advised on sandy soils with a low organic content because of the risk of crop damage if heavy rain follows application.

2.195   **Ioxynil** *as the octanoate ester at 0·7 kg/ha in medium to high volume to control emerged annual broad-leaved weeds.*

The treatment should be applied after the leeks have become established, but not later than 7 days before harvest. Some leaf scorch and distortion may occur but this is transitory except on crops damaged by adverse growing conditions. These should not be sprayed.

2.196   **Ioxynil** *up to 0·56 kg/ha plus* **linuron** *up to 0·56 kg/ha in medium to high volume for the contact and residual control of annual broad-leaved weeds.*

The treatment should be applied after transplants have become established but before the leaves unroll. Some slight leaf scorch may occur especially if the crop has been damaged in any way.

2.197   **Methazole** *1·7–2·1 kg/ha in low or medium volume for contact and residual control of annual broad-leaved weeds (2.353).*

The treatment should not be applied until the crop is established, normally two weeks after planting.

Certain leek varieties are susceptible to methazole but the following may be safely treated although a temporary check to growth may occur:

Artico, Elephant (Oliphant), Empire K7, Goliath, Hubertus, Inverno, Kilima, Lyon, Marble Pillar, Musselburgh, Odin, Rex, Regius, Siberia, Splendid, Titan, Winter Giant, Winter Reuzen.

2.198   **Monolinuron** *0·84 kg/ha in medium to high volume for contact and residual control of annual weeds (2.336).*

This treatment should be applied once the plants are established and providing they are 170 mm high and of pencil thickness.

2.199   **Pyrazone** *1·1 kg/ha plus* **chlorbufam** *0·91 kg/ha on medium soils or pyrazone 1·7 kg/ha plus chlorbufam 1·4 kg/ha on heavy soils and those with high organic content for contact and residual control of annual weeds (3.156).*

The higher dose should be used on medium soils if weeds have reached the 2-leaf stage at the time of application. This treatment is not recommended on light sands or sandy loam soils. On highly organic soils the treatment is only effective against emerged weeds.

2.200   **[For information]** **Simazine** *0·56 kg/ha on light soils or 0·84 kg/ha on* *medium and heavy soils in medium to high volume as soon as the crop has become established for residual control of annual weeds.*

LETTUCE (drilled and transplanted)

PRE-EMERGENCE CONTACT TREATMENTS

2.201   *Contact pre-emergence sprays, using the stale-seedbed technique (2.002—2.003) to kill seedling weeds that emerge before the crop.*

PRE-EMERGENCE RESIDUAL TREATMENTS

2.202   **Chlorpropham** *0·84—1·1 kg/ha in medium to high volume immediately after drilling or as a pre-planting spray to weed-free soil a few days before planting out lettuce under glass or in the open for residual control of some annual weeds (2.139).*

This treatment is not advised on very light sandy soils with a low organic content because of the risk of crop damage if heavy rain follows application. Watering after application should be avoided. Some instances of injury to frame lettuce have been reported when sunny periods, leading to high temperatures under the glass, have followed planting.

2.203   **Propham** *4·4—6·8 kg/ha plus* **diuron** *0·28—0·41 kg/ha plus methyl isopropyl phenyl carbamate 1·1—1·7 kg in high volume for the residual control of annual weeds.*

For the drilled crops the lower rate is recommended from September to May after sowing and the higher dose from May to early August under very warm dry conditions in the summer.

For the transplanted crop the lower dose is used from October to early May and the higher dose from late May to September. In both cases being applied before transplanting. Under very dry soil conditions best weed control will be achieved if the treatment is incorporated.

2.204   **Propyzamide** *1·1 kg/ha in medium to high volume for residual control of annual weeds* (3.156).

Under dry conditions the dose should be increased to 1·4 kg/ha. Many annual weeds are controlled but members of the Compositae and Leguminosae are resistant. Perennial grasses will be suppressed. Optimum weed control is obtained by spraying before weeds have more than 2 true leaves. The crop may be sprayed any time up to 6 weeks before harvest. Propyzamide is persistent particularly at low temperatures and when soils remain dry.

2.205   **Sulfallate** 2·0 kg/ha plus **chlorpropham** *0·28 kg/ha in high volume immediately after drilling for residual control of annual weeds (2.122).*

2.206   **Propyzamide** *1·1 kg/ha in medium to high volume for residual control of annual weeds* (3.156).

Under dry conditions the dose should be increased to 1·4 kg/ha. Many annual weeds are controlled but members of the Compositae and Leguminosae are resistant. Perennial grasses will be suppressed. Optimum weed control is obtained by spraying before weeds have more than 2 true leaves. The crop may be sprayed any time up to 6 weeks before harvest. Propyzamide is persistent particularly at low temperatures and when soils remain dry.

LINSEED and FLAX

PRE-SOWING TREATMENT

2.207   [**For information.**] Trifluralin 1·1 kg/ha in medium volume incorporated for residual control of annual weeds (2.122).

The spray can be applied during soil preparation at any time from 14 days before until immediately before drilling but must be mechanically incorporated into the top 5 cm of soil within 30 min after application.

PRE-EMERGENCE TREATMENTS

2.208   [**For information**] Linuron at doses of 0·84–1·7 kg/ha in medium volume applied on the seedbed pre-emergence has given useful control of annual grass and broad-leaved weeds. The lower dose is used on light soil in high rainfall areas (2.336).

2.209   [**For information.**] Linuron at 0·56–0·85 kg/ha plus lenacil at 0·45–0·67 kg/ha in medium volume has been used successfully to control germinating annual weeds in both linseed and flax.

POST-EMERGENCE TREATMENTS

On flax post-emergence treatments may affect the fibre through a check to growth.

2.210   **MCPA** *at doses up to 1·7 kg/ha applied in medium volume when the crop is less than 50 mm high and not more than 150 mm high to control susceptible broad-leaved weeds in linseed. A check in growth will occur, from which the crop will recover.*

2.211   **Bromoxynil ester** *0·28 kg/ha plus* **MCPA ester** *0·28 kg/ha when the crop is 50–150 mm high to control annual broad-leaved weeds in linseed.*

2.212   [**For information.**] Asulam 1·1 kg/ha, with a non-ionic wetter at 0·2 per cent in the spray solution, when the crop is 50–150 mm high to control Wild-oats and annual grasses in linseed. To this may be added bromoxynil ester 0·21 kg/ha plus MCPA ester 0·21 kg/ha to give control of annual broad-leaved weeds. A slight transient check in growth will occur, but will not affect seed yield. *Stellaria media* (Common chickweed) is not controlled.

MAIZE and SWEET CORN

PRE-SOWING TREATMENTS

2.213   **Atrazine** *split dose application totalling 4·5 kg/ha in medium or high volume to control perennial grasses and annual broad-leaved weeds.*

The first spray of 2·2 kg/ha should be applied to perennial grasses in early spring after commencement of growth. Plough or deep cultivate 1–3 weeks after application. The second spray of 2·2 kg/ha may be applied pre- or post-emergence of the crop.

No crop other than maize or sweetcorn should be grown for 18 months after the second spray of 2·2 kg/ha.

If weed growth indicates the need for control of annual broad-leaved weeds in the second crop of maize or sweetcorn, the dose of atrazine should not exceed 1·1 kg/ha.

2.214   **EPTC** *at 4·5 kg/ha plus protectant in medium volume to control perennial and annual grasses and some annual broad-leaved weeds.*

Application should be made during the two weeks before drilling, but for best control of annual weeds apply immediately pre-drilling. Incorporation followed by rolling must take place within 15 min of application. All soils except those with more than 10 per cent organic matter can be treated. Any crop can be sown or planted after harvest of the maize.

PRE-EMERGENCE CONTACT TREATMENTS

2.215   Contact pre-emergence sprays (2.002–2.003) to kill weeds that emerge before the crop.

PRE-EMERGENCE RESIDUAL TREATMENTS

2.216   **Atrazine** *1·1 kg/ha on very light and light soils or 1·7 kg/ha on medium and heavy soils in medium to high volume to control annual weeds* (3.156).

Weed control is likely to be unsatisfactory on soils high in organic matter. A fine seedbed is desirable and shallow incorporation may improve the activity of atrazine under dry soil conditions. Where crop failure occurs after the application of atrazine, no crop other than maize or sweetcorn should be sown for about 7 months. Under normal conditions it should be possible to sow wheat, barley or beans, but not oats, the following autumn after the necessary interval for degradation of the chemical and full inversion of the soil by mould-board plough.

2.217   **Propachlor** *4·4 kg/ha in medium to high volume or as granules shortly after drilling for the control of annual broad-leaved weeds (2.122).*
Best results are obtained where the seedbed has a fine even tilth and is free of clods. A temporary check to crop growth may occur but recovery is rapid under good growing conditions.

2.218   **Simazine** *1·1 kg/ha on very light and light soils and 1·7 kg/ha on medium and heavy soils in medium to high volume to control annual weeds.*
Weed control is usually unsatisfactory under dry soil conditions when atrazine is to be preferred. Incorporation, using light harrows, will generally improve the efficiency of simazine. As for atrazine, an interval of about 7 months should follow the application of simazine before a cereal crop is sown and the land should first be fully inverted by mould-board plough.

POST-EMERGENCE TREATMENTS

2.219   **Atrazine** *1·7 kg/ha in medium to high volume to control annual weeds.*
The treatment can be applied at any crop stage but seedling weeds should not be larger than 140 mm high.

2.220   **2·4-D-amine** *1·1 kg/ha in medium to high volume to control some annual broad-leaved weeds (1.054).*
2·4-D-amine should be applied when the crop is 75–150 mm high. Some check to the crop may occur.

2.221   [**For information.**] Mixtures of 0·85 kg/ha atrazine plus 0·56 kg/ha 2·4-D-amine have been successfully used post-emergence for the control of seedling and germinating annual weeds. The crop must be at least 75 mm high before treatment. This mixture has the advantage of dealing effectively with broad-leaved seedling weeds under dry conditions when a pre-emergence application of atrazine may be slow in acting. Because of excessive soil residues it should not be recommended after atrazine has been used pre-emergence.

2.222   **Cyanazine** *2·6 kg/ha in medium volume for the control of annual broad-leaved weeds (2.353).*
All mineral soils may be sprayed but not soils with high organic matter content.

OIL-SEED RAPE

PRE-SOWING RESIDUAL TREATMENTS

2.223   **Aminotriazole** *4·5 kg/ha in medium volume to control* Agropyron repens *(Common Couch),* Rumex *spp. (Docks) and* Circium *spp. (Thistles).*
Spray between mid-March and the end of October when the actively growing foliage is 70–100 mm high in the autumn or at least 70 mm high in the spring. Plough 3–6 weeks later, completely inverting the soil.
The crop may be sown as soon as ploughing and cultivations are completed, but, on very light soils and sands, an interval of 6 weeks must lapse between application and sowing. If drought occurs after spraying, planting should not take place until several days after reasonable rainfall.

2.224   **Di-allate** *1·7 kg/ha in medium to high volume incorporated for control of germinating* Avena *spp. (Wild-oats) and* Alopecurus myosuroides *(Black-grass).*
Incorporation 2.049. Field experience indicates that this treatment will not interfere with other soil-applied herbicides used for broad-leaved weed control.

2.225   **TCA** *34·0 kg/ha in medium or high volume at least 4 weeks before drilling to control perennial grass weeds* (12.019).
Spray onto the soil surface and incorporate to 100–120 mm. Cultivations which fragment the rhizomes will greatly improve control.

2.226   **TCA** *7·8–17·0 kg/ha in medium or high volume to suppress perennial grasses and control germinating* Avena fatua *(Wild-oat) and self-sown cereals* (12.019).
An interval of 5–7 days should be allowed between applications and drilling. The lower dose should be used where Wild-oat is the only problem. The herbicide should be incorporated into the soil during seedbed preparation. Control of Wild-oat is variable and depends on the depth of germination and rainfall.

2.227   **Trifluralin** *1·1 kg/ha in medium volume incorporated into the soil for residual control of annual weeds (2.122) on loamy sands, sandy loams, loams and clay loams.*
The treatment can be applied during soil preparation at any time from 14 days before until immediately before drilling but must be mechanically incorporated within 30 min of application. For incorporation details see 2.103.
Trifluralin is not recommended for sands or soils containing 10 per cent or more organic matter.
Only recommended crops should be drilled or planted within 5 months of treatment.

Soil should be thoroughly cultivated to a depth of at least 150 mm before drilling or planting succeeding crops other than recommended crops.

After an autumn application of trifluralin cereal and grass crops should not be sown until the following autumn.

CONTACT PRE-EMERGENCE TREATMENT

2.228 *Contact pre-emergence sprays (2.002–2.003) to kill seedling weeds that emerge before the crop.*

Rape seed normally germinates very rapidly and techniques involving stale seedbeds are unreliable for this crop.

PRE-EMERGENCE RESIDUAL TREATMENTS

2.229 **Nitrofen** *3·4 kg/ha in medium to high volume within 3 days after drilling for residual control of annual weeds (2.122).*

Nitrofen is most effective when there is a fine surface tilth and the soil is moist at the time of weed emergence. Heavy rainfall shortly after spraying may lead to some crop damage.

2.230 **Propachlor** *4·4 kg/ha in medium to high volume or as granules shortly after drilling for the control of broad-leaved weeds (2.122).*

Best results are obtained where the seedbed has a fine even tilth and is free of clods. A temporary check to crop growth may occur but recovery is rapid under good growing conditions.

POST-EMERGENCE TREATMENTS

2.231 **Barban** *0·52 kg/ha in low volume to control* Avena fatua *(Wild-oat).*

The spray should be applied when the majority of the wild oats are at the 1- to 2·5-leaf stage. Best results are obtained from a good competitive crop in narrow rows or broadcast.

2.232 **Benzoylprop-ethyl** *1·1 kg/ha in medium volume to control* Avena spp. *(Wild-oats).*

Apply when oilseed rape is 380–450 mm high in a period of good growing conditions for both the crop and the weed.

2.233 **Carbetamide** *2·1 kg/ha in medium volume for control of mainly grass weeds including* Alopecurus myosuroides *(Black-grass),* Poa spp. *(Meadow-grasses),* Avena spp. *(Wild-oats) self-sown cereals and some broad-leaved weeds.*

Spray during the late autumn and winter months (normally November to end of February) providing the crop has at least 4 true leaves, but not after the crop is growing away in the spring. Annual grasses are controlled pre- and post-weed emergence whilst self-sown cereals are reliably controlled post-emergence only. Susceptible broad-leaved weeds are controlled pre-emergence only, except Common Chickweed and Speedwell which are also controlled early post-emergence. Perennial grasses are suppressed. All soil types except those with over 10 per cent organic matter may be treated.

2.234 **Dalapon-sodium** *3·8 kg/ha in medium volume to control* Avena fatua *(Wild-oat), other annual grass weeds and self-sown cereals.*

The efficiency of the treatment on *Avena fatua* and self-sown cereals will depend on the stage of growth of the weed and activity of growth at the time of application. Cereals beyond the early tillering stage are not well controlled. The younger the weed and more active the growth the better the results. The treatment may arrest the growth of Wild-oat and grass weeds to allow the crop to dominate and smother the weed remnants, particularly when the crop is sown in narrow rows. The treatment may give a slight crop check and should not be applied when frosty periods prevail.

On no account should a high dose be used in any attempt to control perennial grass weeds.

2.235 **Propyzamide** *0·7 kg/ha in medium volume for residual control of self-sown cereals,* Avena spp. *(Wild-oats), annual grasses and some annual broad-leaved weeds in winter oilseed rape* (3.156).

Spray between 1st October and 31st January and as soon as possible after the crop reaches 3 full leaves to obtain optimum weed control. Self-sown cereals, Wild-oats, annual grasses and Common Chickweed are controlled pre-weed emergence up to the established plant stage, whilst other susceptible annual broad-leaved weeds are controlled from germination up to the 2nd leaf stage.

All soil types except those with over 10 per cent organic matter may be treated.

2.236 **[For information.]** Mixtures of carbetamide with dimefuron give control of mixed annual grass and broad-leaved weed populations in oil-seed rape. Application may be made before crop emergence, early post-emergence or after transplants are established.

ONION (drilled)

PRE-SOWING TREATMENT

2.237 **Tri-allate** *1·4–1·7 kg/ha in medium to high volume applied and immediately incorporated into the soil to control germinating* Avena spp. *(Wild-oats) and* Alopecurus myosuroides *(Black-grass).*

For incorporation details see 1.071. Field experience indicates that this treatment will not interfere with other soil-applied herbicides used for broad-leaved weed control.

PRE-EMERGENCE CONTACT TREATMENT

2.238   *Contact pre-emergence sprays (2.002–2.003) to kill seedling weeds that emerge before the crop.*

PRE-EMERGENCE RESIDUAL TREATMENTS

2.239   **Chlorpropham** *1·1–2·2 kg/ha or* **chlorpropham** *1·1 kg/ha plus* **fenuron** *0·28 kg/ha in medium to high volume for residual control of annual weeds (2.139).*

The seedbed should be left with a fine tilth and the crop seed drilled at an even depth. These treatments are not advised on sandy soils with a low organic content because of the risk of crop damage if heavy rain follows application. There is evidence that the risk of damage is least when the spray is applied just before crop emergence.

2.240   **Propachlor** *4·4 kg/ha in medium to high volume or as granules for residual control of annual weeds (2.122).*

The chemical may be applied at any time before or after crop emergence but best results are obtained when the weeds are germinating and just beginning to emerge and when the seedbed has a fine even tilth, free from clods. On black fen soils the residual effect is shorter than on mineral soils; some improvement may be obtained on black fen by increasing the dose to 6·5 kg/ha. A second application can be made if necessary to control late-germinating weeds.

2.241   **Pyrazone** *0·84 kg/ha plus* **chlorbufam** *0·70 kg/ha on light and medium soils or* **pyrazone** *1·1 kg/ha plus* **chlorbufam** *0·91 kg/ha on heavy soils in medium to high volume for contact and residual control of annual weeds (3.156).*

Application on light sands or sandy loam soils is not recommended because of the risk of crop damage. On highly organic soils, the treatment is effective only against seedling weeds that have already emerged. Application may be made at any time after drilling until shortly before emergence, but the crop should not be sprayed during emergence. With bulb onions drilled early in the year it is an advantage to delay spraying until 2–3 weeks after drilling.

2.242   [**For information.**] Tank mixtures of paraquat with propachlor, plus chlorpropham where soil type allows, have given successful contact and residual control of annual weeds. The herbicide manufacturers should be consulted before mixing products.

POST-EMERGENCE TREATMENTS

2.243 **Aziprotryne** *2·0 kg/ha in medium to high volume for contact and residual control of annual weeds (2.122).*
The spray should not be applied until the crop has 3 true leaves. Emerged weeds which have more than 2 true leaves are not effectively controlled, and application should normally follow pre-emergence treatment with another herbicide.

2.244 **Chlorpropham** *1·7 kg/ha in medium to high volume on silt soils for residual control of annual weeds (2.139).*
This treatment should be applied when the crop has 2 to 3 true leaves. It is not recommended for use on light or sandy soils. With the exception of *Stellaria media* (Common Chickweed) and *Urtica urens* (Small Nettle) chlorpropham is not effective against established weeds.

2.245 **Dinoseb-acetate** *2·8 kg/ha in medium volume for the control of seedling broad-leaved weeds (3.336).*
The spray should be applied after the 3-leaf stage of the crop when at least 150 mm high. Crops which are damaged in any way may be scorched.

2.246 **Ioxynil** *as the octanoate ester at 0·7 kg/ha in medium to high volume for contact kill of emerged annual broad-leaved weed.*
Treat after the 3-leaf stage of the crop, but not within 7 days of harvesting. A repeat treatment may be made on bulb onions and autumn sown salad onions. Some leaf scorch and distortion may occur but this is transitory except on crops growing under adverse conditions, which should not be sprayed.

2.247 **Ioxynil** *up to 0·56 kg/ha plus* **linuron** *up to 0·56 kg/ha in medium to high volume for the contact and residual control of annual broad-leaved weeds.*
The spray may be applied after the crops reach the 2·5 leaf stage. Crops which are already damaged in any way may be scorched.

2.248 **Methazole** *1·6−2·5 kg/ha according to soil type applied in 200−400 litres/ha applied at the 2 leaf stage (2½ leaf for salad onions) for the contact and residual control of annual weeds (2.353).*
Methazole has good contact effect on a number of annual weeds and residues persist up to 14 weeks on mineral soil and up to 8 weeks on high organic soils.

2.249 **Pyrazone** *1·2 kg/ha plus* **chlorbufam** *0·91 kg/ha in medium to high volume for contact and residual control of annual weeds (3.156).*
This treatment is not recommended on sands, very light soils or sandy loam soils because of the risk of crop damage. Application should be

made after the crop has passed the crook stage and before the weeds present have more than 2 true leaves. Post-emergence application may follow a pre-emergence spray.

2.250   Sodium monochloroacetate *28 kg/ha in 270 litres/ha applied after the crook stage has been passed but before 4 true leaves have developed, for contact kill of some annual broad-leaved weeds (2.122).*

Wetting agents must not be added to the spray, otherwise crop damage will result. A period of at least 12 hr of fine weather after spraying is essential for success and spraying should not be attempted if frost is imminent.

2.251   Sulphuric acid *at a concentration of 5·5–10 per cent v/v at 1100 litres/ha after the onions have passed the crook stage and have straightened up for contact kill of seedling annual broad-leaved weeds.*

PRE-HARVEST DESICCATION

2.252   Dimexan *19·0–28·0 kg/ha in low to medium volume for pre-harvest desiccation of ware and pickling onions.*

Application should be made when the crop is maturing either to facilitate harvesting at the normal time or to bring forward the time of harvest. The period between treatment and harvesting depends on the weather and the condition of the crop when treated. The crop should be dry at the time of application; late morning is the best time. As early defoliation tends to encourage sprouting of crops stored into the New Year, treated onions should not be stored after the beginning of January.

2.253   [For information.] Cyanazine 1·7 kg/ha has shown promise for the control of annual broad-leaved weeds on soils with over 10 per cent organic matter applied when onions have reached the 2 leaf stage.

ONION (grown from sets)

PRE-PLANTING TREATMENT

2.254   Tri-allate *1·7 kg/ha in medium to high volume applied and immediately incorporated into the soil to control germinating* Avena *spp. (Wild-oats) and* Alopecurus myosuroides *(Black-grass).*

This treatment may also be applied and incorporated soon after drilling but this tends to be less efficient than pre-sowing treatments particularly against *Alopecurus myosuroides* (Black-grass). For incorporation details see 1.071. Field experience indicates that this treatment will not interfere with other soil-applied herbicides used for broad-leaved weed control.

POST-PLANTING TREATMENTS

2.255   **Aziprotryne** *2·0 kg/ha in medium to high volume for contact and residual control of annual weeds (2.122).*
The spray should not be applied until the crop has 3 true leaves. Emerged weeds which have more than 2 true leaves are not effectively controlled, and application should normally follow pre-emergence treatment with another herbicide.

2.256   **Chlorpropham** *1·1–2·2* or **chlorpropham** *1·1 kg/ha plus* **fenuron** *0·28 kg/ha in medium to high volume before shoot emergence for residual control of annual weeds (2.139).*
These treatments are not advised on sandy soils with a low organic content because of the risk of crop damage if heavy rain follows application. On black fen soils especially, it is important that the spray should be applied before the weeds have begun to emerge.

2.257   **Dinoseb-acetate** *2·8 kg/ha in medium volume for the control of seedling broad-leaved weeds after the crop has established (2,336).*
Crops which are previously damaged in any way may be scorched.

2.258   **Ioxynil** *as the octanoate ester at 0·7 kg/ha in medium to high volume to control emerged annual broad-leaved weeds (2.353) after the crop has established.*
Some leaf scorch and distortion may occur but this is transitory except on crops growing under adverse conditions. These should not be sprayed.

2.259   **Ioxynil** *up to 0·56 kg/ha plus* **linuron** *up to 0·56 kg/ha in medium to high volume for the contact and residual control of annual broad-leaved weeds (1.054) after the sets have established.*
Crops which are previously damaged in any way may be scorched.

2.260   **Methazole** *1·6–2·5 kg/ha according to soil type applied in 200–400 litres/ha applied at the 2 leaf stage (2½ leaf for salad onions) for the contact and residual control of annual weeds (2.353).*
Methazole has good contact effect on a number of annual weeds and residues persist up to 14 weeks on mineral soil and up to 8 weeks on high organic soils.

2.261   **Propachlor** *4·4 kg/ha in medium to high volume or as granules for residual control of annual weeds (2.122).*
The chemical may be applied safely pre-emergence of the crop but best results are obtained when applied just prior to weed emergence. On soils with high organic matter the dose should be increased to 6·5 kg/ha.

2.262   **Pyrazone** *1·1 kg/ha plus* **chlorbufam** *0·91 kg/ha on medium soils or pyrazone 1·7 kg/ha plus* **chlorbufam** *1·4 kg/ha on heavy or organic soils* *in medium to high volume for contact and residual control of annual weeds after the sets have established (3.156).*

The higher dose should be used on medium soils if weeds have reached the 2-leaf stage at the time of application. This treatment is not recommended on light sands or sandy loam soils. On high-organic soils the treatment is only effective against emerged weeds.

PARSLEY

PRE-EMERGENCE CONTACT TREATMENT

2.263   *Contact pre-emergence sprays (2.002–2.003) to kill seedling weeds that emerge before the crop.*

PRE-EMERGENCE RESIDUAL TREATMENTS

2.264   **Linuron** *0·55–1·1 kg/ha in medium to high volume for contact and residual control of annual weeds (2.336).*

On light soils 0·55 kg/ha should be applied, on medium soils 0·85 kg/ha and on organic soils 1·1 kg/ha. The parsley seed should be sown at an even depth of not less than 10 mm and on mineral soils application should be made within 4 days after drilling. On peat and peaty soils, linuron may be applied up to crop emergence and best results are obtained when application is made at the time of weed emergence. The soil should be moist at the time of application. Good weed control depends upon sufficient rain falling after treatment to at least maintain soil moisture, but on sandy soils with a low organic content there may be some risk of crop damage if heavy rain follows application. To obtain prolonged freedom from weeds, pre-emergence treatment should be followed by a post-emergence application (2.132).

2.265   [**For information.**] Chlorpropham 0·84–1·1 kg/ha in medium to high volume has given promising results for residual control of annual weeds (2.139). This treatment should not be applied to sandy soils that are low in organic matter.

POST-EMERGENCE TREATMENTS

2.266   **Linuron** *at the doses given above (2.264) in medium to high volume for contact and residual control of annual weeds (2.139).*

Application should be made after the parsley has developed at least 1 true leaf. The selectivity of linuron can be influenced by formulation and certain formulations may not be recommended for post-emergence use on parsley. Application during very hot weather is not advisable because of the risk of some crop scorch.

2.267 Mineral oils *post-emergence as described for carrots* (2.137–2.139). Parsley is rather more susceptible than carrots and should not be sprayed until 2 true leaves have developed.

2.268 Pentanochlor *2·2 kg/ha in high volume for contact kill of seedling annual weeds (2.139).*
Application should be made after the parsley seedlings have fully developed their cotyledons and the first true leaf is showing. The use of a coarse low-pressure spray is desirable. A second application may be made at a later stage of growth if further weeds emerge after treatment.

2.269 Pentanochlor *1·7 kg/ha plus* **chlorpropham** *0·84 kg/ha in high volume for contact and residual control of annual weeds.*
Applications should be made after the parsley seedlings have fully developed their cotyledons and the first true leaf is showing. The use of a coarse low-pressure spray is desirable.

2.270 Prometryne *1·1 kg/ha in medium to high volume for contact and residual control of annual weeds (2.139).*
The spray should be applied after the crop plants have developed at least 2 true leaves or after an established crop has been cut. A period of at least 6 weeks should elapse after spraying before the crop is harvested.

PARSNIP

PRE-SOWING TREATMENTS

2.271 Tri-allate *1·7 kg/ha in medium to high volume applied and immediately incorporated into the soil to control germinating* Avena spp. *(Wild-oats) and* Alopecurus myosuroides *(Black-grass).*
Thorough incorporation is important (1.071). Limited field experience indicates that this treatment is safe and effective and will not interfere with other soil-applied herbicides used for broad-leaved weed control.

2.272 Trifluralin *1·1 kg/ha in medium volume incorporated into the seedbed to control annual weeds (2.122) on mineral soils. Incorporation 2.103.*
A follow up treatment with another herbicide either pre- or post-emergence is recommended where resistant weeds are present.
Trifluralin is not recommended for soils containing 10 per cent or more of organic matter.
Only recommended crops should be drilled or planted within 5 months of treatment.
Soils should be thoroughly cultivated to a depth of at least 150 mm before drilling or planting succeeding crops other than recommended crops.

PRE-EMERGENCE CONTACT TREATMENT

2.273   *Contact pre-emergence sprays (2.002–2.003) to kill seedling weeds that emerge before the crop.*

PRE-EMERGENCE RESIDUAL TREATMENTS

2.274   **Chlorbromuron** *0·55–1·15 kg/ha in medium to high volume for contact and residual control of annual weeds (2.336) on mineral soils.*
Application made as the weeds are just emerging will give optimum control. For prolonged weed control this treatment should be followed by a post-emergence application of chlorbromuron. On peat and other high-organic soils the post-emergence application only is recommended.

2.275   **Linuron** *0·55–1·1 kg/ha in medium to high volume for contact and residual control of annual weeds (2.336).*
The crop seed should be sown at an even depth of not less than 10 mm and on mineral soils application should be made within 4 days of drilling. On peaty and peat soils, linuron may be applied at any time after drilling but preferably at weed emergence. The soil should be moist at the time of application. Good weed control depends upon sufficient rain falling after treatment to at least maintain soil moisture but on very open sandy soils with a low organic content there may be some risk of crop damage if heavy rain follows application. For maximum weed control pre-emergence treatment should be followed by a post-emergence application.

POST-EMERGENCE TREATMENTS

2.276   **Chlorbromuron** *0·55–1·7 kg/ha, in medium to high volume for contact and residual control of annual weeds (2.336).*
The spray should not be applied until the crop has 2 true leaves. On mineral soils, application would normally follow a pre-emergence treatment. Where no pre-emergence treatment has been applied, a single post-emergence application of 1·1 kg/ha on light soils or 1·7 kg/ha on other soils may be made when the crop has 2 true leaves.

2.277   **Linuron** *0·55 kg/ha to 1·1 kg/ha in medium to high volume for contact and residual control of annual weeds (2.336).*
Where a pre-emergence treatment has previously been made, this treatment should be applied when fresh weed germination occurs. If no pre-emergence treatment has been made it should be applied as soon as possible after the parsnips have developed the first true leaf. The selectivity of linuron can be influenced by formulation and certain formulations may not be recommended for post-emergence use on parsnips. Application during very hot weather is not advisable because of the risk of some crop scorch.

2.278   *Certain **mineral oils** for contact kill of seedling annual weeds (2.139).*

Proprietary selective mineral oils are approved by the Agricultural Chemicals Approval Scheme which requires that they shall have a distillation range of between 140 and 210°C and an aromatic content of not less than 15 per cent and not more than 25 per cent of the oil. There is less risk of crop scorch and taint with these selected grades of oil than with tractor vaporizing oils. The doses range from 450 to 900 litres/ha of ground sprayed and should be applied after the parsnips have fully developed their cotyledons and while the weeds are still small. Spraying should not be attempted after they reach 'pencil thickness'.

Most tractor vaporizing oils can be used in a similar manner on main-crop parsnips. These oils should not be applied before the parsnips have 1 true leaf, and spraying during the heat of the day should be avoided. Because different brands and batches of vaporizing oils vary in their effects on plants, a test should be carried out first to verify that the particular oil is satisfactory. Late spraying should be avoided, so as not to incur a risk of tainting the crop.

2.279 **Pentanochlor** *2·2 kg/ha in high volume for contact kill of seedling annual weeds (2.139).*

Application should be made after the parsnips have fully developed their cotyledons and the first true leaf is showing. The use of a coarse low-pressure spray is desirable. A second application may be made at a later stage of growth if further weeds emerge after treatment.

2.280 **Pentanochlor** *1·7 kg/ha plus* **chlorpropham** *0·84 kg/ha in high volume for contact and residual control of annual weeds.*

Application should be made after the parsnips have fully developed their cotyledons and the first true leaf is showing. The use of a coarse low-pressure spray is desirable.

2.281 [**For information.**] Dalapon-sodium up to 7·6 kg/ha in medium volume once the parsnips have reached the 'pencil thickness' stage to suppress perennial grass weeds. As an alternative an application of 4·8 kg/ha followed by a further 4·8 kg/ha 2 weeks later may be used.

2.282 [**For information.**] Prometryne 1·1 kg/ha as a pre- or post-emergence spray used as described for parsley (2.270 and 26) has given good results on parsnips but further evidence of reliability is required before a recommendation can be made.

PEA (vining, drying, picking and field)

PRE-SOWING TREATMENTS

2.283 **Propham** *3·4 kg/ha in medium or high volume, preferably onto a level* *seedbed rather than plough furrows and thoroughly incorporated immediately after spraying at least 5 days before drilling the crop to control* Avena fatua *(Wild-oat) (2.051) and certain other weeds (2.080).*

2.284   **TCA** *7·8 kg/ha in medium or high volume, preferably onto a level seedbed rather than on the plough furrow and thoroughly incorporated, about 2 weeks before drilling to control* Avena fatua *(Wild-oat)* (12.019)

TCA reduces the wax covering on the leaves of peas and not more than half the normal dose of dinoseb formulations should be applied for broad-leaved weed control following its use.

2.285   **Tri-allate** *1·7 kg/ha in medium to high volume applied and immediately incorporated into the soil to control germinating* Avena spp. *(Wild-oats) and* Alopecurus myosuroides *(Black-grass).*

Incorporation 1.071. Applications may be made and incorporated soon after drilling, but tend to be less efficient than the pre-drilling treatments. Alternatively granules at 1·7 kg/ha immediately before or after drilling and incorporate the granules with straight toothed harrows. Post drilling applications are not so effective if the granules are not incorporated or if dry soil surface conditions prevail. Do not make post-emergence applications to emerged *Avena* spp. in spring crops of peas.

PRE-EMERGENCE CONTACT TREATMENT

2.286   *Contact pre-emergence sprays (2.002–2.003) to kill seedling weeds that emerge before the crop.*

Seedling weeds are seldom present before emergence of the peas and the stale seedbed technique is of only limited value for weed control in this crop.

PRE-EMERGENCE RESIDUAL TREATMENTS

2.287   **Chlorpropham** *0·84–1·1 kg/ha plus* **diuron** *0·35–0·42 kg/ha or*
chlorpropham *1·1–1·7 kg/ha plus* **fenuron** *0·28–0·42 kg/ha or*
chlorpropham *1·1–1·7 kg/ha plus* **fenuron** *0·14–0·21 kg/ha or*
chlorpropham *1·12–1·7 kg/ha plus* **fenuron** *0·14–0·21 kg/ha plus*
monolinuron *0·14–0·21 kg/ha in medium or high volume after drilling, but before any weeds have emerged and at least a week before crop emergence, to control annual weeds (3.156).*

The dose is varied according to soil type, the lower doses being used on lighter soils. It is important that the seedbed should be left with a fine even tilth and that the peas are sown not less than 38 mm below the soil surface. This treatment should not be used on very light soils deficient in clay and organic matter since damage may result.

2.288   **Cyanazine** *1·7–2·1 kg/ha depending on soil type in medium to high* *volume shortly after drilling and before crop emergence to control annual weeds (2.353).*

The seedbed should be left with a fine even tilth, preferably rolled and the peas should be drilled to give 10—25 mm of settled soil above the seed. Cyanazine should not be used on highly organic soils or very light soils containing more than 70 per cent sand or 35 per cent coarse sand and on other light soils a split application of 0·88 kg/ha pre-emergence followed by 0·52 kg/ha post-emergence, when the peas are approximately 75 mm high, should be used. The variety Vedette should not be treated.

2.289 **Prometryne** *1·4—1·7 kg/ha in medium or high volume, the higher dose on the heavier soils and the lower dose on medium soils, any time after sowing until 3 days before the crop is expected to emerge, to control annual weeds (2.139).*

Crop damage may result on open-textured soils, particularly on the variety Vedette.

Prometryne should not be used on soils of lighter texture than loamy very fine sand. The herbicide behaves also as a contact pre-emergence treatment that will kill some weed seedlings that have already emerged at the time of application. Prometryne should not be used on very cloddy soils and if used on organic soils there will be little residual action.

2.290 **Terbuthylazine** *0·35—0·51 kg/ha* plus **terbutryne** *0·8—1·2 kg/ha in medium to high volume for control of annual broad-leaved weeds.*

On very light soils, loamy sands and loamy fine sands, some damage may occur when heavy rain follows soon after application. Apply after drilling and until 3 days before the crop is expected to emerge to control annual weeds.

It is important that the seedbed should be left with a fine even tilth and that the peas are sown so that the seed is covered by 30 mm of settled soil. This treatment should not be used on sands, very stony or organic soils. The variety Vedette may be damaged.

2.291 **Trietazine** *0.66—1·1 kg/ha* plus **simazine** *0·09—0·16 kg/ha in medium to high volume for control of annual broad-leaved weeds.*

Apply between drilling and 5 per cent crop emergence. The seedbed should be left fine and even, preferably rolled, and the peas should be covered by 30 mm of settled soil. This treatment should not be used on sands, gravelly or organic soils. The variety Vedette may be checked and recovery may not be complete.

POST-EMERGENCE TREATMENTS

2.292 **Barban** *0·52—0·7 kg/ha in low volume to control* Avena fatua *(Wild-oat).*

The Wild-oats must be at the 1- to 2·5-leaf stage at the time of spraying. Since crop competition following spraying will govern the degree of *Avena fatua* (Wild-oat) control sowing in narrow rows will aid the treatment.

The crop may be checked by the treatment particularly when cold weather follows the application. In the event of a check to the crop the application of dinoseb formulations for broad-leaved weed control should be delayed for 10 days to allow recovery. Barban should not be used in vining peas within 6 weeks of harvest. Because the crop may not provide adequate competition complete suppression of the *Avena fatua* may not be achieved particularly in peas for drying where later harvesting allows the surviving wild oats to set seed.

2.293   **Bentazone** *1·5 kg/ha plus* **MCPB** *1·5 kg/ha in medium volume to control seedling annual broad-leaved weeds (2.353).*

Peas may be sprayed after 3 leaves have expanded until flower buds are present. The warnings given in paragraph 2.299 regarding the conditions of the crop under which treatment should not be carried out apply also where bentazone plus MCPB is used. Applications should not be made before mid-May. Some varieties are sensitive to this treatment and the manufacturers should be consulted on the suitability for specific varieties. Bentazone plus MCPB may be used following applications of pre-emergence herbicides, barban or tri-allate provided the crop is undamaged.

2.294   **Cyanazine** *1·0 kg/ha in medium volume to control seedling broad-leaved weeds (2.353).*

Peas should not be treated before they are 15 cm high or when they are more than 250 mm high. The warnings given in paragraph 2.288 regarding the conditions of the crop under which treatment should not be carried out and those relating to crops treated with TCA or dalapon apply also where cyanazine is used. Cyanazine should not be used on very light soils; on organic soils 2·10 kg/ha should be used. Some varieties are sensitive to cyanazine and the manufacturers should be consulted on the suitability of the treatment for specific varieties.

2.295   **Dinoseb-acetate** *2·8 kg/ha in medium volume to control seedling broad-leaved weeds (2.336).*

The dose should be reduced to 2·1 kg/ha if the land has been previously treated with TCA. Under cool weather conditions or if weeds are advanced beyond the seedling stage a dose of 3·5 kg/ha may be used. Dinoseb-acetate is slightly more selective than dinoseb-amine and is particularly useful for those pea varieties which are susceptible to dinoseb-amine. It may also be used early in the season under cold conditions. The selectivity of dinoseb-acetate can be influenced by formulation and certain formulations are not recommended for early maturing varieties of peas. For best results the weeds should be treated before the seedling stage.

2.296 **Dinoseb-amine** *1·7–2·8 kg/ha in 450 litres/ha or more when the air temperature is not below 7° C and the maximum of the day is not likely to rise above 30° C, on peas for drying and on most varieties for vining and picking to control seedling broad-leaved weeds (2.336).*

If good growing conditions precede spraying and the temperature at the time of application is higher than 18°C, doses between 1·7 and 2·2 kg/ha should be used. Where spraying follows a period of dry cool weather and the weed growth is 'hard' a dose of more than 2·2 kg/ha may be required. The crop may be sprayed at any time after the first true leaf has expanded until the plants reach a height of 250 mm provided the peas are not in flower. It is important that the application is made when the weeds are in the seedling stage particularly where the more resistant weed species are present. The crop should not be sprayed when the foliage is wet and the application should be delayed when the crop has been damaged by high winds, frost or blowing soil until the crop has recovered. Leaf wax can be tested by immersing plants in a solution of crystal violet dye (Appendix II). If the field has been treated with TCA as a pre-sowing application not more than half the normal dose of dinoseb-amine should be applied as excessive damage may occur at higher doses; however there should also be an increase in susceptibility of the weeds and a satisfactory control should be achieved. When barban has been applied for the control of *Avena fatua* (Wild-oat) an interval of at least 10 days should pass before applying dinoseb. Experience has shown that whilst most varieties of peas for drying and peas grown for vining or picking can be sprayed with dinoseb-amine, some varieties, particularly those with soft lax growth, may be more liable to scorch from dinoseb than other varieties.

2.297 **Dinoseb-ammonium** *2·2 kg/ha in high volume when the temperature is not below 13° C and the maximum of the day is not likely to rise above 27° C on dried peas, to control seedling broad-leaved weeds.*

Above and below these limits spraying should not be carried out. Where good growing conditions have prevailed before spraying and pea growth is 'soft' it is necessary, particularly at higher temperatures, to reduce the maximum dose to 1·1 kg/ha to avoid undue scorch to the crop. Peas should be sprayed after 3 leaves have expanded (generally when about 750 mm high) but before the plants reach a height of 250 mm or the flowering stage. The crop should not be sprayed when the foliage is wet. The warnings given in paragraph 2.296 regarding the conditions of the crop under which treatment should not be carried out and those relating to crops treated with TCA or barban apply also where dinoseb-ammonium is used. On vining or picking peas dinoseb-amine is preferable to dinoseb-ammonium as it causes less scorch.

2.298 The addition of approximately 0·14 kg/ha of MCPA-salt to the normal dose of dinoseb-amine or dinoseb-ammonium is sometimes used when *Sinapis arvensis* (Charlock), *Raphanus raphanistrum* (Wild Radish),

Sinapis alba (White Mustard) or *Erysimum cheiranthoides* (Treacle Mustard) are more than 7·5 mm high at the time of spraying or where heavy infestations of these weeds are present. The manufacturers of the two herbicides should be consulted before applying the mixture.

2.299   **MCPB-salt** *2·2 kg/ha in medium volume when the peas have from 3 to 6 expanded leaves to control seedling broad-leaved weeds* (1.054).

Some pea varieties are more susceptible than others. The manufacturers should be consulted on the suitability of the treatment for specific varieties. The treatment is of most use in pea crops where *Chenopodium album* (Fat-hen) or *Cirsium arvense* (Creeping Thistle) are the dominant weeds. For effective control of the latter species spray when the shoots are 150–220 mm high.

2.300   [**For information.**] Cyanazine + MCPB. In dry situations, where weed kill from post-emergence cyanazine is often delayed, or when hardy weeds are present due to size or resistance, a mixture of cyanazine at 1·0 kg/ha + MCPB at 0·56 kg/ha has shown promise in both trials and commercial crops.

Certain pea varieties exhibit high sensitivity to post-emergence herbicides—these are: Hurst Beagle, Nunhem's Parade, Vedette, Surprise and Small Sieve Perfection.

In the moderately tolerant group listed below, the rate of addition of MCPB should be 0·28 kg/ha.

Dart	Orfac	Sprite
Galaxie	Recette	Superfection
Greenshaft	Scout	Tezieridee
Jade	Sparkle	

Crops should not be treated under stress conditions, i.e. soil abraded, lack of wax nor in waterlogged conditions. Peas should be at least 80 mm. high and the mixture should be applied in 400–500 litres of water per hectare.

PRE-HARVEST DESICCATION

2.301   The following treatments should be applied when peas are at a mature stage of development (approximately 45 per cent m.c.). Desiccation will not hasten ripening but is of value to ease harvesting of unevenly ripening or weedy crops.

2.302   **Dimexan** *9·3–13·0 kg/ha in 220 litres/ha on peas to be harvested dry.*

The higher dose should be used when soil conditions are moist and atmospheric conditions humid, where growth is hard or when foliage is dense. Where there is a serious weed problem this treatment is of doubtful value. Use nozzles recommended for 110 litres/ha at 4 bars.

2.303   **Diquat** *0·42–0·5 kg/ha in medium volume on peas to be harvested dry.*
The crop should be harvested as soon as desiccation is complete which
is normally 10 to 14 days after spraying.

2.304   **Sulphuric acid** *70–220 litres/ha undiluted B.O.V. without a wetting agent
on peas to be harvested dry.*
The crop should be harvested as soon as desiccation is complete which
is normally 7–10 days after spraying.

POTATO

PRE-PLANTING TREATMENTS

2.305   **EPTC** *at 4·5 kg/ha in medium or high volume to control grasses and
some annual broad-leaved weeds.*
As the herbicide is volatile it is essential to incorporate deeply into the
soil immediately after application, using rotary or heavy disc cultivation.
Deep ploughing of perennial grass weeds prior to the treatment should be
avoided. Chopping the rhizomes into short lengths either before or during
incorporation is beneficial. Potatoes can be planted immediately or after
an interval of up to 2 weeks. When making potato ridges care should be
taken to avoid exposing untreated soil in the bottom of the furrow so the
ridges should be shallow for 2–4 weeks. This treatment gives reasonable
control of perennial grasses and also annual grasses, Wild-oats, and some
broad-leaved weeds. *Agrostis stolonifera* (Creeping Bent) has been found
on occasions to be less susceptible than other perennial grasses and
control is variable.

2.306   **TCA** *15·0 kg/ha applied in Spring for the control of couch and other
grass weeds; at least 8 weeks before planting.*
Spring treatment is recommended for light soils especially in high
rainfall areas. Thorough incorporation into the soil is normally essential;
prior break up of couch rhizome may assist control. Emergence of the
crop is defined as the emergence of the first shoots above the soil surface,
i.e. as soon as they are visible.

PRE-EMERGENCE CONTACT TREATMENTS

2.307   *Contact pre-crop emergence sprays (2.002–2.003) to kill seedling weeds
that emerge up to the time when the first few potatoes are beginning to
emerge.*
To obtain maximum weed kill, no cultivations should be carried out
after planting so that as many weeds as possible have emerged before the
crop appears. This means that the full ridge must be put up at this time.

If *Avena fatua* (Wild-oat) or other grass weeds are present only paraquat should be used.

While contact pre-crop emergence sprays may achieve adequate control of weeds in certain circumstances, it may well be necessary to follow them with cultivations or a post-crop emergence, foliar acting material. They may well be more effective with early varieties where the crop canopy forms earlier and a shorter period of weed control is necessary.

PRE-EMERGENCE TRANSLOCATED TREATMENTS

2.308 **Barban** at 0·7 kg/ha in low volume to control seedling *Avena fatua* (Wild-oat) and some seedling annual grass weeds which have emerged before the crop.

This treatment can reduce hindrance to subsequent cultivations where a dense growth of early germinating Wild-oats or annual grass weeds is anticipated. The best control is obtained if the grass weeds and Wild-oats are sprayed when in the 1- to 2·5-leaf stage.

2.309 **Dalapon-sodium** *2·9–4·8 kg/ha in low or medium volume before the crop emerges to suppress perennial grasses which are showing sufficient foliage to receive an effective dose.*

Later application or higher doses may reduce the intensity of colour on the tuber of red-skinned varieties. The control of rhizomatous grasses will be partial but will depend on crop vigour soon after application. Cultivations should not be undertaken for at least 2 weeks after spraying.

2.310 **Following crops.** When considering the use of residual herbicides for weed control in potatoes, particularly in early varieties, some thought should be given to the likelihood of residues remaining to affect subsequent cropping. This is of particular importance where catch-cropping follows the growing of early potatoes and it is prudent to consult the manufacturers of individual herbicides for guidance on the best methods of application to minimize any residual effect (Appendix VI).

PRE-EMERGENCE RESIDUAL TREATMENT

2.311 **Metobromuron** *at 1·7 kg/ha on light soils and sands and 2·2 kg/ha on medium or heavy soils, in medium to high volume, to control annual weeds on mineral soils (2.336).*

On early crops the dose should be restricted to 1·7 kg/ha. Some foliar activity on seedling weeds is likely but control at this stage is not reliable.

PRE-EMERGENCE, CONTACT AND RESIDUAL TREATMENTS

2.312 **Ametryne** *1·5–2·2 kg/ha in medium to high volume from about 10 days* *before emergence until 10 per cent of potatoes have emerged and preferably before annual broad-leaved weeds are beyond the cotyledon stage (2.336). The lower dose is recommended for use in early potatoes.* On highly organic soils there is unlikely to be sufficient residual action to control weeds that germinate after spraying. On mineral soils the residual activity is normally short enough to allow crops such as brassicae to be drilled very soon after lifting early potatoes.

2.313   **Chlorbromuron** *1·4–2·0 kg/ha in medium to high volume, the lower dose being used on early potatoes or sandy soils, the higher dose on heavy soils, applied before crop emergence to control germinating or emerged seedling weeds (2.139).*

2.314   **Dinoseb-acetate** *1·7–2·5 kg/ha plus* **monolinuron** *0·57–0·84 kg/ha in medium to high volume to control germinating and seedling annual weeds (2.336).*
         Application on very light sands low in organic matter is not recommended. Application should be made before crop emergence.

2.315   **Dinoseb in oil** *2·5 kg/ha in medium to high volume before crop emergence to control germinating and seedling weeds (2.336).*
         Heavy rainfall soon after application may diminish the effectiveness of this treatment but it is particularly useful where emerged *Galium aparine* (Cleavers) constitutes a problem in potatoes. At these doses the residual activity of dinoseb in the soil is comparatively short and may need to be followed by some cultivation.

2.316   **Linuron** *for main crops at 1·1–2·2 kg/ha to control germinating and seedling weeds (2.336).*
         The lower dose should be used on the lighter soils in each category. On soils with high organic matter 1·7–2·2 kg/ha may be used before crop emergence to control susceptible emerged weeds.

2.317   **Linuron** *0·7–1·3 kg/ha plus* **cyanazine** *0·46–0·9 kg/ha in medium to high volume for the control of annual broad-leaved weeds.*
         Reference to the manufacturers should be made before treating very light soils. Highly organic soils should not be treated.

2.318   **Linuron** *and* **monolinuron** *as a mixture 1·1–2·2 kg/ha on light and medium soils or 1·7–2·2 kg/ha on heavy soils in medium to high volume before crop emergence to control germinating and seedling weeds (2.336).*
         On early crops the dose should be reduced to 0·84–1·1 kg/ha. The lower dose should be used on the lighter soils in each category.

2.319   **Metribuzin** *for main crops at 0·7 kg/ha on light soils, 1·0 kg/ha on heavy soils and organic soils and for earlies at 0·52 kg/ha on light soils,*

0·7 kg/ha on other mineral soils. Applied in medium to high volume to control germinating and seedling weeds (2.336).
Not for use on sands or loamy coarse sands. Residual activity is less on high organic soils to control germinating and seedling weeds.
May be used *before* crop emergence on all varieties; can be used early post emergence in some circumstances. Due to its prolonged residual effect only ryegrass, cereals and winter beans should be sown in the same season and only after ploughing and cultivation to 150 mm but not within 16 weeks of spraying metribuzin.

2.320   **Monolinuron** *for main crops at 1·1–1·7 for earlies, 0·84–1·7 kg/ha applied in medium to high volume before crop emergence to control germinating and seedling weeds (2.336).*
The lower dose should be used on the lighter soils in each category. On soils with high organic matter 1·7 kg/ha may be used before crop emergence to control susceptible emerged weeds.

2.321   **Paraquat** *plus* **monolinuron** *at 0·56 plus 0·78 kg/ha in medium to high volume, to control germinating and seedling weeds (2.336) on all soil types.*
Application should be made not later than 10 per cent emergence of early varieties and 20 per cent emergence of main crop varieties. Residual action is greatest on light soils and least on heavy and high organic soils.

2.322   [**For information.**] Experimental mixtures of paraquat with linuron, ametryne, metobromuron and other residual herbicides have also given successful control of annual weeds in potatoes. Compatibility should be checked and the manufacturers consulted before mixing products.

2.323   **Prometryne** *1·7 kg/ha in medium to high volume before 10 per cent of crop plants have emerged but preferably after early weed growth has developed to control germinating and seedling weeds in early potatoes (2.139).*
The treatment is suitable for use in early potatoes where it is intended to follow with another crop, such as brassicae, very soon after potato lifting.

2.324   **Terbuthylazine** *0·34–0·51 kg/ha plus* **terbutryne** *0·80–1·19 kg/ha for maincrop varieties in medium volume to control annual broad-leaved weeds (2.336).*
Foliar action is limited on weeds which have developed beyond the cotyledon stage. For older weeds and resistant species a tank mix with 0·56 kg/ha paraquat is worthwhile and compatible. On organic soils application should be made only after weed emergence as residual activity is short on such soils.

Potato

2.325

2.325 **Trietazine** *0·7 kg/ha plus* **linuron** *0·7 kg/ha for early varieties and 0·85 to 1·1 kg/ha for maincrop varieties applied in medium volume to control annual broad-leaved weeds up to cotyledon stage (2.336).*
The spray should be applied before weeds exceed the cotyledon stage. Optimum weed control is obtained by spraying soon after planting.

POST-EMERGENCE TREATMENTS

2.326 **Barban** at 0·7 kg/ha in low volume to control seedlings of *Avena fatua* (Wild-oat) soon after crop emergence and when the weed is in 1 to 2·5-leaf stage. The efficiency of this treatment depends on the vigour of the crop soon after application. Treatment later than 6 weeks before the crop is harvested is not recommended.

2.327 **MCPA-salt** *at 0·7 kg/ha in low or medium volume as an emergency measure to control late-growing weed such as* Chenopodium album *(Fathen) and* Cirsium arvense *(Creeping Thistle) which could seriously hinder mechanical harvesting.*
Application should be made from 2 weeks after emergence to just before tuber initiation, i.e. before flowering or before full leaf canopy is reached. Some yield reduction can be expected but certain varieties, e.g. Majestic, tolerate this treatment more than others, e.g. King Edward. Leaf deformity may confuse inspection for virus and variety identification. The treatment is therefore unsuitable for use where potatoes are grown for seed production.

2.328 **Metribuzin** *for maincrop varieties only (other than Maris Piper and Pentland Ivory) at 0·70 kg/ha on light soils and 1·0 kg/ha on heavier soils and organic soils. Applied at medium volume to high volume before the crop is 15 cm high to control germinating and seedling weeds (2.336). Not for use on sands or loamy coarse sands.*
There are limitations as to following cropping in the same season Appendix VI.
For the most effective control of *Polygonum convolvulus* (Black-bindweed) treat at the cotyledon to one true leaf stage, or alternatively use a pre-or early post-emergence treatment followed by a further 0·52 kg/ha when the majority of the *P. convolvulus* has germinated, but before the crop exceeds 150 mm in height.

POST-EMERGENCE CONTACT HERBICIDE AND GROWTH MANAGEMENT

2.329 **Dimexan** *at 9 kg in 220 litres of water per ha. (Use nozzles recommended for 110 litres/ha at 4 bars.)*
Approved for vars.: Desiree, Pentland Crown, Majestic, Bintje, King Edward at about 80 per cent and up to 80 mm tall to kill seedling weeds,

113

increase the yield of medium and small tubers, decrease the number of large tubers.

2.330   **Dalapon-sodium** *at 7·8 kg/ha in low or medium volume for the control of* Agropyron repens *(Common Couch) and other perennial graminaceous plants after the potato haulm has died down.*

This treatment can reduce the hindrances to efficient harvesting operations and give a useful control of perennial grasses and of *Phragmites communis* (Common Reed). Red-skinned potato varieties are liable to loss of pigment if there is uptake of the chemical by the crop prior to harvest.

Since it is possible for abnormal sprout development to occur in tubers that have taken up the chemical, crops of any varieties from which seed tubers are to be taken should not be treated until there is clearer evidence that subsequent growth and yield are not adversely affected.

2.331   Prolonged dry weather renders potatoes conducive to a staining of the vascular ring inside the tubers after defoliation. The internal browning may be quite insignificant but if very severe may lead to heel or neck-end rot. The more severe symptoms may develop during storage and the necrotic areas allow ingress of secondary rotting organisms. It is not known whether subsequent yield is affected if potatoes showing only moderate symptoms are used for seed but where the browning of the vascular ring reaches the eyes of tubers it would be unwise to use them for seed.

The occurrence of internal browning has been noted following all means of haulm desiccation, including mechanical destruction. Chemical desiccation is more likely to produce symptoms particularly when diquat, or to a lesser extent dinoseb, is used. The more severe final condition of stem-end rot has not been recorded as occurring after the use of sulphuric acid or mechanical destruction.

2.332   **Diquat** *at 0·77 kg/ha in medium volume.*

Leaf kill is rapid but stems and tall weeds may be affected much more slowly. Diquat should not be used when the soil is very dry, especially if the haulm shows signs of wilting during the day, otherwise the quality of the tubers may be adversely affected through translocation of the chemical. Stock must be kept out of the treated area for at least 24 hr after spraying.

2.333   **Dinoseb** *formulated in oil as an emulsifiable concentrate, at 2·0–3·0 kg/ha in medium or high volume.*

The higher dose should be applied in high volume where haulm growth is vigorous or where there is a severe weed infestation. Dinoseb should not be used when the soil is very dry as the quality of the tubers may be adversely affected. Spraying should not be carried out during rain or when rain is expected within 24 hr of application. A period of 10 days should elapse between spraying and lifting of tubers. Stock must be kept out of the treated area for a period of at least 10 days after treatment.

2.334   **Sodium chlorate** *at 22·0–34·0 kg/ha where there is no danger of residues damaging succeeding crops.*

In low rainfall areas not more than 22·0 kg/ha should be applied in medium volume increasing to 34·0 kg/ha where rainfall is high. The use of sodium chlorate constitutes a fire hazard and its residues may damage winter cereals sown following late treated potatoes. Haulm death is slower after using sodium chlorate than after the other materials mentioned in this section.

2.335   **Sulphuric acid,** *as a 12 per cent v/v solution, at 1100 litres/ha (i.e. 135 litres of 100 per cent acid in 990 litres/ha of water or 170 litres B.O.V. in 960 litres of water).*

In diluting sulphuric acid, the acid must *always* be added *slowly* to the water and not vice versa. B.O.V. may also be used undiluted at 220 litres/ha. Acid is corrosive to many metals. Stock should be kept out of the treated crop for at least 3 days after spraying. Skin and clothes may be affected for up to 7 days after spraying.

2.336   The susceptibility of annual weeds to herbicides used on potato

This table is intended to provide a general indication of the response of annual weeds to those herbicides used on potatoes at the range of doses given in the relevant paragraphs. The table is divided into response of weeds to soil-applied and foliage-applied treatments and the categories of response are defined as follows:

Soil-applied treatments

S—**Susceptible** Complete or near complete kill.
MS—**Moderately susceptible** Good kill under favourable conditions.
MR—**Moderately resistant** Partial kill.
R—**Resistant** No useful effect.

Foliage-applied treatments

S—**Susceptible** Complete or near complete kill.
MS—**Moderately susceptible** Effective suppression with partial kill.
MR—**Moderately resistant** Temporary suppression, the duration depending on the environment.
R—**Resistant** No useful effect.

They refer to two stages of growth:
Sd—**Seedling stage** Cotyledon to 2 to 3 leaves.
Yp—**Young plant stage** 3 to 4 leaves to early flower-bud stage.

When any of the herbicides are used as foliage-applied treatments residual activity in the soil will also occur, the extent depending upon the herbicide, the soil-type and the weather.

Weeds	Soil-applied							Foliage-applied				
	Ametryne	Dinoseb	Metri-bu-zin	Linuron, mono-linuron	Meto-bro-muron	Ter-butryne/ ter-buthyla-zine	Linuron, tri-etazine	Stage of growth	Ametryne	Dinoseb	Metri-bu-zine	Linuron, mono-linuron
1. *Aethusa cynapium* (Fool's Parsley)	MS	MR	—	MR	—	—	—	Sd Yp	MS —	— —	— —	MS MS

The table below is a weed-susceptibility matrix. Each weed is rated at two growth stages — Sd (seedling) and Yp (young plant) — with ratings S (susceptible), MS (moderately susceptible), MR (moderately resistant) and R (resistant). Cells marked "—" were not recorded. Columns C7–C10 show the rating as Sd / Yp; the rightmost column (R*) carries a footnote mark.

Species	C1	C2	C3	C4	C5	C6	Stage	C7 (Sd/Yp)	C8 (Sd/Yp)	C9 (Sd/Yp)	C10 R* (Sd/Yp)
2. *Alopecurus myosuroides* (Black-grass)	S	—	S	S	—	—	Sd / Yp	MS / —	R / R	MS / MR	S / S
3. *Anagallis arvensis* (Scarlet Pimpernel)	S	S	S	S	—	—	Sd / Yp	S / —	S / S	S / —	S / S
4. *Anthemis arvensis* (Corn Chamomile)	S	S	S	S	—	—	Sd / Yp	R / R	S / MR	— / —	R / R
5. *Anthemis cotula* (Stinking Chamomile)	S	S	S	S	—	—	Sd / Yp	R / R	MS / MR	S / —	MR / MR
6. *Aphanes arvensis* (Parsley-piert)	—	MS	—	MS	—	—	Sd / Yp	— / —	S / MS	— / —	S / MS
7. *Atriplex patula* (Common Orache)	S	MS	S	S	—	—	Sd / Yp	S / —	S / MR	S / MS	R / R
8. *Avena fatua* (Wild-oat)	R	R	R	R	R	R	Sd / Yp	R / R	R / R	MR / R	S / MS
9. *Brassica nigra* (Black Mustard)	MS	S	—	MS	—	—	Sd / Yp	MS / —	S / S	— / —	S / MS
10. *Brassica rapa* ssp. *campestris* (Wild Turnip)	MS	—	—	MS	—	—	Sd / Yp	MS / —	S / S	— / —	S / S
11. *Capsella bursa-pastoris* (Shepherd's Purse)	S	S	S	S	S	—	Sd / Yp	S / —	S / S	S / S	S / MS
12. *Cerastium holosteoides* (Common Mouse-ear)	S	S	—	S	—	—	Sd / Yp	S / —	MR / R	— / —	S / MS
13. *Chenopodium album* (Fat-hen)	S	S	S	S	S	S	Sd / Yp	S / —	S / MS	S / MS	R / R
14. *Chrysanthemum segetum* (Corn Marigold)	S	MR	—	S	—	—	Sd / Yp	R / R	MS / MR	MS / MS	R / R
15. *Erysimum cheiranthoides* (Treacle Mustard)	MS	—	—	MS	—	—	Sd / Yp	MS / —	S / S	— / —	— / —

	Soil-applied							Stage of growth	Foliage-applied			
Weeds	Ametryne	Dinoseb	Metri-bro-zin	Linuron, mono-linuron	Meto-bro-muron	Ter-butryne/ ter-buthyla-zine	Linuron, tri-etazine		Ametryne	Dinoseb	Metri-bu-zine	Linuron, mono-linuron
16. *Euphorbia exigua* (Dwarf Spurge)	R	—	—	—	—	—	—	Sd	MR	—	—	MS
								Yp	—	—	—	MR
17. *Euphorbia helioscopia* (Sun Spurge)	—	—	S	—	—	—	—	Sd	MR	MS	—	MS
								Yp	—	—	—	MR
18. *Euphorbia peplus* (Petty Spurge)	R	—	—	—	—	—	—	Sd	MR	—	—	MS
								Yp	—	—	—	MR
19. *Fumaria officinalis* (Common Fumitory)	S	S	S	MR	R	—	MS	Sd	S	S	S	R
								Yp	—	MS	S	R
20. *Galeopsis speciosa* (Large-flowered Hemp-nettle)	S	—	S	S	—	—	—	Sd	S	S	S	S
								Yp	—	MS	—	MS
21. *Galeopsis tetrahit* (Common Hemp-nettle)	S	S	S	S	—	—	S	Sd	S	S	S	S
								Yp	—	S	—	MS
22. *Galinsoga parviflora* (Gallant Soldier)	S	—	—	S	—	—	—	Sd	S	S	—	S
								Yp	—	S	—	S
23. *Galium aparine* (Cleavers)	MR	MS	R	MR	R	—	R	Sd	RZS	R	R	R
								Yp	R	MS	R	
24. *Geranium dissectum* (Cut-leaved Crane's-bill)	R	MR	—	—	—	—	—	Sd	MR	—	—	—
								Yp	—	—	—	—
25. *Geranium pusillum* (Small-flowered Crane's-bill)	R	—	—	—	—	—	—	Sd	MR	—	—	—
								Yp	—	—	—	—
26. *Lamium amplexicaule* (Henbit Dead-nettle)	S	S	S	MR	—	—	—	Sd	MS	S	S	MR
								Yp	—	—	S	R

Species								Sd/Yp	Sd	Yp	Sd	Yp	Sd	Yp	Sd	Yp
27. *Lamium purpureum* (Red Dead-nettle)	S	S	S	MS	MR	—	—	Sd/Yp	MS	—	S	—	S	S	MS	MR
28. *Lapsana communis* (Nipplewort)	S	S	—	S	—	—	—	Sd/Yp	S	—	S	—	—	—	—	—
29. *Lithospermum arvense* (Field Gromwell)	—	—	—	S	—	—	—	Sd/Yp	—	—	S	MS	—	—	—	—
30. *Lycopsis arvensis* (Bugloss)	—	—	S	MS	—	—	—	Sd/Yp	—	—	MS	—	S	—	—	—
31. *Matricaria matricarioides* (Pineappleweed)	S	S	S	S	—	—	S	Sd/Yp	R	R	S	—	S	S	MR	R
32. *Matricaria recutita* (Scented Mayweed)	S	S	S	S	—	—	—	Sd/Yp	R	R	S	MR	S	S	MR	R
33. *Medicago lupulina* (Black Medick)	—	R	—	MR	—	—	—	Sd/Yp	—	—	—	—	—	—	MS	MR
34. *Myosotis arvensis* (Field Forget-me-not)	—	—	S	MS	—	—	—	Sd/Yp	—	—	S	—	S	MS	MS	MR
35. *Papaver dubium* (Long-headed Poppy)	S	S	—	S	—	—	—	Sd/Yp	S	—	S	—	—	—	S	MR
36. *Papaver rhocas* (Common Poppy)	S	S	S	S	—	—	S	Sd/Yp	S	—	S	MR	S	S	S	MR
37. *Poa annua* (Annual Meadow-grass)	S	MR	S	S	MS	—	S	Sd/Yp	MS	—	R	R	S	MS	MR	R
38. *Polygonum aviculare* (Knotgrass)	MR	MR	S	MR	S	S	S	Sd/Yp	R	R	S	MR	MS	MR	MR	R
39. *Polygonum convolvulus* (Black-bindweed)	S	MS	MS	MS	MS	—	S	Sd/Yp	S	—	S	MR	MS	S	S	MS
40. *Polygonum lapathifolium* (Pale Persicaria)	S	S	S	S	MS	—	S	Sd/Yp	S	—	S	R	S	—	S	MR

Weeds	Soil-applied Ametryne	Dinoseb	Metri-brozin	Linuron, mono-linuron	Meto-bromuron	Ter-butryne/ ter-buthyla-zine	Linuron, tri-etazine	Foliage-applied Stage of growth	Ametryne	Dinoseb	Metri-bu-zine	Linuron, mono-linuron
41. *Polygonum persicaria* (Redshank)	S	S	S	S	MS	—	S	Sd Yp	S —	S MR	S —	S MS
42. *Ranunculus arvensis* (Corn Buttercup)	R	—	—	MR	—	—	—	Sd Yp	MR —	S R	— —	— —
43. *Raphanus raphanistrum* (Wild Radish)	S	S	S	S	—	—	S	Sd Yp	MS —	S MS	S S	S MS
44. *Scandix pecten-veneris* (Shepherd's-needle)	MS	—	—	—	—	—	—	Sd Yp	MS —	S MR	— —	— —
45. *Senecio vulgaris* (Groundsel)	S	S	S	S	S	—	S	Sd Yp	MS —	S MR	S S	S MS
46. *Sinapis alba* (White Mustard)	MS	—	—	MS	—	—	—	Sd Yp	MS —	S S	— —	S MS
47. *Sinapis arvensis* (Charlock)	S	S	S	S	S	—	S	Sd Yp	MS —	S S	S S	S S
48. *Solanum nigrum* (Black Nightshade)	S	MR	R	MS	MR	—	R	Sd Yp	MS —	R R	MS MR	MS MR
49. *Sonchus asper* (Prickly Sow-thistle)	S	S	—	S	—	—	—	Sd Yp	S —	S MR	— —	S MS
50. *Sonchus oleraceus* (Smooth Sow-thistle)	S	S	—	S	—	—	S	Sd Yp	MS —	S MR	— MS	MS MS

Weed	1	2	3	4	5	6	7	Sd	Yp	Sd	Yp	Sd	Yp	Sd	Yp
51. *Spergula arvensis* (Corn Spurry)	S	S	S	S	—	—	S	MS	—	MS	MR	S	S	S	S
52. *Stellaria media* (Common Chickweed)	S	S	S	S	S	S	S	S	—	S	S	S	S	S	S
53. *Thlaspi arvense* (Field Penny-cress)	S	S	S	S	—	—	S	S	—	S	S	S	S	S	MS
54. *Tripleurospermum maritimum* ssp. *inodorum* (Scentless Mayweed)	S	S	S	S	S	—	S	R	R	S	MR	S	S	R	R
55. *Urtica urens* (Small Nettle)	S	MS	S	S	S	—	S	S	—	S	MR	S	—	S	MS
56. *Veronica agrestis* (Green Field-speedwell)	R	S	S	MR	—	—	MS	—	—	S	MR	S	—	MR	R
57. *Veronica arvensis* (Wall Speedwell)	R	S	S	MR	—	—	MS	—	—	S	MR	S	—	MR	R
58. *Veronica hederifolia* (Ivy-leaved Speedwell)	R	S	S	MR	MR	—	MS	—	—	S	MS	S	—	MR	R
59. *Veronica persica* (Common Field-speedwell)	R	S	S	S	MR	S	MS	—	—	S	MR	S	—	MR	R
60. *Vicia hirsuta* (Hairy Tare)	R	R	—	MR	—	—	—	—	—	MR	—	—	—	MR	R
61. *Vicia sativa* (Common Vetch)	R	R	—	R	—	—	—	—	—	MR	R	—	—	MR	R
62. *Viola arvensis* (Field Pansy)	S	MR	S	S	—	—	R	S	—	MS	—	MS	—	S	MS
63. *Viola tricolor* (Wild Pansy)	S	MR	—	S	—	—	—	S	—	MS	—	—	—	MS	MR

SPINACH

PRE-EMERGENCE TREATMENTS

2.337   The recommendations given below arise from field trials and experiences with *Spinacia oleracea* and should be regarded as tentative on *Beta vulgaris* cv. *cicla* or *Tetragonia expansa* which are also sometimes grown as spinach.

2.338   **Chlorpropham** *at 0·9–1·1 kg/ha plus* **fenuron** *at 0·15–0·18 kg/ha according to soil type for residual control of annual weeds (3.156).*
Application should be made when crop has chitted. The lower dose to be used in spring on all soil types. The higher dose may be used on sowings made between June and early August except for crops on sand, very light soils or on soils with a high water table.

2.339   **Dimexan** *5·6 kg/ha plus* **cycluron** *0·31 kg/ha plus* **chlorbufam** *0·21 kg/ha in high volume as a pre-emergence spray for contact and residual control of annual weeds (2.080).*
Application should be made not later than 2–4 days before emergence. This treatment should not be used on very light sandy soils, and on highly organic soils unsatisfactory weed control will be obtained. It is less effective on heavy than on medium soils. For best results rainfall or irrigation should follow application, and residual activity is reduced if there is warm weather after application to summer-drilled crops. Breakdown is sufficiently rapid for other crops to be drilled after harvest.

2.340   **Lenacil** *0·91 kg/ha on very light soils, 1·3 kg/ha on light soils, 1·8 kg/ha fine sandy loams or 2·2 kg/ha on medium soils in medium volume for residual control of annual weeds (2.080).*
Succeeding crops cannot be planted in treated ground for at least 4 months after spraying.

2.341   [**For information.**] Lenacil at the above doses (2.340) reduced by 0·56 kg with 0·84 kg chlorpropham added has given promising results on peat soils.

SWEDES and TURNIPS

PRE-SOWING TREATMENTS

2.342   **Aminotriazole** *4·5 kg/ha in medium volume to control* Agropyron repens *(Common Couch), Docks and Thistles.*

Spray between mid-March and the end of October when the actively growing foliage is 70–100 mm high in the autumn or at least 70 mm high in the spring. Plough 3–6 weeks later, completely inverting the soil.

The crop may be sown as soon as ploughing and cultivations are completed but on very light soils and sands, an interval of 6 weeks must lapse between application and sowing. If drought occurs after spraying, planting should not take place until several days after reasonable rainfall.

2.343 **Di-allate** *1·7 kg/ha in medium to high volume incorporated for control of germinating* Avena *spp.* (Wild-oats) *and* Alopecurus myosuroides *(Black-grass).*

For incorporation details see 2.049. Field experience indicates that this treatment will not interfere with other soil-applied herbicides used for broad-leaved weed control.

2.344 **Dinitramine** *0·25–0·45 kg/ha in 110–170 litres water incorporated for residual control of annual weeds* (2.122).

Spray overall, within 14 days before drilling, onto a weed and clod free seedbed. Thoroughly incorporate into the top 5 cm of soil within 24 hr of spraying.

2.345 **TCA** *33·6 kg/ha in medium or high volume at least 4 weeks before drilling to control perennial grass weeds* (12.019).

The chemical should be sprayed on to the soil surface and incorporated to a depth of 100–120 mm. Cultivations which also fragment the grass rhizomes will greatly improve control.

2.346 **TCA** *7·9–17·0 kg/ha in medium or high volume to suppress perennial grass and control* Avena fatua *(Wild-oat).*

An interval of 5–7 days should be allowed between application and drilling. The lower dose should be used where Wild-oat is the only problem. The herbicide should be incorporated into the soil during seedbed preparation. Control of Wild-oat is variable and depends on the depth of germination and rainfall.

PRE-DRILLING TREATMENTS

2.347 **Trifluralin** *1·1 kg/ha in medium volume incorporated into the soil for residual control of annual weeds on loamy sands, sandy loams, loams and clay loams* (2.122).

The treatment can be applied during soil preparation at any time from 14 days before until immediately before drilling but must be mechanically incorporated within 30 min of application. For incorporation details see 2.103.

Where these crops are to be grown on ridges, trifluralin must be incorporated into the top 100 mm of soil by setting the working depths of rotary cultivators of 100 mm and all other recommended machines to between 150 and 200 mm.

When ridging, care should be taken to ensure that the point of the ridger body does not penetrate below the treated layer, otherwise poor weed control will result.

Trifluralin is not recommended for sands or soils containing 10 per cent or more of organic matter. Only recommended crops should be drilled or planted within 5 months of treatment.

Soil should be thoroughly cultivated to a depth of at least 150 mm before drilling or planting succeeding crops other than recommended crops.

After an autumn application of trifluralin cereal and grass crops should not be sown until the following autumn.

PRE-EMERGENCE CONTACT TREATMENTS

2.348   *Contact pre-emergence sprays (2.002–2.003) to kill seedling weeds that emerge before the crop.*

These treatments are likely to prove more reliable in areas of moderate or high rainfall than in the drier regions of the country.

PRE-EMERGENCE RESIDUAL TREATMENTS

2.349   **Nitrofen** *3·4 kg/ha in medium to high volume within 3 days after drilling for residual control of annual weeds (2.122).*

Recommendations given in 2.174 for kale apply also in the case of swedes and turnips.

2.350   **Propachlor** *4·4 kg/ha in medium to high volume or as granules shortly after drilling for the control of germinating broad-leaved weeds (2.122).*

Best results are obtained when the seedbed has a fine even tilth and is free of clods.

2.351   [**For information.**] Alachlor 1·7–2·1 kg/ha in medium volume shortly after drilling for the control of annual broad-leaved weeds. This treatment is not recommended for direct drilled crops.

POST-EMERGENCE TREATMENT

2.352   [**For information.**] Nitrofen at 1·1 kg/ha has shown promise for the post-emergence control of annual weeds in swedes and turnips. The crop should have at least 1 true leaf and may be scorched or deformed for a time after treatment. Susceptible weeds should be in the cotyledon to 1 leaf stage.

2.353 The susceptibility of annual weeds to herbicides used in various crops

This table is intended to provide a general indication of the response of annual weeds to those herbicides listed below at the range of doses given in the relevant paragraphs. The table is divided into response of weeds to soil-applied and foliage-applied treatments and the categories of response are defined as follows:

Soil-applied treatments
S—**Susceptible** Complete or near complete kill.
MS—**Moderately susceptible** Good kill under favourable conditions.
MR—**Moderately resistant** Partial kill.
R—**Resistant** No useful effect.

Foliage-applied treatments
S—**Susceptible** Complete or near complete kill.
MS—**Moderately susceptible** Effective suppression with partial kill.
MR—**Moderately resistant** Temporary suppression, the duration depending on the environment.
R—**Resistant** No useful effect.

They refer to two stages of growth:
Sd—**Seedling stage** Cotyledon to 2 to 3 leaves.
Yp—**Young plant stage** 3 to 4 leaves to early flower-bud stage.

Weeds	Soil-applied		Stage of growth	Foliage-applied					
	Cyanazine	Meta-mitron		Bentazone	Bentazone + MCPB	Cyanazine	Ioxynil	Meta-mitron	Methazole
1. *Aethusa cynapium* (Fool's Parsley)	—	—	Sd	—	—	—	MS	—	R
			Yp	—	—		MR	—	R
2. *Alopecurus myosuroides* (Black-grass)	S	R	Sd	R	R	S	MR	MR	R
			Yp	R	R	—	R	R	R
3. *Anagallis arvensis* (Scarlet Pimpernel)	S	R	Sd	S	S	S	MS	S	S
			Yp	S	S	S	—	—	MS

Weeds	Soil-applied Cyanazine	Soil-applied Meta-mitron	Stage of growth	Foliage-applied Bentazone	Bentazone + MCPB	Cyanazine	Ioxynil	Meta-mitron	Methazole
4. *Anthemis arvensis* (Corn Chamomile)	S	—	Sd	S	S	MS	S	—	MS
			Yp	S	S	MR	S	—	MR
5. *Anthemis cotula* (Stinking Chamomile)	—	—	Sd	—	—	—	S	—	MS
			Yp	—	—	—	S	—	MR
6. *Aphanes arvensis* (Parsley-piert)	R	—	Sd	—	—	R	MR	—	—
			Yp	—	—	R	—	—	—
7. *Atriplex patula* (Common Orache)	S	S	Sd	S	S	S	S	S	S
			Yp	MS	S	MS	MS	—	S
8. *Avena fatua* (Wild-oat)	MS	R	Sd	R	R	R	R	R	R
			Yp	R	R	R	R	R	R
9. *Brassica nigra* (Black Mustard)	S	—	Sd	—	S	S	S	—	S
			Yp	—	MS	S	—	—	S
10. *Brassica rapa* ssp. *campestris* (Wild Turnip)	S	—	Sd	—	—	S	—	—	S
			Yp	—	—	S	—	—	S
11. *Capsella bursa-pastoris* (Shepherd's Purse)	S	S	Sd	S	S	S	S	S	S
			Yp	S	S	S	MS	—	S
12. *Cerastium holosteoides* (Common Mouse-ear)	S	—	Sd	—	—	S	—	—	—
			Yp	—	—	S	—	—	—
13. *Chenopodium album* (Fat-hen)	S	S	Sd	S	S	S	S	S	S
			Yp	MS	S	MS	MS	—	S
14. *Chrysanthemum segetum* (Corn Marigold)	S	S	Sd	S	S	MS	MR	S	—
			Yp	S	S	R	R	—	—

15. *Erysimum cheiranthoides* (Treacle Mustard)	S	—	Sd	—	—	S	—	—	—
			Yp	—	—	S	—	—	—
16. *Euphorbia exigua* (Dwarf Spurge)	—	—	Sd	—	S	—	MS	—	—
			Yp	—	MR	—	—	—	—
17. *Euphorbia helioscopia* (Sun Spurge)	—	S	Sd	—	S	—	MS	S	S
			Yp	—	MR	—	—	—	MS
18. *Euphorbia peplus* (Petty Spurge)	—	—	Sd	—	S	—	MS	—	S
			Yp	—	MR	—	—	—	MS
19. *Fumaria officinalis* (Common Fumitory)	S	MR	Sd	S	S	S	MS	S	R
			Yp	S	S	MR	MR	—	R
20. *Galeopsis speciosa* (Large-flowered Hemp-nettle)	S	—	Sd	—	—	S	MS	—	—
			Yp	—	—	MS	MR	—	—
21. *Galeopsis tetrahit* (Common Hemp-nettle)	S	—	Sd	R	S	S	MS	—	S
			Yp	R	MR	MS	MR	—	MS
22. *Galinsoga parviflora* (Gallant Soldier)	—	—	Sd	'	—	—	S	—	—
			Yp	—	—	—	MS	—	—
23. *Galium aparine* (Cleavers)	MR	R	Sd	S	S	MS	MS	MR	MS
			Yp	S	S	R	MR	R	MR
24. *Geranium dissectum* (Cut-leaved Crane's-bill)	—	—	Sd	S	S	—	—	—	—
			Yp	S	S	—	—	—	—
25. *Geranium pusillum* (Small-flowered Crane's-bill)	—	—	Sd	S	S	—	—	—	—
			Yp	S	S	—	—	—	—
26. *Lamium amplexicaule* (Henbit Dead-nettle)	S	MS	Sd	R	R	S	'S	S	MR
			Yp	R	R	MS	MR	—	R
27. *Lamium purpureum* (Red Dead-nettle)	S	MS	Sd	R	R	S	MS	S	R
			Yp	R	R	MS	MR	—	R
28. *Lapsana communis* (Nipplewort)	S	—	Sd	—	—	S	S	—	—
			Yp	—	—	MR	MS	—	—

Weeds	Soil-applied		Stage of growth	Foliage-applied					
	Cyanazine	Meta-mitron		Bentazone	Bentazone + NCPB	Cyanazine	Ioxynil	Meta-mitron	Methazole
29. *Lithospermum arvense* (Field Gromwell)	S	—	Sd	—	—	MS	S	—	—
			Yp	—	—	MR	MS	—	—
30. *Lycopsis arvensis* (Bugloss)	—	—	Sd	—	—	MS	MS	—	—
			Yp	—	—	—	MR	—	—
31. *Matricaria matricarioides* (Pineappleweed)	S	—	Sd	S	S	S	S	—	MS
			Yp	S	S	MS	S	—	MR
32. *Matricaria recutita* (Scented Mayweed)	S	—	Sd	S	S	S	S	—	MS
			Yp	S	S	MS	S	—	MR
33. *Medicago lupulina* (Black Medick)	—	—	Sd	—	—	—	—	—	—
			Yp	—	—	—	—	—	—
34. *Myosotis arvensis* (Field Forget-me-not)	S	—	Sd	S	S	S	S	—	—
			Yp	S	S	MS	—	—	—
35. *Papaver dubium* (Long-headed Poppy)	—	—	Sd	—	—	—	—	—	—
			Yp	—	—	—	—	—	—
36. *Papaver rhoeas* (Common Poppy)	S	S	Sd	S	S	S	S	S	S
			Yp	MS	MS	MS	MS	—	S
37. *Poa annua* (Annual Meadow-grass)	S	S	Sd	R	R	S	MR	S	S
			Yp	R	R	MS	R	—	MS
38. *Polygonum aviculare* (Knot-grass)	MS	MS	Sd	R	S	MS	MS	S	S
			Yp	R	MR	MR	MR	—	MS
39. *Polygonum convolvulus* (Black-bindweed)	S	R	Sd	S	S	S	MS	MS	S
			Yp	MS	S	S	MS	—	S

40. *Polygonum lapathifolium* (Pale Persicaria)	S	MS	Sd Yp	S S	S S	S MS	S MS	S —	S MS
41. *Polygonum persicaria* (Redshank)	S	MS	Sd Yp	S S	S S	S MS	S MS	S —	S MS
42. *Ranunculus arvensis* (Corn Buttercup)	—	S	Sd Yp	— —	S MS	— —	— —	S —	— —
43. *Raphanus raphanistrum* (Wild Radish)	S	MR	Sd Yp	S S	S S	S S	MS MR	S —	S S
44. *Scandix pecten-veneris* (Shepherd's-needle)	S	—	Sd Yp	— —	— —	— —	— —	— —	— —
45. *Senecio vulgaris* (Groundsel)	S	S	Sd Yp	S MS	S S	S MR	S S	S —	S S
46. *Sinapis alba* (White Mustard)	MS	—	Sd Yp	S S	S S	S MS	S MS	— —	S S
47. *Sinapis arvensis* (Charlock)	S	MR	Sd Yp	S S	S S	S MS	S M	S —	S S
48. *Solanum nigrum* (Black Nightshade)	MS	MR	Sd Yp	S S	S S	MS MR	— —	MS MR	S S
49. *Sonchus asper* (Prickly Sow-thistle)	—	—	Sd Yp	— —	S MS	— —	S MS	— —	— —
50. *Sonchus oleraceus* (Smooth Sow-thistle)	S	—	Sd Yp	— —	S MS	S MS	S MS	— —	S S
51. *Spergula arvensis* (Corn Spurry)	S	—	Sd Yp	S S	S S	S S	MR R	— —	— —
52. *Stellaria media* (Common Chickweed)	S	S	Sd Yp	S S	S S	S S	MS MR	S —	S S

Weeds	Soil-applied		Stage of growth	Foliage-applied					
	Cyanazine	Meta-mitron		Bentazone	Bentazone + NCPB	Cyanazine	Ioxynil	Meta-mitron	Methazole
53. *Thlaspi arvense* (Field Penny-cress)	S	S	Sd	S	S	S	S	S	S
			Yp	S	S	S	MR	—	MS
54. *Tripleurospermum maritimum* ssp. *inodorum* (Scentless Mayweed)	S	S	Sd	S	S	S	S	S	MS
			Yp	S	S	MS	S	—	MR
55. *Urtica urens* (Small Nettle)	S	S	Sd	S	S	S	MS	S	S
			Yp	S	S	S	MR	—	S
56. *Veronica agrestis* (Green Field-speedwell)	—	—	Sd	R	R	—	MS	—	—
			Yp	R	R	—	—	—	—
57. *Veronica arvensis* (Wall Speedwell)	—	—	Sd	R	R	—	MS	—	—
			Yp	R	R	—	MR	—	—
58. *Veronica hederifolia* (Ivy-leaved Speedwell)	S	MS	Sd	R	R	S	MS	S	MR
			Yp	R	R	S	R	—	R
59. *Veronica persica* (Common Field-speedwell)	S	S	Sd	R	R	S	MS	S	MR
			Yp	R	R	S	MR	—	R
60. *Vicia hirsuta* (Hairy Tare)	—	—	Sd	—	—	—	—	—	—
			Yp	—	—	—	—	—	—
61. *Vicia sativa* (Common Vetch)	MR	—	Sd	—	—	R	—	—	—
			Yp	—	—	R	—	—	—
62. *Viola arvensis* (Field Pansy)	S	MS	Sd	—	S	MS	MR	S	S
			Yp	—	MS	R	MR	—	S
63. *Viola tricolor* (Wild Pansy)	S	—	Sd	—	—	MS	MS	—	—
			Yp	—	—	R	MR	—	—

Chapter 3
Recommendations for the use of herbicides in perennial vegetable crops, fruit, flowers, nursery stock and glasshouse crops

Introduction

3.001 Many recommendations included in this chapter, particularly on minor crops, have evolved from limited experimentation, use in other countries and practical experience of growers and advisers. A few do not appear as label recommendations, or may be listed only as 'growers risk' uses. Growers who apply treatments outside manufacturers' recommendations should ensure that the use has been cleared under the Pesticides Safety Precautions Scheme, and accept that the crop may be at risk.

3.002 Soil-acting herbicides are widely used on most of the crops in this chapter. There are restrictions on their use on extremely light soils, because of the risk of crop damage, and on organic soils because of inadequate weed control. The suitability of a particular herbicide for various soil types should be checked as well as its safety to the crop. Soil moisture plays an important role in determining the activity and selectivity of soil-applied herbicides. Inadequate weed control or crop damage may occur under extreme conditions. Residues of soil-acting herbicides may also persist beyond the life span of the crop and damage a succeeding crop. Check to ensure there is an adequate interval before planting the next crop.

3.003 Perennial weeds present special problems in many of these crops. By confining treatment to where perennial weeds occur both the amount of chemical needed and the area of crop at risk can be reduced.

Most perennial weeds can be greatly reduced, if not eliminated, with pre-planting herbicides or fallow. Detailed control measures for selected perennial weeds are given in Chapter 6 and Chapter 12.

3.004 *Crops grown for processors.* Processors should be consulted about any restrictions which they place on the use of herbicides because of the risk of taint or other problems.

Section I. Vegetables

Artichoke (Globe)

3.005   [**For information.**] Paraquat at 1·1 kg/ha in medium volume as a directed spray during the winter to control annual weeds and *Ranunculus repens* (Creeping Buttercup) and to check other perennial weeds.

3.006   [**For information.**] Simazine at 1·1 kg/ha in medium to high volume as an overall spray in spring to control annual weeds.

Asparagus (seedbeds and freshly-planted crowns)

PRE-EMERGENCE CONTACT TREATMENT

3.007   **Paraquat** *0·6–1·1 kg/ha in medium volume to kill seedling weeds that emerge before the crop.*

PRE-EMERGENCE RESIDUAL TREATMENTS

3.008   **Diuron** *0·9 kg/ha in medium to high volume shortly after sowing to control annual weeds.*
On light soils heavy rainfall may lead to serious crop damage.

3.009   **Linuron** *at 1·1 kg/ha in medium to high volume immediately after sowing to control annual weeds.*

Asparagus (established beds)

PRE-EMERGENCE CONTACT TREATMENT

3.010   **Paraquat** *0·6–1·1 kg/ha in medium volume before the first 'spears' emerge or at the end of the cutting season, immediately following a final cut of all emerged 'spears', to control seedling weeds and* Ranunculus repens *(Creeping Buttercup).*

PRE-EMERGENCE RESIDUAL TREATMENTS

3.011   **Diuron** *0·8–3·4 kg/ha according to soil type in medium to high volume to control annual weeds.*
Apply after the beds have been finally worked in spring, but before the first 'spears' emerge. A second application may be made at the end of the cutting season provided that the dose per application does not exceed 2·8 kg/ha. Treatment is not advisable in the final year when a bed is to be grubbed, because of the risk of damage to the following crop.

3.012   **Lenacil** *1·8–2·2 kg/ha in medium to high volume to control annual weeds.*
Apply overall following the final spring cultivation, but before the 'spears' or weeds emerge. Application may be made in the final year before a bed is grubbed.

3.013   **Simazine** *1·1–1·7 kg/ha according to soil type in medium to high volume to control annual weeds.*
Apply after the beds have been finally worked in spring, but before the first 'spears' emerge. The dose should be reduced in the final year when a bed is to be grubbed, to reduce the risk of damage to the following crop.

3.014   **Terbacil** *2·2–2·7 kg/ha according to soil type in medium to high volume to control annual and some perennial weeds particularly* Agropyron repens *(Common Couch).*
Apply only to crops planted for at least two seasons and do not apply in the 2 years before grubbing.
Apply after the beds have been finally worked in spring but before the first 'spears' emerge. Apply 0·9 kg/ha to control annual weeds including *Polygonum aviculare* (Knotgrass).

POST-EMERGENCE TREATMENTS

3.015   **MCPA-salt** *up to 2·2 kg/ha as a directed spray in summer to control perennial broad-leaved weeds.*
The weeds should be well developed, and the spray should be directed on to the weed foliage, as much as possible avoiding contact with the asparagus stems and fern. This treatment is particularly useful as a spot treatment for *Convolvulus arvensis* (Field Bindweed) and *Ranunculus repens* (Creeping Buttercup).

3.016   **Dalapon-sodium** *9 kg/ha in medium volume to control perennial grasses such as* Agropyron repens *(Common Couch).*
If grass foliage is present in spring before 'spear' emergence, apply overall. In summer, after the cutting season is over, direct the spray on to the weed foliage, as much as possible avoiding contact with the asparagus stems and fern.

Horseradish

PRE-EMERGENCE CONTACT TREATMENTS

3.017   **Paraquat** *0·6–1·1 kg/ha in medium volume as an overall spray before newly planted crops emerge to control annual weeds.*

3.018   **Linuron** *2·2–4·5 kg/ha according to soil-type in medium to high volume in spring before the crop emerges to control annual weeds.*

3.019   **Terbacil** *1·8 kg/ha in medium volume before crop emergence for control of annual and some perennial weeds.*
Apply only to crops growing in black fen soils.

Mint (*Mentha spicata* and *M. piperita*)

CONTACT TREATMENT

3.020   **Paraquat** *0·6–1·1 kg/ha in medium volume to established mint after any cut provided the soil is at or near field capacity.*
Paraquat, in killing the above ground parts of the mint, assists in the control of mint rust (*Puccinia menthae*).

SOIL-APPLIED RESIDUAL TREATMENTS

3.021   **Chloroxuron** *3·4–6·7 kg/ha to established mint in spring or after a cut to control annual weeds.*

3.022   **Lenacil** *1·4 kg/ha in medium to high volume after planting and to established mint to control annual weeds.*
Apply to established crops in early spring or after a cut has been taken. Further applications may be made after subsequent cuts.

3.023   **Simazine** *1·1 kg/ha in medium to high volume to established mint in mid-winter followed by 0·6 kg/ha after the first or second cut to control annual weeds.*

3.024   **Terbacil** *1·3 kg/ha in medium volume to established mint in mid-winter.*
This treatment will control established *Poa annua* (Annual Meadow-grass), *Agropyron repens* (Common Couch) and other grasses.

3.025   **Terbacil** *at 0·4 kg/ha after the first or second cut to control some annual weeds.*

Rhubarb

PRE-EMERGENCE CONTACT TREATMENT

3.026   [**For information.**] Paraquat 0·6–1·1 kg/ha in medium volume as an overall spray when the crop is completely dormant to control annual weeds and *Ranunculus repens* (Creeping Buttercup) and to check other perennial weeds.

3.027 *Mixtures of* **chlorpropham** *2·2 kg/ha plus* **fenuron** *0·6 kg/ha or* **chlorpropham** *2·2 kg/ha plus* **diuron** *0·4 kg/ha in medium to high volume on established rhubarb during the dormant period to control annual weeds.*

Apply in late autumn or in late winter but not after bursting of the pink membrane.

3.028 **Propyzamide** *0·9–1·7 kg/ha in medium volume as an overall spray to control* Agropyron repens *(Common Couch) and certain annual weeds in crops that have been planted for at least one season.*

Apply between the beginning of October and the end of December. The higher dose is required to control perennial grasses and seedling *Galium aparine* (Cleavers).

3.029 **Simazine** *2·2–3·4 kg/ha according to soil type in medium to high volume on established rhubarb during the dormant period to control annual weeds.*

Apply in late autumn or early spring to weed-free soil.

3.030 **Simazine** *1·1–2·2 kg/ha according to soil type in medium to high volume on newly-planted sets.*

3.031 **TCA** *33–56 kg/ha as a high volume spray on established rhubarb during the dormant period for the control of* Agropyron repens *(Common Couch) and other perennial grasses.*

It is not necessary to cultivate after application to incorporate the TCA.

3.032 **Terbacil** *2·4 kg/ha in high volume (e.g. 30 g in 15 litres/125 m²) as a spot treatment only, to control* Agropyron repens *(Common Couch) and* Agrostis *spp. (Bents) in established plantations.*

Crop plants in the treated areas may be severely damaged. Do not apply within 2 years of grubbing because of the risk of residues damaging succeeding crops.

3.033 **Dalapon-sodium** *9·0 kg/ha as a medium volume directed spray during the dormant period for the control of* Agropyron repens *(Common Couch) and other perennial grasses.*

Apply either in autumn or in early spring avoiding the rhubarb crowns.

3.034   **MCPA** *up to 1·7 kg/ha as a high volume directed spray for spot-treatment of perennial broad leaved weeds.*

Sage

PRE-EMERGENCE CONTACT TREATMENT

3.035   **Paraquat** *0·6–1·1 kg/ha in medium volume as an overall spray when the crop is dormant to control annual weeds and* Ranunculus repens *(Creeping Buttercup) and check other perennial weeds.*

PRE-EMERGENCE RESIDUAL TREATMENTS

3.036   **Simazine** *0·6 kg/ha in medium to high volume after planting in September to control annual weeds.*

3.037   **Simazine** *1·1 kg/ha in medium to high volume during March or April on established sage to control annual weeds.*
    This treatment can be used on medium to heavy soils but may cause damage on lighter sandy soils especially if heavy rain follows application. Treatment with simazine can follow overall spraying with contact herbicides during the dormant season.

3.038   [**For information.**] Propachlor 4·5 kg/ha in medium to high volume after planting in September has shown promise for the control of annual weeds.

Section II. Fruit, vines and windbreaks

Apple and pear stoolbeds

PRE-EMERGENCE RESIDUAL TREATMENT

3.039   **Simazine** *0·6–1·1 kg/ha in medium to high volume after the final earthing-up to control annual weeds.*

Apple and pear rootstocks

PRE-EMERGENCE RESIDUAL TREATMENT

3.040   **Chlorpropham** *2·2 kg/ha plus* **fenuron** *0·6 kg/ha 2–3 weeks after planting to control annual weeds.*

Apple and pear orchards

CONTACT TREATMENT

3.041   **Paraquat** *0·6—1·1 kg/ha in medium volume as a directed spray at any time of year to control annual weeds and* Ranunculus repens *(Creeping Buttercup).*
Avoid tree foliage or bark of trees less than 2 years old. Immature bark of older trees may also be damaged. Where the bark is fully mature, wetting by the spray will not cause damage. Paraquat may be mixed with simazine for combined contact and residual effect.

SOIL-ACTING RESIDUAL TREATMENTS

3.042   **Chlorthiamid** *9·2 kg/ha as a strip or tree square treatment to control many established annual and perennial weeds and germinating weeds among apple trees planted for at least 5 seasons.*
Application is normally recommended in February or March, but, autumn treatment is also effective against certain weeds including *Agropyron repens* (Common Couch). Leaf margin chlorosis may develop either in the season of treatment or later. It is caused by a breakdown product of chlorthiamid and does not normally indicate an adverse effect on growth or cropping.

3.043   **Dichlobenil** *5·9—11·0 kg/ha as a tree-base or overall treatment among trees planted for at least 2 seasons, for the control of many established annual and perennial weeds and germinating weeds.*
Application is normally recommended in March and early April, but, late autumn treatment is also effective against certain weeds including *Agropyron repens* (Common Couch). Leaf margin chlorosis may develop either in the season of treatment or later. It is caused by a breakdown product of dichlobenil and does not normally indicate an adverse effect on growth or cropping.

3.044   **Diuron** *2·4—3·2 kg/ha in medium to high volume in early spring to control annual weeds among trees established for at least one season.*
Diuron is more effective than simazine against some weeds such as *Atriplex patula* (Common Orache) and *Polygonum aviculare* (Knotgrass) but less effective against others including *Plantago* spp. (Plantains) and *Senecio vulgaris* (Groundsel).

3.045   **Propyzamide** *0·9—1·7 kg/ha in medium volume to control* Agropyron repens *(Common Couch) and certain annual weeds in trees planted for at least one season.*
Apply between the beginning of October and the end of January. The higher dose is required to control perennial grasses and seedling *Galium aparine* (Cleavers).

3.046   **(i) Simazine** *1·1–2·2 kg/ha according to soil type to newly-planted and established trees to control annual weeds.*

The soil around newly-planted trees should be well firmed. Under favourable conditions simazine is effective at any time of year but best results are usually obtained from treatments in late winter or early spring. A half dose may be applied in the autumn to control many autumn and winter germinating weeds but not *Galium aparine* (Cleavers), *Veronica* spp. and *Viola* spp.

(ii) Simazine *5·6 kg/ha in medium to high volume to trees planted for at least 2 seasons for the longer-term control of annual weeds.*

Some established annuals and shallow-rooted perennial weeds are also controlled. The best time for application is in early spring. This treatment should not be used more than once every two years or within two years of grubbing.

3.047   **(i) Terbacil** *2·7 kg/ha in medium to high volume to control perennial grasses and certain broad-leaved perennial weeds and germinating weeds around apple trees planted for at least 4 seasons.*

Apply in early spring before vigorous grass growth commences. Adequate rainfall after application is essential. Do not use on light sandy soils or those containing less than 1 per cent organic matter or within 2 years of grubbing. Do not use around pears.

(ii) Terbacil *0·9 kg/ha in medium to high volume to control annual weeds among apple trees planted for at least 4 seasons.*

This treatment controls *Polygonum aviculare* (Knotgrass) and *Atriplex patula* (Common Orache) but *Galium aparine* (Cleavers) is resistant. The precautions for the higher dose also apply. Apple is the only tree fruit for which terbacil is recommended.

3.048   **[For information.]** Dichlobenil 16·8 kg/ha as a tree base or overall treatment in late winter or early spring to control persistent perennials and for the prolonged control of annual weeds among trees planted for at least 2 seasons. This treatment should only be applied in alternate years (3.043).

FOLIAGE-APPLIED TRANSLOCATED TREATMENTS

3.049   **Aminotriazole** *4·5 kg/ha in medium volume to control many perennial weeds, including* Agropyron repens *(Common Couch) and* Rumex *spp. (Docks) among trees planted out for at least 4 seasons.*

Apply before the end of June or after picking, when weeds are growing actively. The spray should not contact the crop foliage, freshly-cut wood or injured bark.

Apply 1·1 kg/ha as a tank-mix with other translocated herbicides (3.056) and soil-acting herbicides (3.044 and 3.046) among trees planted for at least one season to contain perennial weeds and control annual weeds.

3.050   *Mixtures of* aminotriazole *4·5 kg/ha plus* simazine *2·2 kg/ha in medium to high volume around trees planted out for at least 2 seasons to control existing weed growth* (3.049) *and germinating weeds.*

Apply before end of June or after picking, when weeds are growing actively. The spray should not contact crop foliage, freshly-cut wood or injured bark.

3.051   **Aminotriazole** *4·5–6·0 kg/ha plus* **diuron** *4·5–6·0 kg/ha in high volume to control existing weeds* (3.049) *and germinating weeds among trees planted for at least 4 seasons.*

The high rate is recommended where perennial weeds are especially dense. The spray should not contact crop foliage, freshly-cut wood or injured bark.

3.052   **Aminotriazole** *3·9 kg/ha plus* **dalapon-sodium** *3·9 kg/ha plus* **diuron** *4·5 kg/ha in medium to high volume to control established weeds* (3.049) *and germinating weeds among trees planted for at least 4 seasons.*

The spray should not contact crop foliage, freshly-cut wood or injured bark.

3.053   **Asulam** *1·7 kg/ha in medium volume to control* Rumex *spp. (Docks).*

Apply as a directed spray. Do not use around the root zones of newly-planted trees. Some grass species may be checked. Seedling and established docks are controlled. Treatment must be made to the expanded leaves when the docks are growing vigorously, either in spring before flowering or in late summer. The chemical works slowly. It may be mixed with MCPA, MCPB or mecoprop to control additional weeds. Do not mow in the 3 weeks before application. Routine mowing of orchards and plantations can recommence 7 days after application. In orchards where there are flowering bulbs, apply in late summer.

3.054   **Dalapon-sodium** *6·7 kg/ha in medium volume to contain* Agropyron repens *(Common Couch) and control annual grasses among trees planted out for at least 4 seasons.*

Apply in autumn or early spring. Grass foliage must be wetted but avoid unnecessary run-off and application to bare soil. There is evidence that Cox's Orange Pippin is less tolerant than other apple varieties and should only be treated in winter.

3.055   **Maleic hydrazide** *5·6 kg/ha in medium volume to check the growth of orchard swards and reduce mowing.*

Apply when grass is growing actively during March/April. The period of suppression depends on weather conditions. Do not apply during drought or when rain is imminent. If necessary a further dose of 4·1 kg/ha may be applied after 6–10 weeks. 3·0 kg/ha may be applied after the last mowing of the season. In cider orchards this facilitates harvesting. Allow 2 weeks between final mowing and spraying.

The addition of 2,4-D will control broad-leaved weeds which might otherwise increase.

3.056 **MCPA-salt** *or* **2,4-D-amine** *up to 2·2 kg/ha,* **MCPB-salt** *up to 3·4 kg/ha or* **dichlorprop-salt** *or* **mecoprop-salt** *up to 2·8 kg/ha alone or in mixtures or mixed with* **dicamba-salt** *at 0·1 kg/ha as directed sprays to control annual and perennial broad-leaved weeds.*

Do not apply when the trees are in blossom. *Avoid drift onto the crop foliage.* Whenever possible avoid ester formulations, especially during hot weather. Pears are particularly susceptible to damage from root-uptake of 2,4-D, this may not be apparent until the year after treatment.

3.057 **2,4,5-T** *1·7 kg/ha as a directed spray around trees planted for more than 4 seasons to control woody weeds such as* Rubus *spp. (Brambles).*

Do not apply when the trees are in blossom. *Avoid drift onto the crop foliage.* Whenever possible avoid ester formulations, especially during hot weather. 2,4,5-T may also be used in oil for the spot treatment of woody weeds, during the winter.

3.058 **Glyphosate** *1·8–2·2 kg/ha in medium volume as a directed spray from November to bud-burst.* To control *Agropyron repens* (Common Couch) and other annual and perennial grass and broad-leaved weeds among trees planted for at least 2 seasons.

Blackcurrant (cuttings)

SOIL-APPLIED RESIDUAL TREATMENTS

3.059 **Simazine** *0·8–1·1 kg/ha according to soil-type in medium to high volume on newly-planted cuttings.*

The cuttings should be inserted at least 150 mm into the ground and the soil well firmed.

3.060 [**For information.**] Lenacil 1·8 kg/ha in medium to high volume on newly-planted cuttings. The cuttings should be inserted at least 150 mm into the ground and the soil well firmed.

Blackcurrant

CONTACT TREATMENT

3.061 **Paraquat** *0·6–1·1 kg/ha in medium volume as a directed spray to control annual weeds, shallow-rooted perennial grasses, and* Ranunculus repens *(Creeping Buttercup).*

140

Apply at any time of year but avoid contact with leaves or dormant buds otherwise damage will result. *Polygonum aviculare* (Knotgrass) and *Atriplex patula* (Common Orache) can be controlled at the 2- and 3-leaf stage but become more resistant with age.

3.062 **Pentanochlor** *2·2–4·5 kg/ha in high volume as a directed spray to control annual weeds.*
Apply at any time of the year but avoid contact with crop leaves as injury may occur. *Chenopodium album* (Fat-hen) and *Polygonum persicaria* (Redshank) are controlled at an advanced stage of development. Other species controlled as seedlings include *Galium aparine* (Cleavers) and *Polygonum aviculare* (Knotgrass).
There is some residual action against a few weed species including *Atriplex patula* (Common Orache), *Chenopodium album* (Fat-hen), *Fumaria officinalis* (Common Fumitory) and *Polygonum persicaria* (Redshank). Chlorpropham may be added to give additional residual effect.

SOIL-APPLIED RESIDUAL TREATMENTS

3.063 **Chlorpropham** *2·2 kg/ha or* **chlorpropham** *2·2–4·5 kg/ha plus* **fenuron** *0·6–1·2 kg/ha in high volume from mid-November to early March.*
These treatments have been largely replaced by more persistent herbicides although they do have the advantage of controlling germinating and established *Stellaria media* (Common Chickweed) and other germinating weeds including *Polygonum aviculare* (Knotgrass). The higher dose of fenuron is more effective against established weeds. The limited persistence of these treatments can be an advantage in the final year of cropping.

3.064 **Chlorthiamid** *up to 9·2 kg/ha in crops planted for at least 2 seasons to control established annual and perennial weeds and germinating annuals.*
Apply in February or March. Do not apply to cut-back bushes.

3.065 **Dichlobenil** *up to 11·2 kg/ha in crops planted for at least 2 seasons to control established annual and perennial weeds and germinating annuals.*
Application is normally recommended in March or early April but it may be applied in November for the control of *Agropyron repens* (Common Couch). Do not apply to cut-back bushes.

3.066 **Diuron** *1·8–2·4 kg/ha according to soil type, in early spring or autumn to control annual weeds on bushes planted for at least one season.*
It is more effective than simazine against weeds such as *Atriplex patula* (Common Orache) and *Polygonum aviculare* (Knotgrass) but less effective against others including *Plantago* spp. (Plantains) and *Senecio vulgaris* (Groundsel). Do not apply as an overhead spray after bud-burst.

3.067 Propyzamide *0·9–1·7 kg/ha in medium volume to crops planted for at least one season to control* Agropyron repens *(Common Couch) and certain annual weeds.*

Apply from the beginning of October to the end of January. The higher dose is required to control perennial grasses and seedling *Galium aparine* (Cleavers).

3.068 Simazine *1·1–2·2 kg/ha according to soil type in medium to high volume to newly-planted or established crops to control annual weeds.*

Best results are normally obtained with late winter or early spring application. A half-dose may be applied in the autumn to control many autumn and winter germinating weeds but not *Galium aparine* (Cleavers), *Veronica* spp. and *Viola* spp.

3.069 [For information.] Lenacil 1·8–2·2 kg/ha according to soil type in medium to high volume to control annual weeds. It is more effective than simazine against *Atriplex patula* (Common Orache) and *Polygonum aviculare* (Knotgrass).

FOLIAGE-APPLIED TRANSLOCATED TREATMENTS

3.070 Asulam *1·7 kg/ha in medium volume as a directed spray to established plants before fruit set or after picking to control* Rumex spp. *(Docks) as described in 3.053.*

3.071 Dalapon-sodium *4·5–9·0 kg/ha as a directed spray in medium volume from autumn until within about 2 weeks before bud-burst in early spring to control grasses.*

The lower dose, which can be used in bushes planted for one season, will control annual grasses. The higher dose, which is required for *Agropyron repens* (Common Couch) and other perennial grasses, should only be used on bushes planted for at least 3 seasons.

Soil-acting herbicides are now available which are at least as good against couch, also control certain broad-leaved weeds and may be applied overall.

3.072 MCPB-salt *2·5–3·4 kg/ha in medium to high volume to control perennial broad-leaved weeds including* Convolvulus arvensis *(Field Bindweed),* Cirsium arvensis *(Creeping Thistle) and* Ranunculus repens *(Creeping buttercup).*

Avoid unnecessary contact with the bushes by directing the spray onto the alleys and the base of the bushes except where the bushes are covered with weed. Apply as soon as possible after growth has stopped, and before the weeds are damaged by frost.

Small patches of weed may be spot-treated with carefully directed sprays in May and June.

Gooseberry (cuttings)

SOIL-APPLIED RESIDUAL TREATMENTS

3.073   [For information.] Lenacil 1·8 kg/ha in medium to high volume on newly-planted cuttings. The cuttings should be inserted at least 150 mm into the ground and the soil well firmed.

3.074   [For information.] Simazine 0·8−1·1 kg/ha according to soil-type in medium to high volume on newly-planted cuttings. The cuttings should be inserted at least 150 mm into the ground and the soil well firmed.

Gooseberry

CONTACT TREATMENTS

3.075   Paraquat *0·6−1·1 kg/ha in medium volume as an overall spray when the crop is dormant or as a directed spray at other times to control annual weeds, shallow-rooted grasses and* Ranunculus repens *(Creeping buttercup).*

Avoid contact with leaves and developing buds. *Polygonum aviculare* (Knotgrass) and *Atriplex patula* (Common Orache) can be controlled at the 2- to 3-leaf stage but become more resistant with age. Simazine may be added for a combined contact and residual treatment.

3.076   Pentanochlor *2·2−4·5 kg/ha in high volume as a directed spray to control annual weeds.*

Apply at any time of the year but avoid contact with crop leaves as injury may occur. *Chenopodium album* (Fat-hen) and *Polygonum persicaria* (Redshank) are controlled at an advanced stage of development. Other species controlled as seedlings include *Galium aparine* (Cleavers) and *Polygonum aviculare* (Knotgrass).

There is some residual action against a few weed species including *Atriplex patula* (Common Orache), *Chenopodium album* (Fat-hen), *Fumaria officinalis* (Common Fumitory) and *Polygonum persicaria* (Redshank). Chlorpropham may be added to give additional residual effect.

SOIL-APPLIED RESIDUAL TREATMENTS

3.077   Chlorpropham *2.2 kg/ha or* chlorpropham *2.2−4.5 kg/ha plus* fenuron *0·6−1·2 kg/ha in high volume from mid-November to early March.*

These treatments have been largely replaced by more persistent herbicides although they do have the advantage of controlling germinating and established *Stellaria media* (Common Chickweed) and other germinating weeds including *Polygonum aviculare* (Knotgrass). The higher dose of fenuron is more effective against established weeds. The limited persistence of these treatments can be an advantage in the final year of cropping.

3.078   Chlorthiamid *up to 9·2 kg/ha in crops planted for at least 2 seasons to control established annual and perennial weeds and germinating annuals.*
Apply in February or March. Leaf margin chlorosis may develop either in the season of treatment or later. It is caused by a breakdown product of chlorthiamid and does not normally indicate an adverse effect on growth or cropping. Do not apply on light sandy soils.

3.079   Dichlobenil *up to 10·9 kg/ha in crops planted for at least 2 seasons to control established annual and perennial weeds and germinating annuals.*
Application is normally recommended in March or early April but it may be applied in November for the control of *Agropyron repens* (Common Couch). Leaf margin chlorosis may develop either in the season of treatment or later. It is caused by a breakdown product of dichlobenil and does not normally indicate an adverse effect on growth or cropping.

3.080   Diuron *2·4–3·2 kg/ha according to soil type in medium volume to control annual weeds in bushes planted for at least one season.*
Diuron is more effective than simazine against weeds such as *Atriplex patula* (Common Orache) and *Polygonum aviculare* (Knotgrass) but less effective against others including *Plantago* spp. (Plantains) and *Senecio vulgaris* (Groundsel).

3.081   Propyzamide *0·9–1·7 kg/ha in medium volume to crops planted for at least one season to control* Agropyron repens *(Common Couch) and certain annual weeds.*
Apply from the beginning of October to the end of January. The higher dose is required to control perennial grasses and seedling *Galium aparine* (Cleavers).

3.082   Simazine *1·1–2·2 kg/ha according to soil type in medium to high volume to newly-planted or established crops, to control annual weeds.*
Best results are normally obtained with late winter or early spring application. A half-dose may be applied in the autumn to control many autumn and winter germinating weeds but not *Galium aparine* (Cleavers), *Veronica* spp. and *Viola* spp.

FOLIAGE-APPLIED TRANSLOCATED TREATMENTS

3.083   Dalapon-sodium *4·5–9·0 kg/ha as a directed spray in medium volume in*

144

the dormant season to control grasses.

The lower dose is used in bushes planted for one season, to control annual grasses. Apply the higher dose, for *Agropyron repens* (Common Couch) and other perennial grasses before the end of December and only to bushes planted for at least 3 seasons.

Soil-acting herbicides are now available which are at least as good against couch, also control certain broad-leaved weeds and may be applied overall.

3.084   **MCPB-salt** *2·5–3·4 kg/ha in medium to high volume to control perennial broad-leaved weeds including* Convolvulus arvensis *(Field Bindweed) and* Calystegia sepium *(Hedge Bindweed),* Cirsium arvense *(Creeping Thistle) and* Ranunculus repens *(Creeping Buttercup).*

Avoid unnecessary contact with the bushes by directing the spray on to the alleys and the base of the bushes, except where the bushes are covered with weed. Apply as soon as possible after growth has stopped, and before the weeds are damaged by frost.

Small patches of weed may be spot-treated with carefully directed sprays before or after the picking period.

3.085   [**For information.**] Asulam 1·7 kg/ha in medium volume as a directed spray to control *Rumex* spp. (Docks) as described in 3.053.

Hop

CONTACT TREATMENT

3.086   **Paraquat** *0·6–1·1 kg/ha in medium volume after weed germination is finished in autumn and before the hop shoots emerge in spring or as a directed spray in July to control annual weeds and* Ranunculus repens *(Creeping Buttercup) and to check other perennials.*

When applying in July avoid drift on to the upper parts of the plant; contact with the base of the bine at this time does not affect the crop.

PRE-EMERGENCE RESIDUAL TREATMENTS

3.087   **Lenacil** *1·8–2·2 kg/ha according to soil type in medium to high volume, to established crops in late winter or early spring to control annual weeds including* Polygonum aviculare *(Knotgrass).*

3.088   **Simazine** *1·1–2·2 kg/ha according to soil type in medium to high volume in late winter or early spring to control annual weeds in established hops.*

3.089   **Simazine** *1·1 kg/ha in medium to high volume, in propagation nurseries planted with layered cuts, but not recently mist-propagated plants, to control annual weeds.*

Damage has occasionally occurred on excessively sandy soil or where the layered cuts have been planted with the buds less than 50 mm below the soil surface.

3.090 **[For information.]** Terbacil 0·9 kg/ha in medium to high volume for control of annual weeds in hops including *Polygonum aviculare* (Knotgrass).

Do not apply to crops planted less than 2 seasons. Damage may occur particularly on light soils or under wet conditions or where there is overdosing.

FOLIAGE-APPLIED TRANSLOCATED TREATMENTS

3.091 **Asulam** *1·7 kg/ha in medium volume as a directed spray in established hops to control* Rumex *spp. (Docks).*

Apply to the expanded leaves when the docks are growing vigorously either in the spring before flowering or in late summer. Seedling and established docks are controlled. It works slowly. More than one application may be needed for complete eradication. Hop sets and 'weaker' hills should not be treated.

3.092 **MCPB-salt** *3·3 kg/ha or* **2,4-D-amine** *1·1–2·2 kg/ha in medium volume as a directed spray to control perennial broad-leaved weeds.*

Apply from June onwards to control *Cirsium* spp. (Thistles), *Convolvulus arvensis* (Field Bindweed) and *Calystegia sepium* (Hedge Bindweed). *Polygonum aviculare* (Knotgrass) will be controlled if paraquat 0·6–1·1 kg/ha is mixed with 2,4-D-amine or sprayed one day after the 2,4-D.

Drift on to any part of the hop plant in June will cause damage but during August the base of the bine may be sprayed safely.

3.093 **[For information.]** Dalapon-sodium 9·0 kg/ha as a medium volume directed spray during November for the control of *Agropyron repens* (Common Couch) and other perennial grasses. The use of dalapon later than November may cause damage.

3.094 **[For information]** Glyphosate at 1·3 kg/ha in medium volume as an overall spray to dormant hops for the control of annual and perennial weeds including *Agropyron repens* (Common Couch).

Loganberry and blackberry

CONTACT TREATMENTS

3.095 **Paraquat** *0·6–1·1 kg/ha in medium volume, as a directed spray to control*

annual weeds, shallow-rooted perennial grasses and Ranunculus repens *(Creeping Buttercup).*
Apply at any time of year but avoid contact with leaves, dormant buds and stems. *Polygonum aviculare* (Knotgrass) and *Atriplex patula* (Common Orache) can be controlled at the 2- to 3-leaf stage but become more resistant with age.

3.096 **Bromacil** *2·2—3·0 kg/ha in medium to high volume to control perennial grass and suppress broad-leaved perennial weeds in crops planted for at least 2 seasons, as for raspberries* (3.115).

3.097 **Chlorpropham** *2·2 kg/ha plus* **fenuron** *0·6 kg/ha in high volume from the beginning of October to the end of December to established crops to control annual weeds, as for raspberries* (3.116).

3.098 **Dichlobenil** *5·6—10·9 kg/ha in early spring before bud movement to control established annual and perennial weeds and germinating annuals in crops planted for at least one season.*

3.099 **Diuron** *1·8—2·4 kg/ha according to soil type, in early spring or autumn to control annual weeds on bushes planted for at least one season.*
It is more effective than simazine against some weeds such as *Atriplex patula* (Common Orache) and *Polygonum aviculare* (Knotgrass) but less effective against others including *Plantago* spp. (Plantains) and *Senecio vulgaris* (Groundsel).

3.100 **Propyzamide** *0·9—1·7 kg/ha in medium volume to crops planted for at least one season to control* Agropyron repens *(Common Couch) and certain annual weeds.*
Apply from the beginning of October to the end of January. The higher dose is required to control perennial grasses and seedling *Galium aparine* (Cleavers).

3.101 **Simazine** *1·1—2·2 kg/ha according to soil type in medium to high volume to newly-planted or established crops to control annual weeds.*
Best results are normally obtained with late winter or early spring application. A half-dose may be applied in the autumn to control autumn and winter germinating weeds.

FOLIAGE-APPLIED TRANSLOCATED TREATMENTS

3.102 **Dalapon-sodium** *4·5—9·0 kg/ha* Agropyron repens *(Common Couch) as for raspberries* (3.121).

3.103 **MCPB-salt** *2·2—3·4 kg/ha to control perennial broad-leaved weeds, as for gooseberries* (3.084).

Plum and cherry

CONTACT TREATMENTS

3.104   **Paraquat** *0·6–1·1 kg/ha in medium volume as a directed spray at any time of the year to control annual weeds, shallow-rooted grasses and* Ranunculus repens *(Creeping Buttercup).*

Avoid wetting foliage or bark of trees less than 2 years old. Where bark is fully mature wetting by spray will not cause damage.

3.105   **Pentanochlor** *2·2–4·5 kg/ha in high volume as a directed spray to control annual weeds.*

Apply at any time of the year but avoid contact with crop leaves as damage may occur. *Chenopodium album* (Fat-hen) and *Polygonum persicaria* (Redshank) are controlled at an advanced stage of development. Other species controlled as seedlings include *Galium aparine* (Cleavers) and *Polygonum aviculare* (Knotgrass).

There is some residual action against *Atriplex patula* (Common Orache), *Chenopodium album* (Fat-hen), *Fumaria officinalis* (Common Fumitory) and *Polygonum persicaria* (Redshank). The addition of chlorpropham increases the residual effect.

SOIL-APPLIED RESIDUAL TREATMENTS

3.106   **Propyzamide** *0·9–1·7 kg/ha in medium volume to plums planted for at least one season to control* Agropyron repens *(Common Couch) and certain annual weeds. Do not apply to cherries.*

Apply from the beginning of October to the end of January. The higher dose is required to control perennial grasses and seedling *Galium aparine* (Cleavers).

3.107   [**For information.**] Simazine 1·1–2·2 kg/ha in medium volume to weed-free soil has been used successfully around plum and cherry trees and is frequently applied to nursery stock. These trees, however, do not possess the same degree of tolerance as apple and pear, and although the treatment may be safe, the absence of more positive information and the frequent occurrence of marginal chlorosis, precludes a firm recommendation.

FOLIAGE-APPLIED TRANSLOCATED TREATMENTS

3.108   **Asulam** *1·7 kg/ha in medium volume to control* Rumex spp. *(Docks).*

This treatment is recommended for plum but at present it is not recommended for cherry.

Apply as a directed spray. Do not use around the root zones of newly-planted trees. Some grass species may be checked. It is effective against seedling as well as established docks. Treatment must be made to the expanded leaves when the docks are growing vigorously, either in spring before flowering or in late summer. The chemical works slowly. Do not mow in the 3 weeks before application. Routine mowing of orchards and plantations can recommence 7 days after application. In orchards where there are flowering bulbs apply in late summer.

3.109 [**For information.**] Glyphosate 1·8–2·2 kg/ha in medium volume as a directed spray from November to bud-burst to control *Agropyron repens* (Common Couch) and other annual and perennial grassland broad-leaved weeds among trees planted for at least two seasons.

Raspberry

CONTACT TREATMENTS

3.110 **Paraquat** *0·6–1·1 kg/ha in medium volume as a directed spray to control annual weeds, shallow rooted perennial grasses and* Ranunculus repens *(Creeping Buttercup) and suckers.*

Application to the cane base in late winter before bud-burst will control over-wintered weeds without crop injury.

In non-cultivated plantations, suckers between the rows may be controlled by an application made when growth is 100–150 mm high. Further emergence will occur and 2 or 3 applications are normally required before fruit harvest. Drift of paraquat on to fruiting cane or replacement canes can cause serious damage and must be avoided by the use of appropriate equipment. This herbicide is not suitable for regulating the growth of replacement canes in the crop row.

3.111 [**For information.**] Dinoseb-in-oil at 3·0 kg/ha in high volume as a directed spray applied to run-off to control suckers between the rows. Drift on to fruiting canes or replacement canes can cause serious damage and must be avoided by use of appropriate equipment. Further emergence will occur and 2 or 3 applications at 100–200 mm height may be required.

Promising results have also been obtained by applying this treatment to the first flush of replacement canes in tall growing, vigorous plantations where access and height is a problem. This treatment should only be applied to healthy well-established plantations and must achieve complete 'burn-off' of treated canes to encourage further emergence of healthy canes. Dinoseb-in-oil also controls annual weeds.

SOIL-APPLIED RESIDUAL TREATMENTS

(i) Preplanting

3.112 **Trifluralin** *1·1 kg/ha applied in medium volume and incorporated 1–14 days before planting to control annual weeds.*

Trifluralin is less dependent on soil moisture than most soil-acting herbicides. Other soil-acting herbicides may be used after planting to extend the range of weeds controlled (see below).

Thorough incorporation within 30 min of application is essential. Depth of incorporation depends on planting method, but untreated soil should not be exposed after planting.

(ii) Post-planting

3.113   *(i)* **Atrazine** *1·1–2·2 kg/ha according to soil type in medium to high volume for the control of annual weeds in newly-planted and established crops.*

Apply in late winter or early spring. This treatment is more effective than simazine under dry conditions and also controls seedling weeds.

(ii) **Atrazine** *2·2–3·4 kg/ha according to soil type in medium to high volume for the control of perennial grasses and broad-leaved weeds in crops planted for at least 2 seasons.*

3.114   **Atrazine** *1·4 plus* **cyanazine** *1·4 kg/ha in medium to high volume to control annual weeds in newly-planted crops.*

Apply in late winter or early spring. This treatment is more effective than atrazine alone on *Galium aparine* (Cleavers) and *Polygonum* spp. and has greater contact effect on seedling weeds.

3.115   *(i)* **Bromacil** *1·1 kg/ha in medium to high volume in newly-planted and established plantations for the control of annual weeds.*

Treatment of newly-planted crops in England has occasionally resulted in crop injury. Until further local information is available this recommendation only applies to crops growing in Scotland.

(ii) **Bromacil** *2·2–3·0 kg/ha in medium to high volume for the control of perennial grasses and suppression of broad-leaved perennial weeds in crops planted for at least 2 seasons.*

Best results are obtained when the soil is moist and rain follows application. Application should be made in early spring before bud-break and new canes emergence. If application is delayed new canes may show transient yellowing but subsequent growth should be normal.

Do not use in the last 2 years before grubbing in order to avoid damage to subsequent crops.

If for any reason the plantation has to be ploughed in before the bromacil has completely disappeared, frequent cross-cultivation and ploughing, preferably at right angles will help to reduce to a minimum the possible hazards to following crops. Crops extremely sensitive to bromacil include carrot, lettuce, beet, leeks and brassicas.

3.116   **Chlorpropham** *2·2 kg/ha plus* **fenuron** *0·6 kg/ha in high volume from the beginning of October to the end of December to established crops to* *control annual weeds.*

This treatment has been largely replaced by more persistent herbicides although it has the advantage of controlling germinating and established *Stellaria media* (Common Chickweed) and other germinating weeds including *Polygonum aviculare* (Knotgrass). The limited persistence can be an advantage in the final year of cropping.

3.117 *(i)* **Chlorthiamid** *4·5 kg/ha in February or March before bud movement in established plantations and immediately after planting out new plantations to control annual weeds.*

If cane emergence has begun before treatment severe stunting of new canes may occur. Until further local information is available treatment of newly-planted crops in England is not recommended.

(ii) **Chlorthiamid** *6·7–9·2 kg/ha in February or March before bud movement to control established annual and perennial weeds and germinating annuals on crops planted for at least 2 seasons.*

Treatment after cane emergence has begun may result in severe stunting of young canes.

3.118 **Dichlobenil** *5·6–10·9 kg/ha in early spring before bud movement to control established annual and perennial weeds and germinating annuals in crops planted for at least one season.*

Treatment after cane emergence has begun may result in severe stunting of young canes.

3.119 **Propyzamide** *0·9–1·7 kg/ha in medium volume to crops planted for at least one season to control* Agropyron repens *(Common Couch) and certain annual weeds.*

This recommendation is only for crops growing in England. Apply from the beginning of October to the end of January. The higher dose is required to control perennial grasses and seedling *Galium aparine* (Cleavers).

3.120 **Simazine** *1·1–2·2 kg/ha according to soil type in medium to high volume to newly-planted and established crops and spawn beds to control annual weeds.*

Best results are normally obtained with late winter or early spring application. A half-dose may be applied in the autumn to control autumn and winter germinating weeds.

FOLIAGE-APPLIED TRANSLOCATED TREATMENTS

3.121 **Dalapon-sodium** *4·5–9·0 kg/ha as a directed spray in medium volume from mid-November to mid-June to control grasses.*

This treatment has been largely superceded. The low dose controls annual grasses but has been replaced by directed sprays of paraquat. The higher rate is necessary for control of *Agropyron repens* (Common Couch) and presents some risk of crop damage. Soil-acting herbicides are available which are at least as good against couch, also control certain broad-leaved weeds and may be applied overall.

3.122   **MCPB-salt** *2·2–3·4 kg/ha in medium to high volume to control perennial broad-leaved weeds including* Convolvulus arvensis *(Field Bindweed) and* Calystegia sepium *(Hedge Bindweed) and* Ranunculus repens *(Creeping Buttercup).*

Avoid unnecessary contact with the canes by directing the spray on to the weed. Apply in late August or early September when cane growth has slowed down and before the weeds are damaged by frost.

Redcurrant (cuttings)

SOIL-APPLIED RESIDUAL TREATMENTS

3.123   [**For information.**] Lenacil 1·8 kg/ha in medium to high volume of newly-planted cuttings. The cuttings should be inserted at least 150 mm into the ground and the soil well firmed.

3.124   [**For information.**] Simazine 0·8–1·1 kg/ha according to soil-type in medium to high volume on newly-planted cuttings. The cuttings should be inserted at least 150 mm into the ground and the soil well firmed.

Redcurrant

CONTACT TREATMENTS

3.125   **Paraquat** *0·6–1·1 kg/ha in medium volume as a directed spray as for blackcurrants* (3.061).

3.126   **Pentanochlor** *2·2–4·5 kg/ha in high volume as a directed spray to control annual weeds as for blackcurrants* (3.062).

SOIL-ACTING RESIDUAL TREATMENTS

3.127   **Chlorpropham** *up to 4·5 kg/ha plus* **fenuron** *1·2 kg/ha in high volume from mid-November to early March as for blackcurrants* (3.063).

3.128   **Dichlobenil** *up to 10·9 kg/ha in crops planted for at least 2 seasons for general weed control as for blackcurrants* (3.065).

3.129 **Propyzamide** *0·9–1·7 kg/ha in medium volume to crops planted for at least one season to control* Agropyron repens *(Common Couch) and certain annual weeds as for blackcurrants* (3.067).

3.130 **Simazine** *1·1–2·2 kg/ha according to soil type to control annual weeds as for blackcurrants* (3.068).

Strawberry

CONTACT TREATMENT

3.131 **Paraquat** *0·6–1·1 kg/ha in medium to high volume as a directed, inter-row spray to control annual weeds and unwanted runners in established strawberries.*

Apply at any time from the end of picking to the start of flowering. Two sprays are usually required to control runners, one in August and another in October, or when growth has recommenced in March or April. Drift of paraquat on to the crop plants can cause serious damage and must be avoided by the careful use of appropriate equipment. The use of discs on both sides of the crop row severs or weakens the runners and reduces the risk of translocation.

This treatment can also be used for a modified stale seedbed technique 3 to 4 days before planting.

RESIDUAL TREATMENTS

(i) Pre-planting

3.132 **Chlorpropham** *1·1 kg/ha plus* **fenuron** *0·6 kg/ha in high volume 10–14 days before planting to control annual weeds.*

3.133 **Trifluralin** *1·1 kg/ha applied in medium volume and incorporated 1–14 days before planting to control annual weeds.*

Trifluralin is less dependent on soil moisture than most soil-acting herbicides. Other soil-acting herbicides may be used after planting to extend the range of weeds controlled. (See post-planting treatments.)

Thorough incorporation within 30 min of application is essential. Depth of incorporation depends on planting method but untreated soil should not be exposed after planting.

(ii) Post-planting

3.134 **Chloroxuron** *4·5–5·6 kg/ha according to soil type in high volume two weeks after planting or to established fruiting crops and runner beds to control annual weeds.*

Established crops may be treated in the 6–8 weeks before strawing, but not later than mid-April, or after picking. Cloched crops should be treated 2 weeks before being covered and there should be rain or irrigation in this period.

Apply to runner beds shortly before the onset of runner production.

3.135 **Chlorpropham** *1·1 kg/ha or* **chlorpropham** *1·1 kg/ha plus* **fenuron** *0·3 kg/ha in high volume in late autumn or early winter to established crops to control annual weeds.*

The crop should be dormant otherwise there may be damage, particularly to Cambridge Vigour. These treatments have been largely replaced by more persistant herbicides although they do have the advantage of controlling established *Stellaria media* (Common Chickweed) and other germinating weeds including *Polygonum aviculare* (Knotgrass).

3.136 **Lenacil** *1·8–2·2 kg/ha according to soil type in medium to high volume to newly-planted and established crops at any time of year and to runner beds to control annual weeds.*

Its use is restricted to certain soil types. Damage may occur on certain light soils especially when there is a lot of rain shortly after treatment. It may be used on cold-stored runners; the moisture conditions required for good weed control are particularly critical at this period. Apply to runner beds shortly before the onset of runner production.

3.137 **Propyzamide** *0·9–1·4 kg/ha in medium volume from October to December inclusive to crops planted for at least one year to control* Agropyron repens *(Common Couch) and certain annual weeds.*

The higher dose which is needed to control perennial grasses and seedling *Galium aparine* (Cleavers) *should not be used on matted rows* or on light soils.

3.138 *(i)* **Simazine** *1·1–1·7 kg/ha according to soil type as a single or split application in medium to high volume to established crops from July to December inclusive and to runner beds to control annual weeds.*

Apply to runner beds shortly before the onset of runner production.

Spring planted crops should not normally be treated for 6 months and autumn/winter planted crops for 9 months. For maximum effectiveness and safety to the crop, apply half in July–September and half in November or December. Do not exceed the half dose in December.

(ii) **Simazine** *0·6–0·8 kg/ha according to soil type in medium to high volume to newly-planted runners that were dipped in activated charcoal, before planting, to control annual weeds.*

Field trials and commercial experience indicate that runners which have been dipped in activated charcoal are able to tolerate simazine applied one or two weeks after planting.

(iii) [**For information.**] Simazine is used on recently-planted strawberries but there is insufficient information for an *overall UK* recommendation. Use of the following treatments, which are regularly used in certain strawberry growing areas, particularly on the heavier soils, should be based on local experience:

(a) 0·6—0·7 kg/ha soon after planting in summer
(b) 0·8 kg/ha in November or December to August and September planted crops with 3 new leaves.
(c) 0·8—1·1 kg/ha to spring planted crops in the south-west of England and eastern Scotland that have produced 3—4 new leaves.

3.139 **Terbacil** *1·9 kg per treated ha as a spot application only, in established crops to control* Agropyron repens *and* Agrostis *spp. (Common Couch).*
Early spring application gives best results. Treated areas of crop may be damaged or killed, therefore large areas should not be treated. The dose is equivalent to 30 g of the 80 per cent w/w wettable powder formulation per 125 m². Residues may affect succeeding crops if this treatment is applied in the last two years of a crop.

3.140 **Trietazine** *1·0—1·5 kg/ha plus* **simazine** *0·14—0·21 kg/ha according to soil-type in medium to high volume to crops planted for at least one season.*
Although there is some contact action on seedling weeds it is preferable that crops are weed-free when treated. There may be transitory marginal chlorosis but the crop normally recovers. Crops to be protected should not be covered for at least 14 days after treatment.

3.141 [**For information.**] Chlorthal-dimethyl 6·0—8·3 kg/ha in medium volume incorporated pre-planting, or as a surface application post-planting or to established crops except between flowering and harvest, for the pre- and post-emergence control of *Veronica* spp. (Speedwells), and the pre-emergence control of some annual weeds.

SELECTIVE FOLIAGE-APPLIED TREATMENTS

3.142 **Phenmedipham** *1·0—1·1 kg/ha according to weather in not more than 220 litres/ha to control annual weeds.*
Many weeds are controlled only at the cotyledon or first true-leaf stage. Larger weeds may be controlled by applying the lower dose and repeating the treatment after 2—3 days. Do not apply between the start of flowering and harvest. Transient yellowing of some leaves may occur. Do not use on crops growing in polythene tunnels or cloches.

3.143 [**For information.**] By adding an adjuvant oil to phenmedipham it is possible to reduce the dose for the same level of weed control, or control larger weeds with the normal dose. This technique is used in sugar beet. The adjuvant may increase the leaf symptoms on the crop.

3.144 [**For information**] 2,4-D-amine 1–2 kg/ha in medium to high volume to control perennial broad-leaved weeds. Promising results have been obtained on established crops sprayed after harvest and on spring-planted runners sprayed in May or June in the year of planting. The crop may be damaged, therefore confine treatment to weedy areas. Early summer application is more effective against the weeds, but in fruiting crops causes damage and mis-shapen fruits in the year of treatment.

Vines (outdoor)

The following treatments are based on recommendations from abroad and limited commercial experience in England.

CONTACT TREATMENT

3.145 **Paraquat** *0·6–1·1 kg/ha in medium volume as a directed spray to control annual weeds.*

SOIL-APPLIED RESIDUAL TREATMENTS

3.146 **Dichlobenil** *5·9–10·9 kg/ha when the crop is dormant to control established annual and perennial weeds and emerging annuals in crops planted for at least two seasons. Avoid local overdosing especially near the stem of the vines.*

3.147 **Simazine** *1·1–2·2 kg/ha in medium to high volume to control annual weeds.*

POST-EMERGENCE TREATMENTS

3.148 [**For information.**] 2,4-D-amine 1–2 kg/ha in medium to high volume as a carefully-directed spray, after the crop has flowered for the control of perennial broad-leaved weeds.

Windbreaks

Experience has shown that herbicides safe on fruit crops may cause damage on the surrounding windbreaks. For instance alder (*Alnus* spp.) is reported to have been damaged by simazine and terbacil. *Alnus incana* has been damaged by aminotriazole when the suckers have been sprayed. *Alnus glutinosa* and *A. cordata* do not sucker. The following treatments are used on most species including alder, willow, hazel, Lawsons and

Leylands cypress, beech, poplar, plum and damson. Further information is available in 3.223–234 and Chapter 7.

CONTACT TREATMENT

3.149 **Paraquat** *0·6–1·1 kg/ha in medium volume as a directed spray at any time of year to control annual weeds and Ranunculus repens (Creeping Buttercup) and check other perennials.*

Avoid wetting immature bark of trees or foliage particularly of conifers.

SOIL-APPLIED RESIDUAL TREATMENTS

3.150 **Simazine** *1·1–3·4 kg/ha depending on soil type, age and species, in medium to high volume to control annual weeds.*

Best results are achieved when applied to weed-free ground or in conjunction with a contact or foliage-acting herbicide in late winter or early spring. A half-dose in autumn will prevent annuals establishing in the autumn and winter. Apply a low dose to newly-planted and less-tolerant species such as alder and *Prunus* spp. especially on lighter soils. Some leaf margin chlorosis may occur but growth is not normally reduced.

3.151 **Dichlobenil** *up to 9 kg/ha to control established annual and perennial weeds and germinating annuals in wind-breaks established for at least 2 seasons.*

Apply in late winter or early spring before growth starts. Consult manufacturer's leaflet for list of susceptible 'crop' species. Avoid local overdosing particularly near the stem. Some leaf margin chlorosis may occur but this is not normally associated with reduced growth.

3.152 [**For information.**] Propyzamide 1·7 kg/ha in medium volume from October to January (inclusive) to wind-breaks planted for at least one season to control *Agropyron repens* (Common Couch) and certain annual weeds.

FOLIAGE-APPLIED TRANSLOCATED TREATMENTS

3.153 **Aminotriazole** *2·2–4·5 kg/ha in medium volume as a directed spray to wind-breaks established for at least 2 seasons to control many annual and perennial weeds.*

Apply to actively growing weeds. The lower dose controls annual and checks perennial weeds. Avoid contact with foliage, fresh-cut wood, injured bark and prevent drift onto neighbouring crops. *Alnus incana* (grey alder) has been damaged when suckers have been sprayed.

Aminotriazole 1·1 kg/ha as a tank mixture with other translocated and soil-acting herbicides among trees planted for at least one season.

3.154   **MCPA-salt** *or* **2,4-D-amine** *1·1—2·2 kg/ha or* **dichlorprop** *or* **mecoprop-salt** *2·8 kg/ha alone, or in mixture or mixed with* **dicamba** *0·1 kg/ha in medium to high volume as a directed spray to control annual and perennial weeds.* **2,4,5-T** *at 1·7 kg/ha may be used to control woody weeds.*

Avoid contact with foliage, freshly-cut wood, injured bark and prevent drift of spray particles and vapour onto neighbouring crops especially during blossom.

3.155   **[For information.]** Glyphosate 1·8—2·2 kg/ha in medium volume as a directed spray from November to bud-burst to control *Agropyron repens* (Common Couch) and other annual and perennial grasses and broad-leaved weeds among trees planted for at least two seasons.

3.156   The susceptibility of weeds to soil-applied herbicides in fruit and ornamental crops

This table is intended to provide a general indication of the response of annual and perennial weeds to those herbicides used in fruit and ornamental crops in the range of doses given in the relevant paragraphs.

Soil-applied treatments

S—Susceptible	Complete or near complete kill.
.MS—Moderately susceptible	Good kill under favourable conditions.
MR—Moderately resistant	Partial kill.
R—Resistant	No useful effect.

Weed	Chloro-xuron	Chlor-propham plus fenuron	2,4-DES	Dichlo-benil, Chlorthia-mid
1. *Aegopodium podagraria* (Ground-elder)	R	R	R	MS
2. *Aethusa cynapium* (Fool's Parsley)	R			
3. *Agropyron repens* (Common Couch)	R	R	R	MS
4. *Agrostis* spp. (Bentgrass)	R	R	R	MS
5. *Alopecurus myosuroides* (Black-grass)			R	S
6. *Anagallis arvensis* (Scarlet Pimpernel)	S	MS	MS	
7. *Anthemis arvensis* (Corn Chamomile)				
8. *Anthemis cotula* (Stinking Chamomile)				S
9. *Anthriscus sylvestris* (Cow Parsley)				
10. *Anthoxanthum odoratum* (Sweet Vernal-grass)				MR
11. *Aphanes arvensis* (Parsley-piert)				
12. *Atriplex patula* (Common Orache)	MR	MS		S
13. *Avena fatua* (Wild-oat)	R	S	R	S
14. *Brassica nigra* (Black Mustard)	S			
15. *Brassica rapa* (Wild Turnip)	S			

Diuron	Lenacil	Propy-zamide	Pyrazon plus chlor-bufam	Simazine, Atrazine	Terbacil, Bromacil	Trieta-zine plus simazine	Tri-fluralin
R	R		R	R	MR	R	
S				MS	MS	S	R
R	R	S	R	MS*	S	R	
R	R		R		S	R	
		S	S	S		MR	S
S	S	R	MR	S	S	S	S
S	S	R		S		S	R
S	S	R		S		S	
					MS		
				S		S	R
S	S	S		MS	S	MS	MS
	R	S	MR	MS	S	R	MS
				S			R
				S			R

*atrazine

Weed	Chloro-xuron	Chlor-propham plus fenuron	2,4-DES	Dichlo-benil, Chlorthia-mid
16. *Bromus sterilis* (Barren Brome)				MR
17. *Calystegia sepium* (Hedge Bindweed)		R		MR
18. *Capsella bursa-pastoris* (Shepherd's-purse)	S	S	S	MS
19. *Cardaria draba* (Hoary Cress)				MS
20. *Cerastium holosteoides* (Common Mouse-ear)	S		S	S
21. *Chenopodium album* (Fat-hen)	S	MS	S	S
22. *Chrysanthemum segetum* (Corn Marigold)				S
23. *Cirsium* spp. (Thistle)	R	R	R	S
24. *Convolvulus arvensis* (Field Bindweed)	R	R	R	MR
25. *Dactylis glomerata* (Cocks-foot)				MS
26. *Eleocharis* spp. (Spike-rush)				MR
27. *Epilobium* spp. (Willowherb)	S			S
28. *Equisetum arvense* (Field Horsetail)	R	R	R	S
29. *Erysimum cheiranthoides* (Treacle Mustard)				
30. *Euphorbia exigua* (Dwarf Spurge)				
31. *Euphorbia helioscopia* (Sun Spurge)				
32. *Euphorbia peplus* (Petty Spurge)	S			
33. *Fumaria officinalis* (Common Fumitory)	MR	MS	S	
34. *Galeopsis speciosa* (Large-flowered Hempnettle)				
35. *Galeopsis tetrahit* (Common Hempnettle)	S	MS	R	

Diuron	Lenacil	Propy-zamide	Pyrazon plus chlor-bufam	Simazine, Atrazine	Terbacil, Bromacil	Trieta-zine plus simazine	Tri-fluralin
					S		
	R	R			MR	R	
S	S	MS	S	S	S	S	R
S				S			S
S	S	S	S	S	S	S	S
S	S			S			R
R	R	R	R	R	MS	R	
R	R	R	R	R	R	R	
					S		
S				MS	MS		
R	R		R	R	R	R	
		R		S			
	R			S		MS	MS
	R			MR		MS	MS
	R					MS	MS
R	S	MS	MR	MS	S	MS	S
				S			
	MR	R	R	S	S	MS	S

Weed	Chloro-xuron	Chlor-propham plus fenuron	2,4-DES	Dichlo-benil, Chlorthia-mid
36. *Galinsoga parviflora* (Gallant Soldier)	S		S	
37. *Galium aparine* (Cleavers)	R	MS		MS
38. *Geranium dissectum* (Cat-leaved Crane's-bill)				R
39. *Geranium pusillum* (Small-flowered Crane's-bill)				R
40. *Heracleum sphondylium* (Hogweed)	R	R	R	R
41. *Holcus mollis* (Creeping Soft-grass)				S
42. *Hordeum murinum* (Wall Barley)				
43. *Humulus lupulus* (Hop)				R
44. *Juncus bufonius* (Toad Rush)				MR
45. *Lamium amplexicaule* (Henbit Dead-nettle)				
46. *Lamium purpureum* (Red Dead-nettle)	MR	R	R	
47. *Lapsana communis* (Nipplewort)		R		
48. *Lithospermum arvense* (Field Gromwell)				
49. *Lolium perenne* (Perennial Ryegrass)				MS
50. *Lycopsis arvensis* (Bugloss)				
51. *Malva sylvestris* (Common Mallow)				S
52. *Matricaria matricarioides* (Pineappleweed)	MR			
53. *Matricaria recutita* (Scented Mayweed)	MR		S	
54. *Medicago lupulina* (Black Medick)	R			MR
55. *Medicago sativa* (Lucerne)				MR

164

Diuron	Lenacil	Propy-zamide	Pyrazon plus chlor-bufam	Simazine, Atrazine	Terbacil, Bromacil	Trieta-zine plus simazine	Tri-fluralin
S		R		S	S		
MR	R	S	S	MR	MS	R	R
				MR			
R	R		R	R	MR	R	
					S		
MR			S	S			S
MR	MR	R		S	S	S	MS
				S			
					S		
	MS			S			R
S	S	R		S		S	R
S	S	R		S			R
S		R		MS			
					S		

Weed	Chloro-xuron	Chlor-propham plus fenuron	2,4-DES	Dichlo-benil, Chlorthia-mid
56. *Mercurialis annua* (Annual Mercury)				MS
57. *Myosotis arvensis* (Field Forget-me-not)				
58. *Papaver dubium* (Long-headed Poppy)	S			S
59. *Papaver rhoeas* (Common Poppy)	S			S
60. *Phragmites communis* (Common Reed)				MR
61. *Plantago* spp. (Plantain)				S
62. *Poa annua* (Annual Meadow-grass)	MR	S	R	S
63. *Poa pratensis* (Smooth Meadow-grass)				S
64. *Poa trivialis* (Rough Meadow-grass)				MS
65. *Polygonum aviculare* (Knotgrass)	MR	S	MR	MS
66. *Polygonum convolvulus* (Black-bindweed)	MR	S	MS	MS
67. *Polygonum lapathifolium* (Pale Persicaria)	MS			
68. *Polygonum persicaria* (Redshank)	MS	S	MS	MS
69. *Potentilla reptans* (Creeping Cinquefoil, silver weed)				MR
70. *Pteridium aquilinum* (Bracken)	R		R	MS
71. *Ranunculus arvensis* (Corn Buttercup)				
72. *Ranunculus repens* (Creeping Buttercup)	R	R	R	MR
73. *Raphanus raphanistrum* (Wild Radish)	MS		S	
74. *Rorippa sylvestris* (Creeping Yellow-cress)	R		R	MS
75. *Rumex crispus* (Curled Dock)				S

Diuron	Lenacil	Propy-zamide	Pyrazon plus chlor-bufam	Simazine, Atrazine	Terbacil, Bromacil	Trieta-zine plus simazine	Tri-fluralin
	S		S	S			
	S			S			
S	S	R		S		S	MS
R				S	S		
S	S	S	MS	S	S	MS	S
MS	S	S	S	MR	S	S	S
MS	S	S	S	MS	S	MS	S
	S		S	MS	S	S	S
	S	S	S	MS	S	S	S
					R		
R			R	R	R	R	
	S			R			
MR	R	MS		MR	R	R	
S	S		S	S		S	R
R			R	R			
		MR			MS		

Weed	Chloro-xuron	Chlor-propham plus fenuron	2,4-DES	Dichlo-benil, Chlorthia-mid
76. *Rumex obtusifolius* (Broad-leaved Dock)	R		R	S
77. *Rubus fruticosus* (Bramble)	R	R	R	R
78. *Scabiosa columbaria* (Small Scabious)				R
79. *Scandix pecten-veneris* (Shepherd's-needle				
80. *Scirpus lacustris* (Common Club-rush)				MR
81. *Senecio vulgaris* (Groundsel)	S	MS	MR	S
82. *Sinapis alba* (White Mustard)	MS			
83. *Sinapis arvensis* (Charlock)	MS		S	S
84. *Sisymbrium officinale* (Hedge Mustard)				S
85. *Solanum dulcamara* (Bittersweet)				
86. *Solanum nigrum* (Black Nighthsade)	S	MS	MS	R
87. *Sonchus arvensis* (Perennial Sowthistle)				
88. *Sonchus asper* (Prickly Sowthistle)	MS			S
89. *Sonchus oleraceus* (Smooth Sowthistle)	MS	R	S	S
90. *Spergula arvensis* (Corn Spurrey)	S	S	MR	S
91. *Stellaria media* (Common Chickweed)	S	S	S	S
92. *Taraxacum officinale* (Dandelion)	R	R	R	S
93. *Thlaspi arvense* (Field Pennycress)	S			S
94. *Torilis arvensis* (Spreading Hedge-parsley)				
95. *Trifolium* spp. (Clover)				MR

Diuron	Lenacil	Propy-zamide	Pyrazon plus chlor-bufam	Simazine, Atrazine	Terbacil, Bromacil	Trieta-zine plus simazine	Tri-fluralin
R		MR	R	R	MS		
R	R	R	R	R	R	R	R
				S			R
MS	MS	R	S	S	MS	S	R
S				S		S	R
S	S	R	S	S	S	S	R
					S		
S	R	S		S	S	MS	R
					S		
MS				S	S		R
MS	S	R	S	S	S	S	R
S	S			MS		S	MS
S	S	S	S	S	S	S	S
R	R	R	R	MR	R	R	
S	S		S	S		S	R
					MS*		
		R					

*terbacil

Weed	Chloro-xuron	Chlor-propham plus fenuron	2,4-DES	Dichlo-benil, Chlorthia-mid
96. *Tripleurospermum maritimum* spp. *inodorum* (Scentless Mayweed)	MR	S	MR	S
97. *Tussilago farfara* (Colt's-foot)				MS
98. *Urtica dioica* (Common Nettle)				MS
99. *Urtica urens* (Small Nettle)	MS	S	S	S
100. *Veronica agrestis* (Green Field-speedwell)	MS	MR	MS	MS
101. *Veronica arvensis* (Wall Speedwell)	MR	MR		MS
102. *Veronica hederifolia* (Ivy-leaved Speedwell)	MR	MR		MS
103. *Veronica persica* (Common Field-speedwell)	MS	MR		MS
104. *Vicia hirsuta* (Hairy Tare)	R			
105. *Vicia sativa* (Common Vetch)	R			
106. *Viola arvensis* (Field Pansy)		R	MR	
107. *Viola tricolor* (Wild Pansy)	MR			
108. Volunteer Cereals	MR	S	R	S

Diuron	Lenacil	Propy-zamide	Pyrazon plus chlor-bufam	Simazine, Atrazine	Terbacil, Bromacil	Trieta-zine plus simazine	Tri-fluralin
S	S	R	S	S	S	S	R
					MR		
				R	MS		
S	MS	S	S	S	S	S	MS
R	MR	S	S	MR	S	S	S
R	R	S	S	MS	S	S	S
R	R	S	S	MS	S	S	S
R	MR	S	S	MS	S	S	MS
				MR			R
			S	MR			R
	R			MS		MS	
			S	MS			
	S	S	·	S			S

Section III. Flower crops and nursery stock

3.157   This section covers a great number of crops grown in a large number of varieties and with widely different growing methods. The nature of many of the crops is such that weed problems are particularly serious and there is a great demand for information on chemical control methods. As the areas involved are relatively small, intensive research is rarely possible and the main source of information is often trials carried out by growers. Therefore, some of the recommendations in this section are based on less experience than other recommendations in this book. Even with treatments which have been in general use for several years, developments in growing methods, new varieties or extension of the crop on to different soil types might result in considerable changes in safety and effectiveness.

Anemone

PRE-EMERGENCE CONTACT TREATMENT

3.158   **Paraquat** *0·6–1·1 kg/ha in medium volume to anemones grown from corms or seeds just before the first leaves emerge, to control seedling weeds.*

PRE-EMERGENCE RESIDUAL TREATMENTS

3.159   **Fenuron** *1·1 kg/ha plus* **chlorpropham** *0·6 kg/ha in high volume immediately after planting corms to control annual weeds.*
   The treatment may cause a slight check to growth so that it may be necessary to plant 10–14 days earlier. The mixture should not be used on light, sandy soils deficient in organic matter or under drought conditions. *Veronica* spp. (Speedwells) are not well controlled.

3.160   **Simazine** *0·6–0·8 kg/ha in medium to high volume immediately after planting corms to control annual weeds.*
   The treatment may cause a slight check to growth so that it may be necessary to plant 10–14 days earlier. The treatment should not be used on light, sandy soils deficient in organic matter.

Annual, biennial and perennial flowers grown from seed and bedding plants

PRE-EMERGENCE CONTACT TREATMENT

3.161   **Paraquat** *0·6–1·1 kg/ha in medium volume to control seedling weeds which appear before the emergence of crops grown from seed and between the final cultivation and planting of transplants.*

172

PRE-EMERGENCE RESIDUAL TREATMENTS

3.162 **Chlorpropham** *1·1 kg/ha in medium to high volume immediately after drilling has been used successfully in the following crops for the control of annual weeds: acroclinium, annual chrysanthemum, china aster, coreopsis, strawflower, calendula, sweet sultan, African and French marigolds.*

3.163 *(i)* **Chlorpropham** *0·8 kg/ha plus* **fenuron** *0·15 kg/ha in medium to high volume applied 4 or 5 days after sowing the following crops to control annual weeds—calendula, viola, zinnia, lupin, wallflower, polyanthus, myosotis, annual chrysanthemum, cornflower, foxglove, delphinium, canterbury bell.*
(ii) **Chlorpropham** *1·1 kg/ha plus* **fenuron** *0·2 kg/ha in medium to high volume to weed free soil 5–7 days before transplanting polyanthus, wallflower, viola, delphinium, canterbury bell and lupins, to control annual weeds.*
Avoid unnecessary soil disturbance when planting.

3.164 *(i)* **Chloroxuron** *4·5–5·6 kg/ha in medium to high volume to weed-free soil after planting out violas and pansies, to control annual weeds.*
(ii) **Chloroxuron** *4 kg/ha in medium to high volume to weed free soil 10 days after transplanting sweet william, to control annual weeds.*
Promising results indicate that the following crops may also be treated: carnations, primula, pelargoniums, pansies, viola, fuchsia, petunia, ageratum, lobelia, salvia, centaurea, cleome, mesembryanthemums, tagetes and zinnia.

3.165 **Linuron** *0·6 kg/ha in medium to high volume as a pre-emergence treatment in cornflower, nasturtium, mignonette and* Linum perenne, *to control annual weeds.*

3.166 *(i)* **Propachlor** *4·5 kg/ha in medium to high volume to weed-free soil immediately after drilling wallflower to control annual weeds.*
(ii) **Propachlor** *4·5 kg/ha as a granular formulation to weed-free soil anytime after planting many bedding-out plants including wallflower, geranium, fuchsia, stocks and antirrhinums, to control annual weeds.*
Do not apply to ageratum or salvia.

Bulbous crops

PRE-EMERGENCE CONTACT TREATMENT

3.167 **Paraquat** *0·6–1·1 kg/ha in medium volume after planting until shortly before crop emergence to control annual weeds, shallow-rooted perennial grasses and* Ranunculus repens *(Creeping Buttercup).*

This treatment is generally used in conjunction with the residual treatments listed below.

Narcissus, tulip, iris (dutch) and gladiolus

PRE-EMERGENCE RESIDUAL TREATMENTS

(i) *Pre-crop emergence*

3.168   **Chlorpropham** *4·5 kg/ha or* **chlorpropham** *2·2 kg/ha plus either* **diuron** *0·9 kg/ha or* **fenuron** *0·6 kg/ha in medium to high volume any time after planting until crop emergence, to control annual weeds.*

With the exception of *Stellaria media* (Common Chickweed), established weeds are not controlled. Other weeds can be controlled with paraquat.

Chlorpropham 1·1–2·2 kg/ha may be used on crops under glass but the treatment should not be used if other crops are being grown in the same block of houses because of the risk of damage from volatilization of the herbicide.

3.169   **Linuron** *1·1 kg/ha plus* **chlorpropham** *2·2 kg/ha or* **linuron** *0·8 kg/ha plus* **lenacil** *0·9 kg/ha any time after planting until shortly before crop emergence, to control annual weeds.*

Linuron controls some emerged weeds, but all treatments are most effective against established weeds when used in combination with paraquat.

3.170   **Lenacil** *1·8–2·2 kg/ha according to soil type in medium to high volume to narcissus and tulip any time before crop emergence, to control annual weeds.*

Emerged weeds are not controlled and should be treated with paraquat.

3.171   **Pyrazone** *1·1–2·2 kg/ha plus* **chlorbufam** *0·9–1·8 kg/ha according to soil type and duration of weed control required in high volume for the control of annual weeds.*

The treatment is effective against many species of emerged weeds, provided that they have not developed beyond the cotyledon stage when the lower dose is used or have not more than two true leaves when the higher dose is used. Where weeds are larger use in conjunction with paraquat.

3.172   **Simazine** *0·8 kg/ha in medium volume on narcissus and iris on medium and heavy soils in south-west England before the crop emerges, to control annual weeds.*

This treatment is not recommended for silts and lighter soils because of a reduction in bulb yield.

(ii) *Post-crop emergence*

3.173 **Chlorpropham** *2·0 kg/ha alone or with* **diuron** *0·9 kg/ha in medium to high volume to narcissus up to 10 cm high, tulip with leaves still furled and iris with 2 to 3 leaves and not more than 12 cm long to control annual weeds.*

With the exception of *Stellaria media* (Common Chickweed) emerged weeds are not controlled.

3.174 **Linuron** *1·1 kg/ha plus* **chlorpropham** *2·2 kg/ha or* **linuron** *0·8 kg/ha plus* **lenacil** *0·9 kg/ha in medium to high volume to narcissus up to 10 cm high and iris with 2 to 3 leaves and not more than 12 cm high to control annual weeds.*

Linuron controls some emerged weeds at the seedling stage.

3.175 **Lenacil** *1·8–2·2 kg/ha in medium to high volume to narcissus and iris shortly after crop emergence to control annual weeds.*

Emerged weeds are not controlled.

3.176 [**For information.**] Metoxuron *4·0 kg/ha in medium volume to narcissus up to 10 cm high and tulip before the leaves unfurl, to control annual weeds.*

It gives post-emergence control of a number of annuals including *Matricaria* spp. and *Tripleurospermum maritimum* ssp. *inodorum* (Mayweed) and *Veronica* spp. (Speedwells).

3.177 **Pyrazone** *1·1–2·2 kg/ha plus* **chlorbufam** *0·9–1·8 kg/ha in high volume post-emergence on narcissi at any stage other than during flowering, on tulips whilst the leaves are still furled and on iris with 2 to 3 leaves and not much more than 12 cm high. Gladioli may be treated at the lower rate before the flower spike emerges.*

The treatment is effective against many species of emerged weeds, provided that they have not developed beyond the cotyledon stage when the low dose is used or have not more than 2 true leaves when the high dose is used. *Matricaria* spp. and *Tripleurospermum maritimum* ssp. *inodorum* (Mayweed) are only controlled pre-emergence.

This treatment may also be applied to narcissus and tulip after planting. Do not exceed the low dose on tulip.

SENESCENCE TREATMENTS

3.178 **Dimexan** *9·4–28·0 kg/ha to narcissus and iris to desiccate the foliage and stems of both crop and weeds, to facilitate lifting.*

3.179 **Dinoseb** *formulated in oil as an emulsifiable concentrate at 3 kg/ha in medium to high volume to desiccate foliage and stems of narcissus and iris and weeds to facilitate lifting.*

3.180   **Sulphuric acid** *as a 12 per cent v/v solution at 1100 litres/ha to desiccate the foliage and stems of narcissus and weeds to facilitate lifting.*

3.181   **Aminotriazole** *4·5 kg/ha in medium volume to narcissus and iris after the crop has died back and the dead foliage has been separated by flailing, to control annual and perennial weeds.*
Can be used in crops that are to remain *in situ* for another season. Should be applied as soon as there is enough weed growth and before crop growth recommences.

3.182   **Asulam** *4·5 kg/ha in medium volume to narcissus after the crop has died back and the foliage has been separated by flailing to control* Rumex *spp. (Docks).*
Apply when the expanded leaves of the docks are growing vigorously but before the dock flower shoot emerges.

3.183   **Paraquat** *1·1–2·2 kg/ha in medium to high volume to clear weeds from narcissus and iris after the crop foliage has died down.*
Where weed growth is dense use the high volume. It is important that no bulb foliage, living or dead, is showing above ground at the time of spraying, otherwise the bulb can be seriously damaged. The treatment is safe after cultivation has detached the dead foliage from the bulbs and covered them with soil, but should not be applied to bulbs growing on very sandy soil. For crops which are being left *in situ* for a further season, this treatment, followed by a similar spray in late autumn to kill the next flush of weeds, will often keep the crop very clean until the following spring.

3.184   [**For information.**] MCPA-salt or 2,4-D-amine up to 2·2 kg/ha or dichloprop-salt or mecoprop-salt up to 2·8 kg/ha have been used successfully after the crop had died down to control perennial broad-leaved weeds. The crop may be damaged if the herbicide is washed down to root level, therefore treatment should be confined to affected area.

Miscellaneous bulbous crops (Scilla, Muscari, Chionodoxa, Crocus, Galanthus, Iris reticulata)

3.185   **Chlorpropham** *4·0 kg/ha or* **chlorpropham** *2·2 kg/ha plus* **diuron** *0·9 kg/ha in medium to high volume at any time after planting until the crop leaves are 50 mm high, to control annual weeds.*
With the exception of *Stellaria media* (Common Chickweed),

established weeds are not controlled. When application is before the crop emerges these treatments can be applied with paraquat. Where they are to be applied after the crop emerges, paraquat should be applied pre-emergence.

3.186   **Linuron** *1·1 kg/ha alone or with* **chlorpropham** *2·2 or* **linuron** *0·3 kg/ha plus* **lenacil** *0·9 kg/ha in medium to high volume any time after planting until the crop leaves are about 50 mm high, to control annual weeds.*

    Linuron controls some emerged weeds but the control of established weeds is better with paraquat, but this must be applied before the crop emerges.

3.187   **Pyrazone** *1·1–2·2 kg/ha plus* **chlorbufam** *0·9–1·8 kg/ha in medium to high volumes any time after planting until the crop leaves are about 50 mm high, to control annual weeds as in narcissus (3.171).*

Freesia (corms or seed)

3.188   **Chloroxuron** *4·5 kg/ha in medium volume to weed-free soil when shoots are 50 mm high to control annual weeds.*

Lily

    Work with mid-century hybrids indicates the following treatments suitable for control of annual weeds.

PRE-EMERGENCE RESIDUAL TREATMENTS

3.189   **Lenacil** *2·2 kg/ha in medium to high volume to moist weed-free soil after crop emergence (April/May), to control annual weeds.*

3.190   **Simazine** *0·6 kg/ha plus* **lenacil** *1·1 kg/ha in medium to high volume to moist weed-free soil before crop emergence in early spring (February), to control annual weeds.*

Chrysanthemum

CONTACT TREATMENT

3.191   **Pentanochlor** *2·2–4·5 kg/ha in high volume as a directed spray, to control annual weeds.*

    Apply at any time; keep spray to the base of the crop taking great care to avoid the tops of the crop. *Chenopodium album* (Fat-hen) and *Polygonum persicaria* (Redshank), *Stellaria media* (Common Chickweed), *Urtica urens* (Small Nettle) are controlled at an advanced stage of development. Other species controlled as seedlings include *Galium aparine* (Cleavers) and *Polygonum aviculare* (Knotgrass).

There is some residual action against *Atriplex patula* (Common Orache), *Chenopodium album* (Fat-hen), *Fumaria officinalis* (Common Fumitory) and *Polygonum persicaria* (Redshank). Chlorpropham may be added for additional residual effect.

SOIL-APPLIED RESIDUAL TREATMENTS

(i) *Preplanting*

3.192 **[For information.]** *Trifluralin 1·1 kg/ha in medium volume and incorporated 1–14 days before planting to control annual weeds.*

Thorough incorporation within 30 min of application is essential. Depth of incorporation depends on planting method but untreated soil should not be exposed after planting.

(ii) *Post-planting*

3.193 **Chloramben** *1·4–2·8 kg/ha in high volume as an overhead spray or as a granular formulation to weed-free soil in established chrysanthemums, to control germinating weeds.*

On young plants with soft growth only the lower dose is recommended and the range of weeds controlled by this dose is limited. Chloramben is most effective when applied to moist soil, but heavy rain after application can greatly reduce activity.

3.194 **Chloroxuron** *4·5–5·6 kg/ha in medium volume as an overhead spray to weed-free soil three or more days after planting to control germinating weeds.*

This treatment has been widely used on many varieties. In some cases slight marginal leaf chlorosis has occurred but this appears to have no effect on growth or cropping. Chrysanthemums under glass have also been successfully treated.

3.195 *(i)* **Chlorpropham** *1·1–2·2 kg/ha in medium to hig volume as a directed spray to weed-free soil in chrysanthemums which have been planted out for 10 days or more to control germinating weeds.*

Overhead treatments have also been used successfully on many varieties, but Chatsworth has been temporarily checked.

(ii) **Chlorpropham** *1·1 kg/ha in medium to high volume at any time in the two weeks before planting rooted cuttings to control annual weeds.*

3.196 **2,4-DES** *4·5–6·7 kg/ha in high volume as an overhead spray to weed-free soil in chrysanthemums which have been planted out for 10 days or more for the control of annual weeds.*

The herbicide is most effective when applied to soil which is moist and warm, under prolonged dry conditions results are poor. Of the large number of varieties on which 2,4-DES has been tested only Chatsworth, Pauline Shepherd and New Princess have been injured (the injury consisting of growth distortion typical of the effects of growth-regulators) and these varieties should not be treated.

3.197 [**For information.**] Propachlor 4·4 kg/ha as a granular formulation applied to weed-free soil after planting out chrysanthemums for the control of annual weeds.

3.198 [**For information.**] Propyzamide 1·1 kg/ha for the control annual weeds. Apply to weed-free soil.

Dahlia

PRE-EMERGENCE RESIDUAL TREATMENTS

3.199 **2,4-DES** *4·5–6·7 kg/ha in high volume as an overhead high-volume spray to weed-free soil in crops planted for 10 days or more, to control annual weeds.*
Best results are obtained under moist, warm soil conditions.

3.200 **Lenacil** *1·8–2·2 kg/ha in medium to high volume as an overall spray to weed-free soil soon after planting, to control annual weeds.*
This treatment has been widely used and most varieties may be treated although damage has occasionally occurred on very small plants on light soils when heavy rain followed application.

3.201 [**For information.**] Propachlor 4·4 kg/ha as a granular formulation applied to weed-free soil after planting out, for the control of annual weeds.

Lavender

SOIL-APPLIED RESIDUAL TREATMENTS

3.202 [**For information.**] Terbacil 0·9 kg/ha on light soil has given good control of *Agropyron repens* (Common Couch) and other weeds in established lavender for oil production. Higher rates may be required on heavier soils.

3.203 [**For information.**] Trifluralin 1·1 kg/ha incorporated before planting, to control annual weeds.

Perennial herbacous plants

CONTACT TREATMENT

3.204   **Paraquat** *0·6—1·1 kg/ha as a directed spray during the growing season or as an overall spray in the dormant season to species which have died down completely, to control annual weeds, shallow-rooted perennial weeds and* Ranunculus repens *(Creeping Buttercup).*

A wide range of crops that do not die down completely in the winter have also been safely sprayed in the dormant period. Application after February has sometimes caused a considerable check.

SOIL-APPLIED RESIDUAL TREATMENTS

3.205   **Lenacil** *1·8—2·2 kg/ha according to soil-type in medium to high volume as an overall spray to weed-free soil to control annual weeds.*

This treatment has been found to be safe in transplanted and established plants of a wide range of perennial flowers, but it is possible that some species or varieties may be susceptible (3.217).

3.206   **Simazine** *0·6—1·1 kg/ha according to soil type in medium to high volume to weed-free soil to control annual weeds.*

Susceptibility varies greatly among cultivars, for guidance see paragraph 3.217. Well-established plants are usually more tolerant than those that are small or newly planted.

3.207   [**For information.**] Chloroxuron at 3·4—4·5 kg/ha in medium to high volume as an overhead spray to a weed-free soil after planting out. Many herbaceous plants appear to be safe but further information is required before firm recommendations can be made (3.217).

3.208   [**For information.**] Propachlor at 4·5 kg/ha as a granular formulation applied to weed-free soil for the control of annual weeds in phlox, michaelmas daisies and pyrethrums. Further information is required before comment can be made for other herbaceous perennials.

3.209   [**For information.**] Trifluralin 1·1 kg/ha incorporated before planting hasgiven good results against annual weeds in a wide range of herbaceous perennials (3.217).

Rose and rose stocks

CONTACT TREATMENTS

3.210   **Paraquat** *at 0·6—1·1 kg/ha in medium to high volume as a directed spray at any time of the year, for the control of emerged weeds.*

3.211   [**For information.**] Paraquat 0·6–1·1 kg/ha has given good results when applied as an overall application in late winter to rootstocks which have been headed back.

SOIL-APPLIED RESIDUAL TREATMENTS

3.212   **Atrazine** *1·1–1·7 kg/ha according to soil type on newly planted rootstocks, after budding and in the spring after heading back, to control annual weeds.*
Three applications may be made over 2 years. Atrazine is more soluble than simazine and is more effective under dry conditions. It will control weeds up to 4 cm high.
Rosa multiflora appears more susceptible than other stocks. It may be scorched, but the plants soon recover.

3.213   **Dichlobenil** *4·2–9·4 kg/ha depending on the weeds to be controlled, applied before crop growth starts in spring, to crops established for at least 2 seasons, to control established annual and perennial weeds and germinating annuals.*
When this treatment has been used after heading back, the primary growing point of the 'bud' has sometimes been damaged. The laterals develop normally in bush roses.

3.214   **Lenacil** *1·8–2·2 kg/ha according to soil type in medium to high volume applied soon after planting, after budding and after heading back, to control annual weeds.*
This treatment is more effective than simazine against *Atriplex patula* (Common Orache) and *Polygonum aviculare* (Knotgrass) but it does not give such persistent control of other weeds.

3.215   **Propyzamide** *0·8–1·4 kg/ha in medium volume from October to February inclusive to crops planted for at least one season to control* Agropyron repens *(Common Couch) and certain annual weeds.*
The higher dose is needed to control perennial grasses and seedling *Galium aparine* (Cleavers).

3.216   *(i)* **Simazine** *1·1–1·7 kg/ha according to soil-type in the medium to high volume spray to newly-planted stocks, after budding and in the spring after heading-back to control annual weeds.*
Three applications may be made over the 2 years roses are being propagated.
(ii) **Simazine** *1·1–2·2 kg/ha according to soil type in medium to high volume to established crops in the spring to control annual weeds.*

3.217   The susceptibility of perennial herbaceous plants to residual herbicides

Key: T = tolerant; S = susceptible; I = intermediate.
The normal dose is indicated in the text

Perennial herbaceous	Simazine	Lenacil	Chloroxuron	Trifluralin
Achillea	I	I	T	T
Aconitum	T	T		
Agapanthus	S	I		
Alchemilla	S	T	T	T
Allium	T			
Anaphalis	S	T		
Anchusa		T		
Anthemis		T		
Aquilegia	S	T		T
Armeria	T	T		T
Aster	I	T	T	
Astilbe	I	I		
Aubretia	S	I		
Bergenia	T	T	T	
Buphthalmum	T			
Campanula	I	I	T	T
Centaurea	S	I	T	T
Chrysanthemum maximum	I	T	T	T
Coreopsis	I	T		T
Delphinium	I	T		T
Dicentra		T		
Digitalis	T	I		
Dianthus	I	T	T	
Doronicum	I	T		
Echinops	T			T
Erigeron	I	T	T	
Eryngium		T		T
Euphorbia	I	T	T	
Gaillardia	S	T	T	
Galega	T			
Geranium	I	I		
Geum	S	T		
Gypsophila	I	T	T	
Helenium	S	I		
Helianthus	I	I	T	
Heliopsis	T			
Helleborus		T		
Hemerocallis	T			T
Heuchera	S	T	T	T
Hosta	T	T	T	
Hypericum	T	T	T	
Iris	I	I	T	
Kniphofia	I	T		T
Lavendula		T		T
Liatris	T	T		
Lupinus	I	I		T
Lychium		T		
Lythrum		T		
Mentha		T		T
Monada	S	S		

Perennial	Simazine	Lenacil	Chloroxuron	Trifluralin
Nepeta	T	T		
Oenothera	I	I		
Paeonia	T	T		
Pennisetum	T			
Penstemon	T			
Phlox	S	I		
Platycodon	T			
Polygonum	I	T		
Potentilla	I	T		
Primula			T	T
Prunella	T			
Pyrethrum	I	T		T
Ranunculus	I	T	T	
Rudbeckia	T	I	T	T
Salvia		T		
Scabiosa	T	T		
Santolina	S	T	T	
Sedum	T	T		T
Sidalcea	T	T		
Solidago	T	T		T
Stachys	S	T	T	
Statice	I	T		
Thalictrum	T			
Thymus				T
Tradescantia		T		
Trollius		T		
Vallisneria			T	
Verbascum		T		
Veronica	I	T		
Vinca	I	T		
Viola		T	T	

Section III. Shrubs and trees

Nursery stock in containers

3.218   Most composts are free of weed seeds, but seeds can be introduced with transplants, in water and in the wind. The most troublesome weeds in containers are *Cardamine hirsuta* (Hairy Bittercress), *Epilobium* spp. (Willowherbs), *Marchantia* spp. (Liverworts), *Poa annua* (Annual Meadow-grass), *Salix* spp. (Willows) and *Senecio vulgaris* (Groundsel). All have efficient methods of seed distribution. If these weeds are controlled in other parts of the nursery and surrounding areas the problem is greatly reduced.

3.219   **Chloroxuron** *2·2 kg/ha in very high volume to weed-free containers to control germinating weeds.*

Chloroxuron controls the most important weeds of containers but *Poa annua* (Annual Meadow-grass) is moderately resistant. Many growers apply chloroxuron in a volume of 3000 litres/ha. Some scorch and damage has occurred on *Berberis, Buddleia, Hydrangea* and heathers, particularly the varieties with golden foliage. The risk of scorch is greatest under glass or polythene and on crops that are not hardened-off. Scorch is reduced if chloroxuron is applied in dull or wet weather and the spray is washed off the foliage immediately with clear water. Do not use on alpine plants as flowering many be inhibited.

This treatment can be repeated every 6–12 weeks according to site and season.

3.220   [**For information.**] Simazine at 1·4 kg/ha has been used on many species with the method described for chloroxuron. It is more effective against *Poa annua* (Annual Meadow-grass) but less effective against *Epilobium* spp. (Willowherbs) and *Marchantia* spp. (Liverworts). Simazine is not as safe as chloroxuron on many species. In trials *Senecio greyii, Deutzia x rosea* and *Weigela florida 'Variegata'* have been damaged or killed.

3.221   [**For information.**] Chloroxuron has been applied to empty sand beds to prevent weeds establishing in the sand.

3.222   [**For information.**] Paraquat 0·6–1·1 kg/ha has been applied to empty sandbeds that are weedy. Care should be taken as excessive numbers of applications can lead to the presence of 'free' paraquat that can be taken up in the containers and damage the plants.

Field-grown nursery stock

3.223   **Paraquat** *0·6 to 1·1 kg/ha in medium to high volume as a directed spray at any time of year to control annual weeds and* Ranunculus repens *(Creeping Buttercup).*

There is no risk of damage to field-grown crops from root uptake. Contact with crop leaves can be very injurious and should be avoided by careful application with appropriate equipment. On many deciduous species slight wetting of well-protected dormant buds is unlikely to cause damage. The mature bark of many species tolerates paraquat, but avoid stems less than 2 years old, and those that are older and are still green. *Tilia euchlora* is particularly susceptible.

SOIL-APPLIED RESIDUAL TREATMENTS

3.224 **Chlorpropham** *2·2–4·4 kg/ha plus* **fenuron** *0·6–1·2 kg/ha in high volume, November to early March (before bud-burst), to control annual weeds.*

The lower dose will only control established *Stellaria media* (Common Chickweed). The higher dose will control many more established weeds. Do not spray over conifers or evergreen foliage. The addition of dalapon at 3·5 kg/ha will check perennial grasses.

3.225 **Dichlobenil** *5·9–9·2 kg/ha according to the weed spectrum before new growth starts in the spring, to crops planted for at least two seasons in their final position to control established annual and perennial weeds and germinating annuals.*

The manufacturer's recommendations stipulate that crops should have been established two years after final planting and only certain genera should be treated. Many nursery stock growers have used it in nurseries on crops. In most cases this has been successful although serious damage can occur on some species.

Damage has occurred to the collar of a number of species, mainly conifers, which has sometimes lead to death. This has usually been associated with localized overdosing and late application. Where dichlobenil is to be used outside label recommendations, up-to-date local advice should be sought (3.232).

3.226 **Lenacil** *1·8–2·7 kg/ha according to soil type in medium to high volume to newly and established trees or shrubs, to control annual weeds.*

This treatment is more effective than simazine against *Atriplex patula* (Common Orache) and *Polygonum aviculare* (Knotgrass) but does not give such long term control of other weeds (3.232).

3.227 **Propyzamide** *0·8–1·4 kg/ha in medium volume from October to January inclusive to crops planted for at least one season, to control* Agropyron repens *(Common Couch) and certain annual weeds.*

The higher dose is needed to control perennial grasses and seedling *Galium aparine* (Cleavers). This treatment has been used satisfactorily in a wide range of species but it is still relatively new and up-to-date local advice should be sought.

3.228 **Simazine** *1·1–1·7 kg/ha according to soil type in medium to high volume to weed-free soil to control annual weeds in a wide range of coniferous and broad-leaved nursery stock.*

The reaction of different species is influenced by such factors as size of plant, age, variety, length of time established, soil type and growing conditions, so that it is difficult to classify species satisfactorily according to resistance. In general, newly-planted stock or very small plants are more liable to suffer injury than established or larger plants and the chance of injury is greater on light, sandy soils deficient in organic matter than on heavier or more organic soils, especially under very wet conditions. On the less resistant species a directed spray in the inter-rows is less likely to cause damage than an overall spray. With newly-planted stock it is important that the soil should be firm around the roots before treatment is applied (3.232).

3.229   [**For information.**] Diuron 1·7 kg/ha plus paraquat 0·6 kg/ha formulated as a proprietary mixture as a directed spray between nursery rows for contact and residual control of annual weeds. This mixture should not be used on species known to be susceptible to diuron.

3.230   [**For information.**] Propachlor 4·4 kg/ha applied as an overall spray or as a granular formulation over a range of liner shrubs for control of annual weeds.

3.231   [**For information**] Trifluralin 1·1 kg/ha incorporated before planting has given good results against annual weeds and no damage to a limited range of hardwood species.

3.232   The susceptibility of nursery stock to residual herbicides

Key: T = tolerant; S = susceptible; I = intermediate.

These recommendations should be regarded as tentative. In several genera there are many cultivars which have not been tested. Damage depends on plant size and soil, and is most likely to occur with young plants on sandy soil low in organic matter.

Genus	Simazine at up to 1·1 kg/ha (except where shown)	Lenacil at up to 3·4 kg/ha	Dichlo-benil at 6·7 kg/ha 2-year plants	Remarks
A. Lined out broad-leaved species				
Abelia	T			
Acacia	0·56 kg/ha			
Acer	T			
Aesculus	I			
Ailanthus	T		T	
Alnus	T			
Amelanchier	T			
Amorpha	T			
Ampelopsis	T			
Andromeda	T			
Aralia	T			
Arbutus	T			
Aronia	T			
Artemisia	T		T	
Arundinaria	T			
Atriplex	T			
Aucuba	T		T	
Azalea (see *Rhododendron*)				
Azara	T			
Berberis	T	T	T	*B. stenophylla* is susceptible to dichlo-benil but *B. wilsonae* is less so
Betula	I–T		T	*B. pendula* is sensitive to simazine
Buddleia	T	T		
Buxus	T	T		
Callicarpa	T			
Callistemon	T			
Calluna	T	T	T	
Camellia	T			
Caragana	0·56 kg/ha			
Carpinus	T	T	T	
Caryopteris	0·56 kg/ha			
Cassinia	T	T	T	
Castanea	T			
Catalpa	T			

Genus	Simazine at up to 1·1 kg/ha (except where shown)	Lenacil at up to 3·4 kg/ha	Dichlo-benil at 6·7 kg/ha 2-year plants	Remarks
Ceanothus	T			
Celtis	T			
Cercis	I–S			Susceptible to simazine for up to 2 years
Chaenomeles	T		I–T	
Chimonanthus	I			
Choisya	S	T		
Cistus	0·56 kg/ha			
Clerodendron	I			
Clethra	T			
Colutea	T			
Cornus	I		T	C. alba 'Spaethii', C. mas 'Aura' and C. mas Elegantissima' are susceptible to sima-zine
Corokia	T			
Corylopsis	0·56 kg/ha			
Corylus	0·56 kg/ha			
Cotoneaster	I–T	T	T	C. franchetii and C. cornubia are susceptible to simazine
Crataegus	T	T	T	
Cydonia	T			
Cytisus	T		T	
Daboecia	0·56 kg/ha			
Davidia	T			
Decaisnea	T			
Deutzia	S		T	0' kg/ha simazine is used on some nurseries D. gracilis, D. rosea and D. scabra are particularly susceptible
Diervilla	I–T			D. florida 'Variegata' is susceptible to simazine
Dipelta	T			
Elaeagnus	T	T	T	
Enkianthus	T			
Erica	T	T	T	
Escallonia	T	T	T	
Eucalyptus	T			
Euonymus	I–T		T	E. hamiltonianus, yedoensis and alata are susceptible to simazine
Eucrpyhia	T			

Genus	Simazine at up to 1·1 kg/ha (except where shown)	Lenacil at up to 3·4 kg/ha	Dichlo-benil at 6·7 kg/ha 2-year plants	Remarks
Exochorda	I–S			E. giraldii and korolkowii more susceptible to simazine
Fagus	T		T	
Fatsia	T			
Forsythia	S	S	T	Plants grow out of marginal chlorosis when 0·6 kg/ha simazine used on some soils
Fothergilla	0·6 kg/ha			
Fraxinus	I	T	T	F. excelsior tolerant of 1·1 kg/ha simazine but other species susceptible.
Fuchsia	0·6 kg/ha			
Gaultheria	T			
Genista	T			
Gleditschia	T			
Grevillea	T			
Griselinia	T			
Halesia	I			
Halimodendron	T			H. argenteum usually grafted on Caragana is more susceptible
Hammamelis	T		T	
Hebe (Veronica)	I	T		H. brachysiphon (Veronica traversii) and H. subalpina may be more susceptible to simazine
Hedysarum	T			
Helianthemum	T			
Hibiscus	I		T	
Hippopheae	T		T	
Hoheria	0·6 kg/ha			
Holodiscus	T			
Hydrangea	0·6 kg/ha		T	
Hypricum	T	T	T	
Ilex	T	T	I	
Illicium	T			
Indigofera	S			
Jasminum	T			
Juglans	T			
Kalmia	T			
Kerria	I			
Koelreuteria	T			
Kolkwitzia	T			Susceptible when small

Genus	Simazine at up to 1·1 kg/ha (except where shown)	Lenacil at up to 3·4 kg/ha	Dichlobenil at 6·7 kg/ha 2-year plants	Remarks
Laburnocytisus	T			
Laburnum	T		T	
Laurus	T			
Lavandula	0·6 kg/ha	S		
Leptospermum	T			
Leucothoe	T			
Leycesteria	I			
Ligustrum	0·6 kg/ha	T	T	
Liquidambar	T			
Liriodendron	T	S		
Lithospermum	0·6 kg/ha			
Lonicera	I		T	
Lupinus	T			
Magnolia	T		I	*M. soulangeana* is susceptible to dichlobenil
Mahonia	T		T	
Malus	T		T	
Mespiulus	T			
Morus	0·6 kg/ha			
Myrtilus	T		T	
Nandina	T			
Neillia	T			
Nothofagus			T	
Olearia	0·6 kg/ha	T		
Osmanthus	T		T	
Osmarea	T	T		
Pachysandra	T			
Pernettya	T	T		
Perowskia	T			
Philadelphus	0·6 kg/ha	T	T	
Phillyrea	T			
Photinia	T			
Physocarpus	0·6 kg/ha			
Pieris	0·6 kg/ha			
Pittosporum	T			
Platanus	T			
Poncirus	S			
Populus	T		T	
Potentilla	T	T		
Prunus	I–T	T	T	Although widely treated *P. amygdalus, P. avium, P. laurocerasus* and *P. glandulosa* are slightly susceptible to simazine
Pterostyrax	S			
Pyracantha	T			

Genus	Simazine at up to 1·1 kg/ha (except where shown)	Lenacil at up to 3·4 kg/ha	Dichlo-benil at 6·7 kg/ha 2-year plants	Remarks
Pyrus	T		T	
Quercus	T	T		
Rhamnus	T			
Rhododendron (and Azalea)	T	T		
Rhus	T	T		
Ribes	I–T		T	
Robinia	T			
Romneya	T			
Rosmarinus	T			
Rubus	T			
Ruscus	T			
Ruta	T	S		
Salix	T	T		
Salvia	T	T		
Sambucus	I		S	
Santolina	T	S–I		
Sarcococca	T			
Senecio	I–T	T		
Skimmia	T			
Solanum	T			
Sophora	T			
Sorbaria	T			
Sorbus	T		T	
Spartium	T			
Spiraea	I–T	T	T	
Staphylea	T			
Stephanandra	T			
Stranvaesia	T			
Sycopsis	T			
Symphoricarpus	T	T		Simazine and dichlobenil can damage young plants
Syringa	0·6 kg/ha	T		
Tamarix	T		T	
Teucrium	T			
Tilia	I–T			
Ulex	T			
Ulmus	T			
Vaccinium	T			
Veronica now Hebe				
Viburnum	I–T	T	T	V. fragrans, V. × bodnantense and V. × candidissum are more susceptible to simazine
Vinca	T	T		
Weigela	I–T	I	T	

191

Genus	Simazine at up to 1·1 kg/ha (except where shown)	Lenacil at up to 3·4 kg/ha	Dichlo-benil at 6·7 kg/ha 2-year plants	Remarks
Yucca	T			
Zenobia	T			
B. Conifers				
Abies	T			
Araucaria	T			
Cedrus	I–T			
Chamaecyparis	I–T			
Cryptomeria	T			
Cunninghamia	T			
Cupressocyparis	T	T		
Cupressus	T			
Ginko	I–T			
Juniperus	T	T		
Larix	I–T		S	
Libocedrus	T			
Metasequoia	I–T			damage possible on very light soil
Phyllocladus	T			
Picea	T	T	S	
Pinus	T			
Pseudotsuga	T			
Sequoia	T			
Sequoiadendron	T			
Taxus	I–T			
Thuya	I–T	T		
Tsuga	T			

Established trees and shrubs

3.233   *The recommendations in paragraphs 3.223–3.230 can be used on established trees and shrubs with less risk of damage.*

3.234   **Aminotriazole** *3·7 kg/ha plus* **simazine** *7·3 kg/ha in medium to high volume as a directed spray to control established perennial and annual weeds and germinating annuals.*

    Do not treat varieties that are susceptible to simazine. Apply in spring or early summer when weeds are at a susceptible stage.

3.235   [**For information.**] Maleic hydrazide for the suppression of hawthorn and privet hedges and suckers in trees is described in Chapter 11.

Section IV. Weed control in glasshouses and plastic covered structures

3.236 **Soil sterilization.** Although chiefly used for pest and disease control, sterilization has an ancillary value in controlling weeds, and is sometimes used primarily for this purpose. The main treatments are as follows:

(i) STEAM STERILIZATION

The soil temperature is raised by steam to about 100°C for periods varying between 10 min and (in some parts of the profile) 4 h. This effectively kills seeds and perennial roots in the treated area. Where only annual weed is likely to be a problem, steaming to a depth of 75–100 mm is quite often adequate.

(ii) CHEMICAL STERILIZATION

The most widely used materials are dazomet, metham-sodium and methyl bromide. When applied correctly, they give satisfactory control of most weed seeds. To ensure the best level of control the soil must be moist and temperatures adequate for seed germination for some days before application, and the sterilant must be applied uniformly.

Lettuce

SOIL-APPLIED RESIDUAL TREATMENTS

3.237 **Chlorpropham** *0.8–1.1 kg/ha in medium to high volume as a pre-planting spray to weed-free soil in a few days before planting to control annual weeds.*

Damage can occur from herbicide vapour with high temperatures and inadequate ventilation. The treatment should not be used if there are sensitive crops in the same block.

3.238 [**For information.**] Trifluralin 0.6 kg/ha in medium volume and incorporated 1–14 days before planting to control annual weeds. Thorough incorporation within 30 min of application is essential. Depth of incorporation depends on planting method but untreated soils should not be exposed after planting.

Tomato

SOIL-APPLIED RESIDUAL TREATMENT

3.239 [**For information.**] Trifluralin 1.1 kg/ha in medium volume and incorporated 1–14 days before planting to control annual weeds. Thorough incorporation within 30 min of application is essential. Depth of incorporation depends on planting method but untreated soils should not be exposed after planting.

CONTACT TREATMENT

3.240   Pentanochlor *2·2–4·5 kg/ha in 300–500 litres/ha as a low pressure directed spray to control annual weeds.*
Avoid spraying the crop foliage as damage may occur. *Chenopodium album* (Fat-hen) and *Polygonum persicaria* (Redshank) are controlled at an advanced stage of development. Other species controlled as seedlings include *Galium aparine* (Cleavers) and *Polygonum aviculare* (Knotgrass). There is some residual action against *Atriplex patula* (Common Orache), *Chenopodium album* (Fat-hen), *Fumaria officinalis* (Common Fumitory) and *Polygonum pericaria* (Redshank).

Chrysanthemum

CONTACT TREATMENT

3.241   Pentanochlor *2·2–4·5 kg/ha in 60p–1100 litres/ha as a low pressure directed spray to control annual weeds as in paragraph 3.240.*
Avoid spraying the crop foliage as damage may occur.

SOIL-APPLIED RESIDUAL TREATMENTS

(i) *Preplanting*

3.242   [For information.] Trifluralin 1·1 kg/ha in medium volume and incorporated 1–14 days before planting to control annual weeds. Thorough incorporation within 30 min of application is essential. Depth of incorporation depends on planting method but untreated soils should not be exposed after planting.

(ii) *Post-planting*

3.243   Chloroxuron *4·5–5·6 kg/ha in medium to high volume as an overhead spray to weed-free soil soon after planting out to control annual weeds.*
Some marginal chlorosis has occurred on a few varieties.

Bulbs (narcissus, tulip, gladioli and bulbous iris)

PRE-EMERGENCE RESIDUAL TREATMENT

3.244   Chlorpropham *1·1–2·2 kg/ha in medium volume at any time between planting and crop emergence for the control of annual weeds.*
The treatment should not be used where sensitive crops are in the same block due to the risk of volatilization at high temperatures.

Freesia

3.245 [**For information.**] Chloroxuron 4·5 kg/ha in medium volume to weed-free soil when freesia shoots are 50 mm high.

Rose

SOIL-APPLIED RESIDUAL TREATMENT

3.246 **Simazine** *1·1 kg/ha in medium to high volume immediately after planting and firming the soil or simazine up to 1·68 kg/ha in medium to high volume to weed-free soil.*

Under benches

3.247 [**For information.**] Ammonium sulphamate has been used to control established weeds. Bromacil, sodium borate plus bromacil, simazine and diuron have been used for residual control. Avoid heating pipes and areas close to them to reduce the risk of volatilization.

Control of weeds around glasshouses

3.248 Care is needed in selecting herbicides for use on a glasshouse holding. Volatile materials should be avoided. *Dichlobenil, chlorthiamid, 2,4-D ester* and *2,4,5-T-ester* are examples of unsuitable materials. Whenever possible keep ventilators and doors closed when applying any foliar acting herbicides.

3.249 **Ammonium sulphamate** *at 1 kg in 1 l of water sprayed to run-off controls many woody weeds including* Rubus fruticosus *(Bramble). It may also be applied as dry crystals as described in Chapter 7.*

3.250 **Aminotriazole** *4·5 kg/ha in high volume to control established perennial and annual weeds.*

3.251 **Paraquat** *0·6–2·2 kg/ha in medium to high volume to control annual weeds, shallow-rroted perennial grasses and* Ranunculus repens *(Creeping Buttercup).*

3.252 **Simazine** *2·2–5·6 kg/ha in medium to high volume for the residual control of annual weeds.*
    Avoid areas from which there could be run-off into glasshouses and mastic-covered structures. Some established annual weeds are controlled if the application is made in late winter or early spring.

Chapter 4
Recommendations for the control of weeds in crops grown for seed

4.001 The special problems of crops grown for seed are discussed in this chapter which deals mainly with the use of herbicides in producing weed-free crops. It is important to realize that whilst herbicides can be invaluable in controlling weeds in seed crops, chemical weed control will not necessarily produce a crop clean enough for seed purposes. Some details of seed production schemes and the tolerance of weed seed contamination under these schemes is given in Volume I, Chapter 11.

This chapter is divided into three sections, (i) Herbage Seed Crops, (ii) Cereal Seed Crops and (iii) Root and Vegetable Seed Crops. In the year of establishment many of the weed control problems of seed crops are common to the same crop when grown as an arable crop. The recommendations made in Chapters 5, 1 and 2 respectively for the three sections of this chapter are not repeated, and reference should be made to the appropriate chapter in addition to the recommendations made specifically for seed crops.

Grass, clover and lucerne seed crops

4.002 Herbage seed crops, especially those to be grown in wide drills or at low plant populations—as is often advisable for the best seed yields—*should be sown on clean land, preferably following a crop in which weeds have been effectively destroyed before seeding.*

4.003 Of particular importance is the freedom from rhizomatous grass weeds (*Agropyron repens* (Common Couch) and *Agrostis gigantea* (Black Bent)), the control of which must be undertaken before a seed crop is sown by exhausting the rhizomes by a series of cultivations or by herbicides, or by a combination of both methods (12.13–12.26). The presence of *A. repens* can be markedly reduced if the stubbles of the preceding spring barley crop are vigorously cultivated soon after harvest. Alternatively, some control is achieved if the stubbles are treated with paraquat. There is no effective method of control of these weeds once the crop is established and they tend to increase with age of the crop. Special attention should also be given to headlands and areas from which such weeds are likely to spread.

4.004 Trials have shown that successive spring barley crops can be used as cleaning crops on land infested with dormant seed of *Poa trivialis* (Rough

Meadow-grass) provided all overwintering plants left over from previous crops are destroyed by good ploughing and seedbed cultivations.

The standard of cultivations must be of a high order since carry-over of *Poa trivialis* can occur by vegetative means, as well as by seed. In spring barley, *Poa trivialis* germinating along with the crop is unvernalized and therefore incapable of producing seed heads. The addition of fresh seed to that already in the soil is thus prevented. Surviving overwintered *Poa trivialis* plants from previous crops however, are vernalized and capable of producing seed. It is imperative therefore that these plants are not allowed to survive and establish themselves in the new barley crop.

4.005 Herbage seed crops are sown at any time between March and October. The spring-sown crops are frequently undersown in cereals. *Alopecurus myosuroides* (Black-grass) in spring cereals is not treated because of the lack of suitable materials and as a consequence by the autumn after cereal harvest, the black-grass population can be at various stages of development from one leaf through to fully mature plants with seed set. *No recommended herbicides can be used in herbage seed crops which are effective against black-grass when the weed has passed the four-leaf stage and fields should be examined closely to ascertain the growth stage of the weed before herbicide use is contemplated.*

4.006 Much the same set of conditions arises in the case of *Avena fatua* and *Avena ludoviciana* (Wild-oat) infestation in that the period of germination and establishments of the weed is extended from six months under the cereal to more than a year under the herbage seed crop. This is because the wild-oat germinates during the autumn and the spring following cereal harvest. The wild-oat plants can therefore be at many stages of growth from the one-leaf stage through the growth stage six by the late autumn in the herbage seed crop.

4.007 The control measures which should be considered at particular stages in the life of a seed crop are given below. (See also N.I.A.B. Herbage Seed Grower's Leaflet No. 6, *Weed control and the use of herbicides in herbage seed crops*. Welsh Plant Breeding Station *Technical Bulletin No. 1*. Ministry of Agriculture, Fisheries and Food, *Bulletin 204*.)

Year of sowing

Treatment of undersown cereal crops is dealt with in Chapter 1 and newly-sown leys in Chapter 5.

Various pre-sowing and pre-emergence treatments are possible at sowing.

4.008 **Paraquat** *0·6−1·1 kg/ha in medium to high volume on a stale seedbed or between sowing and emergence of the crop.*

The low rate should be used where the weeds have no more than 2 true leaves. Where the weed density is high and they have more than 2 true leaves the higher rate should be used.

4.009   *Shallow inter-row cultivations started as early as possible in a direct-sown wide-drilled crop.*
A marker such as mustard or lettuce, sown around 200 g of seed/ha with the crop seed, may help by showing the rows early.

4.010   **Paraquat** *0·6–1·1 kg/ha applied by dribble-bar or a shielded spray between the rows.*
This avoids disturbance of the soil which may induce more weeds to germinate, although the absence of residual effect may necessitate more than one spraying.

4.011   **Methabenzthiazuron** *1·2 kg/ha applied post-emergence to direct-sown perennial ryegrass crops at the 3-leaf stage to control* Poa trivialis *and* Poa annua *(Meadow-grasses) germinating along with the crop.*
Some broad-leaved weeds including *Stellaria media* (Common Chickweed), *Veronica* sp. (Speedwell), and some Mayweeds are also controlled. If the crop and meadow grass are between the 3-leaf stage and the start of tillering, control is still possible with an increased rate of 1·6 kg/ha. This increased rate should not however be used on thin or light soils. Treatment should only be applied to *well- and evenly-germinated crops* sown into clean seedbeds. Uniform germination is aided by rolling the crop immediately after sowing.
Many factors influence the safe use of methabenzthiazuron on herbage seed crops. The application rate is critical and therefore boom overlapping must be avoided and there must be good agitation in the tank before and during spraying. If the crop is poorly established or under stress from drought, frost damage, pest damage (fruit fly/shoot fly complex), poor seedbed consolidation or liquid fertilizer application, damage can occur which may or may not be outgrown.

4.012   **Methabenzthiazuron** *1·2 kg/ha to control* meadow-grasses *in perennial ryegrass undersown to spring barley and wheat.*
The crop is best treated shortly after drilling and rolling, using a pre-emergence treatment only as some damage to the barley crop is likely if post-emergence treatment is used. The same precautions should be observed as outlined in 4.011.

4.013   In narrow-drilled crops soon after sowing, or in such crops soon after removal of the cover crop, a herbicide treatment may be necessary and Chapter 5 should be consulted for the treatments and tolerances of grass and clover seedlings to herbicides. When undersown crops in wide drills are cleared of the cover crop, they may be inter-row cultivated or treated with paraquat as in 4.010 above.

4.014 Topping-over when the crop is established will help to control some broad-leaved weeds but several cuts will be needed if *Avena fatua* (Wild-oat) or *Alopecurus myosuroides* (Black-grass) are to be prevented from seeding.

Hand-removal of grass weeds in summer and autumn in crops sown in the spring may be practicable if numbers are small. This should be done and the plants removed before they set seed. Spot treatment with a herbicide such as sodium chlorate or paraquat is a possible alternative. Headlands should be ploughed, cultivated or sprayed as often as necessary to prevent encroachment of weeds such as *Agropyron repens* (Common Couch), *Agrostis gigantea* (Black Bent) and *Anisantha sterilis* (syn. *Bromus sterilis*) (Barren Brome).

4.015 [**For information.**] Prometryne $1 \cdot 7 - 2 \cdot 2$ kg/ha overall on well-established crops of grass in autumn, winter or spring to control seedlings of *Alopecurus myosuroides* (Black-grass) and other grass weeds when they appear.

The selectivity of the treatments depends on differences in plant size and root depth between crop and weed.

The following factors are important:

(i) The grass weeds should have germinated but it is most important that the majority of seedlings should not have more than 3 to 4 leaves. With seedlings, complete kill can be expected but frequently the weed is present as well-tillered plants and under these conditions prometryne is ineffective. Particular care should therefore be taken to inspect a crop before recommending treatment.

(ii) The crop grass must be well established and would normally need to be at least 4 months old, i.e. crops sown direct in spring may normally be safely sprayed in autumn; those sown in summer should only be sprayed late in the year of sowing, if at all; and crops undersown in spring may or may not be sprayed in autumn according to their development under the cover crop.

(iii) Only perennial ryegrass, cocksfoot, timothy, meadow fescue and tall fescue can be sprayed at the stage described.

(iv) It is not safe to use this treatment at all on Italian ryegrass.

(v) $1 \cdot 7 - 2 \cdot 2$ kg/ha is recommended for medium and heavy soils. There is insufficient information for recommendations to be made for light soils, and the treatment should not be used at all on highly organic soils. Crop damage can be caused by over-lapping of the spray swaths or by repeating the treatment before the residual effect of the first treatment has disappeared.

(vi) The treatment is less effective if heavy rain falls soon after application and, whenever possible, a weather forecast should be obtained before the treatment is applied.

(vii) Application should be done before the grass crop forms a complete canopy which will shelter the weed grasses.

4.016   Methabenzthiazuron *In autumn 3·1 kg/ha on well established perennial ryegrass crops to control* Poa spp. *(Meadow-grasses) and* Alopecurus myosuroides *(Black-grass).*

Application should be after removal of the cereal cover crop but before the ryegrass forms a complete canopy. An application will control tillered plants of *Poa trivialis* and *Poa annua* together with volunteer seedlings of spring barley. Black-grass seedlings up to the 2-leaf stage are also controlled. Treatment can be made up to mid September but should only be applied to well-established tillering crops which are growing vigorously. The same degree of care should be observed as in 4.011.

4.017   Mecoprop-salt *2·2 kg/ha. Early treatment will give good control of* Stellaria media *(Common Chickweed) in the autumn.*

Year of harvest

General weed control

4.018   Inter-row work may be continued in later winter or early spring on light land. On heavy land such cultivations may not only bring up large clods but also cause the germination of blackgrass and other weeds. In such cases and as a general alternative, inter-row application of paraquat or a diquat/paraquat mixture may be used, as in 4.010.

Grass crops

4.019   [**For information.**] In trials, ethofumesate at 1·7 kg/ha when applied to established perennial ryegrass crops in spring before harvest has given good control of *Alopecurus myosuroides* (Black-grass) (3–4 tiller stage), *Poa annua* (Annual Meadow-grass) and *Stellaria media* (Common Chickweed). Early applications have given better control than later ones. Germination of harvested seed and crop vigour do not seem to be affected.

4.020   [**For information.**] In trials, benzoyl propethyl at 1·1 kg/ha applied at the first node stage of *Avena fatua* (Wild-oat) in spring has given good control in perennial ryegrass seed crops with little or no effect on crop vigour or seed germination.

4.021   [**For information.**] In trials, difenzoquat at 1·0 kg/ha has given good control of *Avena sativa* and *Avena fatua* (Wild-oat) in perennial ryegrass crops in spring with little or no effect on crop vigour or seed germination.

4.022 The herbicides listed in paragraph 4.024 can be used for controlling broad leaved weeds but the time of application is important and recommendations for different varieties are shown. Spraying should normally be carried out within the 4- to 5-week period before the heads begin to emerge from their sheaths except for S.48 timothy which should be sprayed 6 to 7 weeks before head emergence. Spraying should never be later than mid-May for any variety unless less damage is likely to result from late spraying than from allowing a heavy weed infestation to go unchecked.

4.023 In paragraph 4.024 are the relative heading and recommended safe spraying times for the S. grass varieties bred at the Welsh Plant Breeding Station, Aberystwyth. Also included are other varieties (not in italics) which have yet to be tested for their reaction to herbicide. It is thought, however, that these are unlikely to react differently from the tested Aberystwyth S. varieties. These dates based on experience at NIAB, Cambridge, somewhat according to season and district and must be adjusted accordingly. Safe spraying periods for any other variety can be calculated if its normal time of head emergence is known.

4.024   Suggested periods for using broad-leaf weed herbicides in spring before seed harvest on grass varieties at present being grown

	Doses kg/ha
MCPA-salt	1·6
2,4-D-amine	1·4
Mecoprop-salt	2·8
Dichlorprop-salt	2·8
MCPA- + 2,3,6-TBA-salt	0·8 + 0·3 (see note * below)
MCPA- + dicamba-salt	1·3 + 0·1 (see note * below)

Variety	Normal start of head emergence (Cambridge)	Approximate extent of recommended period (all dates apply to Cambridge and may need to be adjusted for other places)
Perennial Ryegrasses in order of heading		
Devon Eaver	4th week April to 1st week May	April
Gremie *Aberystwyth S.24†* Cropper Houba Premo	1st week May	
Barvestra Reveille Stadion Monta Itermo	2nd week May	2nd week April to 1st week May
Barstella Barlara Taptoe Kelvin *Aberystwyth S.321†* Hora Ladi Sceempter Hay Kent Indigenous Agresso Animo Combi Terhoy Barlenna *Aberystwyth S.101†* Talbot Mettra R.v.P. Tresceaver	3rd to 4th week May	Late April to mid-May

Variety	Normal start of head emergence (Cambridge)	Approximate extent of recommended period (all dates apply to Cambridge and may need to be adjusted for other places)
Scotia Fingal Caprice Pelo Spirit Romney *Aberystwyth S.23*† Fortis Semperweide Wendy Petra Barpastra Compas	4th week May	
Perma Lamora Barenza Angela Melle Terpas Endura	4th week May to 1st week June	

Italian Ryegrasses in order of heading

Note. These guide lines are only relevant if there has not been a conservation cut.

Variety	Normal start of head emergence (Cambridge)	Approximate extent
Sabel Sabrina Meritra R.v.P. Maris Ledger Terli Tetila Delecta	4th week April to 1st week May	April
R.v.P. Sabalan Tiara Optima Lema Milamo Combita *Aberystwyth S.22*†	2nd week May	2nd week April to 1st week May
Fescues in order of heading *Aberystwyth S.59*† *Aberystwyth S.170*†	4th week April to 1st week May	April

Variety	Normal start of head emergence (Cambridge)	Approximate extent of recommended period (all dates apply to Cambridge and may need to be adjusted for other places)
Aberystwyth S.215† Rossa Comtessa Bundy Admira	2nd week May	2nd week April to 1st week May
Cockfoots in order of heading Scotia Norton Tenderbite Aberystwyth S.37† Saborto Flaxmere	1st week May	April
Prairial Aberystwyth S.26†	2nd week May	2nd week April to 1st week May
Baraula Aberystwyth S.143†	2nd to 3rd week May	Mid-April to mid-May
Timothy in order of heading Aberystwyth S.352† Aberystwyth S.50†	4th week May to 1st week June	Late April to mid-May
Erecta	1st week June	Late April to mid-May
Aberystwyth S.51†	1st to 2nd week June	
Aberystwyth S.48*† Pastremo Oakmere	2nd to 3rd week June	

* For S.48 timothy and perhaps for other varieties of timothy, special care is needed with MCPA/2,3,6-TBA and MCPA/dicamba. Spray at least 6 and preferably 7 weeks before head emergence, otherwise yield and germination may be seriously reduced.

† Only the Aberystwyth varieties have been tested experimentally.

4.025 [**For information.**] Herbicides not yet tested on grass seed crops in the year of harvest include: 2,4-D-ester, dinoseb-amine, benazolin-salt, ioxynil-salt and -ester, bromoxynil-ester.

4.026 [**For information.**] Linuron at $1 \cdot 1 - 2 \cdot 2$ kg/ha has given promising results when applied in the spring or autumn to timothy seed crops grown in central Scotland for the control of *Holcus lanatus* (Yorkshire-fog).

Post-harvest weed control

4.027 When grass seed crops infested with *Poa trivialis* (Rough Meadow-grass) are to be ploughed up, the incorporation of viable seed into the soil can be prevented by delaying stubble cultivations for as long as possible after harvest. This delay is important since most of the seed will only germinate in the presence of light. A delay of 6–12 weeks should allow sufficient time for the seed to germinate on the surface and the addition of new potentially dormant seed to the soil is avoided. During this period, other grass weeds such as *Poa annua* (Annual Meadow-grass), *Agropyron repens* (Common Couch) and *Agrostis gigantea* (Black Bent) can be suppressed by spraying the crop aftermath with paraquat 4 weeks after harvest. Three weeks later the dead dry foliage, including any *A. repens* regrowth, can then be set on fire. With an efficient burn most of the remaining ungerminated seed of *P. trivialis* is killed.

4.028 This cultural technique coupled with the use of spring barley as in 4.004, has proved effective in reducing infestations of *Poa trivialis* in field crops of meadow fescue and perennial ryegrass grown for seed. One such example is illustrated in 4.029.

4.029   Field Control of *Poa trivialis* in Meadow Fescue Seed Crops.

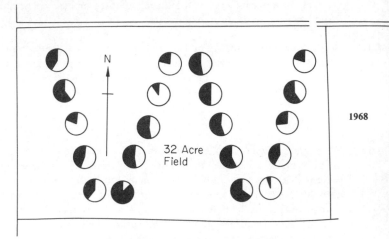

1968

Mean = 937 **Meadow Fescue** + 802 *Poa trivialis* seeds heads/yd^2
15 Plants of *Poa trivialis*/yd^2 each with 53 heads/plant
Crop yield 3·7 cwt/ac

SPRING BARLEY **1969**

1971

Mean = 1320 **Meadow Fescue** + 15 *Poa trivialis* seed heads/yd^2
4 Plants of *Poa trivialis*/yd^2 each with 4 heads/plant
Crop yield 5·6 cwt/ac

Key. Sample area of 1 yd^2

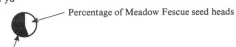

Percentage of Meadow Fescue seed heads

Percentage of *Poa trivialis* seed heads

Red clover

4.030 **Carbetemide** *2·1 kg/ha to control* Holcus lanctus *(Yorkshire-fog)*, Alepecurus myosuroides *(Black-grass) and* Avena spp. *(Wild-oats) in red clover seed crops.* Treatment in February to mid-March appears to be preferable. *Stellaria media* (Common Chickweed) and some *Veronica* spp. (Speedwells) are also controlled. The *Compositae* are only poorly controlled.

4.031 [**For information.**] Propyzamide *0·75 kg/ha has been used experimentally on red clover crops with no apparent damage.* Treatment between October and the end of February are suggested. Weeds controlled are similar to those controlled by carbetemide. Spring applications of up to 1·0 kg/ha are tentatively indicated.

White clover

4.032 *For grass weeds or suppression of a companion grass in white clover, paraquat 0·6—1·1 kg/ha as soon as the weeds or grass and the crop start active growth (usually late March or early April).*
All species will be scorched and some fodder will be lost but the clover will recover quickly and become dominant. A cut 3—4 weeks after spraying will leave the crop in good condition for seed production.

4.033 Because of the risk of damaging the clover, treatment with paraquat should not be applied to young establishing crops in which the plants have not started to produce runners.

4.034 **MCPB** *2·2 kg/ha early enough in the season to precede flower-bud formation and to allow, during the 2—3 weeks after spraying, grazing or a forage cut before the crop is shut up for seed, to control broad-leaved weeds.*
Because it is best to shut up a crop for seed not later than mid-May (in a normal season) and because flower-buds are normally formed during April (becoming visible in early May), spraying needs to be done in March or early April to satisfy these requirements. The crop should be rested from grazing or cutting for 1—2 weeks before spraying to allow weeds to grow enough foliage to absorb the herbicide. The defoliation (cutting or grazing) after spraying is intended to remove the spray-treated clover foliage and avoid any herbicide effect on flower production.

4.035 **Carbetemide** *2·1 kg/ha on white clover seed crops.* Can be used in the same manner as in 4.030.

4.036 [**For information.**] Propyzamide 0·75 kg/ha has been used experimentally on white clover with little apparent damage.

Pre-harvest desiccation

Legumes (red and white clover and lucerne)

4.037   Some herbicides applied to legume seed crops at the stage when maximum yield can be expected will stop further development of the seed, kill off the foliage and stems and make harvesting and threshing easier. A quick-acting chemical is needed and desiccation is most useful in hot dry weather to allow quick harvesting before the weather breaks. In wet weather which prevents harvesting at the appropriate time and causes continuing delay, regrowth will progressively lessen the value of the treatment.

4.038   By using the long-range forecast service the grower can plan his spraying to coincide with a 48-h dry spell. Usually there is a period of about 10 days when clover seed crops are at the right stage for cutting. This is the period in which to spray and harvest, if possible. Red clover can usually be combined direct, preferably within 2–3 days of spraying. White clover must usually be cut first and then picked up with the combine. It is often possible to spray one day and to cut the next, picking up the crop 2–3 h after cutting. In really good weather it is possible to spray in the morning, cut in the afternoon and combine later the same day. If harvest is delayed too long after spraying, white clover heads will fall to the ground and be lost. When the crop is very short, desiccation is not necessary and may even make the problem of harvesting more difficult.

4.039   Clover and lucerne seed viability is not affected by the treatments listed below, although the proportion of hard seeds may sometimes be increased.
   To ensure thorough penetration of the crop, a high spraying pressure should be used.

4.040   **Diquat,** *formulated with a wetter, at 0·4–0·6 kg/ha in medium volume.* The higher rate should be used if the foliage is dense.

4.041   **Dinoseb,** *as an emulsifiable oil formulation, at 1·5–2·1 kg/ha in medium volume.*

4.042   **Sulphuric acid,** *as 8–9 per cent solution with a wetting agent, at 1100 l/ha or as undiluted B.O.V. (77 per cent v/v solution) without a wetting agent at 170–220 l/ha.*
   In diluting sulphuric acid, the acid must always be added slowly to the water and not vice versa. Acid is corrosive to many metals.

4.043   **Pentachlorophenol** *at 5·6 kg/ha in medium volume.*
   For better results dilute in 10–15 gal of tractor fuel oil rather than

water. This treatment acts more slowly than the others.

(*Caution:* Where diquat has been used, a minimum time interval of 4 days after spraying must be observed before the straw is fed to stock or stock are allowed to enter the harvested field.

When dinoseb or pentachlorophenol are used straw should not be fed to stock; they should not be allowed to enter the harvested field for 10 days after spraying with dinoseb and 14 days after spraying with pentachlorophenol.)

Cereal seed crops

4.044   Weed control in cereal seed crops presents few special problems. Chapter 1 describes herbicide treatments for cereal crops.

In seed crops it is particularly essential that the correct dose is applied at the correct growth stage. Incorrect dose or application during susceptible periods can cause ear distortion and this may prevent satisfactory identification of the crop variety as required under an inspection scheme. In cases where damage has occurred the crops are normally rejected for seed purposes.

4.045   Rogueing weed plants such as *Avena* spp. (Wild-oat) out of seed crops is a regular practice on certain seed-growing farms. This can be an effective way of ensuring that crops are approved but is practicable only when the original weed population is low and is of value only if the whole weed plant is removed from the crop.

4.046   *Code of practice in using* **chlormequat** *on wheat and oat seed crops entered in the British Cereal Seed Scheme.*

When growing cereal crops for seed it is essential to ensure that the produce is true to variety. This feature must be checked at field inspections and anything which alters the varietal characteristics of the growing crop must be used with care.

Chlormequat depends for its effect on increasing stem strength, which is accompanied by a reduction in length of straw (altering the straw length). There may also be a change in the density of the ear in wheat and possibly in the maturity of the crop. In the field this effect should not pose inspection problems, provided the effect is regular and provided the main identification features remain unchanged throughout the crop. There may be a problem however when a crop is contaminated with an admixture of another variety, if there is a mixture of spring and winter varieties or if the two varieties present were at different stages of growth at the time of treatment. This might, for example, result in a levelling out of the heights of the two varieties so that an impurity which would normally be easily visible because it was taller would, when treated, become more difficult to assess because its height was similar to that of the crop.

4.047   Because of the potential economic advantages in using chlormequat its use on wheat and oat crops in the Scheme is permitted. Care must however be taken to ensure that:

(1) The spray is applied at the correct growth stage of the crop and at the rate of application recommended by the manufacturer.

(2) The application is made evenly throughout the field with a well-maintained sprayer.

(3) Chlormequat is not applied when the crop is wet or if rain is imminent.

(4) The crop is sprayed uniformly and a control area left unsprayed. It should consist of an area of not less than 3 m wide taken across the drill rows. Inspectors should note and apply Rule 6(a) when spraying is uneven (crops which are so weedy, diseased, stunted, deformed or damaged that adequate inspections are impossible should be rejected).

(5) The crop is inspected with great care, particularly bearing in mind the possibility of contamination masked by the treatment.

The Executive Officer should be informed of all wheat and oat seed crops entered in the British Cereal Seed Scheme as soon as they are sprayed with chlormequat.

Fodder, root and vegetable seed crops

4.048   Recommendations for the control of weeds in these crops are given in Chapter 2. Most of the crops, except peas and beans, are biennials when grown for seed and the recommendations in Chapter 2 apply only to the first year vegetative growth. Although the husbandry practices in this first year are often somewhat different for seed crops, the same principles apply.

Except for sugar beet, little research has been devoted to weed control in the second year of the biennial crops and firm recommendations can be made only for sugar beet. However, sufficient is known of the likely action of some herbicides to warrant trial use by growers on other crops and some suggestions can be made.

Brussels sprouts, cabbage, winter cauliflower, broccoli (sprouting) and kale

First year

4.049   Limited data suggest that the parent lines of the F_1 hybrid kale Maris Kestrel show differential responses to desmetryne and the proportions of the parents in the seed crop could be substantially changed. For complete safety desmetryne should not be used on seed crops of this variety even though under some conditions it appears that 0·3 kg/ha may be satisfactory.

Second year

4.050 [**For information.**] Inter-row cleaning should be undertaken just before spring growth starts while it is still possible to work a tractor in the crop. This can be by either application of paraquat, at 0·5—1·0 kg/ha or paraquat plus diquat, at 0·6—1·1 kg/ha using either a dribble-bar or a directed coarse spray, or by cultivation. The advantage of the chemical method is that a tilth for the germination of weed seeds is not produced. The higher rate should be used if the weed population is dense and advanced.

4.051 [**For information.**] Simazine at 0·6—1·1 kg/ha applied to the cleaned land should control spring weed growth normally without damaging the crop but there is insufficient evidence to make a recommendation. It will not control perennial or large established weeds and there could be a risk of crop damage if very heavy rain, such as a thunderstorm, fell soon after application.

Rape, turnip and swede

Second year

4.052 [**For information.**] Inter-row cleaning should be carried out as for Brussels sprouts, etc., above. It is not known what effect simazine has on this group of crops but it is possible that it might give adequate seedling weed control without crop damage.

Mangel and red beet

Second year

4.053 [**For information.**] No recommendations can be made for the second season but, in limited trials, simazine at 0·9—1·1 kg/ha has given good weed control without crop damage in red beet when applied soon after transplanting in the spring provided the stecklings are covered by enough soil to prevent the spray falling on them.

Carrots

4.054   [**For information.**] Linuron at 0·8 kg/ha applied soon after planting the stecklings, followed by a repeat application if necessary, has shown promising results in limited trials.

4.055   [**For information.**] Dalapon-sodium at 10·0 kg/ha applied in October has shown promise for killing grass weeds in steckling beds.

Onions

4.056   [**For information**] Chapter 2 describes the use of chlorpropham for controlling weeds in onion sets. Limited information suggests that this treatment could be applied to onion bulbs planted into clean land in the spring.

Sugar beet

Crops grown *in situ* in the open

4.057   Only a very small proportion of the sugar beet seed crops are grown in this way. Generally such crops are sown in July and August. Weed problems and the conditions in which herbicides must be used vary according to the previous cropping and the amount of rainfall received during the period.

4.058   *Contact pre-emergence herbicides applied where a good flush of weeds emerge before the crop, usually 3–6 days after drilling.*
Higher rates should be used if the weed population is dense and advanced.

4.059   **Pyrazone** *1·4–4·0 kg/ha according to soil type (2.139).*
Current commercial literature should be consulted for the dose. Best results would normally be expected if the herbicide is worked into the seedbed immediately before drilling.

4.060   **Lenacil,** *at 0·9–2·2 kg/ha depending on soil type, immediately after drilling (2.139).*
Activity will be reduced by dry and warm weather after application. Current commercial literature should be consulted for the dose.

4.061   **Pyrazone** *at 2·7–3·1 kg/ha after crop emergence to control weeds still in the seedling stage. (2.139).*
Generally pyrazone is less effective applied in this way than as recommended in paragraph 4.000. The lower dose should be used on

medium loams and silts and the higher dose on heavy soils. The addition of a suitable wetter is required.

4.062 **Phenmedipham** *1·1 kg in 240 l/ha as a post-emergence treatment for the control of broad-leaved weeds in direct-sown sugar beet stecklings or in* situ *seed crops.*

Leaf scorch may occur if phenmedipham is applied during hot weather, and the dose should be reduced to 1·0 kg/ha.

4.063 It is essential to apply the phenmedipham as a fine spray. Weed species vary in susceptibility; some are killed up to the 4-leaf stage while others are killed only at the cotyledon stage. Weeds not satisfactorily controlled include *Tripleurospermum maritimum* ssp. *inodorum* (Scentless Mayweed) and annual grasses.

Improved and more rapid control of *Polygonum* spp. may be obtained with a tank of mix of 1·1 kg/ha phenmedipham and 0·35 kg/ha barban.

For the combined control of broad-leaved weeds and *Avena fatua* (wild-oat) a tank mix of 1·1 kg/ha phenmedipham and 0·70 kg/ha barban may be used.

4.064 [**For information.**] 0·8 kg/ha or 1·1 kg/ha phenmedipham as a tank mix with 2·8 litres/ha or 5·6 litres/ha adjuvant oil is used in the sugar beet root crop and should give similar results in appropriate seed crops. Current commercial literature should be consulted for the dose which depends on the growth of the beet and weeds and the prevailing weather conditions.

Crops grown in situ *under a cover crop, usually barley*

4.065 Most of the sugar beet seed crops are grown by this method and are usually sown during April.

4.066 Frequently a drill is used which drills beet and barley in separate rows in one operation with usually 2 or sometimes 3 rows of barley between the beet rows. This system allows a band application of herbicides over the sugar beet rows without effect on the barley cover crop. At this time of year conditions for herbicide activity are the same for the seed crop as for the root crop and reference should be made to Chapter 2 for current recommendations. With this method of growing the beet seed crop, spraying the cereal cover crop for weed control should not normally be undertaken (4.068).

4.067 [**For information.**] As an emergency measure phenmedipham at 1·1 kg in 240 litres/ha has been found to be successful in controlling heavy infestations of volunteer mustard and of *Stellaria media* (Common

Chickweed) without obviously affecting the vigour of the barley. If the beet have emerged leaf scorch may occur if phenmedipham is applied during hot weather.

4.068 After the cover crop has been removed, freshly-germinating weeds and volunteer barley may be controlled by the use of TCA, propham, or mixtures of the two. If temporary crop scorch is acceptable up to 22 kg/ha of TCA, up to 6·7 kg/ha of propham, or a mixture of 11·2 kg/ha TCA and 4·5 kg/ha propham may be used according to soil type and the weeds present. As TCA may have an effect on the germination of the beet seed produced if applied to growing plants, application should be made when the plants are dormant and never later than the end of December.

4.069 **Dalapon** *8·5 kg/ha in 300 litres/ha to control grass weeds and volunteer barley.*
Dalapon should be applied early enough in September to allow for translocation before growth ceases. When applied in the spring there is evidence of a depression of the germination of the beet seed and therefore dalapon should not be applied after mid-December.

4.070 [**For information.**] Simazine has been used successfully at 0·8 kg/ha for general weed control after removal of the cover crop. Best results have been obtained when the beet plants are entering the dormant phase which is usually at the end of September.

4.071 [**For information.**] In trials carbetamide at 2·2 kg/ha or propyzamide at 0·8 kg/ha applied in November have given encouraging results for general weed control. Current commercial literature should be consulted before use.

Transplanted crops

Very few seed crops are grown in this way. The young plants are usually transplanted between November and April so that a wide range of soil and weather conditions may be encountered.

4.072 **Pyrazone** *at 1·4–4·0 kg/ha according to soil type applied to clean land following transplanting for the control of annual weeds* (2.139).

4.073 [**For information**] 0·6–1·1 kg/ha simazine according to the manufacturer's instructions, has given good results in trials on red beet and it might be effective for sugar beet but there is insufficient evidence to make a recommendation.

4.074 [**For information**] Lenacil at 0·90—2·2 kg/ha according to soil type applied to clean land following transplanting for the control of annual weeds may give acceptable results (2.139).

4.075 **Phenmedipham** 1·1 kg/ha in 240 litres/ha as a post emergence treatment for the control of broad-leaved weeds (2.066).

4.076 [**For information.**] 0·8 kg/ha or 1·1 kg/ha phenmedipham as a tank mix with 2·8 litres/ha or 5·6 litres/ha adjuvant oil (4·064).

Chapter 5
Recommendations for weed control in grassland and herbage legumes

5.001 General principles of weed control in grassland are given in Volume 1, Chapter 12. It needs to be emphasized that the recommendations given in this present chapter will only be effective if the causes of excessive weediness are removed. These could include poor drainage, acidity or nutrient deficiencies in the soil or faulty management such as over-grazing or under-grazing, excessive or late cutting for hay, or by combinations of these. It may be more economic to control weeds by altering these factors than by a direct attack. If a herbicide is to be used where such conditions exist it is important to rectify them so far as possible, or weed control may be disappointing or short lived.

The recommendations given in the chapter are laid out in sequential order, namely weed control prior to sowing the crop, in the seedbed, in the newly-sown crop and in the mature crop. Throughout a clear distinction is made between grass-only crops, grass/legume mixtures and legume crops. A final section is devoted to the control of individual problem weeds found commonly in grassland

The chapter is laid out as follows:

Site preparation prior to sowing

Grass after cereals

5.002 *Surface cultivation of arable stubbles for general weed control.*
Following cereal crops, most broad-leaved weeds and the common non-rhizomatous grasses *Agrostis stolonifera* (Creeping Bent), *Poa annua* (Annual Meadow-grass), *P. trivialis* (Rough Meadow-grass) and *Alopecurus myosuroides* (Black-grass) may be reduced by surface cultivations after harvest and in early spring. The control of rhizomatous grasses *Agropyron repens* (Common Couch) and *Agrostis gigantea* (Black Bent) is discussed in paragraph 5.010.

5.003 *Stubble cleaning by* **paraquat** *0·5–0·8 kg/ha or* **dalapon-sodium** *5·6 to 6·7 kg/ha or* **glyphosate** *1·4 kg/ha used as an alternative to surface cultivations following cereal crops.*
These chemicals can be used to kill off weeds in the stubble. They may be sprayed at any time after harvest provided there is sufficient green and growing leaf to absorb the chemical. Dalapon will only kill grasses. Established perennial weeds may only be checked by dalapon and paraquat. Glyphosate will give good control of *Agropyron repens* (Common Couch).
Following stubble cleaning with paraquat, but not dalapon, reseeding can then take place either by drilling direct in a one-pass operation or by minimal cultivations as described in paragraph 5.005. The advantage of direct-drilling is that the seed can be sown without delay as soon as the straw and other loose trash is cleared, and without further risk of soil moisture loss. Labour and machinery involvement is small at this busy time of year and thus early establishment is ensured before the winter sets in. These quick seeding techniques avoid the need for undersowing, with all its attendant disadvantages both to the grass and the cereal crop. Where dalapon is used for stubble cleaning, sowing should be delayed for at least 6 weeks. With glyphosate drilling can take place 14 days after spraying.

Grass after grass

5.004 *Site preparation by ploughing and cultivations.*
Major infestations of broad-leaved weeds should be controlled prior to ploughing using the appropriate herbicide recommendation (12.088).
The best way to prevent or minimize invasion of new grass by grass weeds is to plough the old grass or weedy stubble in such a way that the weed grasses cannot grow through. This calls for a good deal more care and often a technique different from normal ploughing in an arable rotation. Every effort should be made to bury the surface under as much soil as possible and so skim coulters should always be used. Ploughing

should not be too shallow—about 175–200 mm deep—and the body type, furrow proportions and speed of work chosen so that the furrow slices are well turned with no gaps in them through which grass weed can grow. On heavy land, this result is achieved by turning flat unbroken furrow slices using a long body of the general purpose type, furrow slices that are at least twice as wide as they are deep and a low ploughing speed. As the land becomes lighter, it is possible to get adequate surface burial with shorter bodies, narrower furrows and higher speeds; but quality of ploughing should never be sacrificed for output. Further, some pretreatment of old grass or a very weedy stubble with disc harrows or a rotary cultivator will usually facilitate good ploughing. Ridges or open furrows are weak points in conventional ploughing where grass tends to grow through. One-way ploughs give a better control of grass weeds.

Cultivations after ploughing should be kept shallow to avoid bringing old turf to the surface.

In light soils rotary cultivation may be used as an alternative to ploughing and has given good control of *Agropyron repens* (Common Couch). In general, however, rotary cultivation is more reliable when used in conjunction with a chemical spray.

5.005   *Chemical sward destruction prior to re-seeding*

Chemicals can be used as alternatives to ploughing grass swards. Where the sward is open and non-matted seed can often be direct drilled without any soil disturbance, although disc or tine harrows may improve the seedbed. Where the sward is matted it can either be sprayed in the late summer and left to break down during the winter, or be rotovated 7–14 days after spraying in the summer.

At spraying the sward should be short and well growing, with a minimum of surface trash. Accurate spraying at volumes between 200 and 500 litres/ha depending on the density of the sward is essential to obtain a complete kill. After re-seeding, rolling with a heavy roller has been found beneficial, and suitable anti-slug treatment should be applied.

5.006   **Paraquat** *1·1–1·7 kg/ha for chemical sward destruction prior to re-seeding.*

Paraquat is most effective for quick desiccation of the old turf. 1·1 kg/ha of paraquat is normally sufficient but 1·7 kg/ha may be necessary if *Dactylis glomerata* (Cock's-foot), *Deschampsia caespitosa* (Tufted Hair-grass), or fine-leaved fescues are present. The best control of these species is obtained by spraying in the autumn with a view to re-seeding in the spring. Splitting the application of paraquat, and applying two thirds of the dose first, followed by one third of the dose from 9 days (or up to 150 days later where swards are left sprayed over winter), will mean that 1·4 kg/ha will suffice where the more resistant species are present. However, recovery of some deep-rooted broad-leaved perennial species may often occur, and these should be removed from the sward by the use of selective weedkillers prior to spraying with paraquat.

Spraying may be carried out at any time of the year provided 50–75 mm of fresh growth is present, i.e. there should not be an excessive amount of trash present, nor should the sward be bare immediately following cutting. A better kill will be obtained where spraying is carried out in conditions of low light intensity, e.g. late afternoon or evening or in overcast conditions. Accurate spraying at volumes of between 200 and 560 litres/ha, depending on the density of the sward, and at least 2·1 bar pressure is essential to obtain a complete kill. Re-seeding should not take place until 3 days, preferably 10 days, after spraying.

5.007 **Glyphosate** *1·4–2·1 kg/ha for chemical sward destruction prior to re-seeding.*

Glyphosate is a foliage absorbed herbicide which is rapidly translocated to all parts of plants soon after spraying. Results are dependant upon adequate green leaf being present at the time of spraying. Grasses are very susceptible and are generally killed at lower rates than broad-leaved spp. Applications made during the summer months, when the weeds are at or near maturity, particularly broad-leaved spp. are most effective. Glyphosate is slow acting but re-seeding may take place as soon as the foliage of the weeds changes colour. It is most effective on swards containing rhizomatous spp.

Grass clover leys from 1 to 6 years old, including those containing *Agropyron repens* (Common Couch) may be effectively killed with 1·4 kg/ha. On old permanent grassland containing mostly grass spp. the rate should be increased to 1·8 kg/ha. Where many broad-leaved spp. occur in old permanent grassland, a rate of 2·1 kg/ha is most effective. If perennial broad-leaved weeds such as *Rumex* and *Cirsium* spp. are a problem, then applications made from June onwards are most effective. Ploughing can take place two weeks after spraying. Allow two weeks after spraying leys and 4 weeks after spraying old permanent grass, before direct drilling.

5.008 **Dalapon-sodium** *8·9–11·02 kg/ha for chemical sward destruction prior to re-seeding.*

Dalapon is slower in action than either paraquat or glyphosate. It is not very effective against broad-leaved weeds but gives good control of grasses, especially from late summer onwards. Because it is relatively slow in action and persistent, re-seeding is not recommended until 6 weeks after spraying; hence, dalapon is normally used in the autumn prior to re-seeding in the spring. Subsequently, a spring treatment of paraquat may be required to kill plants that have grown during the winter.

5.009 **[For information.]** Aminotriazole 4·5 kg/ha for autumn sward destruction prior to re-seeding in the spring.

Good control of many broad-leaved weeds, including *Rumex* spp. (Docks) have been achieved with this treatment, which is also very effective on most grasses.

5.010   The susceptibility of established grasses and legumes to herbicides

R = good tolerance, good recovery
MR = some check, reasonable recovery
MS = severe check, poor recovery
S = very severe check, practically no recovery
(All susceptibility ratings refer to herbicides applied at the recommended time of year.)

Grasses	Dalapon-sodium (kg/ha)		Paraquat (kg/ha)		Glyphosate kg/ha	Asulam (kg/ha)
	2·8	5·5–11	0·3–0·6	0·6–1·2	1·4	1·1–2·2
Agropyron repens (Common Couch)	MR	MS	MR	MS	S	R
Agrostis gigantea (Black Bent)	MS	MS	MS	MS	S	MR
Agrostis stolonifera (Creeping Bent)	MS	MS	S	S	S	MR
Agrostis tenuis (Common Bent)	MS	S	MS	S	MS	MR
Alopecurus pratensis (Meadow Foxtail)	MR	MR	MR	MR	MS	MS
Bromus mollis (Soft-brome)	—	MS	MR	MS	S	R
Cynosurus cristatus (Crested Dog's-tail)	MR	MS	MR	MS	S	—
Dactylis glomerata (Cock's-foot)	R	MR	MR	MS	S	MR
Deschampsia caespitosa (Tufted Hair-grass)	R	MR	MR	MS	MS	R
Festuca ovina (Sheep's-fescue)	MR	MS	MR	MR	MS	MR
Festuca pratensis (Meadow Fescue)	MR	MS	MS	S	MS	R
Festuca rubra (Red Fescue)	MR	MS	MR	MR	S	R
Holcus lanatus (Yorkshire-fog)	MS	S	MS	S	MR	MS
Holcus mollis (Creeping Soft-grass)	MR	MS	MR	MS	S	—
Lolium multiflorum (Italian Rye-grass)	MR	S	MS	S	S	R
Lolium perenne (Perennial Rye-grass)	R	MS	MS	S	S	R
Phleum pratense (Timothy)	MR	MR	MR	MS	S	MR
Poa annua (Annual Meadow-grass)	MS	S	MS	S	S	S
Poa trivialis (Rough Meadow-grass)	MS	S	MS	S	S	MS
Legumes						
Medicago sativa (Lucerne)	R	S	MS	S	MS	R
Trifolium repens (White Clover)	R	MS	MS	S	MS	R
Trifolium pratense (Red Clover)	MS	S	MS	S	S	MR

Controlling weeds in the seedbed

Cultural weed control

5.011   The annual weed problem can be reduced by sowing during a period of minimum weed germination, e.g. July. For information regarding the seasonal distribution of germination of annual weeds see Volume I, 1.038. Some species, though capable of germination during most months are more serious weeds at certain seasons. *Stellaria media* (Common Chickweed) is more competitive in the cool wet conditions of autumn than when emerging in spring and summer. *Chenopodium album* (Fathen) germinating in summer competes less with the sown species than do the more vigorous plants resulting from spring germination. Undersowing usually results in fewer weed seeds establishing compared with direct-sowing, while broadcast crops are often cleaner than drilled crops, especially if high seed rates are used. Including a companion species like Italian ryegrass or red/white clover, can also reduce weed ingress.

Chemical weed control

5.012   *Pre-emergence spraying of* **paraquat** *0·6 kg/ha or* **glyphosate** *1·4 kg/ha to control seedling weeds that emerge before the grass.*

The herbicide may be sprayed not less than 3 days before sowing, or after sowing but at least 3 days before emergence of the grass seedlings, provided no excessive trash is present. These treatments are not suitable for crops undersown in cereals.

5.013   *Pre-emergence spraying of* **ioxynil** *0·42 kg/ha plus* **bromoxynil** *0·42 kg/ha, as esters, in low volume, to control seedling broad-leaved weeds.*

Undersown crops may also be treated provided the cereal is at least at the 3-leaf stage, and the undersown seeds have either not been sown or not emerged. The cereal crop should not be rolled within 7 days of application. The 'seeds' may be drilled or broadcast, but trefoil should not be treated post-sowing.

Useful control is given of such weeds as *Chrysanthemum segetum* (Corn Marigold), *Stellaria media* (Common Chickweed) and *Tripleurospermum* and *Matricaria* spp. (Mayweeds), but *Galium aparine* (Cleavers) and *Spergula arvensis* (Corn Spurrey) are resistant.

5.014   *Pre-emergence spraying of* **methabenzthiazuron** *1·2 kg/ha to control* Poa *spp. (Meadow-grass) establishing in perennial ryegrass.*

This treatment can also be used in perennial ryegrass undersown in spring barley, provided the crop is treated shortly after drilling and rolling. Care should be taken to avoid spray overlapping. Some broad-leaved weeds, e.g. *Stellaria media* (Common Chickweed), *Veronica* spp. (Speedwell) and some *Tripleurospermum* and *Matricaria* spp. (Mayweeds) are also controlled.

5.015 [**For information.**] Ethofumesate applied pre- or post-emergence at 1·5–2 kg/ha in 200–400 litres/ha to the seedbed of direct sown perennial or Italian ryegrass has given good control of grass weeds including *Alopecurus myosuroides* (Black-grass), *Avena fatua* (Wild-oat), *Hordeum murinum* (Wall Barley), *Poa annua* (Annual Meadow-grass) and volunteer cereals, and of certain broad-leaved weeds including *Galium aparine* (Cleavers) and *Stellaria media* (Common Chickweed). Weed grasses are generally best controlled in their early growth stages.

Application should preferably be in autumn, but February–March treatments have also given good results when followed by adequate rainfall.

Controlling weeds during establishment

5.016 *Cutting for broad-leaved weed control.*

Weeds with an upright habit of growth can be controlled by an early mowing or grazing. The degree of control depends on the vigour of the establishing sward. It is less with a slow-establishing crop or with low soil fertility. Prostrate weeds, or those producing a rosette of leaves at ground level, are little affected and may even be encouraged by the reduction of competition from a taller-growing crop. Examples of weeds which are fairly resistant to defoliation are *Capsella bursa-pastoris* (Shepherd's-purse), *Galium aparine* (Cleavers), *Polygonum aviculare* (Knotgrass), *Stellaria media* (Common Chickweed) and *Veronica* spp. (Speedwells). With most perennial weeds, defoliation is ineffective, since they remain inconspicuous rosettes during the year of establishment. Hence, their control has to be achieved by herbicides.

5.017 *Grass seedling tolerance to herbicides*

Resistance of grass seedlings to herbicides increases with age, and spraying at the 2- to 3-leaf stage may cause a temporary check or depression which would not occur at the tillering stage (i.e. when a first tiller appears, 5.018). The number of leaves showing at tillering and the interval between sowing and tillering vary according to species and the conditions of establishment. Tillering is generally about 3–7 weeks after sowing, when there are 3–5 leaves. Large-seeded species, such as ryegrass, usually tiller sooner than small-seeded species, such as timothy. Unfavourable growing conditions will increase the period between sowing and tillering.

The recommended maximum doses for seedling grasses at different growth stages are given in 5.027.

(The tolerance of legume seedlings to herbicides is dealt with in paragraph 5.028.)

5.018   Grass seedling beginning to tiller.

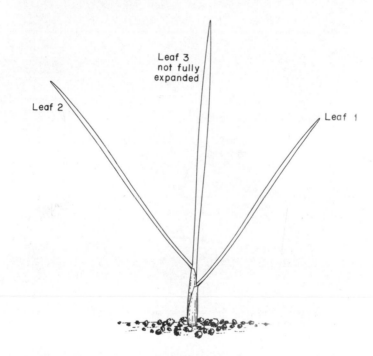

Leaf 3
not fully
expanded

Leaf 2

Leaf 1

a. Grass seedling with 2 fully expanded leaves (ZCK Growth stage: 12–See appendix V).

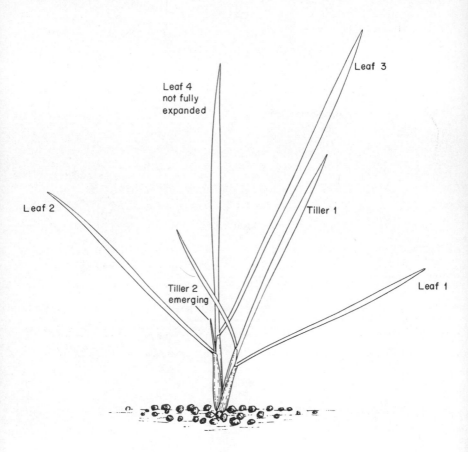

b. Grass seedling with 3 fully expanded leaves and one tiller (ZCK Growth Stage: 13, 21–See appendix V).

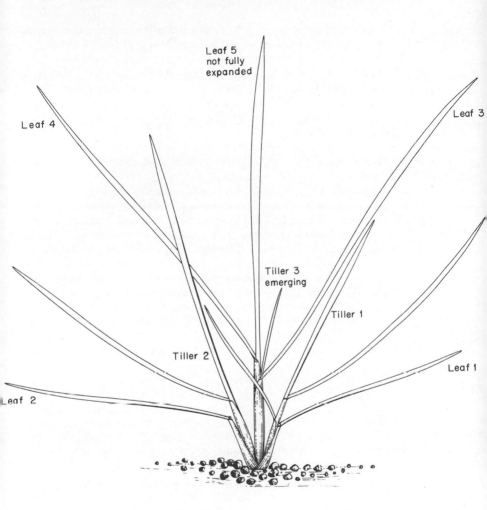

c. Grass seedling with 4 fully expanded leaves and two tillers. (ZCK Growth Stage: 14, 22–See appendix V).

Weed control in establishing grass-only leys

(NB) If the grass is undersown in a cereal crop then care must be taken to ensure that the cereal has reached the correct stage of growth, 1.002.

5.019   MCPA-salt *1·4 kg/ha,* **2,4-D-amine** *0·84 kg/ha or* **2,4-D-ester** *0·49 kg/ha for the control of weed seedlings in establishing grass.*

This treatment will also control the regrowth from root or shoot fragments of perennial weeds. (For grasses undersown in cereal crops, see Chapter 1.)

5.020   Mecoprop-salt *1·4–2·8 kg/ha for general weed control in establishing grass.*

Controls many broad-leaved weeds especially seedlings and young plants of *Rumex* spp. (Docks) and *Stellaria media* (Common Chickweed). Where *S. media* has established itself well, before the grass is advanced enough to spray, it is necessary to use up to 2·7 kg/ha mecoprop to obtain control. This often happens following an autumn re-seed on a soil in fertile conditions. Spraying may be carried out in this case during any open, frost-free, spell, during the winter months when the ground will bear the weight of the sprayer, without excessive wheeling damage. If allowed to grow unchecked, the *S. media* may dominate, and eventually smother large areas of the sward, causing the re-seed to fail.

5.021   Dichlorprop-salt *2·2 kg/ha for general weed control in establishing grass.*

5.022   *Mixtures of* dicamba *with* mecoprop, MCPA-salt, *with or without* 2,3,6-TBA *for general weed control, when the grass has 2–3 leaves.*

This treatment is useful against *Stellaria media* (Common Chickweed), *Cirsium arvense* (Creeping Thistle) and many other broad-leaved weeds.

5.023   *Mixture of* 2,3,6-TBA, dicamba, MCPA-salt *and* mecoprop *for the control of broad-leaved weeds.*

This treatment can be used to attack a range of broad-leaved weeds when they are larger than the ideal stage, e.g. *Matricaria* spp. (Mayweeds), *Galium aparine* (Cleavers) and *Stellaria media* (Common Chickweed).

5.024   Ioxynil *and* bromoxynil esters *at up to 0·84 kg/ha total.*

This mixture is of particular value for the control of *Chrysanthemum segetum* (Corn Marigold) and *Tripleurospermum* and *Matricaria* spp. (Mayweed).

Grass weeds

5.025   **Methabenzthiazuron** *1·2 kg/ha applied post-emergence to direct-sown perennial ryegrass crops at the 3-leaf stage to control* Poa trivialis *and* P. annua *(Meadow-grasses) germinating along with the crop.*

Some broad-leaved weeds including *Stellaria media* (Common Chickweed), *Veronica* sp. (Speedwell), and some mayweeds are also controlled. If the crop and meadow grass are between the 3-leaf stage and the start of tillering, control is still possible with an increased rate of 1·5 kg/ha.

5.026   [**For information.**] Ethofumasate 1·5–2·0 kg/ha applied post-emergence to direct-sown crops of perennial and Italian ryegrass has given good control of several annual grass and broad-leaved weeds.

5.027   Recommended maximum doses of herbicides for newly-sown grasses and legumes

NR = Not recommended.
* Provided that the majority of seedlings are sheltered by the weeds.
† See Fig. 5, 6 and 7.
‡ Chlorpropham may also be used, see paragraph 5.040.
§ Used pre-emergence of legumes.

Crop	Growth stage†	Herbicide and dose (kg/ha)								
		MCPA-salt	2,4-D-amine	2,4-D-ester	2,4-DB-salt	MCPB-salt	Dinoseb-amine	Benazolin-salt	Mecoprop-salt	Ioxynil + bromoxynil
Grasses	2nd-3rd leaf	1·4	0·84	0·49	2·2	2·2	1·1	0·21	1·4	0·84
	Tiller	1·4	0·84	0·49	2·w	2·2	1·1	0·42	2·8	0·84
White	Unifoliate leaf	NR	NR	NR	NR	NR	NR	NR	NR	0·84§
clover	1st trifoliate leaf	NR	0·56*	NR	2·2	2·2	2·2	0·21	NR	0·84§
	2nd trifoliate leaf	NR	0·56*	NR	2·2	2·2	2·2	0·21	NR	0·84§
	3rd to 4th trifoliate leaf	0·56*	0·56*	NR	2·2	2·2	2·2	0·42	NR	0·84§
Red	Unifoliate leaf	NR	NR	NR	NR	NR	NR	NR	NR	0·84§
clover	1st trifoliate leaf	0·56*	NR	NR	2·2	2·2	2·2	0·21	NR	0·84§
	2nd trifoliate leaf	0·56*	NR	NR	2·2	2·2	2·2	0·21	NR	0·84§
	3rd to 4th trifoliate leaf	12*	NR	NR	2·2	2·2	2·2	0·21	NR	0·84§
Lucerne‡	Unifoliate leaf/1st trifoliate leaf	NR	NR	NR	NR	NR	NR	NR	NR	0·84§
	2nd/4th trifoliate leaf	NR	NR	NR	2·2	2·2	2·2	NR	NR	0·84§
Sainfoin	1st compound leaf	NR	NR	NR	NR	NR	NR	NR	NR	0·84§
	2nd compound leaf	NR	NR	NR	2·2	2·2	2·2	NR	NR	0·84§

Weed control in establishing grass/legume mixtures

(NB If the grass/legume mixture has been undersown in a cereal crop then care must be taken to ensure that the cereal has reached the correct stage of growth, 1.002.)

5.028 *Legume seedling tolerance to herbicides*

Herbicides should not be applied before *all* the sown species have reached a stage of growth tolerant to the dose to be used. Legume seedlings are more likely to be permanently damaged than grass seedlings. Where both are present the stage reached by the legume should decide the time and dose.

The development of legume seedlings is described in terms of the number of expanded leaves. On emergence, two small round or oval cotyledons are apparent. These are sometimes called 'seed' leaves, but are not true leaves. They are followed by a single leaf which is the unifoliate leaf or 'spade' leaf. All subsequent leaves of clovers and lucerne have 3 leaflets; these are called trifoliate leaves.

In sainfoin, the cotyledons are followed by a single unifoliate or spade leaf; after this appear 2 trifoliate leaves (like lucerne), then all subsequent leaves have 5 or more leaflets.

Seedlings of clover, lucerne and sainfoin are illustrated in 5.030 and 5.031.

The recommended maximum doses for seedling legumes at different stages of growth are shown in 5.027.

5.029 **MCPB**-salt *and* **2,4-DB**-salt *2.2 kg/ha for the control of seedling weeds in establishing grass/legume mixtures.*

The tolerance of legumes to these herbicides is the main reason for their use in young grass/legume mixtures. 2,4-DB is slightly more toxic than MCPB to red clover. It may cause leaf deformities but these do not persist more than 6–8 weeks. MCPB-salt is not recommended for use on newly-sown lucerne.

These two herbicides can be applied soon after the appearance of the second true (first trifoliate) leaf. Where the seed mixture contains both red and white clover, care should be taken to verify that both species have reached the resistant stage.

Because of their limited effectiveness on weeds these chemicals are now chiefly used in mixtures with MCPA or 2,4-D (see below).

5.030   Legume seedlings at the first trifoliate-leaf stage: (a) clover; (b) lucerne.

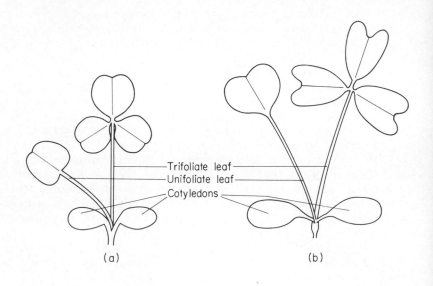

Trifoliate leaf
Unifoliate leaf
Cotyledons

(a)   (b)

5.031   Sainfoin seedling with third compound leaf.

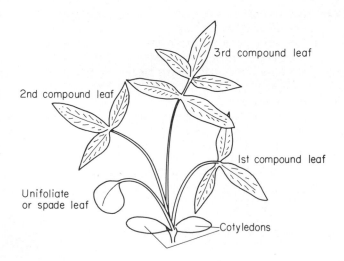

3rd compound leaf

2nd compound leaf

1st compound leaf

Unifoliate
or spade leaf

Cotyledons

5.032 *Mixtures of* **MCPA-salt** *or* **2,4-D-amine** *or* **-ester** *with* **MCPB-salt** *or* **2,4-DB-salt** *for the control of seedling weeds in establishing grasses/legume mixtures.*

Mixtures including MCPA may be used with both red and white clover, but not lucerne; 2,4-D should not be used on red clover. With these mixtures the dose of the constituent chemicals should never exceed the maximum doses given in 5.027.

5.033 **Dinoseb-amine** *2·2 kg/ha for the control of seedling weeds in establishing grass/legume mixtures.*

Dinoseb-amine should not be applied before the clovers have reached the second trifoliate leaf stage. This treatment will cause some leaf scorch and should only be used when the weed problem makes it essential. Doses should be reduced when spraying in warm weather (e.g. by 0·5 kg/ha at over 21°C).

Young grass-legume mixtures

5.034 **Dinoseb-acetate** *2·8 kg/ha for the control of seedling weeds in establishing grass/legume mixtures.*

The clovers should have at least 1–3 true leaves and the grasses 3–4 leaves when sprayed. This herbicide is less affected by extremes of temperature than is the amine formulation.

5.035 *Mixtures of* **benazolin-salt** *(0·21 kg/ha) with* **MCPA** *(0·31 kg/ha) and* **2,4-DB** *(0.18 kg/ha) or* **MCPB** *for the control of seedling weeds in establishing leys containing clover.*

Benazolin is only available in mixtures. These give good control of *Stellaria media* (Common Chickweed) and *Galium aparine* (Cleavers). Mixtures with benazolin can be used on undersown or direct-sown clovers from the first trifoliate leaf stage. The mixture containing benazolin, 2,4-DB and MCPA is not recommended for use in red clover beyond the third trifoliate leaf stage. White clover can be sprayed at any stage after one trifoliate has appeared.

If *Polygonum convolvulus* (Black-bindweed), *P. aviculare* (Knotgrass) or *P. persicaria* (Redshank) are present, the mixture containing 2,4-DB should be used. If *Galeopsis tetrahit* (Common Hempnettle) is a major weed the mixture with MCPB is more satisfactory.

Weed control in establishing legume crops

(NB If the legume is establishing in a cereal cover crop then care must be taken to ensure that the cereal has reached the correct stage of growth, 1.002.)

5.036 **MCPB**-salt *or* **2,4-DB**-salt *2·2 kg/ha for the control of broad-leaved weeds in establishing white clover.*

These herbicides can be used soon after the appearance of the second true (first trifoliate) leaf. 2,4-DB is slightly more toxic than MCPB.

5.037 **MCPB**-salt *2·2 kg/ha for the control of broad-leaved weeds in establishing red clover.*

Same timing as 5.036 above. (2,4-DB is not normally used on red clover because it may cause some deformities although these do not persist for more than 6–8 weeks.)

5.038 *Mixtures of* **MCPB** *or* **2,4-DB** *with* **MCPA** *for the control of broad-leaved weeds in establishing red and white clover.*

Because MCPB and 2,4-DB are rather limited in their effectiveness on weeds they are usually combined with some MCPA, although the dose of the constituent chemicals in the mixture should never exceed the maximum doses given in 5.027. For timing, with both clovers, see 5.036 above.

5.039 **2,4DB**-salt *2·24 kg/ha for controlling weeds in establishing lucerne.*

The optimum time of treatment is between the first and fourth trifoliate leaf stages; this is also the period of maximum sensitivity of the crop to weed competition. Treatment after development of the fourth trifoliate leaf may produce deformity and reduced vigour in subsequent lateral and tiller growth. Although this deformity will disappear within 6–8 weeks of spraying, the loss of vigour will affect the ability of the lucerne to compete with semi-resistant weeds, particularly if the crop is sown in late summer.

5.040 **Chlorpropham** *2·2 kg/ha for controlling* Stellaria media *(Common Chickweed) in newly sown lucerne.*

This treatment can be applied from the fourth trifoliate leaf onwards. It is slow in action on established plants and the full effect may not be evident for several weeks. It will seriously check any grasses present.

5.041 **Dinoseb-amine** *2·2 kg/ha for the control of seedling weeds in establishing clovers and lucerne.*

For clovers, see 5.033. With lucerne this treatment can be applied either during the first 3 days after drilling the lucerne, or after the lucerne has developed at least 2 trifoliate leaves.

5.042 **Dinoseb-acetate** *2·8 kg/ha for controlling weeds in newly sown clovers and lucerne.*

For clovers, see 5.034. With lucerne, spraying should be carried out at the 1–3 trifoliate leaf stage in newly-sown crops. When undersown, the treatment can be applied at any time between the 3-leaf and 'shooting' stage.

5.043 [**For information.**] Carbetamide 2·1 kg/ha, applied autumn to early spring, for the control of grass weeds in establishing clovers and lucerne. The treatment will also control volunteer cereals and *Stellaria media* (Common Chickweed). Clovers should be at, or beyond, the first trifoliate-leaf stage.

Controlling weeds in established grasses and legumes

Weed control in established grass-only swards

5.044 Weeds in grassland include unproductive or unpalatable grasses as well as broad-leaved plants. Weed infestations are often associated with deficiencies in soil fertility, management or utilization. Unless these are corrected, lasting results from weed control measures will not be achieved. Management factors which may need attention are summarized below.

1. *Drainage.* Lasting improvement and freedom from weeds cannot be achieved on very wet land until it is drained.

2. *Fertility.* Weeds are generally better adapted to acidity and low nutrient status than are sown grasses or good permanent pasture species. Lime, phosphate and potash levels should be sufficient for vigorous growth. Regular nitrogen applications, or a good clover content make grass more vigorous and so help to suppress most broad-leaved weeds.

3. *Control of grazing.* Controlled systems which maintain high stocking levels, but which avoid seasonal extremes of over- or under-grazing, will tend to prevent weed incursion.

4. *Topping.* Regular cutting-over after grazing to remove uneaten patches reduces the spread of unpalatable grasses and weeds.

5. *Alternation of mowing and grazing.* Rotating the management where possible will discourage weeds associated with repeated cutting or repeated hard grazing.

6. *Sward damage.* Avoid poaching and mechanical damage where possible.

Weed species such as *Poa* spp. (Meadow-grasses), *Rumex* spp. (Docks) and *Stellaria media* (Common Chickweed) occupy bare ground more quickly than sown grasses. Mole hills also provide opportunities for weeds, for example, *Agrostis stolonifera* (Creeping Bent), to establish or spread.

Broad-leaved weeds in all-grass swards

5.045 Spraying of broad-leaved perennials is usually carried out during their period of maximum growth, especially when the majority of species are beginning to form flower buds. The best time for spraying can vary according to weed species and herbicide. The best results from the use of herbicides will be gained if vigorous crop growth is encouraged at the same time by fertilizer application. This will reduce the recovery of weeds only checked by the spray.

Where grass is to be cut for hay, the herbicides can be applied either in early spring, e.g. for the control of *Ranunculus* spp. (Buttercups) or delayed until re-growth of the weed after mowing, e.g. for the control of *Cirsium arvense* (Creeping Thistle).

5.046 Where poisonous weeds are not present, animals can usually graze with safety within a day or so after spraying—although confirmation of safety should always be sought by checking the instructions on the herbicide container.

It should be remembered that wilting vegetation is often more palatable to livestock and animals may eat weeds more readily after spraying.

If poisonous weeds are present, fields should not be grazed until the weeds are dead and the foliage has disappeared. This restriction applies particularly in the case of *Senecio jacobaea* (Common Ragwort). Other weeds that can be poisonous to stock are *Ranunculus* spp. (Buttercup), *Pteridium aqualinum* (Bracken), *Equisetum arvense* (Field Horsetail), *Digitalis purpurea* (Foxglove), *Conium maculatum* (Hemlock) and *Atropa belladonna* (Deadly Nightshade).

5.047 **MCPA-salt** *1·6 kg/ha,* **2,4-D-amine** *1·4 kg/ha or* **2,4-D-ester** *1·0 kg/ha or* **mecoprop** *2·8 kg/ha for general broad-leaved weed control in established grasses.*

5.048 *Mixture of* **mecoprop** *with* **MCPA** *and* **dicamba** for general broad-leaved weed control in all-grass swards.

5.049 Recommendations for the control of specific broad-leaved weeds in all-grass swards are given in paragraph 5.065 onwards.

Grass weeds in all-grass swards

5.050 **Dalapon-sodium** *2·8 kg/ha applied in July for the selective suppression of weed grasses in perennial ryegrass.*

Weed grasses which are most effectively controlled by this treatment include *Agrostis stolonifera* (Creeping Bent), *P. trivialis* (Rough Meadowgrass) and *Holcus lanatus* (Yorkshire Fog). *Festuca rubra* (Red Fescue) and *Deschampsia caespitosa* (Tufted Hair-grass) are relatively unaffected by dalapon. (This treatment can also be recommended for controlling grass weeds in swards of cocksfoot but not timothy.)

Where broad-leaved weeds are likely to be a problem they should be controlled before the dalapon is applied; also, any drainage problems should be rectified. The ryegrass content in the pre-sprayed sward should be at least as high as the weed grass content, with the ryegrass plants being fairly uniformly distributed; the presence of some ryegrass in three out of four random throws of a 6-inch square quadrat is a useful guide. At the time of spraying, when the sward should be about 10 cm high, 40–50 kg/ha of nitrogen should be applied to encourage the ryegrass to occupy the spaces left by the weeds. Normal grazing can be resumed as soon as the sward contains sufficient growth, usually after 3–5 weeks. Sward growth is checked initially, depending on weather and soil conditions, and the proportion of weed grasses present. Some scorch is to be expected, with the more susceptible species becoming progressively yellower and moribund. White clover is not harmed and usually increases in proportion.

5.051   *Spot treatment of* Deschampsia caespitosa *(Tufted Hair-grass) in the autumn by dalapon-sodium solution 0·45 kg in 45 litres water.*

5.052   **Methabenzthiazuron**   *3·2–4·7 kg/ha   on   well-established   perennial ryegrass swards, applied in the autumn, before mid-November, for the control of* Poa spp. *(Meadow-grasses) and seedling* Alopecurus myosuroides *(Black-grass).*

5.053   [**For information.**] Linuron at 1·1–1·2 kg/ha has given useful control of *Holcus lanatus* (Yorkshire-fog) in timothy. Ethofumesate at 1·0–1·5 kg/ha has been used successfully to control *Hordeum murinum* (Barley Grass) in perennial ryegrass pastures.

Weed control in established grass/legume swards

Broad-leaved weeds

5.054   **MCPB-salt** *2·2 kg/ha,* **2,4-DB-salt** *2·2 kg/ha or* **dinoseb** *2·2 kg/ha for general broad-leaved weed control in established grass/legume swards.*

5.055   *Mixtures of* **MCPA-salt** *0·56 kg/ha, or* **2,4-D-amine** *0·56 kg/ha, or* **2,4-D-ester** *0·28 kg/ha, plus up to 1·4 kg/ha of either* **MCPB-salt** *or* **2,4-DB-salt** *for controlling broad-leaved weeds in established grass/legume swards.*

When red clover is present in the mixture, 2,4-D is not recommended. The rates quoted for MCPA and 2,4-D are the maximum safe doses that can be applied without checking the legume content of the sward.

5.056   **Benazolin-salt** *0·42 kg/ha with* **MCPA** *0·63 kg/ha and* **2,4-DB** *3·5 kg/ha for general broad-leaved weed control in established grass/legume swards.*

Treatments may take place at any time during the growing season when weeds are in an active stage of growth. When *Rumex* spp. (Docks) are present (5.095).

5.057   Recommendations for the control of specific broad-leaved weeds in established grass/legume swards are given in paragraph 5.065 onwards.

Grass weeds

5.058   **Dalapon-sodium** *2·8 kg/ha applied in July for the selective suppression of weed grass in perennial ryegrass/white clover leys.* See paragraph 5.050.

5.059   [**For information.**] Carbetamide 0·6–1 kg/ha in medium volume applied in early spring will help to restore the clover content of a long-term ley or pasture.

Leys most suitable for this improvement technique contain a small percentage of clover and some perennial ryegrass which will be largely unaffected, and weed grasses such as *Holcus lanatus* (Yorkshire-fog) and *Poa trivialis* (Rough Meadow-grass) which will be selectively suppressed.

Other herbicides useful for this purpose include paraquat 0·5 kg/ha, propyzamide 0·8 kg/ha and glyphosate 0·6 kg/ha.

For use of carbetamide in controlling grass in legume crops, see paragraph 5.063.

Weed control in established legume crops

Broad-leaved weeds

5.060   *White clover. Established stands of white clover will tolerate treatments of* **MCPB** *or* **2,4-DB** *(5.036), mixtures of* **MCPB** *or* **2,4-DB** *with* **MCPA** *(5.038), and* **dinoseb-amine** *(5.041). Where a seed crop is to be taken only* **MCPB** *at 2·2 kg/ha is recommended (4.026).*

5.061   *Red clover. As for white clover, with* **2,4-DB** *being more damaging than* **MCPB**.

None of these herbicides are recommended for established red clover prior to seed harvesting.

5.062   *Lucerne. Established stands of lucerne will usually tolerate* **2,4-DB** *(5.039) and* **dinoseb-amine** *(5.051). If Rumex spp. (Docks) are present* **asulam** *1·7 kg/ha can be used when the dock leaves are fully expanded, with an allowance of 1 week between application and cutting.*

Grass weeds

5.063   **Carbetamide** *2·1 kg/ha or* **dalapon-sodium** *5·6–6·7 kg/ha or* **paraquat**

0·4–0·8 kg/ha for controlling weed grasses in established lucerne and clovers.

These herbicides are best applied when the legumes are dormant but the grasses growing, late-winter application usually being better than autumn. Paraquat is particularly effective for the control of *Poa* spp. (Meadow-grasses) and *Stellaria media* (Common Chickweed). Carbetamide gives useful control of *Lolium perenne* (Perennial Rye-grass), *Alopecurus myosuroides* (Black-grass) and *Stellaria media* (Common Chickweed). All treatments should result in comparative freedom from grass competition during the following season, but re-colonization by grasses or broad-leaved weeds may occur when the lucerne again becomes dormant.

5.064   [**For information.**] Propyzamide 1·2 kg/ha and metribuzin 1·0 kg/ha, applied in late-winter, have proved useful in controlling grass weeds in legume forage crops, including lucerne.

Notes on some common grassland weeds and their control

Cirsium arvense (Creeping Thistle)

5.065   Creeping thistle is one of the most persistent and troublesome perennial weeds of grassland. It spreads by lateral roots which may remain dormant for many years if deeply buried under a vigorous sward. Later, under the right conditions, they may readily produce new shoots. Creeping thistle is usually most troublesome in pastures where there is a tendency to overgraze in winter or early spring and undergraze in summer.

5.066   *Cultural control.*

The control of creeping thistle in pasture is often attempted by cutting in the flower-bud stage, but unless cutting is done regularly eradication is seldom achieved. A change in management to mowing, especially for silage will reduce the amount of the weed.

5.067   *Chemical control*

Chemical treatment is usually more satisfactory, but the degree of success is influenced by the situation. On re-seeded grassland the disturbance of the roots by the cultivations used in preparing the seedbed usually leads to an abundant emergence of shoots. The ratio of the number of shoots to the amount of main roots is then high and in this condition the weed may be particularly vulnerable to herbicides. In established grassland the ratio of shoots to roots may be low and control of the weed more difficult.

5.068   MCPA-salt *1·7 kg/ha,* **2,4-D-amine** *1·4 kg/ha or* **2,4-D-ester** *1·0 kg/ha for controlling* Cirsium arvense *(Creeping Thistle) in established grass.*
MCPA and 2,4-D can give a good suppression of shoots in the first and perhaps second year after spraying. They do not completely kill the root system and gradual reinfestation is likely to occur. The best time for spraying with MCPA or 2,4-D is in the early flower-bud stage, although spraying in later summer has also been successful.

5.069   MCPB-salt *2·2 kg/ha,* **2,4-DB-salt** *0·84 kg/ha for controlling* Cirsium arvense *(Creeping Thistle) in established grass/legume swards.*
The MCPB or 2,4-DB should be sprayed when the shoots are 100–200 mm high.

Deschampsia caespitosa (Tufted Hair-grass)

5.070   A serious perennial grass weed of wet grazing land, spreading by seed. It needs moist conditions for initial establishment but can persist as a mature plant even after drainage is improved. Older plants are almost completely avoided by stock, and quickly form characteristic large clumps.

5.071   *Cultural control*
The most effective control, where it is possible, is a change of management to cutting for hay or silage. On land that can only be grazed, regular hard cutting several times a year, combined with better fertilizer (not necessarily high nitrogen) and grazing management, will weaken and reduce an infestation and may eventually eliminate it. Digging and removal alone is usually unsuccessful as new plants germinate in the bare patches. In severe infestations rotovation is necessary, followed by re-seeding with densely tillering grasses.

5.072   *Chemical control*
Selective chemical control is not yet practicable. Dalapon-sodium at 6·7 kg/ha will control the weed fairly well if applied at medium volume in the autumn, but this application will also kill or seriously check many good pasture grasses and encourage the spread of broad-leaved weeds. It should therefore be used only where the farmer is prepared to re-seed afterwards.

5.073   *Spot treatment of* Deschampsia caespitosa *(Tufted Hair-grass) in established grass by* **dalapon** *or* **paraquat.**
Spot treatment may be practicable if plants are present in small numbers. A complete wetting with a solution of 0·45 kg dalapon-sodium per 45 litres water, or 1·7 kg/ha of paraquat, should be given with a lance or knapsack sprayer. Improved control will be obtained if the tussocks

can be cut hard, i.e. with a flail mower or harvester, 6–8 weeks before spraying. This will allow new softer green growth, which is much more susceptible to paraquat or dalapon than the harder, older leaves. The dead plants should later be cut over to encourage the surrounding sward to invade the clumps.

Equisetum spp. (Horsetail)

5.074 The two most important species are *Equisetum arvense* and *E. palustre,* both of which are poisonous to stock. They are a considerable hazard in hay, dried grass or silage. *E. palustre* is the more important species in grassland and thrives in damp situations.

5.075 **MCPA-salt** *1·6 kg/ha,* **2,4-D-amine** *1·4 kg/ha or* **2,4-D-ester** *1·0 kg/ha for controlling* Equisetum *spp. (Horsetail) in established grass.*

The shoots of both species are readily killed by these herbicides but there is generally strong regrowth from underground parts in the year following treatment. The best time for spraying is when the shoots have made maximum growth. Long-term reduction of both species by spraying is most likely if competition from the sward is increased by good management.

To give a kill of shoots of *Equisetum* spp. in grassland required for hay or silage, the field may be sprayed a week or more before the grass is to be cut with MCPA or 2,4-D at two-thirds the doses given above.

(See paragraph 5.054 if legumes are present.)

5.076 **Asulam** *2·2 kg/ha for controlling* Equisetum *spp. (Horsetail) in established grass to be ploughed.*

Spray in the late spring just before the shoots have made maximum growth, and leave undisturbed for 1 week. This rate of asulam is damaging to grass. Any subsequent crop should not be sown sooner than 6 weeks after treatment.

Juncus spp. (Rushes)

5.077 Rushes are closely associated with wet land and very often poor drainage is responsible for their presence. Improvement of drainage is of fundamental importance. In areas of high rainfall and heavy soils, rushes may be prevalent on reasonably well-drained land because of poor vigour of the sward due to low fertility. The spraying of the rushes should then be combined with increased fertilizer applications.

The soil on which rushes grow almost always contains dormant seeds which will germinate in moist conditions if brought to the surface or exposed to light. Poaching by animals or ploughing are equally undesirable unless the drainage of the land has previously been improved. Cutting of rushes without other treatments is unlikely to be worthwhile.

(For further details on the control of rushes, see MAFF Advisory Leaflet 433.)

5.078 **MCPA-salt** *1·6 kg/ha,* **2,4-D-amine** *1·4 kg/ha or* **2,4-D-ester** *1·0 kg/ha for controlling* Juncus effusus *(Soft Rush) in established grass.*

Spraying should take place before flowering and when the rushes are growing vigorously. The rushes should be cut about 4 weeks after treatment to improve the control and help the sward to develop over the dead rush clumps. Cutting may alternatively be done a month before spraying, but the cut litter must then be removed to prevent shielding from the spray. Spraying uncut rushes can also give satisfactory results, particularly when the rushes have been cut in previous years.

Juncus effusus (Soft Rush), which is distinguished from other rushes by having continuous pith inside its green flowering stems, which are devoid of green leaves, is the only rush species which is readily killed by this treatment.

Pteridium aquilinum (Bracken)

5.079 Bracken is a dominant plant over considerable areas, generally on light acid soils, in both woods and grassland. It is persistent and troublesome, being usually avoided by grazing animals, and spread very extensively by means of underground rhizomes. Cases of bracken poisoning are fairly common, resulting in severe losses in cattle and disorders in sheep.

5.080 *Cultural control.*

Cultural measures for controlling bracken are given in the Ministry of Agriculture Advisory Leaflet No. 190. Bracken on ploughable land can be satisfactorily controlled by ploughing in the summer, followed by heavy discing and application of lime and fertilizers. The land is sown in late summer to a pioneer crop, such as rape, turnips or Italian ryegrass which is grazed in the autumn, and disced in during December. The following spring the land should be fit for potatoes, a suitable cereal crop or for direct re-seeding. On unploughable land bracken can be greatly reduced in quantity and vigour, if not eliminated, by cutting or bruising the fronds twice a year for a number of years.

5.081 **Asulam** *4·4 kg/ha in very low to medium volume for the control of* Pteridium aquilinum *(Bracken) in grassland, hill land and other agricultural areas.*

Treatment must be made at or just before full frond expansion, but before the onset of senescence (bronzing), i.e. within the period early July to late August. The fronds should not be damaged by stock, frost or cutting before spraying. Slight yellowing and distortion may be seen in the year of treatment, but normally the bracken dies back as usual and the herbicidal effect is shown as little or no regrowth next season. Persistence of effect for up to three years after treatment has so far been recorded. Heavy rain during or immediately after application may adversely influence the degree of control.

Most grasses and a few herbs, e.g. sorrells, *Bellis perennis* (Daisy) and *Saxifraga* spp. (Saxifrages) will be severely damaged at this rate although the bracken canopy can reduce the damage. Other ferns are susceptible and *Ulex minor* (Dwarf Gorse) is slightly sensitive, but rushes, sedges and most shrubs, e.g. *Vaccinium myrtillus* (Bilberry), *Ulex europaens* (Gorse) and *Calluna vulgaris* (Heather) are practically unaffected. Some young trees may exhibit chlorosis and a slight check to growth if sprayed directly while actively growing but mature trees will be unharmed.

Large areas may be treated from the air by helicopter or fixed-wing aircraft using 45 litres of water per ha. Small areas can be spot-treated (dilution 20 g asulam/5 litres) with knap-sack or hand-lance, spraying to run off.

Cutting within 14 days after spraying would affect the degree of control—preferably leave the bracken undisturbed until late autumn, when appropriate after-care may begin. A programme of one or a combination of, the following practices may take place: burning of litter, fertilizer application, cultivation, re-seeding, fencing. It is important that the reclaimed pasture should be well stocked and grazed to prevent other weeds coming in or incursion of bracken from unsprayed areas.

5.082   [**For information.**] Glyphosate 1–1·5 kg/ha has given good control of *Pteridium aquilinum* (Bracken), when sprayed at full frond emergence in late July to early August. These rates kill any grasses.

5.083   [**For information.**] Good results have been obtained with 5·6–8·4 kg/ha aminotriazole, applied just before the fronds fully unroll. At these rates aminotriazole is toxic to clover and may kill or damage grasses.

Ranunculus spp. (Buttercups)

5.084   Buttercups are common in permanent pastures but also invade leys. Stock will not readily eat them and their presence may discourage the grazing of neighbouring grasses. As the three most important species differ in their reactions to herbicides, it is necessary to identify those present before treatment. *R. bulbosus* (Bulbous Buttercup), the earliest flowering of the three, is recognized by the swollen stem base found just underground (except in early spring) and by the sepals which are bent downwards away from the open flower. *R. repens* (Creeping Buttercup) can be distinguished from the others during the summer months by its runners. It has furrowed flower stalks and the apical lobe of the basal leaves is long-stalked and projects beyond the other two lobes. In *R. acris* (Meadow Buttercup) the flower stalks are not furrowed and the 3 lobes of the basal leaves all radiate from a single point. The sepals of *R. repens* and *R. acris* are spreading and not bent downwards during flowering. Unlike the other two species *R. bulbosus* dies down after flowering in the spring and is dormant in the summer; new leaves do not appear again until the autumn.

5.085   **MCPA-salt** *1·6 kg/ha,* **2,4-D-amine** *1·4 kg/ha or* **2,4-D-ester** *1·0 kg/ha for controlling* Ranunculus *spp. (Buttercup) in established grass.*

R. repens* is the most susceptible of the three species, while *R. bulbosus* is the least susceptible. *R. acris* responds better to MCPA than 2,4-D. The best time for spraying *R. repens* and *R. acris* is in spring or early summer before flowering. Treatment of *R. bulbosus* in spring will usually prevent flowering that year, but will not reduce significantly the population the following year. It may be preferable to spray in the autumn when new leaves appear and germination occurs.

(See paragraph 5.054 if legumes are present.)

Rumex spp. (Docks)

5.086   The most widespread species of dock occurring as a weed of grassland is *Rumex obtusifolius* (Broad-leaved Dock), the leaves of which are oval. It is often found with *R. crispus* (Curled Dock), which has long, comparatively narrow leaves the margins of which are markedly wavy. Hybrids of these two species, with intermediate characteristics, are also common.

Dock seed may be spread in a number of ways, including the out-feeding of contaminated hay and straw to stock, the application of muck or slurry, and the winter flooding of low-lying fields. 'Open' swards, poaching, and dung-pats provide favourable opportunities for seed germination, and after only 3 months a new plant with a tap-root can become established. Root fragments produced by cultivations and treading are easily spread and will generate fresh shoots when conditions are suitable. Dock plants thrive under high nitrogen conditions, but will also tolerate poor nutritional conditions.

Docks are most frequently found on heavily-stocked dairy farms, where high levels of nitrogen fertilizers are used, in combination with the return of slurry, especially in fields cut for silage.

The spread of dock seed by the methods indicated above should be avoided wherever possible; to this end, the flowering shoots should be cut off before seed is set. The encouragement of a dense sward helps to prevent seedling establishment.

(For further details of docks, see MAFF Advisory Leaflet 46.)

5.087   **MCPA-salt** *or* **2,4-D-amine** *at less than 0·8 kg/ha for the control of seedling* Rumex *spp. (Docks) in grass.*

5.088   **MCPA-salt** *1·7 kg/ha,* **2,4-D-amine** *1·4 kg/ha or* **2,4-D-ester** *1·0 kg/ha for controlling mature* Rumex *spp. (Docks) in grass.*

These herbicides should be used either pre-flowering in May or any time after defoliation, so long as the docks are growing vigorously.

5.089   **Mecoprop** *mixture with* **dicamba** *and* **MCPA**-**salt** *with or without* **2,3,6-TDA** *for the control of seedling* Rumex *spp. (Docks) and early regrowth from root fragments, in young or establishing swards of grass alone.*

5.090   **Asulam** *1·2 kg/ha in low volume for controlling mature and seedling* Rumex *spp. (Docks) in established grass and grass/clover swards.*

The asulam must be sprayed on the expanded leaves when the docks are growing vigorously—but not flowering—any time between April and September, as grassland management permits. A second application may be necessary to give satisfactory control of heavy or long-established infestations; because the chemical acts slowly the interval between spraying should not be less than 10 months.

To minimize possible damage to the pasture, and to allow the docks to regrow, at least 3 weeks must elapse between mowing or grazing and applying asulam.

After treatment, the docks must be left undisturbed for at least a week so that the herbicide is satisfactorily translocated from leaf to root. A cut for silage may then be made or grazing resumed, but a cut of hay is not advised.

If the above conditions are observed, established ryegrasses and clovers can safely be treated with asulam. When it is used on bents, fescues, meadow grasses and timothy swards, with or without ryegrasses, treatment may be followed by yellowing and a temporary check to growth. Cocksfoot and *Holcus* spp. can be severely checked. The 'balance' of species in the sward may be altered after using asulam and there can be varietal differences in grass tolerance.

If it is desired to break up a sward, allow at least 2 weeks between spraying and carrying out any cultivation (or ploughing) which would disturb the dock roots. When preparing the seedbed the roots should not be chopped up (e.g. by rotary cultivator) otherwise regeneration may occur from the fragments produced. Paraquat should not be applied before asulam treatment, nor during the week after application. It is safe to sow or plant any crop 6 weeks after spraying asulam.

Small areas or clumps of docks may be spot-treated (dilution 10 g asulam/5 litres) with knapsack or hand-lance. If docks occur in lucerne, see paragraph 5.062.

5.091   *Mixtures of* **asulam** *1·2 kg/ha with* **MCPA** *1·7 kg/ha or* **MCPB** *2·2 kg/ha or* **mecoprop** *1·7 kg/ha for the control of* Rumex *spp. (Docks) and other broad-leaved weeds in established grass.*

The mecoprop mixture is best used when docks and *Stellaria media* (Common Chickweed) occur together; the other two mixtures give good control of *Cirsium arvense* (Creeping Thistle) and *Ranunculus bulbosus* (Creeping Buttercup).

5.092   Mecoprop *2·8 kg/ha for the control of* Rumex *spp. (Docks) in grass-only swards.*

This treatment has given good control of established docks in grassland where it has been applied to the docks in late summer. The docks should be allowed to flower in July, and the flowers cut before seeding to weaken the roots reserve. Mecoprop should be sprayed on the regrowth leaves from 14 days cutting the flowering heads off.

5.093   Dicamba *mixture with* **mecoprop** *(with or without* **MCPA-salt***) for the control of established* Rumex *spp. (Docks) in established, grass-only swards.*

Spraying can be carried out at any time the docks are making active growth, prior to seed-setting. Repeat applications may be necessary to control well-established infestations. Provided very recently grazed or mown swards are not sprayed, grasses are unlikely to be damaged.

5.094   Dicamba *mixture with* **2,4,5-T** *and* **mecoprop** *for the control of established* Rumex *spp. (Docks) in all-grass swards.*

5.095   Benazolin-salt *0·42 kg/ha with* **MCPA-salt** *0·63 kg/ha and* **2,4-DB** *3·5 kg/ha for the control of* Rumex *spp. (Docks) in established grass/legume swards.*

Docks should be treated when the stem has elongated just prior to flowering. Older growth with flowers or seed heads and plants at the rosette stage will not be controlled properly. For best results the weed should grow actively; spraying can take place at any time during the growing season. After grazing it is advantageous to close-mow in an endeavour to obtain uniform growth of docks. This is important since stock tend to graze docks differentially so that all stages are available at the time of spraying.

The mixture has a very high degree of safety to grasses and only has a temporary effect on clover. Normal clover levels are maintained. Retreatment will be essential in the following season to control regrowth.

5.096   [**For information.**] Glyphosate 1·5 kg/ha has given good control of *Rumex* spp. (Docks), but all grasses that are sprayed will be killed.

Senecio jacobaea (Common Ragwort)

5.097   Ragwort is scheduled as an injurious weed under the Weeds Act of 1959. It is poisonous to cattle and horses as a growing plant, when conserved in hay or silage or when dying after cutting or spraying.

Ragwort is most commonly found on neglected or overgrazed old pastures, but it may also rapidly invade young leys, particularly after direct-re-seeding. If undisturbed, ragwort is biennial. The rosette stage may be indefinitely prolonged by cutting or trampling and the plant may then become branched and considerably enlarged. Seed production is prolific and vegetative propagation may take place by means of shoots arising from root fragments. Seeds germinate quickly under suitable conditions but can remain viable for several years in the soil.

Senecio aquaticus (Marsh Ragwort) occasionally occurs as a weed of wet pastures.

(For further details about ragwort see MAFF Advisory Leaflet 280.)

5.098   *Cultural control.*

Heavy stocking with sheep for short periods will reduce a ragwort infestation. Control is often attempted by cutting the flowering shoots when in full flower. Although seeding is prevented, the treatment has no other beneficial effect and may encourage ragwort to perennate. The cut shoots should be removed from the field, both to prevent formation of viable seed and because they become more palatable when wilted and may cause stock poisoning.

Seedling establishment is the most vulnerable phase of the life history; a high level of grassland husbandry giving a dense sward can prevent a serious invasion by suppressing the seedlings. The most effective method of cultural control of established ragwort is to plough for an arable rotation before sowing down again to grass under a cover crop. Direct-reseeding should be avoided.

5.099   **MCPA-salt** *and* **2,4-D-amine** *2·2 kg/ha or* **2,4D-ester** *1·6 kg/ha for controlling* Senecio jacobaea *(Common Ragwort) in grassland.*

These herbicides will normally kill ragwort plants at all stages of growth up to the early bud stage; 2,4-D has usually been better than MCPA. Results may be masked because (i) the flowering shoots if sprayed too late may continue to produce flowers and viable seed in the season of spraying, (ii) new seedlings or regrowth from roots may appear soon after spraying. The success of spray treatment depends largely on whether the field becomes re-colonized after spraying. A single treatment may not be successful and repeat applications may be necessary.

The best time for treatment is in June in southern counties, when the flowering shoot is developing rapidly and seedlings and rosettes are growing strongly. Spraying should be carried out before the flower buds are well formed. *As ragwort becomes more palatable after spraying, it is essential to prevent stock from having access to treated fields until the ragwort plants have disappeared.*

5.100   [**For information.**] Mecoprop and dichlorprop 2·8 kg/ha have been reported as giving good control of ragwort, although clovers will be killed by these herbicides. Asulam 1·1 kg/ha, which is safe to clovers, has also given good control when applied in the spring at the rosette stage, before the flower buds have appeared.

Stellaria media (Common Chickweed)

5.101   Chickweed has increased in importance as a grassland weed in recent years. It is found chiefly in the wetter, low-lying or poorly drained pastures and in other intensively stocked areas receiving high rainfall. Mild poaching, overgrazing, and 'open' swards provide conditions for establishment, and the weed proliferates readily from seed during the growing season. The characteristic light-green clumps which quickly develop are particularly competitive with grasses under the cool wet conditions of the autumn.

(For further details of chickweed, see MAFF Advisory Leaflet 528.)

5.102   **Mecoprop** *2·5 kg/ha in low volume for controlling* Stellaria media *(Common Chickweed) in grass.*

This treatment should be carried out when the chickweed is growing vigorously and not shielded by grass, usually in late summer or autumn. Mecoprop will damage any clover that is present.

5.013   **Mecoprop** *mixtures with* **dicamba** *and* **MCPA-salt** *(with or without 2,3,6-TBA) to control* Stellaria media *(Common Chickweed) in young or established grass-only swards.*

5.104   **Benazolin** *mixtures for controlling* Stellaria media *(Common Chickweed) in newly-sown leys* (5.027).

Urtica dioica (Common Nettle)

5.105   *Cultural control*

Regular cutting for hay or silage will eliminate *Urtica dioica* (Common Nettle) in pastures that have been continually grazed. Nettles generally indicate a loose soil structure and systematic trampling by cattle will often control them. Ploughing followed by an arable rotation before re-seeding will also eliminate nettles.

(For further details about nettles, see MAFF Advisory Leaflet 47.)

5.106   **MCPA-salt** *1·6 kg/ha,* **2,4-D-amine** *1·4 kg/ha or* **2,4-D-ester** *1·0 kg/ha for controlling* Urtica dioica *(Common Nettle) in grass.*

These herbicides will provide only temporary control of top growth; new shoots will soon appear. The repeated spraying necessary for eradication will cause severe damage to clovers if MCPA or 2,4-D are used, unless it is feasible to spray only the nettle clumps.

5.107   **Mecoprop** *or* **2,4,5-T** *0·23 kg/45 litres of water applied at high volume to isolated clumps or pure stands of* Urtica dioica *(Common Nettle).*

Spraying should be carried out when the nettles are growing well but not in flower. This treatment is very effective when repeated in the autumn

246

as the nettles die down. The stems and base of the clumps should be thoroughly wetted. These chemicals are very toxic to clovers. It is desirable to sow grass seed on the sprayed area otherwise seedling nettles will quickly establish again.

5.108   *Mixtures containing* **2,4-D-ester** *and* **2,4,5-T ester,** *in water or oil, applied at high volume to control vigorously growing* Urtica dioica *(Common Nettle).*

5.109   *A mixture containing* **dicamba, 2,4-D-amine** *and* **2,4,5-T** *for the control of* Urtica dioica *(Common Nettle) in grass.*

5.110   **Sodium chlorate** *2·2 kg/45 litres of water for spot-control of* Urtica dioica *(Common Nettle).*

5.111   The susceptibility of weeds to herbicides used on established grassland

Category	Effect of chemical		Requirement of supporting management
S	Consistently good control (both shoot and roots)		Chemical treatment normally sufficient
MS	Aerial growth usually killed and a useful measure of long-term control obtained under suitable conditions		Extent of long-term control dependent on improved follow-up management
MR	Variable effect on aerial growth; appreciable long-term control unlikely		Radical changes of environmental conditions necessary to achieve control
R	No useful effect		

Weed species	Herbicide and dose (kg/ha)					
	MCPA-salt	2,4-D-amine/-ester	MCPB/2,4-DB-salt	Mecoprop-salt	Asulam	Benazolin/MCPA/2,4-DB
	1·6	1·4/1·0	2·2/2·2	2·8	1·2	4·5
Achillea millefolium (Yarrow)	MR	MR	R	MR	R	—
Allium vineale (Wild Onion)	MR	MR	—	MR	—	—
Bellis perennis (Daisy)	MS	MS	MR	MS	S	MS
Carex spp. (Sedges)	R	R	R	—	R	—
Centaurea nigra (Common Knapweed)	MS	MS	—	—	—	—
Cirsium acaule (Dwarf Thistle)	MR	MR	—	—	—	—
Cirsium arvense (Creeping Thistle)	MS	MS	MS	MS	R	MS
Cirsium vulgare (Spear Thistle)	MS	MS	MS	MS	R	—

Species						
Deschampsia caespitosa (Tufted Hair-grass)	R	R	R	R	R	R
Equisetum spp. (Horsetails)	MR	MR	MR	MR	MS	R
Filipendula ulmaria (Meadowsweet)	MR	MR	R	R	—	—
Hypochaeris radicata (Cat's Ear)	MS	MS	MS	MS	MS	—
Juncus articulatus (Jointed Rush)	R	R	R	R	R	—
Juncus conglomeratus (Compact Rush)	MS	—	MS	MS	—	—
Juncus effusus (Soft Rush)	MS	MS	MR	MR	MR	—
Juncus inflexus (Hard Rush)	MR	MR	R	R	R	—
Juncus squarrosus (Heath Rush)	R	R	R	R	R	—
Leontodon autumnalis (Autumn Hawkbit)	MS	S	S	MS	MR	MR
Plantago spp. (Plantains)	S	S	S	S	R	—
Prunella vulgaris (Self-heal)	MS	MS	MS	—	—	—
Pteridium aquilinum (Bracken)	R	R	R	R	S*	R
Ranunculus acris (Meadow Buttercup)	MS	MS	MS	MS	R	MS
Ranunculus bulbosus (Bulbous Buttercup)	MR	MR	MR	MR	R	MR
Ranunculus repens (Creeping Buttercup)	S	S	S	S	R	S
Rhinanthus minor (Yellow Rattle)	MR	MR	MR	—	—	—
Rumex acetosa (Common Sorrel)	MR	MR	MR	—	MS	—
Rumex acetosella (Sheep's Sorrel)	MR	MR	MS	MR	MS	—
Rumex crispus (Curled Dock)	MS	MS	MS	R	S	MS
Rumex obtusifolius (Broad-leaved Dock)	R	R	R	R	S	MS
Senecio jacobaea (Common Ragwort)	MR	MR	MR	MR	MS	—
Sonchus arvensis (Perennial Sow-thistle)	MR	MR	MR	—	MS	—
Taraxacum officinale (Dandelion)	MR	MS	MR	MR	MR	—
Urtica dioica (Common Nettle)	MS	MS	MS	MS	R	MS

* Use 4·4 kg/ha.

Chapter 6
Recommendations for weed control by herbicides in sports turf and lawns

Introduction

6.001   The use of herbicides is only one aspect of turf management and should not replace normal essential cultural operations. The application of herbicides cannot be expected to achieve desired results unless drainage, aeration, feeding and cultivation are correctly carried out. Information on turf management and some individual weed species is given in Volume I, Chapter 13. This chapter only contains recommendations for the chemical control of weeds, particularly with growth-regulator herbicides. The response of the commonest broad-leaved weeds to these herbicides, alone or in mixtures, is given in paragraph 6.016. Most paragraphs in this chapter relate only to organic herbicides—either for selective treatment of turf or non-selective use in seed bed preparation. There are, however, some paragraphs which deal with the use of ammonium sulphate and calcined ferrous sulphate in lawn sand.

Application of herbicides

6.002   Doses of active material are given either as the most commonly recommended dose or the range that may be used according to season, growth stage of weeds and turf, soil conditions and other factors. With commercial formulations, always follow the manufacturer's label recommendation. Too low rates of application for the sake of economy may be ineffective. Too high rates may kill off the tops of weed plants before the chemical can be translocated to the roots, at the same time damaging the turfgrasses.

For most herbicide application, except on small areas, it is normal to use a pressurized sprayer at medium volume (230–680 l/ha) and this volume is appropriate for applying all recommended treatments by sprayer, except where shown otherwise. When there is special need to wet the target plants thoroughly, this can be done with wetting agents or by spraying at volume rates of 500–1000 l/ha, provided that pressure is not increased so much as to cause drift hazards. For small areas a watering can fitted with a dribble-bar or a fine rose is often satisfactory, giving relatively little risk of drift (particularly with the dribble-bar) and applying volumes up to 2500 l/ha or even more. There are also special no-drift application machines which transfer liquid from the tank to the turf by means of a fluted roller. Some herbicides and herbicide/fertilizer mixtures are formulated as granules, and can be applied with a drop spreader where there are risks to adjacent areas. To reduce spray drift even in normal conditions, pressures should not exceed 2 bars. To minimize the effects of misses or overlaps, particularly on some fine turf areas where appearance is important, it is advisable to apply herbicides in two half-doses, one at right angles to the other.

Spot treatment of individual weeds such as *Plantago* spp. (Plantains) can be a risky procedure. Special equipment (e.g. aerosol packs) or special herbicide formulations are helpful, especially for non-professional use. If ordinary herbicide formulations are applied, whether with a watering can, a knapsack sprayer or a paint brush, even a professional user may have difficulty in ensuring accurate safe and effective treatment.

Chapter 13 in Volume I gives more information on method and volume of application and notes on season of application, weather conditions, and herbicide treatments in relation to times of fertilizer application and mowing.

Precautions

6.003   After spraying with growth-regulator herbicides, any grass clippings removed from the turf at the first four mowings should not be used directly as a mulch round broad-leaved plants or shrubs but may be incorporated into compost heaps, provided that they remain there for at least six months before use as compost for broad-leaved plants or shrubs. After the first four mowings no special precautions are needed.

Normal care is needed in all matters relating to drift onto adjacent susceptible plants, cleaning sprayers, safe storage of herbicides and operator safety as described in Volume I. Reminders on some important points are given below; more detail is given in Volume I, Chapter 13:

1 Avoid all drift of spray or vapour onto vegetables, flowers, fruit trees, bushes and shrubs. For plants and shrubs near to or overhanging lawn edges use no-drift application methods or protect with hardboard sheets, plastic bags, etc.; beware of drips.

2 Take great care near glasshouses, even with doors and ventilators closed.

3 Avoid contaminating water in tanks etc., by dipping into them watering cans or other equipment used for herbicides.

4 Store herbicides well away from other garden materials and all seeds and planting materials.

Preparations for sowing or turfing

6.004   **Paraquat** *1·1 kg/ha in medium volume to control most weeds.*
Established perennial weeds may be only checked. Diquat is more effective against some broad-leaved weeds but paraquat is preferable

where grass weeds predominate. Sowing or turfing three days after spraying is safe.

6.005 **[For information]**. Partial sterilization of the soil with materials such as methyl bromide or dazomet is effective in killing weed seeds. Methyl bromide can only be applied by specialist contractors; dazomet has not this limitation though safety recommendations must be followed. Soil temperature and other factors are important in treatments with both materials.

6.006 **[For information]**. Glyphosate at 1·5 kg/ha will control many grass weeds, particularly rhizomatous spp. such as *Agropyron repens* (Common Couch) and *Agrostis* spp. (Bents) and some broad-leaved weeds. Applications are most effective when made at or near the flowering period of the weeds. A good leaf area is essential for best results and if applications are made early in the season, or if broad-leaved weeds predominate, then rates should be increased to 1·8—2·2 kg/ha. The lack of persistence in the soil makes this a potentially useful treatment for seed bed preparation.

Seed beds

6.007 **Paraquat** *0·56—1·1 kg/ha in medium volume not less than three days before sowing.*
The lower rate of application can be used if only seedling weeds are present in the seed bed; otherwise the higher rate should be applied. Weeds that appear after sowing but before emergence of the grass seedlings may also be treated, though great care is needed in deciding the safety of such a treatment.

Newly sown turf

6.008 **MCPA-salt** *at 1·4 kg/ha;* **2,4-D-amine** *at 0·84 kg/ha;* **2,4-D-ester** *(low volatile) at 0·49 kg/ha;* **mecoprop-salt** *(alone or in mixture) at 1·4 kg/ha;* **dicamba-salt** *(only in mixture) at 0·14 kg/ha, to control weeds in (a) grass mixtures containing mainly ryegrass or other strong-growing grasses (e.g. creeping red fescue and timothy) which have at least two to three expanded leaves, (b) grass mixtures containing fine grasses (e.g. Chewings fescue and bents) after the sward is satisfactorily established and regular mowing has begun under normal good management.*
Doses should be determined by the stage of growth of the slowest developing species in the sward, and particular care is needed when applying herbicide mixtures. Turf sown in spring or early summer may be

ready for spraying after about two months, but turf sown in late summer or autumn should not be sprayed until growth is resumed in the following spring, perhaps eight months after sowing.

A young sward is very sensitive to environmental stresses and although herbicides can be used at an early stage, sward strength must be satisfactory, otherwise not only can direct damage occur, but the sward may also be affected in the long term. The doses recommended above can be increased as the grasses develop, up to the higher rates given in paragraph 6.016. Further information on the spraying of the coarser grasses is given in Chapter 5.

6.009   **Ioxynil-salt** *1·1 kg/ha on seedling grasses which have at least two fully expanded leaves.*

All species of commonly used turfgrasses with the exception of crested dogstail may be safely treated. One application is likely to kill seedlings of, among others, *Stellaria media* (Common Chickweed), *Matricaria* spp. (Mayweeds), *Cerastium holosteoides* (Common Mouse-ear), *Senecio vulgaris* (Groundsel), *Capsella bursa-pastoris* (Shepherd's-purse), and *Veronica* spp. (Speedwells). Seedlings of *Trifolium repens* (White Clover) and *Polygonum aviculare* (Knotgrass) are checked.

6.010   [**For information**]. Morfamquat at 1·7 kg/ha to control a range of seedling weeds, including *Medicago lupulina* (Black Medick), *Trifolium dubium* (Lesser Trefoil), *Lotus corniculatus* (Common Bird's-foot-trefoil) and *Veronica* spp. (Speedwells). It is not advisable to use it less than six weeks after sowing.

Newly laid turf

6.011   Newly laid, good quality turf should not be treated with selective herbicides until it is well established and growing normally; turf laid in autumn or winter should not be sprayed until the following spring.

Established turf

6.012   **MCPA-salt** *or* **2,4-D-amine** *or* **-ester** *(low volatile);* **mecoprop-salt** *or* **dichlorprop-salt;** *mixtures of* **2,4-D** *with* **mecoprop, dichlorprop, fenoprop** *or* **dicamba,** *and* **ioxynil-salt** *with* **mecoprop,** *for control of broad-leaved weeds at doses given in paragraph 6.016, during the growing season (normally April to September for most species) but avoiding periods of drought.*

Many common broad-leaved weeds are adequately controlled by 2,4-D. Mecoprop or dichlorprop are useful against *Trifolium repens* (White Clover), *Sagina procumbens* (Procumbent Pearlwort) and

Cerastium holosteoides (Common Mouse-ear). These are not adequately controlled by 2,4-D, which, on the other hand, does control weeds such as *Taraxacum officinale* (Dandelion), *Leontodon* spp. (Hawkbits), and *Bellis perennis* (Daisy) that are not well controlled by mecoprop or dichlorprop. When weeds from the two groups occur together mixtures of 2,4-D with mecoprop or dichlorprop should be used. The higher doses of mecoprop may give some temporary damage to the turf. Dicamba is particularly effective against *Polygonum aviculare* (Knotgrass). Ioxynil with mecoprop is specially useful against *Veronica* spp. (Speedwells), *Aphanes arvensis* (Parsley-piert) and the commonly occurring clovers and trefoils.

The weed responses in paragraph 6.016 may differ from those shown elsewhere in this Volume, as weeds in turf often need higher rates for control than in agricultural situations. If complete control of weeds is not obtained with one application of a herbicide treatment, further applications should be given at intervals of four to six weeks. Responses shown in Table 6.016 are of plants present at treatment, and do not take account of recolonization from seed or vegetative spread.

6.013   Growth-regulator herbicides are most effective if the weeds and grass are growing vigorously: the weeds are killed more rapidly and the grasses can fill the bare patches better. For this reason application of nitrogenous fertilizer 7–14 days before spraying is recommended. Compound mixtures of fertilizer and selective herbicide are available for greater convenience and economy of labour. They do not give any stimulus to the growth of grass or weeds before application of herbicide but grass growth is increased afterwards. Rain falling soon after treatment may make them less effective than separate applications, first of fertilizer then of herbicide.

6.014   Care is needed in relating herbicide treatments to mowing. On infrequently mown turf it is advisable to delay treatment until a few days before a cut is due, to give weeds time to produce maximum leaf area to absorb herbicide. On frequently mown turf, this point is less appropriate and although it is prudent to defer treatment if possible until the day after mowing—in case of any possible effect of herbicide on newly cut grass—many greenkeepers and groundsmen in fact mow fine turf and spray it the same day with apparent safety. After treatment, turf should not be mown for at least one day, and preferably two or three, to allow herbicide absorption by the weeds.

6.015   Some of these herbicides are liable to persist in the soil for a few weeks after treatment. Therefore, if bare patches have to be resown shortly after spraying, a higher seeding rate than normal is needed to compensate for any impaired germination that might be caused by the herbicide. However, where reseeding is not urgent, a six-week period between application and sowing is normally safe.

6.016 The susceptibility to herbicides of broad-leaved weeds in turf

Categories of weed susceptibility refer to the following herbicide doses:

MCPA	1·4 –2·8 kg/ha
2,4-D	1·1 –2·2 kg/ha
Mecoprop	2·2 –3·4 kg/ha

Herbicide mixtures:

2,4-D 0·75–1·7 kg/ha + { Mecoprop 1·5 –3·4 kg/ha
Dichlorprop 2·2 kg/ha
Fenoprop 1·1 –2·2 kg/ha
Dicamba 0·141–0·28 kg/ha }

Ioxynil-salt 0·63 kg/ha + Mecoprop 1·9 kg/ha

S = Consistently killed by one application
MS = Sometimes killed by one application but may require a second treatment to give complete control
MR = Some effect from one application but two or three often required to give an adequate control
R = No useful effect

Weed	MCPA-salt	2,4-D-amine and -ester	Mecoprop-salt	2,4-D plus mecoprop, dichlorprop, fenoprop or dicamba	Ioxynil plus mecoprop
Achillea millefolium (Yarrow)	MR	MR	MS*	MS*	MS
Aphanes arvensis (Parsley-piert)	R	R	MS*	MS*	S
Armeria maritima (Thrift)	S	S	S	S	—
Bellis perennis (Daisy)	MR	MS	MR	MS	MR
Cerastium holosteoides (Common Mouse-ear)	MS	MR	S	S	S
Cirsium acaule (Dwarf Thistle)	MS	MS	MR	MS	MS
Crepis capillaris (Smooth Hawk's-beard)	MS	MS	MS	MS	—
Erodium cicutarium (Common Stork's-bill)	MS	MS	MS	MS	—

6.016   The susceptibility to herbicides of broad-leaved weeds in turf (cont.)

Weed	MCPA-salt	2,4-D-amine and -ester	Mecoprop-salt	2,4-D plus mecoprop, dichlorprop, fenoprop or dicamba	Ioxynil plus mecoprop
Erodium maritimum (Sea Stork's-bill)	MS	MS	—	MS	—
Galium saxatile (Heath Bedstraw)	MS	MS	MS	MS	MS
Geranium molle (Dove's-foot Crane's-bill)	R	R	MR	MR	MS
Glaux maritima (Sea-milkwort)	MS	MS	S	S	—
Hieracium pilosella (Mouse-ear Hawkweed)	S	S	S	S	MS
Hydrocotyle vulgaris (Marsh Pennywort)	MS	MS	MR	—	—
Hypochaeris radicata (Cat's-ear)	MS	MS	MS	MS	MS
Juncus bufonius (Toad Rush)	R	R	R	MS	MS
Leontodon autumnalis (Autumn Hawkbit)	MS	MS	MR	MS	—
Leontodon hispidus (Rough Hawkbit)	MR	MS	MR	MS	—
Lotus corniculatus (Common Bird's-foot-trefoil)	R	R	MR	MR	MS
Luzula campestris (Field Wood-rush)	R	R	MR	MR	MR
Medicago lupulina (Black Medick)	R	R	MS	MS	MS
Plantago major (Greater Plantain)	S	S	S	S	s
Plantago media (Hoary Plantain)	S	S	S	S	s
Plantago lanceolata (Ribwort Plantain)	S	S	S	S	s
Plantago maritima (Sea Plantain)	S	S	MS	S	MS
Plantago coronopus (Buck's-horn Plantain)	S	S	S	S†	s
Polygonum aviculare (Knotgrass) { seedlings	MR	MR	MR	S†	s
mature plants	R	R	R	S†	MR

Species					
Potentilla anserina (Silverweed)	MS*	MS*	MS*	MS*	MS
Potentilla reptans (Creeping Cinquefoil)	MS*	MS*	MS*	MS*	MS
Prunella vulgaris (Selfheal)	MR	MR	MS	MS	MS
Ranunculus bulbosus (Bulbous Buttercup)	MS	MS	MR	MS	MR
Ranunculus ficaria (Lesser Celandine)	MS	MR	MR	MR	—
Ranunculus repens (Creeping Buttercup)	S	S	MR	S	MS
Rumex acetosa (Common Sorrel)	MS	MS	R	MS	MS
Rumex acetosella (Sheep's Sorrel)	MS	MS	R	MS	MS
Rumex crispus (Curled Dock)	MS	MS	MR	MS	—
Sagina procumbens (Procumbent Pearlwort)	MR	MR	S	S	S
Senecio jacobaea (Common Ragwort)	MS	MS	—	MS	—
Sherardia arvensis (Field Madder)	R	—	MS	MS	—
Soleirolia soleirolii (Mind-your-own-business)	R	R	MR	MR	MS
Stellaria media (Common Chickweed)	MS	MS	S	S	S
Taraxacum officinale (Dandelion)	MS	MS	MR	MS	MR
Trifolium dubium (Lesser Trefoil)	R	R	MR	MS*	MS
Trifolium repens (White Clover)	MR	R	MS	MS	S
Veronica chamaedrys (Germander Speedwell)	R	R	MR	MR	S
Veronica filiformis (Slender Speedwell)	R	R	MR	MR	S
Veronica serpyllifolia (Thyme-leaved Speedwell)	R	R	MR	MR	S

* Sometimes MR: doses at high end of range likely to be needed for MS.
† Dicamba mixtures.

Special weed problems (See also Volume I, Chapter 13)

Clovers and trefoils

6.017 **Ioxynil-salt** *0·63 kg/ha with* **mecoprop** *at 1·9 kg/ha to control* Lotus corniculatus *(Common Bird's-foot-trefoil)*, Medicago lupulina *(Black Medick)*, Trifolium dubium *(Lesser Trefoil) and* Trifolium repens *(White Clover)* (6.016).

6.018 **Mecoprop-salt** *2·2 to 3·4 kg/ha or mixtures of* **mecoprop, dichlorprop, fenoprop** *or* **dicamba** *with* **2,4-D** *(6.016), to control* Trifolium repens *in early summer when it is growing vigorously, and for partial control of the other species listed above.*

6.019 The two perennial species *Lotus corniculatus* and *Trifolium repens* can be adequately controlled by a single treatment per season of the appropriate herbicide, although some regrowth may occur in the following season, especially if the sward has not been treated with a nitrogenous fertilizer. Treatment of the two annual species *Medicago lupulina* and *Trifolium dubium* may be less successful, as they can re-establish at any time from seed in the ground.

Achillea millefolium (Yarrow)

6.020 **Mecoprop-salt** *at 2·2 kg/ha or mixtures of* **mecoprop, dichlorprop, fenoprop** *or* **dicamba** *with* **2,4-D***, or* **ioxynil** *with* **mecoprop** *(6.016).*
More than one application is likely to be necessary, and even then this weed is difficult to control, frequently showing vigorous regrowth from stolons.

Aphanes arvensis (Parsley-piert)

6.021 **Ioxynil-salt** *0·63 kg/ha with* **mecoprop-salt** *1·9 kg/ha on closely mown turf in the spring or autumn.*

6.022 **Lawn sand** *140 g/m² as recommended for moss (6.029) at any time during the growing season, but preferably late spring or early summer. If rain does not fall within two days, water thoroughly.*

Sagina procumbens (Procumbent Pearlwort)

6.023 **Mecoprop-salt** *2·8 kg/ha in high volume.*

Veronica filiformis (Slender Speedwell)

6.024 **Ioxynil-salt** *0·63 kg/ha with* **mecoprop** *at 1·9 kg/ha (formulated with* *wetting agent) to control* Veronica filiformis *(Slender Speedwell) on closely mown turf.*

Application should be made in the early spring (e.g. late March or early April) before the blue flower heads have formed. Heavy infestations will require repeat treatment. Application in early autumn will suppress the weed, but is less successful than in early spring. It is important to wet the foliage thoroughly; in addition to the wetting agent, application should be made with a pressurized sprayer, with a spray volume of 350 l/ha.

6.025 Lawn sand *as recommended for moss (6.029).*

Grass weeds

6.026 Certain weed species such as *Poa annua* (Annual Meadow-grass), *Holcus lanatus* (Yorkshire-fog) and *Holcus mollis* (Creeping Soft-grass) regularly occur in turf where they are unsightly and can seriously interfere with the playing qualities of sports turf. There is no adequate chemical control of these grasses but establishment of dense turf in a clean seed bed is the principal measure, followed by hand-weeding where practical and justified. There is further discussion of these weeds in Volume I, Chapter 13.

Moss

6.027 Moss can be controlled adequately only by a combination of cultural and chemical methods. Cultural treatments which contribute to the control of moss in turf, mainly by ensuring vigorous grass growth, are summarized below and discussed further in Volume I, Chapter 13.

   (i) Improvement of drainage (surface and sub-soil).
   (ii) Avoidance of unnecessary compaction.
   (iii) Correct fertilizer treatment.
   (iv) Liming over-acid soils.
   (v) Aeration.
   (vi) Not mowing too closely or scalping on uneven surfaces.
   (vii) Reduction of shade.

Although cultural practices can help to maintain freedom from moss, these alone are not always enough and chemical control becomes necessary. It is important to emphasize that chemical control may only be temporary. In order to obtain a permanent effect cultural treatments must also be practised.

6.028 Mosskillers can vary in effect from a quick contact 'scorch' of the moss (e.g. calcined ferrous sulphate) to a long-term effect, particularly by control of reproductive spores (mercurous chloride). Mixtures may be used, to combine both actions, and fertilizer added to stimulate grass growth. Nitrogen, particularly in spring, does much to ensure effective control. The combination of ferrous sulphate and nitrogen is generally described as a lawn sand; the same with the addition of mercurous chloride is mercurized lawn (or turf) sand; ferrous sulphate and mercurous chloride with little or no nitrogen is mercurized mosskiller. All these are bulked up with sand or other inert carrier.

Materials containing mercurous chloride will give more lasting control of moss than ordinary lawn sand, by persisting over several months and preventing re-establishment from spores. They can, therefore, be effectively applied throughout the year, although mercurized lawn sands containing more than slight amounts of nitrogen should not be used when nitrogen application is inadvisable, e.g. late autumn.

6.029 **Lawn sand** *140 g/m² on a dewy morning when the soil is moist and the weather fine and warm; at any time during the growing season but preferably in the early spring.*

If rain does not fall within two days, water thoroughly.

A suitable lawn sand mixture consists of:
  1 part calcined ferrous sulphate
  3 parts ammonium sulphate
 10 parts carrier (sand).

This treatment will control moss, but only temporarily. It may need to be followed by vigorous scarifying about two weeks after application to remove dead moss.

Formulations of balanced compound turf fertilizers with ferrous sulphate are also available.

6.030 **Mercurous chloride (calomel):** *(a) alone, at 0·7–1·2 g/m², or up to 2·2 g/m² for very heavy infestations, at any time of year but preferably in early autumn, (b) no less than 0·6 g/m² and desirably at least 1·0 g/m² in mercurized mosskillers or mercurized lawn sands (see 6.028 for definitions), preferably in spring.*

6.031 **[For information].** Dichlorophen at 1·7 g/m² kills moss in turf. Application may be made at any time but ideally in spring or autumn. Sprayer application being made in approximately 0·2 l/m² water or watering can application in 1·5 l/m².

Chapter 7
Recommendations for the control of herbaceous vegetation in non-agricultural land

Vegetation control

7.001   This chapter contains recommendations for the control or maintenance of herbaceous vegetation on roadside verges, grassed and planted areas on motorways, railway embankments, canal and river banks; also grassed areas on airfields, earthworks forming part of dams and reservoirs, golf course roughs, cemeteries, greens and commons, non-intensively managed areas round housing estates, military camps and similar areas. It complements the information given in the relevant chapters of Volume I of the handbook.

7.002   Management requirements are influenced by the considerations that, whilst the land may have a greater or lesser structural importance in relation to the primary land use, it is non-productive and the botanical composition of the vegetation is not of particular interest to the land manager. Chapters 5 and 6 refer to grassland situations where productivity and/or species composition are important.

7.003   Management of non-agricultural areas is aimed at vegetation control to broadly defined standards (e.g. of height or appearance), whilst weed control, as generally understood in other chapters of this handbook, does not apply except in very particular circumstances described below.

Objectives

7.004   Objectives of management are not often well defined. The over-riding factor in the future is likely to be cost. Costs can be justified where the management is practised for the sake of the primary land use (e.g. safety, prevention of obscuration of signs, fire hazard); they can also be justified in the interests of good neighbourliness and especially where there is a real need to control the spread of weeds and pests. Control for tidiness (including litter control) and amenity are becoming less easy to justify economically in rural areas, but are still important in built up areas. Conservation of wildlife (which can be accepted as an important secondary use of the land) benefits from less intensive management, and incidentally provides a useful additional argument for low cost programmes.

7.005   Thus when labour, money and materials are scarce it is important to define clearly the objectives of management for the various land uses. Once the objectives have been clearly decided, it will be possible to set the standards of management to satisfy them.

7.006   In some instances no cost-justifiable objectives may be found as, for example, on the lower slopes of rail and motorway embankments. If there are no objectives for management it is entirely reasonable to let the area grow wild.

Standards

7.007   It will be found that four simple standards of management cover the majority of objectives. These are related to the ecology of the vegetation, and its characteristic patterns of growth and development.

Standard a.   Coarse herbaceous vegetation with occasional control of encroaching scrub at intervals of more than one growing season. Where scrub is not controlled there will be a natural progression to secondary woodland with attendant problems of taller growth and additional shading. This standard is appropriate to the less easily seen areas, or as a contrast to more intensively managed vegetation.

Standard b.   Once yearly control of coarse herbaceous vegetation. This standard is appropriate where both scrub control and a once yearly tidy-up of plant growth are required. This is a common situation at the back of rural road verges. It is often necessary in order to give access to boundaries (hedges, fences, walls) and to ditches for their maintenance. On roads it is also of general importance in the overall preservation of the highway, which extends from boundary to boundary.

Standard c.   Maintenance of grass swards to an average height of 30–40 cm. This is appropriate to untrampled areas where the tallest vegetation is not acceptable. It is generally perfectly adequate for sight lines on roads, and again as a contrast to more intensively managed amenity and landscaped areas. This standard is related to the control of culm (flowering stem) growth of grasses and the height to which leaves of most British grasses grow as explained in Volume I, Chapter 14. It is the most economical standard involving regular management, needing only two (or at the most three) cuts with a mowing machine, or one application of a suitable growth retarder such as MH (Maleic hydrazide)*, and a subsequent cut.

---

* Maleic hydrazide is the only growth retarder commercially available at the time of writing.

Standard d. Maintenance of grass swards to an average height of 15–20 cm. This is appropriate again to untrampled areas but where, usually for amenity purposes, a higher standard of control than c) is thought necessary. Because the natural height to which most grasses grow is greater than 20 cm, a continuous mowing programme is necessary throughout the season, leading to considerably increased costs.

7.008 Standards of grass maintenance calling for control of growth at heights below 15 cm are management intensive and outside the scope of this chapter (see Chapter 6).

Management

7.009 The standards described above are generally quite easily achieved, although where timing is important there may be conflicts with scarcity of labour or machines, and priority given to the most important areas. As vegetation adapts over a period of years to the management it receives, it is an ecological principle that any area should consistently receive the same treatment each year. Thus, for the most economical and efficient management in the medium and long term the treatment for individual areas should be as carefully timed as possible, with the intention that similar timing should continue from season to season.

7.010 *Standard a.* Management for coarse vegetation with occasional scrub control depends on whether scrub has already invaded the area or not. Once scrub (particularly hawthorn, blackthorn, elm, privet, bramble and wild rose) is established it is increasingly difficult to manage the older it is (because of the bulk of material), and difficult to eradicate (because of the extensiveness of the root systems). The aim should be therefore to prevent establishment of bramble and scrub. This can be achieved by mowing (or burning where appropriate as on railway banks) as frequently as is necessary, depending on the locality and on seasonal inspections to determine the presence of seedlings in the vegetation. Control of established scrub is discussed in Chapter 8. There are a number of alternative methods employing hand labour, (heavy) machinery, or chemicals, alone or in combination.

Neither hand nor mechanical methods will kill scrub species except where the roots are physically dug out, involving considerable soil disturbance.

7.011 *Standard b.* Once yearly control of herbaceous vegetation. This can be achieved by burning or mowing. Burning is best done in the late winter (when it is often quite dry) and the sap is well down. Late autumn (end of August/September) and any dry periods during the winter are also suitable times for mowing, again when the sap is out of the taller herbaceous vegetation. With side-arm mowers, and particularly flails on extensible arms, ground conditions are not necessarily limiting, although they would be for rear mounted machines. Cutting in June or July when the vegetation is lush and full of growth is the most difficult and unsuitable period.

7.012   *Standard c.* The 30–40 cm height of vegetation standard can be achieved in most years in most parts of the country by mowing in mid- to late May and again in June, four to six weeks later. The date of the first cut depends on the season but it should not be made too early. Cutting in April is generally too early and has little influence on growth later in the season. In many seasons a single well-timed cut late in May is sufficient, but may be followed by a cut late in the season (late August onwards) to tidy up for the winter.

Chemical growth retarders such as Maleic hydrazide (MH) can be used in place of mowing (see paragraph 7.035) but it is usually necessary to cut or respray the vegetation in order to be sure of whole season control.

7.013   *Standard d.* The 15–20 cm height standard can be achieved by cutting or by use of chemicals. The frequency of management in any season depending upon growing conditions. However, with cutting it will probably be necessary to start in early May and continue at intervals of less than four weeks up to September. Where chemical control using MH is used, at least two applications will be required, probably with mowing of the vegetation at the beginning of the season before the first treatment.

Weeds

7.014   There are two classes of weeds in non-agricultural areas: these are broadly those plants that interfere with the primary land use, and those injurious agricultural weeds that might spread to neighbouring land.

7.015   So far as the first category is concerned many plants are called weeds because of their association with other land uses, but not because of any economic effects they might have on non-agricultural land. However, certain plants when they occur in particular situations (such as tall-growing Umbellifers on sight lines) might then be called weeds and justifiable measures taken to control them in those particular situations. Otherwise there are no plants that can be described generally and ubiquitously as weeds of the primary, non-agricultural land uses discussed in this chapter.

7.016   The control of the spread of *Rumex crispus* (Curled Dock), *Rumex obtusifolius* (Broad-leaved Dock), *Cirsium arvense* (Creeping Thistle), *Cirsium vulgare* (Spear Thistle) and *Senecio jacobaea* (Ragwort) is covered by the statutory provisions of the Weeds Act, 1959. The operation of this Act and a statement by the Ministry of Agriculture, Fisheries and Food about how it should be interpreted with reference to road verges and other non-agricultural areas are discussed in Volume I, Chapter 14. In no case is there an insistence on the eradication of plants, but only control of the spread of those weeds that might be the cause of an economic infestation in neighbouring crops. This presupposes that the weeds are not already present in the crop.

7.017   It is otherwise generally true to say that weeds as plants that have an economic effect on the land use are not an important component of the vegetation of non-agricultural areas. There is, therefore, no general requirement to manage the land for their control; especially where management is likely to unnecessarily affect the establishment of species and development of communities of otherwise innocuous and desirable wild plants.

Weed control

7.018   Weed control may be total or selective. Total weed control such as is required on railway tracks, around structures, sometimes in such places as under the guard rails of motorways, and to prevent obscuration of signs, is discussed in Chapter 9.

7.019   Selective weed control. Selective weed control is aimed at killing individual species without affecting others in the same sward. However, neither mechanical, nor chemical methods (with very rare exceptions), are so sophisticated that only the target species is affected and all others left alone as a result of a general treatment. For this reason *overall* cutting programmes or chemical spray applications are not recommended for the control of individual weed species on roadsides and similar places. The Department of the Environment specifically advises against overall selective spraying in its advice to County Councils on the management of road verges, in favour of localized spot applications by hand held equipment to individual specimens or clumps of the weed concerned. This is not so tedious as might appear and effects considerable savings in materials, cartage of water, and of labour.

NEWLY ESTABLISHED OR DISTURBED SWARDS

7.020   Whereas few plants in established non-productive grassland can be described as weeds, once the sward is disturbed, or when newly formed areas are sown, considerable populations of annual weedy plants may appear in the first two or three years after the event. In some circumstances the presence of these plants may represent a hazard to agricultural land, but more often their control is important in the interests of the development of the grass sward itself. It is recommended therefore that appropriate weed control measures should be taken in these situations over the first one to three years after sowing where weeds are interfering with sward development. However, as most of the species concerned depend upon soil disturbance and some element of open ground conditions, they will disappear naturally over a period of time. The matter of their control depends upon whether their presence can be tolerated for a limited period. Populations of many of these plants are also affected by the conventional mowing regimes likely to be used in the early stages of sward establishment, but there may nevertheless be a need for more specific measures including the use of herbicides (see below).

HAY AND SILAGE

7.021   There has been a steady decline since the end of the war in the usage of roadside grass for animal feed. Crops of grass for silage or animal feed have, on the other hand, been taken from grassed areas of military and civilian airfields for many years. The wastage of grass represented by the non-productive management of road and, more recently, motorway banks has caused some comment. It is recommended, in face of all the practical difficulties (including some pollution by lead and other chemicals), that advantage should be taken of any opportunity to manage the land by taking a crop from it.

Application of herbicides and growth regulators

7.022   Because of the dangers of spray drift and other hazards, the use of granular formulations of herbicides is recommended, where commercially available, in preference to sprays. Otherwise high volume (670–1100 l/ha) applications using low pressures, with special nozzles that operate efficiently down to 0·7 bars, are most safe and, because of the good coverage of the target plants, most effective. The alternative is to put the work out to specialist contractors.

Many of the treatments discussed below are for spot application (i.e. to individual plants) or localized application (i.e. generally to clumps of an individual species such as thistle or nettle), and it is visualized that these will be mostly made by knapsack sprayer. With these treatments timing of application and adequate coverage of the target plants are of the greatest importance. Rates of application are usually given in terms of weight of active material per unit area, but may in practice refer to dilution rates of active material in given volumes of water.

Employees and contractors who do the work should be properly briefed in the objectives, in the dangers to wildlife and amenity from incorrect applications, and instructed to stop work if there is any danger of spray drift onto adjoining land or contamination of water courses. Manufacturer's label recommendations for the use of commercial products should always be followed.

Specific weed problems

(See also Chapters 5 and 12 for detailed recommendations.)

INJURIOUS WEEDS LISTED IN THE WEEDS ACT, 1959

7.023 *Cirsium arvense* (Creeping Thistle) (12.045). Perennial. A characteristic plant of unmanaged coarse grassland, waste places and unimproved agricultural grassland. Quite easily controlled by mowing (Chapter 5), especially when large numbers of shoots arising from fragments of rhizomes have reached a height of about 45 mm, or soon after shoots have reappeared following a previous cut. Depending upon the age of the plants it is sensitive or moderately sensitive to MCPA at 1·7 kg/ha, and 2,4-D amine at 1·4 kg/ha. Complete kill may not be obtained from the first application and subsequent retreatments may be necessary. Commercial formulations of picloram at 0·29 kg/ha and 2,4-D amine at 1·1 kg/ha, or 2,4-D acid at 2·8 to 5·6 kg/ha in oil are effective at the respective manufacturer's recommended rates of application. Thistles are also susceptible to a wide range of other herbicides, many of which are not, however, generally available for non-agricultural uses (7.036). Where carefully controlled spot treatment of the individual plant is proposed, formulations of total herbicides are effective. Care must be taken to ensure that the persistence of some of these materials does not affect the colonization by more desirable plants of the area surrounding the dead plants.

7.024 *Cirsium vulgare* (Spear Thistle). Biennial spreading by seed and usually occurring as spaced individual plants, but may appear in colonies if the land is undermanaged. Suppression of flowering by mowing may lead to the vegetative rosette stage persisting for more than one season. Spear Thistle is sensitive or moderately sensitive, depending on stage of growth, to MCPA at 1·7 kg/ha, 2,4-D amine at 1·4 kg/ha and also to commercial formulations of picloram at 0·29 kg/ha plus 2,4-D amine at 1·1 kg/ha, or 2,4-D acid at 2·8 to 5·6 kg/ha in oil, at manufacturers recommended rates of application.

7.025 *Rumex crispus* (Curled Dock), *Rumex obtusifolius* (Broad-leaved Dock) (10.075, 12.075). Docks are perennial plants spread by seed which may remain viable in soil for upwards of 30 years. Seed may be spread by wind or water, in bird droppings, or in vegetation or soil transferred from one place to another. They can also be spread by regeneration of fragments of roots. The plants are able to establish and flower in the same season, even if regeneration is delayed until quite late in the season. They are serious weeds of grassland but are usually adequately controlled by normal husbandry in arable crops. Docks are not controlled by cutting which only stimulates proliferations of new growth from the crown at ground level. Established docks have deep tap roots and once these have developed the plants are difficult to kill in uncultivated land, even by chemicals. However, in the seedling or early regrowth from root fragment stages they can be killed quite easily by application of mecoprop, dichlorprop, or dicamba (normally available only in mixtures with other herbicides) at agricultural rates. Asulam at 1·1 to 1·7 kg/ha at full leaf stage (e.g. before the flowering stem is present), or dicamba at 0·84 kg/ha are effective against established docks, asulam being the more specific. However, complete control is unlikely from a single application and retreatment is almost certain to be required in the same or later seasons. Mecoprop at 2·8 kg/ha and dichlorprop at 2·8 kg/ha or commercial formulations containing mecoprop and dicamba, with or without MCPA, have been recommended for control of established docks. A commercial formulation of 2,4-D amine at 1·1 kg/ha and picloram at 0·29 kg/ha reduces regrowth more effectively than 2,4-D alone, whilst control has also been obtained from autumn or spring applications of maleic hydrazide at the equivalent of 5·6 kg/ha. As with thistles, directed spot treatments of total herbicides such as chlorthiamid or dichlobenil, atrazine, simazine, bromacil or terbacil will also kill dock (see Chapter 12).

7.026   *Senecio jacobaea* (Ragwort) (5.097). Ragwort is a biennial or perennial plant, the change in status occurring if normal flower stem and flower production is prevented (*inter alia*) by trampling or cutting in the second year. The plant is spread by seed or vegetatively by regeneration from root fragments. It is poisonous to cattle and horses and is avoided by rabbits. It is a plant of uncultivated places and is also characteristic of overgrazed grassland. Cutting and mowing only serve (as with docks) to stimulate adventitious buds, and to proliferate the stems arising from any one rootstock. Plants can be removed by pulling but must be carted away from any area where stock may have access to them, as they are as toxic (and often more attractive because of the relative increase in sugar content) in the wilted state, as living. Pulling is in any case a tedious process and one that land managers will wish to avoid where possible. Invasion of clean areas can be reduced or prevented by management that encourages a physical barrier (of dense grass growth) to weed seed germination and establishment. Ragwort can be controlled by MCPA salt or 2,4-D amine at 2·2 kg/ha or 2,4-D acid at 2·8 to 5·6 kg/ha in oil. Mecoprop or dichlorprop at 2·8 kg/ha, or a commercial formulation of picloram at 0·59 kg/ha plus 2,4-D amine at 2·3 kg/ha, are also effective. The same dangers of poisoning to stock from sprayed plants apply as to pulled plants, so that chemical treatment cannot be used on Common land (e.g. in the New Forest or Port meadows at Oxford) where removal of stock in the period after application is not possible.

INVASIVE PLANTS

7.027 *Anthriscus sylvestris* (Cow Parsley), *Heracleum sphondylium* (Hogweed) and some other tall growing Umbellifers are objected to by highway engineers where they obstruct sight lines. There are also other species in the family such as *Pastinaca sativa* (Wild Parsnip) which contain allergens to which certain people are sensitive; for this reason the plants are undesirable in the close proximity of housing. Several of the species with which we are concerned are biennials that are liable to behave as perennials if prevented from flowering in the second year. Others are perennial. They can generally be controlled by mowing and populations can be reduced over a number of years by mowing regimes that span the period of their maximum growth. Where this is impracticable or ineffective 2,4-D acid at 5·6 kg/ha in oil is effective or a commercial formulation of 2,4-D amine at 2·3 kg/ha with picloram at 0·59 kg/ha, applied at the manufacturers' recommended rate. Maleic hydrazide at 5·6 kg/ha applied at the appropriate time for the suppression of grass growth will also suppress *A. sylvestris* actively growing at the same time. Species such as *H. sphondylium* which develop later in the season are less likely to be satisfactorily controlled by April/May applications of maleic hydrazide.

7.028 *Epilobium hirsutum* (Great Willowherb), *Chamaenerion angustifolium* (Rosebay Willowherb). Both plants are perennials that spread aggressively under suitable conditions by seed, and vegetatively by creeping underground stems (stolons) or shoots from roots (rhizomes). *E. hirsutum* is commonly a weed of water courses and of damp ground, whilst *C. angustifolium* is an early colonizer of bare ground. Neither are serious weeds of agriculture although both can be a local problem in perennial horticultural crops. Neither species can be controlled by occasional cutting, but will disappear after a period of time if subjected to more intensive mowing regimes. Selective herbicides are not very effective but higher rates of the common total herbicides will kill the plants. Where applications of maleic hydrazide at 5·6 kg/ha plus 2,4-D at 3·9 kg/ha for grass growth control coincide with the susceptible growing stages of *E. hirsutum* and *C. angustifolium* control can be obtained after a number of seasons of treatment.

7.029 *Urtica dioica* (Common Nettle). Perennial spreading by seed and vegetatively by creeping stems. Usually an indicator of previous soil disturbance and high fertility. Not a weed of arable farming nor of improved grasslands. Mainly an amenity weed but valuable for wildlife;

also an occasional weed of the primary land use in non-agricultural land where height of vegetation is of serious concern. Can be controlled over a period of time by regular cutting and also by trampling to consolidate the ground. Top kill can be obtained by spraying with MCPA salt at 1·7 kg/ha or 2,4-D amine at 1·4 kg/ha, but repeated applications are necessary to kill complete plants. Mecoprop or 2,4,5-T at 0·23 kg/45 litres of water as drenching sprays in the autumn to isolated clumps or pure stands of nettle are effective; commercial mixtures of 2,4-D at 1·1 to 2·0 kg/ha with 2,4,5-T at 0·98 to 2·2 kg/ha in 273 to 455 litres of water to run-off as spot applications are considered to be even more efficient. There are also recommendations for the use of aminotriazole in late spring to reduce heavy infestations to a level where they can be dealt with easily by hand cutting, or before treatment with MCPA or 2,4-D at rates shown above.

7.030   *Pteridium aquilinum* (Bracken) (5.079). Perennial plants spreading by spores but mainly vegetatively by rhizomes. A very invasive plant on acidic soils in areas of former grass or heather, or in moderately shaded woodland. A serious weed of marginal agricultural land, poisonous to pigs and cattle and less severely to sheep. Also an amenity weed in non-agricultural land suppressing more useful or attractive vegetation, and a fire risk in some circumstances. *P. aquilinum* can be controlled by mowing or bruising twice a year over a number of years. It is not generally susceptible to the phenoxyacetic and related herbicides except at very high rates of application. It can, however, be controlled by asulam at 4·5 kg/ha in the period mid-July to mid-August, and by dicamba at 4·5–6·7 kg/ha. Aminotriazole at 5·6–8·4 kg/ha, and picloram at 2·2–3·4 kg/ha early in the season, have also given good results. In all cases, timings of application are quite specific: the different chemicals being effective at different stages in the development of the plants.

7.031   Scrub and bramble. Detailed recommendations are given in Chapter 8.

7.032   Control of dense infestations of the plants (especially nettle and bracken) noted in paragraphs 7.027 to 7.031 will often reveal very sparsely vegetated ground beneath them. It may be necessary to consider scarifying the ground to encourage invasion by grasses, or to seed these areas with desirable species before they become reinfested by the original plant or invaded by other weedy plants.

OTHER 'UNDESIRABLE' PLANTS

7.033   In addition to the species mentioned above there are a certain number of other plants about which complaints are made from time to time. Most of these are plants of bare or disturbed ground and may be either (a) like *Papaver* spp. (Poppies) or *Sinapis arvensis* (Charlock) agricultural weeds appearing ephemerally in the first few seasons after disturbance but very susceptible to common herbicides, or (b) like *Matricaria* and *Tripleurospermum* spp. (Mayweeds) and *Polygonum* spp. (Bindweeds and Knotgrasses) more persistent species that are resistant to the most commonly used chemicals. Others such as *Taraxacum officinale* (Dandelion) are natural constituents of occasionally to intensively managed grassland, or, like *Polygonum cuspidatum* (Japanese Knotweed) are alien species spreading throughout the country, notably in this instance along railway tracks.

7.034   In general, none of these plants pose economic problems. The disturbed ground plants will disappear naturally with the establishment of the grass sward. Dandelions are weeds of gardens and turf and, it can be argued, should be controlled there; they are naturally occurring wild plants of less intensively managed grassland. In addition they are often confused with other small yellow composites especially from the genera *Hieracium, Hypochoeris, Crepis* and *Leontodon* (Hawkweeds, Catsears, Hawksbeards and Hawkbits) that are quite innocuous.

   Polygonum cuspidatum is a very invasive tall growing plant, if at present not very widespread. It will probably respond over a period of time to cutting but, like the other Polygonaceae is resistant to the commoner selective herbicides and also to the urea and triazine total herbicides. It is moderately susceptible to higher rates (9·0–12·0 kg/ha) of bromacil, and can be controlled in the early pre-emergent stages by picloram at 0·84 kg/ha, or post-emergence after the beginning of May by picloram at 1·4–2·2 kg/ha plus 2,4-D at 3·4 kg/ha. Dicamba at 4·5 kg/ha applied in the spring when the weed is 1·0–1·5 metres high has also been found to be effective.

Growth retarders (See also Chapter 13)

7.035   Growth retarders may be either cell division inhibitors such as maleic hydrazide, or morphactins which interfere with plant co-ordination and inhibit apical growth such as chlorflurecol-methyl. Both types of compound are likely to be critical as to the timing of their application and the most sensitive stage of growth. The objective in their application is to slow down the growth of the plants and suppress flowering, rather than to kill them.

   In the process of inhibiting growth, aggressive, dominant, species tend to be affected more than the less aggressive. This can lead to interesting ecological changes in a sward as a result of which tall growing grasses and other plants may be replaced by species that are naturally shorter growing. In this way height of the sward can be reduced both by inhibiting growth, and by selecting for lower growing species. However, changes of this kind only occur over a number of years of continuous treatment, and it has to be recognized that the most efficient use of growth-retarders involves this element of continuity. If, after a period of years of use of maleic hydrazide, its use is stopped, there may be quite a rapid return to the pre-existing situation with the re-establishment of aggressive, taller growing species.

Maleic hydrazide is applied at 5·6 kg/ha in the period mid-March to early May, depending upon growing conditions, for control of grass growth over the next 10–14 weeks. The aim is to apply the material to plants at an active stage of growth but before they have put on too much growth, and in particular before culm (flower stem) extension has begun. If application is too early, the culm primordia may not have been formed or it may not be in a susceptible stage.

A disadvantage of maleic hydrazide in the past has been the possibility of the material being washed off plants by heavy rain falling within 12–18 h of application. Recent formulations are claimed to be rainfast within 2 h of application. Nevertheless, so far as it is practicable, as long a rain-free period as possible should be looked for immediately after application.

Where tall growing herbaceous plants are present in the sward and are known not to be affected by maleic hydrazide, the selective weedkillers MCPA or 2,4-D at 3·9 kg/ha may be added to the spray. There are indications that the height of vegetation sprayed with the mixture remains shorter than vegetation sprayed with maleic hydrazide alone. This may be due to the effect of the 2,4-D or MCPA on broadleaved plants, and possibly as well to a synergistic effect of the mixture on the principal grasses. However, the relatively small extra benefit obtained in this way has to be set against the wide range of non-target wild plants that will be killed by the selective herbicides. For this reason there are strong arguments on conservation grounds against the widespread practice of adding 2,4-D to maleic hydrazide, unless there are over-riding economic reasons for doing so.

In the past, recommendations have also existed for the standard inclusion of 2,4-D with maleic hydrazide in order to increase the rainfastness of the latter (2,4-D being rapidly absorbed by susceptible plants). With the modern formulations of maleic hydrazide referred to above there is no longer a need to add 2,4-D for this purpose.

Selective herbicides

7.036   Earlier paragraphs have noted the usefulness of 2,4-D and other selective herbicides *as localized or spot applications* to particular problem plants in non-agricultural land. At the same time it has been emphasized, and is again here, that *overall general sprays* of these materials on the areas referred to in this chapter are not recommended, whether applied alone or in mixtures with maleic hydrazide or other compounds.

In other sections of the handbook dealing with agricultural situations more compounds are recommended for individual weed problems than have been listed in this chapter. The intention here has been to mention only those materials that are currently and satisfactorily in use, and are commercially available for non-agricultural situations. Thus, for example, ester formulations of 2,4-D have been deliberately excluded because of the volatility problems (however slight) associated with them. This has been done partly because local authorities and other public bodies are especially sensitive to public criticism; any herbicide damage arising in an area where these chemicals had been used might well be blamed onto them, whether they were in fact responsible or not. Nevertheless, it is recognized that the lower volatile formulations such as butoxy ethyl and iso-octyl esters of 2,4-D do present a minimal hazard and might be considered for use at 0·98 to 1·5 kg/ha for control of troublesome species such as *Senecio jacobaea* (Ragwort) in areas (but not for instance on roadsides) where there was unlikely to be criticism from individuals or the public generally. The application of these materials in the quite different situations presented by lawns and sports turf is discussed in Chapter 6.

Chapter 8
Recommendations for the use of herbicides in forestry and for scrub control

Section I Forest nurseries

Index to herbicides

8.001 The following table covers the main herbicides recommended for forest nurseries.

Type of treatment	Herbicide	Weeds controlled	Paragraph
Seedbeds Pre-sowing:	Formalin	May reduce viable weed	8.002
	Dazomet	seeds	8.003
	White spirit/ vaporizing oil	Seedling weeds	8.004
	Paraquat		8.005
Seedbeds Pre-emergence:	White spirit/ vaporizing oil		8.006
	Simazine	Germinating weeds	8.008
	Paraquat		8.009
Seed beds Post-emergence:	White spirit/ vaporizing oil		8.011–8.012
	Simazine (on seedlings > 1 year old and > 5 cm tall)	Germinating weeds	8.013
Transplant lines	Atrazine	Germinating weeds	8.017
	Simazine		8.018
	Paraquat	Seedling weeds	8.019
	White spirit/ vaporizing oil	Seedling weeds	8.021
Poplar and willow cutting and seed beds	White spirit/ vaporizing oil	Seedling weeds	8.023
	Simazine (not poplar	Germinating weeds	8.024
Established poplar and willow	Simazine	Germinating weeds	8.025
			8.026
Beds	Dalapon	Established grasses	
Ornamental trees	See Chapter 3		8.030
Fallow land	TCA Aminotriazole Sodium Chlorate MCPA/2,4-D Paraquat	Established annual and perennial weeds choice depends on whether grasses or broad leaved predominate	8.031
Non-crop land			8.033

Seedbeds

PRE-SOWING TREATMENTS

8.002 **Formalin,** *for soil sterilization as a soil drench applying 250 litres/ha of commercial 38 per cent formalin.*

Applied to the seedbed at least 3 weeks and preferably 6 weeks before sowing to improve growth of tree seedlings, particularly on light-medium loam soils which are neutral or only slightly acid. Such treatments may also reduce the emergence of weeds during the season of treatment.

8.003   **Dazomet** *220–340 kg/ha granular formulation incorporated in the soil to a depth of 150–200 mm in September to November in the year before sowing.*

Soil temperatures should be 7°C or over at the time of incorporation. Immediately after incorporation the soil surface should be 'sealed', preferably with plastic sheeting, or alternatively by watering and rolling. The seal must be effective for at least 2 weeks. The soil should be rotovated to break the seal and release toxic gases at least 6 weeks before sowing.

This chemical is used as a soil sterilant, and where control of weeds only is required more effective and less-costly herbicides should be used.

8.004   **Vaporizing oil** *400–700 litres/ha at any time to within 4 or 5 days of sowing for control of most weeds which have emerged.*

The seedbed should be prepared early in the season, several weeks in advance of sowing, to allow weed seeds to germinate.

8.005   **Paraquat** *0·5–1·0 kg/ha formulated with a wetter at medium volume for control of most weeds which have emerged.*

The higher doses are recommended where weeds are beyond the seedling stage.

PRE-EMERGENCE TREATMENTS

8.006   **Vaporizing oil** *as a contact herbicide 400–700 litres/ha 3–4 days before crop emergence to kill most annual weeds that have emerged.*

If, on excavation, germinating crop seeds have radicles 12 mm long, they will probably begin to emerge in 3–4 days; this simple test gives a guide to the latest safe date for spraying. In many cases earlier spraying will be justified, and in general, spraying should be done as soon as an appreciable number of weeds have emerged. It is quite safe to apply two or more sprays as long as the last one is applied no later than 3–4 days before crop seedling emergence.

8.007   [**For information.**] Nitrofen can be applied at 4 kg/ha immediately after sowing direct onto the surface of the seed bed for the control of germinating weeds. It is only effective when applied to moist soils.

8.008   **Simazine** *2·2 kg/ha pre-emergence to seedbeds of oak, beech and sweet chestnut (i.e. large-seeded hardwood species which are covered with 25–50 mm of soil following sowing) and before weeds emerge.*

Simazine has seldom been used on hardwood beds but this reflects the very small proportion of hardwoods currently used in forestry.

8.009 **Paraquat** *0·5 kg/ha formulated with a wetter as a contact herbicide at medium volume 3–4 days before crop emergence to seedbeds of either hard wood or coniferous species to kill weeds that have emerged.*

While pine species in particular can be treated with vaporizing oil with little ill-effect, immediately after emergence, when the seedcoats are still attached, paraquat used in the same way will cause severe losses. Very little work has been done on hardwood seedbeds, where seed is covered with soil instead of grit. However, there is no reason to expect that these recommendations will not be equally satisfactory.

8.010 [**For information.**] Diphenamid at 4·0 kg/ha applied immediately after sowing as a pre-emergent spray direct onto the surface of the seed bed has been successfully used. Diphenamid is most effective when applied to a moist soil. It is only recommended for use on tolerant conifer spp. in seed beds.

POST-EMERGENCE TREATMENTS

8.011 *Petroleum distillate/white spirit*

White spirit of the type similar to those used for spraying carrots (Chapter 2) *to control annual weeds in seedbeds of several conifer species.*
Tree species can be grouped according to their resistance to such oils.

Group I. Resistant (dose: 280 litres/ha):

Chamaecyparis lawsoniana	(Lawson Cypress)
Picea abies	(Norway Spruce)
Picea sitchensis	(Sitka Spruce)
Pinus mugo	(Mountain Pine)
Pinus nigra var. *maritima*	(Corsican Pine)
Pinus sylvestris	(Scots Pine)
Thuja plicata	(Western Red-cedar)

Group II. Moderately resistant (dose: 168 litres/ha):

Abies procera	(Noble Fir)
Abies grandis	(Giant Fir)
Larix decidua	(European Larch)
Larix leptolepis	(Japanese Larch)
Pinus contorta	(Lodgepole Pine)
Pseudotsuga taxifolia	(Douglas Fir)
Tsuga heterophylla	(Western Hemlock)

Group III. Sensitive (should not be sprayed):
Hardwood species.

The first application may normally be made no sooner than 4 weeks after emergence is complete. Generally, the resistance of the trees increases with age, although the most resistant species can safely be sprayed while the cotyledons are enclosed in the seed coats. While the seed coats are being shed and immediately afterwards, there is a period of extreme susceptibility, but this will pass in 3 or 4 weeks as the tree develops, depending on growing conditions; freshly acquired resistance is usually accompanied by a slight darkening in colour. Seedlings must not be sprayed in times of drought or very bright, hot sun. The soil should be moist (natural or by watering) though the foliage should be dry. If the foliage of crop and weed seedlings is wet, the treatment will be somewhat less effective than under cool, dry conditions but it will not damage the crop species. If damage occurs it usually consists of scorched leaves or slight stunting of growth without scorch.

It is important that normal hand-weeding is not neglected during the period when sprays cannot safely be applied, as the first permissible spray will be effective only against newly-germinated weeds. Frequency of spraying will be governed by the development of the weed population and sprays should be applied as required up to a maximum of six in one season. Weeds surviving two spray treatments should be regarded as resistant and be removed by hand. The doses recommended will control most annual weeds while they are young, the best control being obtained when they are in the cotyledon (seed-leaf) stage. Older annual weeds and perennial weeds may be scorched and checked in growth but will usually survive.

8.012 **White spirit** *to seedbeds in their second year at the same doses as for first-year beds* (8.012) *at any time except in the 4 weeks following bud-break.*

Sprays are likely to be ineffective if there is a dense cover of seedling foliage to prevent the spray reaching the young weeds. White spirit has been used on a small scale for over 12 years.

8.013 **Simazine** *to seedbeds in their second year 1·0 kg/ha in medium to high volume subject to the same provisions that are made for transplants* (8.018).

Simazine is not widely used on second-year seedbeds.

8.014 [**For information.**] Diphenamid has shown promise at 4·0 kg/ha applied after full emergence of crop seedlings for the control of germinating weeds. Repeated applications can be made at intervals of 6 weeks.

8.015 [**For information.**] Nitrofen at 4·0–6·0 kg/ha has shown promise when applied after full emergence of crop seedlings. Cool moist conditions are necessary for weed control.

8.016 [*For information.*] Propyzamide at 1·6 kg/ha has been successfully used after seedlings have hardened off in the months of October to December. This treatment is useful in standover seed beds and will control annual as well as perennial weeds.

Transplant lines

POST-PLANTING TREATMENTS

8.017 **Atrazine** *4·0–6·0 kg/ha in medium volume or as granules to transplants from February to May to control most fine grasses and some seedling broad-leaved weeds.*

Most tree species tolerate atrazine although Norway Spruce, Western Hemlock and European Larch should only be treated at the lowest dose.

8.018 **Simazine** *1·0–2·2 kg/ha in medium to high volume to transplants at any time in late winter or spring when the soil surface is moist for the control of annual weeds* (Chapter 3).

The ground should be free from weeds at the time of spraying.

A second spray at the lower dose may be applied in July, August or September to ground carrying crops that will not be disturbed until the following spring, provided that a minimum period of 4 months has elapsed from the first spray. Simazine may be applied as late as October or November to crops which are to remain undisturbed in the succeeding year. A second application should only be made when it is clear that young weeds have recently germinated and have become established. Existence of a few healthy large weeds, especially of deep-rooted species, is no indication that simazine has disappeared. Before any second application, the ground should be lightly cultivated to kill those weeds present.

The following species may be sprayed:

Norway and Sitka spruce, Scots, Corsican and Lodgepole pine, Douglas fir, Lawson cypress, Western red cedar, Western hemlock, Hybrid and Japanese larch, Noble fir, Grand fir, oak, birch, beech and Sweet chestnut.

European larch and *Picea omorika* are more susceptible and should not be sprayed with simazine at more than 1·1 kg/ha in medium to high volume.

The following must not be sprayed:

(i) Ash, unrooted cuttings of poplar.
(ii) All plants less than 50 mm tall at the time of spraying.

Simazine has been widely used in transplant lines for 9–10 years. It has generally supplanted directed mineral oil sprays (8.021).

8.019   **Paraquat** *0·5–1·0 kg/ha formulated with a wetter in medium to high volume as a directed inter-row application using special application equipment which shields the spray and prevents it reaching the crop.*
Paraquat is used only to a limited extent in transplant lines.

8.020   [**For information.**] Diuron 1·82 kg/ha plus paraquat 0·56 kg/ha, as a formulated mixture, has been used successfully with negligible crop damage. It has been sprayed at medium to high volume as a directed inter-row application using similar equipment to that required by paraquat alone (8.019).
A wide range of seedling grasses and herbaceous broad-leaved weeds are controlled, and the persistence of diuron helps to prevent re-invasion.

8.021   **White spirit** *or* **vaporizing oils** *directed to the spaces between the rows of plants, minimizing the amount reaching young tree foliage, to most common conifer species at any time.*
Hardwood species may only be sprayed in the dormant season. It is important to treat weeds at an early stage of development. A week or a fortnight later the area should be weeded by hand or machine to remove any surviving large weeds. Thereafter, if subsequent spray applications are properly timed, little hand-weeding should be necessary.
White spirits or vaporizing oils may be used as inter-row sprays as follows:

	Bud-break to mid-June	*Mid-June to end of season*	*Dormant season*
Hardwoods	Not safe	Not safe	Vaporizing oil 450 litres/ha
Douglas fir	White spirit,	White spirit,	Vaporizing oil,
Larches	300 litres/ha	450 litres/ha	450 litres/ha
Pine		or	
Tsuga		vaporizing oil,	
Firs (*Abies* spp.)		300 litres/ha	
Spruces	White spirit	White spirit	Vaporizing oil,
Lawson cypress	or	or	450 litres/ha
Thuja	vaporizing oil,	vaporizing oil,	
	300 litres/ha	450 litres/ha	

NB. Plants of any species less than 125 mm in height should not be sprayed at doses exceeding 300 litres/ha during the growing season.

8.022   [**For information.**] Propyzamide at 1·5 kg/ha (Scotland and Northern England) and 2·0 kg/ha (S. England and Wales) as a 4 per cent granule or as a 50 per cent wettable powder has been successfully used for weed control in transplant lines of Sitka spruce, Norway spruce, Corsican pine, Scots pine, *Larix* spp., Douglas fir, *Quercus* and *Fagus* spp., when applied between mid October and late January.

Poplar and willow cutting beds, nursery stool-beds and lines

8.023 **Vaporizing oil** *680 litres/ha, or pentachlorphenol 2·2 to 4·5 kg/ha in cutting beds of willow and cutting and transplant lines of poplar and willow as a directed spray to control annual weeds.*
The treatment may be repeated as often as required during the growing season.

8.024 **Simazine** *2·2 kg/ha in medium volume in first-year beds of willow (but not poplar) in the spring to control annual weeds soon after insertion of cuttings.*

8.025 **Simazine** *2·2–4·5 kg/ha in the spring in established stool-beds of poplar and established beds of willow to control annual weeds.*

8.026 **Dalapon-sodium** *10·0–13·0 kg/ha in medium volume as a directed spray in poplar stool-beds shortly before bud-break of the crop to control perennial grasses.*
See paragraphs 8.095–8.097 for control of weeds in commercial basket-willow beds.

8.027 [**For information.**] Glyphosate at 2·0 kg/ha has been successfully used for the control of annual and perennial weeds in poplar stool beds. The spray must be directed to avoid contact with any poplar growth.

8.028 [**For information.**] Paraquat can be applied at 1·0 kg/ha to poplar stool beds for the control of annual weeds and foliage of perennial weeds. The spray must be directed to avoid any foliage or new bark of the poplar.

8.029 [**For information.**] Propyzamide has been successfully used in medium volume in first year beds of poplar cuttings and stool beds at 1·5 kg/ha. Application must be made from October to December and annual and perennial grass weeds will be controlled.

Areas carrying ornamental trees

8.030 Recommendations for weed control in beds of ornamental species are made in Chapter 3.

Fallow land

8.031 The fallow area in the nursery rotation provides a useful opportunity for attacking the perennial weed population by a combination of cultivation and chemical control. *Agropyron repens* (Common Couch) and

Ranunculus repens (Creeping Buttercup) present in the nursery can be reduced or eradicated using dalapon, TCA, aminotriazole or sodium chlorate for the former, and MCPA or 2,4-D for the latter, following the recommendations given in Chapter 12 for these particular species. Aminotriazole will also control certain perennial broad-leaved weeds. Where dalapon or aminotriazole are used, sowing or transplanting should normally be deferred for 8 weeks after application or, if exceptionally dry, for 12 weeks. Other perennials, for example *Rumex acetosella* (Sheep's Sorrel), can be controlled by sodium chlorate applied at a dose of 250 kg/ha as spray. This treatment will also control any established annual weeds present at the time of spray. Notes on the use of sodium chlorate and the relative susceptibility of weeds to it are given in Chapter 9. Six months should be left between application of sodium chlorate and sowing or transplanting.

Where annual weeds only are present, these may be controlled most cheaply by regular cultivation. Another effective but more expensive method of control is sprays of paraquat at 1·1 kg/ha formulated with a wetter in medium volume. This should be applied as an overall spray to fallow land after encouraging maximum weed emergence. Repeated applications will often be necessary and these should be applied soon after weed regrowth is observed. Such repeat treatments may be applied to individual weedy patches (spot treatments) or may need to be applied over the whole area. Sowing or transplanting can be carried out immediately after the final treatment.

8.032   Glyphosate at 1·4 kg/ha, as a 36 per cent w/v concentrate can be used to control grasses and herbaceous broad-leaved weeds in fallow land.

Non-crop land in and around forest nurseries

8.033   Weeds on uncultivated land, notably paths, fence lines, and the surrounds of buildings, are often overlooked as important sources of weed seed infection in forest nurseries. Weeds in such situations are frequently difficult to control by cutting or cultivation, and non-selective, persistent herbicides, can be used with advantage in early spring to control most annual weeds and keep the sites free from seedling weeds for 12 months or more. Such chemicals can be applied close to the boundaries of cultivation without risk to crops, as there is little or no lateral movement of the chemical in the soil.

Fuller details of treatment are given in Chapter 9.

Section II Forests

Equipment

8.034   For most of these operations, agricultural spraying equipment is unsuitable because of the topography. Knapsack sprayers or other specialized portable equipment, whether motorized, pneumatic, continuously pumped, powered by electric batteries or emptied by gravity are very widely used. Most spraying is at medium volumes and the lowest possible working pressure. Most frequently selective materials are used, but on occasion, selectivity for non-selective materials is obtained by using guards which prevent the spray reaching the tree, whilst treating the immediately adjacent vegetation.

There are few opportunities for aerial application of herbicides in forestry; although in the private sector 2,4,5-T or proprietary 2,4-D/2,4,5-T mixtures are sometimes applied, by fixed wing aircraft or helicopter. They are applied from the air to check the growth and reduce the shade cast by large woody weeds, for example, trees of oak or coppice regrowth of hazel. 2,4,5-T or 2,4-D/2,4,5-T mixtures are also sometimes applied aerially for the control of large areas of *Ulex* spp. (Gorse) *Sarothamnus scoparius* (Broom) or *Betula* spp. (Birch) either prior to planting or selectively in young plantations of softwoods. There are also occasions when 2,4-D or 2,4-D/2,4,5-T mixtures are applied by air in order to control large areas of *Calluna vulgaris* (Heather) either prior to planting or more commonly in spruce plantations. The smaller areas are commonly treated by motorized knapsack mistblowers. Herbicides based on 2,4,5-T and 2,4-D have been specially formulated for ultra-low volume application, without the addition of water, by means of hand-held rotary atomizers. Rotary atomizers may also be used to apply suspension concentrate formulations of atrazine as very low volume sprays for the control of grassy weeds or mixtures of cyanazine/atrazine for the control of grassy and herbaceous non-woody broad-leaved weeds.

While granular herbicides may be applied by hand, this often leads to inaccuracies both in application and distribution. Motorized knapsack granular applicators are now widely used, and on level ground tractor mounted granular applicators are preferred to knapsacks.

Index to herbicides

8.035   The herbicides used for controlling weeds in forests are most conveniently considered according to the weed type first, and then the situation as follows:

Weed type	Situation	Herbicide	Paragraph
Grasses and herbaceous weeds	Pre-planting	Dalapon	8.041
		Paraquat	8.042–8.043
		Chlorthiamid	8.045
		Dichlobenil	8.046
		Atrazine	8.048
		Cyanazine/Atrazine	8.049
		Glyphosate	8.050
		Propyzamide	8.044
	Post-planting	Dalapon	8.051
		Paraquat	8.052
		Chlorthiamid	8.053
		Dichlobenil	8.054
		Atrazine	8.055
		Cyanazine/Atrazine	8.056
		Propyzamide	8.057
Bracken	Pre-planting	Asulam	8.062
		MCPA	8.063
	Post-planting	Asulam	8.064
		Chlorthiamid/	8.065
		Dichlobenil	8.065
		Paraquat	8.066
Heather	Pre-planting	2,4-D	8.077
(*Calluna* and *Erica* spp.)		Paraquat	
	Post-planting	2,4-D	8.080
		Paraquat	8.084
Woody weeds			
(i) Foliage spraying	Pre-planting	2,4,5-T/2,4-D/	8.075–8.078
		2,4,5-T mixtures.	
		Ammonium sulphamate	
	Post-planting	2,4,5-T/2,4-D/	8.079–8.083
		2,4,5-T mixtures.	
(ii) Dormant shoots	Pre-planting	2,4,5-T	8.085
(iii) Basal-bark sprays	Pre- and post-planting	2,4,5-T	8.086
(iv) Frill girdling, notching or tree injection	Pre- and post-planting	2,4,5-T	8.087–8.089
		Ammonium sulphamate	
		2,4-D	
(v) Cut stumps	Pre- and post-planting	2,4,5-T	8.090
		Ammonium sulphamate	8.091

Grasses and herbaceous broad-leaved weeds

8.036   Grasses, either in pure stands, or mixed with herbaceous broad-leaved weeds are widespread in young plantations and by competing with the young trees for light, water and nutrients can have a detrimental effect upon the annual growth of the trees. There is the added danger that a lush weed growth may smother the trees in the autumn.

It is not common to find herbaceous broad-leaved weeds without grasses—though areas of pure *Chamaenerion angustifolium* (Rosebay Willowherb) for example, often occur locally.

Chemicals available to control such weeds are paraquat, dalapon, chlorthiamid, dichlobenil, atrazine, cyanazine/atrazine and propyzamide. These herbicides are used mainly post planting. Dalapon and atrazine have little effect upon broad-leaved weeds. Chlorthiamid, dichlobenil, cyanazine/atrazine and propyzamide will control both grasses and herbaceous broad-leaved weeds.

The susceptibility of common forest grasses to herbicides

8.037 Grass weeds are of much greater importance than herbaceous broad-leaved weeds and the dominant spp. of grass should dictate the choice of herbicide.

In the following table the susceptibility of common forest grasses to recommended herbicides is given on the basis of satisfactory weed control persisting for one growing season after application of the herbicide. It is

S = Susceptible: control should be excellent.
MS = Moderately susceptible: control should be adequate.
MR = Moderately resistant: control often inadequate.
R = Resistant: little effect or control obtained.

Grass species	Paraquat 1·1 kg/ha	Dalapon 11·2 kg/ha	Chlorthiamid/ dichlobenil 4·5 kg/ha	Atrazine 4 5 6 7 kg/ha kg/ha
Agropyron repens	MR	MS	MS	MR
Agrostis gigantea	MS	MS	MS	MS
Agrostis spp.	MS	S	S	S
Anthoxanthum odoratum	MS	S	MR	S
Arrhenatherum elatius	MS	S	S	MR
Calamagrostis epigejos	R	MR	MR	R
Dactylis glomerata	MR	MS	MS	MR
Deschampsia caespitosa	MS	MS	MS	R
Deschampsia flexuosa	S	S	S	S
Festuca arundinacea	MS	MS	S	MS
Festuca pratensis	MS	MS	S	MS
Festuca ovina	MS	MS	S	S
Festuca rubra	MS	MS	S	S
Holcus lanatus	MS	S	S	MS
Holcus mollis	MR	MS	MS	MR
Molinia caerulea	S	S	MS	R
Poa annua	MS	MS	S	S
Poa pratensis	MS	MS	S	MS
Poa trivialis	MS	MS	S	S

accepted that the performance of each herbicide will vary with soil type, weather conditions and time of application. The relative susceptibilities are a guide only, and assume that the herbicide will be used as recommended in the text.

8.038   [**For information.**] Cyanazine—atrazine mixtures can be used at combined rates of 5·4—7·2 kg/ha as either a wettable powder or suspension concentrate for the control of forest-grass weeds including *Anthroxanthum odoratum* (Sweet Vernal-grass).

8.039   **Propyzamide** *as a 50 per cent wettable powder or a 4 per cent granule applied at 1·5—2·0 kg/ha gives the same control of the common forest grasses as that with chlorthiamid or dichlobenil.*

8.040   In forestry the total area is rarely treated. The young trees are usually planted at a spacing of about 2 × 2 m, and the herbicides are applied to strips or patches with the young trees planted in the middle of the treated areas. This substantially reduces the cost of chemical per hectare planted.

Grass and herbaceous broad-leaved weed control before planting

8.041   **Dalapon-sodium** *12·5 kg/ha in medium volume up to 3 weeks before planting without serious risk of damage to the crop while the grass is growing at least fairly vigorously.*
    Best results are likely if the spray is applied not more than 6 weeks before planting. Sprays may be applied in September or October for autumn planting, or in March or early April for spring planting. Application should not be made immediately before or after rain. A more compete kill of rough deep swards is obtained by burning, grazing or mowing to encourage fresh growth before spraying, and then at least one season may elapse before broad-leaved weeds and re-invading grasses begin to interfere with the crop seriously.

8.042   **Paraquat** *1·0 kg/ha in medium volume up to 2—3 days prior to planting.*
    The grass must be green when treated, as paraquat cannot move through any parts of the grass above ground which are dead at the time of spraying. If plentiful, such dead grass can effectively screen the live parts and protect them. Paraquat is not translocated to rhizomes nor to developing shoots which have not yet emerged out of the grass mat. After treatment in the spring, perennial grasses can be expected to shoot again and application should be left as late as possible so as to delay recovery.

8.043   **Paraquat** in the autumn or winter on grasses remaining green has been effective and killed a higher proportion of some grasses than when these have been sprayed in the spring. However, the grasses have a longer time in which to 'seed in' or recover before the end of the following season.

8.044 **Propyzamide** *at 1·5—2·0 kg/ha as a 50 per cent wettable powder or 4 per cent granules.* This treatment has given good control of grasses and broad-leaved herbaceous weeds when applied post planting in the period October—January. This herbicide could also be suitable for pre-planting treatments, but has not yet been adequately tested in this situation.

8.045 [**For information.**] Chlorthiamid at 3·4—4·5 kg/ha applied up to 1 month before planting as 7·5 per cent granules has been successfully used as a pre-planting treatment when the crop is to be of a resistant species (8.053).

Much less is known about the safety of pre-planting applications of chlorthiamid. Otherwise, crop and weed sensitivities and the optimum application times are expected to be the same as for post-planting applications.

8.046 [**For information.**] Dichlobenil at 3·0—4·0 kg/ha applied up to 1 month before planting as 6·75 per cent granules is expected to give similar results to an identical treatment with chlorthiamid (8.045).

Trials and experience with dichlobenil is limited and less is known about its reliability in forest situations. The proposed crop should be of a species resistant to dichlobenil.

8.047 [**For information.**] Dichlobenil at 2·7—4·0 kg/ha plus dalapon sodium at 4·0—6·0 kg/ha as a combined granule applied 1 month before planting is known to give better control of perennial grasses than dichlobenil alone. The amount of information on pre-plant-treatments is low.

8.048 [**For information.**] Atrazine at 4·0—6·0 kg/ha as a wettable powder or suspension concentrate in a medium volume has provided good control of a range of fine and soft grasses when applied in February to April post-planting, with negligible crop damage (8.055).

This herbicide might also be suitable for re-planting treatments, but it has not been adequately tested in this situation.

8.049 [**For information.**] Cyanazine plus atrazine 5·40—7·20 kg/ha as a formulated wettable powder or suspension concentrate mixture has provided good control of grasses and broad-leaved herbaceous weeds, when applied post-planting from February to May. This mixture is also suitable for pre-planting treatments but has not yet been adequately tested in this situation.

8.050 **Glyphosate** at 1·4 kg/ha in medium volume has given good control of grasses and herbaceous broad-leaved weeds. Allow three days to elapse before planting.

Grass and herbaceous broad-leaved weed control in planted areas

8.051   **Dalapon-sodium** *10·0 kg/ha in medium volume only when young plantations are dormant.*

As weed grasses need to be actively growing to get a satisfactory kill, the best time for application is in March or early April, just before the tree crop begins to grow. Spray should be directed so as to minimize wetting the crop. Application should not be made immediately before or after rain.

8.052   **Paraquat** *1·0 kg/ha in young plantations only where both the stem and foliage of the trees can be protected from direct contact with the spray.*

In the early part of the growing season, the bark of many conifer species can be damaged by paraquat.

Paraquat must be applied in early summer before the weeds have become large; such weeds will often recover by late summer but will not grow tall. Alternatively, weeds remaining green may be sprayed in the autumn or winter (see 8.043). Normally, grasses are too tall for paraquat to be usefully applied in July and August. The tall stems may transfer paraquat to young trees as they move in the wind; also spraying is unduly slowed by the extra time needed to place the spray shield in tall weeds.

8.053   **Chlorthiamid** *3·4–4·5 kg/ha (as 7·5 per cent granules) from January to March in the south or from January to April in the north, only in crops of tolerant species.*

The lower rate is suitable for light weed situations, or when crops are tall enough to require less than complete weed control to release it from competition for light. Also, since control tends to be better at the later dates of application, lower rates can be favoured for March–April applications.

Crop species which are known to tolerate chlorthiamid as recommended above are Sitka spruce, Norway spruce, Corsican, Lodgepole and Scots pine, oak, ash, beech and sycamore.

Douglas fir, Western hemlock, Larix and abies spp. should not be treated. There is insufficient evidence on other species to make recommendations.

8.054   **Dichlobenil** *3·0–4·0 kg/ha (as 6·75 per cent granules) in February to April only in crops of tolerant species (as chlorthiamid see 8.053).*

Experience with dichlobenil is much less than with chlorthiamid. Less is known about its reliability in forest situations, and the susceptibility of crop species.

8.055   **Atrazine** *at 4·5–6·7 kg/ha as wettable powder or suspension concentrate in medium volume during February to May for weed control in conifers only.*

It can be safely applied over the foliage of the young trees, treatment can be made in the first spring after planting and repeated annually if necessary.

The higher rate may be used on all coniferous species grown for timber, except Norway spruce, Western hemlock and European larch where the lower dose only should be used. Some needle browning may occur especially on larch, but this is unlikely to affect subsequent tree growth. Grasses vary in their susceptibility to atrazine. For moderately resistant grasses rates above 4·50 kg/ha will be required for adequate control.

8.056 Cyanazine *plus atrazine 5·40–7·20 kg/ha as a wettable powder or suspension concentrate, for the control of grasses and herbaceous broad-leaved weeds when applied post-planting from February to May.* Species successfully treated are: Sitka spruce, Norway spruce, Corsican, Lodgepole and Scots pine, oak, ash, beech, sycamore, maple, alder, birch, Douglas fir, Serbian spruce and Larix spp.

8.057 [**For information.**] Propyzamide at 1·5 kg/ha (Scotland and Northern England) and 2·00 kg/ha (S. England and Wales) as a 50 per cent wettable powder or a 4 per cent granule applied from mid October to late January has been successfully used for the control of perennial and annual grasses and some broad-leaved weeds. Species treated without damage are Sitka spruce, Norway spruce, Corsican pine, Scots pine, Lodgepole pine, Larix spp., Douglas fir, Western hemlock, oak and beech. Other species have not been evaluated.

8.058 [**For information.**] Atrazine and cyanazine/atrazine as suspension concentrate formulations have been successfully applied at the recommended rates (see paragraphs 8.055 and 8.056) as very low volume application by means of rotary atomizers.

8.059 [**For information.**] Dichlobenil at 2·7–4·0 kg/ha plus dalapon sodium at 4·0–6·0 kg/ha, as a combined granule has been successfully used in February to April for the control of perennial grass weeds and annual weeds in tolerant species (as per chlorthiamid 8.053). Better control of perennial grasses is to be expected from this combined formulation compared to dichlobenil alone.

8.060 [**For information.**] Glyphosate at 1·4 kg/ha has been successfully used for the control of most weeds post-planting. Sprays must be directed to miss the crop trees and a guard must be used if this cannot be done.

Bracken control

8.061 This section deals only with herbicide treatments on bracken in the forest. See also Chapter 12 for the control of bracken on agricultural land.

Bracken is a serious problem in plantations on the better forest soils in many hill and lowland areas.

Asulam has shown promise in controlling this weed before planting. A number of other chemicals are undergoing trials as pre-planting herbicides for bracken control, but cannot be used post-planting.

Three herbicides, which may be used for post-planting selective control of bracken are, asulam, chlorthiamid and dichlobenil.

In forests, bracken is nearly always accompanied by an understorey of grass. After control of the bracken the grass usually spreads to create a greater problem than the original bracken. Ideally, therefore, the herbicide which is used should also control the understorey of grasses.

BRACKEN CONTROL BEFORE PLANTING

8.062   **Asulam** 3·0–4·0 kg/ha of a 40 per cent w/v concentrate applied ultra low, low or medium volume after most of the bracken fronds have fully extended (late June–July) to well before any sign of senescence (early August). Ultra low and low volume applications will tend to give a better control than medium volume, but an even coverage of the fronds is essential.

This treatment will control grass reached by the spray.

8.063   [For information.] Winter application of MCPA at 35·0–45·0 kg/ha at medium volume have provided a good initial control of bracken without damage to crops planted the following March or April. This treatment will not control grass.

BRACKEN CONTROL IN PLANTED AREAS

8.064   *Asulam* at 2·0–4·0 kg/ha of a 40 per cent w/v concentrate applied ultra low, low or medium volume after most of the bracken fronds have fully extended, (late June–early July), to well before any sign of senescence (mid August). Ultra low and low volume applications tend to give a better control than medium volume, but an even coverage of the fronds is essential. The softwoods Corsican pine, Scots pine, Norway spruce, Sitka spruce, Douglas fir, Grand fir and *Larix* spp., and beech and elm of the hardwoods have shown good tolerance to Asulam, though some chlorosis and check may occur at the highest rate combined with the earliest date of application.

Western hemlock will not tolerate more than 2·8 kg/ha at the latest possible spraying date (August onwards).

8.065   [For information.] When the primary objective is to control grass and herbaceous broad-leaved weeds, the use of chlorthiamid or dichlobenil at 3·4–4·5 kg/ha will often provide useful control of any bracken present. These herbicides should only be used if the crop species are suitable (8.053).

8.066 [**For information.**] Paraquat applied in May or June at 1·0–2·2 kg/ha will defoliate bracken but has no effect beyond the season of application.

Woody weeds

8.067 While woody weeds are a particular problem in forestry, they may encroach on agricultural land and on to roadsides, ditches, fire-breaks, fences and railway embankments. This section deals with woody weeds in forests, but because the recommendations are equally applicable to scrub control in many other situations, it is used extensively as a reference in the later section on the control of scrub in other situations.

The treatments recommended here will kill or check the species treated; none of them will directly hasten the rotting of the stump. Where removal is required, bulldozing, winching or blasting of the whole tree, stump and root together should be considered, rather than the use of a herbicide. Machines exist which can grind or chip even large stumps away in a few hours. If blasting is unsafe and machinery cannot reach the site, stumps may be impregnated with sodium or potassium nitrate by packing crystals of these compounds into holes made with an auger. After several months the stumps may be soaked in paraffin and burnt in situ. The salt is applied by boring 2 to 4 holes 18 mm diameter in the stump so that the holes slope down towards the pith. These holes are then packed with about 28 g of the salt in each and plugged with clay or putty. It is important that the stump is protected from persons and animals during the period between treatment and firing. It may be necessary to kill the live stump before treatment for firing.

HERBICIDES

8.068 While many herbicides affect woody species, those mainly used in Britain are low volatile ester formulations of 2,4,5-T, 2,4-D + 2,4,5-T mixtures or ammonium sulphamate. Ester formulations of 2,4-D alone are usually confined to the control of heather (*Calluna* and *Erica* spp.) either before planting, in areas planted with spruce, or for the control of certain herbaceous weeds.

8.069 2,4,5-T and 2,4-D + 2,4,5-T.
These growth regulator herbicides are effective for the control of many woody species when applied by the methods detailed below. Although some success has been achieved from the application of water soluble metallic salts or amine derivatives, the ester formulations are superior for woody weed control.

The specific ester may vary from product to product but low volatile esters should always be used, to reduce the hazard of vapour drift on to susceptible crops.

Butyl esters have been commonly used and can be classed as moderately volatile. However, these are now being replaced by less volatile esters, which should always be preferred in hazardous situations.

2,4,5-T is effective on the majority of woody weeds and commercial mixtures of 2,4-D and 2,4,5-T usually in the proportion 2 : 1 are economical and valuable for foliage spraying where there are mixed stands of woody and herbaceous weeds. Products based on 2,4,5-T or 2,4-D + 2,4,5-T esters are available formulated as emulsifiable concentrates which can be mixed in water for foliage spraying or dissolved in mineral oil for application to the bark of standing stems, cut stems or to cut stumps. A special ultra low volume formulation of 2,4,5-T low volatile ester has been developed for application, without the addition of water, by means of hand-held rotary atomizers.

Cheaper unformulated esters of 2,4,5-T are also available for use only in solutions of oils such as diesel oil, paraffin, gas oil or vaporizing oil. Diesel and gas oils are cheapest but more highly refined, less noxious paraffins have recently been preferred because of operator complaint. In order to be genuinely less noxious such paraffins must comply with BSS 2869 Class C1.

2,4-D and 2,4-D + 2,4,5-T

8.070   These mixtures are effective for the control of heather (*Calluna* or *Erica* spp.). The 2 : 1 mixtures of 2,4-D + 2,4,5-T should be used where a mixture of herbaceous and woody weeds requires to be controlled for example, *Chamaenerion angustifolium* (Rosebay Willow-herb) and *Rubus* spp. (Blackberries etc.) 2,4-D ester is available formulated as an emulsifiable concentrate. A special ultra low volume formulation of 2,4-D low volatile ester has been developed for application, without the addition of water by means of hand-held rotary atomizers.

8.071   Spray systems capable of spraying invert emulsions of oil soluble amines of 2,4-D and 2,4,5-T have recently been developed. Such emulsions are more viscous than oil-in-water types and are less liable to spray-drift. Oil soluble amines of 2,4-D and 2,4,5-T are also of extremely low volatility and such emulsions therefore overcome the hazard of vapour drift mentioned in paragraph 8.069. A further advantage is that the spray droplets are visible on plant surfaces for a short time after application and act as a marker thus assisting accurate application.

While they have been known for a number of years, invert emulsions cannot be sprayed through conventional spraying equipment because they become too thick and clog the pump and spray lines. However, in the recently devised bifluid system, the difficulties have been overcome. See also Volume I, Chapter 13.

8.072   [**For information.**] Sodium alginate or hydroxyethyl cellulose at 0·25−0·5 per cent w/w also increase the viscosity of water-borne herbicides and reduce the spray drift. No evidence from Britain is available on whether these more viscous solutions increase the activity of the herbicides carried in them, although this is claimed.

Ammonium sulphamate

8.073 This chemical is effective against a wide range of woody plants including several important species such as *Rhododendron ponticum, Crataegus monogyna* (Hawthorn) and *Fraxinus excelsior* (Ash) which are relatively resistant to 2,4-D and 2,4,5-T. It is a very soluble crystalline solid which absorbs moisture readily when exposed to damp air. Ammonium sulphamate can act both as a contact and translocated herbicide being used in aqueous solution for spraying low growth, or in solution or as dry crystals on stumps and in notches or frill-girdles cut in stems of standing trees. Treatment should be made to fresh cut stumps, notches or frill-girdles on a dry day so that the plant has an adequate opportunity to absorb the herbicide before it is washed away by rain.

Ammonium sulphamate can kill trees and shrubs rooting in the soil beneath plants treated with this herbicide and should therefore only be applied in plantations to notches or frills cut in the weed species. Where an area of ground has been cleared of *Rhododendron ponticum* and *Fraxinus excelsior* (Ash) and the stumps treated with ammonium sulphamate, an interval of at least 8 and preferably 12 weeks should elapse between application and planting near treated stools. Ammonium. sulphamate is of low toxicity to animals. In solution, it is extremely corrosive to copper, brass and other copper alloys; it also corrodes galvanized iron, mild steel and lead. Stainless steel or plastic spraying equipment is recommended. Sodium benzoate at $15 \cdot 5$ g/5 litres of solution should be added to reduce the rate of corrosion of brass, but sprayers must still be washed out immediately after use.

Ammonium sulphamate has been in use since 1957, mostly against *Rhododendron ponticum*.

8.074   The susceptibility of common woody weeds to ester formulations of 2,4,5-T and 2,4-D and to ammonium sulphamate

Recommended ranges of doses for esters of 2,4,5-T and 2,4-D.

Overall summer foliage sprays 2·2–4·5 kg/ha in water.

Overall winter shoot sprays—17·0–22·0 kg/ha in 1100 litres oil applied to run off.

* Basal-bark and cut-stump treatments—17·0–22·0 kg in 1100 litres oil applied to run off.

1·50–2·0 kg in 100 litres oil for small areas.

Ammonium sulphamate—2 kg/5 litres of water applied to run-off, or used in dry crystalline form.

The categories of response for these doses:

S—Consistently good control by suggested technique with little resprouting.

MS—Good control of aerial growth by suggested technique but generally requiring a higher dose or concentration than for 'S' category. Small plants killed; big ones may recover.

MR—Some useful effect from the higher dose or concentrations, but recovery usual.

R—No useful effect at the highest doses quoted.

	Diluent								
	Water	Oil						Ammonium sulphamate to stump or stem	
	Foliage	Dormant shoot	Frill-girdle or basal-bark		Stump		All seasons*	Remarks
Species	2,4-D	2,4,5-T	2,4,5-T	2,4-D*	2,4,5-T*	2,4-D*	2,4,5-T*		
Acer campestre (Field Maple)	—	MS	S	MS	S	—	S	—	
Acer pseudoplatanus (Sycamore)	—	MS	—	—	MS	—	MS	—	
Aesculus hippocastanum (Horse-chestnut)	MS	MS	—	MR	S	—	S	S	
Alnus spp. (Alder)	MS	S	S	MS	MS	S	S	S	
Betula spp. (Birch)	MS	MS	S	MS	S	S	S	S	
Buxus sempervirens (Box)	—	MS	—	—	—	—	—	—	
Calluna vulgaris (Heather)	MS*	MR	—	—	—	—	—	—	*Apply June–Aug. 4·00–6·00 kg in 670 litres/ha See para. 8.071

* Where basal-bark and cut-stump treatments are concerned it is only possible to give the dilution rates, as the rate per hectare will depend upon the density of scrub to be controlled.

Species	1	2	3	4	5	6	7
Carpinus betulus (Hornbeam)	—	—	MS	MS	—	S	—
Castanea sativa (Sweet Chestnut)	MS	—	S	S	MS	S	S
Clematis vitalba (Traveller's-joy)	MS	—	—	—	—	S	—
Corylus avellana (Hazel)	MS	R	MS	MS	MS	S	S
Crataegus spp. (Hawthorn)	R	—	S	MR	MR	MR	—
Fagus sylvatica (Beech)	MS	—	S	—	—	—	S
Fraxinus excelsior (Ash)	MR	—	MS	MR	MR	MS	—
Hedera helix (Ivy)	R	—	S	—	—	—	—
Ilex aquifolium (Holly)	R	—	MR	—	—	—	—
Juniperus communis (Juniper)	R	—	—	—	—	MS	—
Ligustrum vulgare (Wild Privet)	MS	—	MS	—	MR	MS	—
Lonicera periclymenum (Honeysuckle)	MR	—	—	—	—	—	—
Pinus sylvestris (Scots Pine)	R	MS	—	MS	—	—	—
Populus spp. (Poplar)	MS	—	S	S	S	S	S
Prunus spinosa (Blackthorn)	S	—	MS	MS	MR	S	S
Pyrus communis (Wild Pear)	MS	—	—	—	—	S	S
Quercus spp. (Oak)	R	—	MS	MS	MS	S	S
Rhamnus catharticus (Buckthorn)	MS	—	S	—	—	MS	MS
Rhododendron ponticum (Rhododendron)	R	—	S†	MR†	R	MS†	S
Rosa spp. (Briar)	MR	—	S	—	—	S	—
Rubus spp. (Bramble, etc.)	MR	—	S	—	—	S	—
Salix spp. (Willow)	S§	—	S	MS	—	MS	S
Sambucus nigra (Elder)	MS	—	S	—	S	S	S
Sarothamnus scoparius (Broom)	S	—	S	S	—	S	S
Sorbus aucuparia (Rowan)	MS	—	—	S	—	MS	—
Thelycrania sanguinea (Dogwood)	—	—	MS	—	—	MS	S
Tilia spp. (Lime)	MS	—	—	—	—	S	—
Ulex spp. (Gorse)	MR	—	S‖	—	MR	S	—
Ulmus spp. (Elm)	MR	—	S	—	MS	S	—
Vaccinium spp. (Bilberry)	MS	—	—	—	—	—	—

† Use 16·8–22·4 kg in 500 litres diluent

‡ Good control at 1·12–2·24 kg/ha. Old canes more susceptible than young

§ Good control at 1·12–2·24 kg/ha

‖ see para. 8.083

* All woody species listed here are susceptible to ammonium sulphamate. Where no symbol is given in the table, 2,4-D or 2,4,5-T are preferable because of lower cost. Where these materials are used, planting close to treated woody species does not have to be deferred for a period whereas in similar situations planting should be delayed by 3 months following treatment with ammonium sulphamate.

8.075   Foliage sprays should be applied evenly to all parts of the weed to be killed—foliage, branches and stem down to soil level. Leaves will obviously receive by far the largest part of the spray but, especially with more resistant species, the aim should be to cover all parts of the plant.

Because woody weeds are unevenly distributed in most places where they occur, foliage sprays are seldom 'overall' sprays (see Glossary). Only with species such as heather is a foliage spray applied overall. Foliage sprays are extravagant in herbicide and diluent when applied to the point of run-off.

Foliage applications are normally made at low volume using a mist-blower as this reduces the cost of transporting water to inaccessible sites. Ultra low volume (ULV) applications of 7–10 litres/ha may be used giving further substantial reductions in the cost of transporting diluents. Application should be made by means of hand-held rotary atomizers at a height of 1 metre above the vegetation to be treated.

When deciduous species are being sprayed the foliage must be healthy and functional. Foliage sprays are not so effective when applied to leaves which are rapidly expanding at the beginning of the growing season and may be wasted if applied shortly before leaf-fall even if leaf-fall has been prematurely induced, e.g. by drought.

Where coppice sprouts are to be treated, a substantial leaf area must be present, especially if the coppice stump is large. Coppice shoots should not normally be treated by foliage spraying until there is 3 years' growth present.

After foliage-spraying, treated shoots must not be cut for at least a month, to allow time for the herbicide to be translocated into the woody tissues, otherwise stumps may resprout.

Foliage sprays have been applied on a fairly small scale and in forestry almost always post- rather than pre-planting.

FOLIAGE SPRAYING IN ABSENCE OF FOREST CROP

8.076   2,4,5-T-ester or 2,4-D + 2,4,5-T mixtures at 2·2–4·5 kg/ha applied in water in low or medium volume for species shown in 8.074 as susceptible or moderately susceptible, at any time between when leaves are first fully expanded until late August (or the first signs of leaf-fall, if earlier).

Up to 20 per cent of oil by volume, added to the 2,4,5-T or 2,4-D + 2,4,5-T concentrate before diluting with water, may increase the effectiveness on the more resistant species. The oil must be well mixed with the concentrate before diluting with water.

8.077   2,4-D Ester 5·6 kg/ha or paraquat 1·0–2·2 kg/ha in low or medium volume applied in June to August for control of *Calluna vulgaris* and *Erica* spp. (Heather).

The higher dose of paraquat is generally necessary to kill *Calluna vulgaris* in Scotland. The higher volume rate usually gives a better kill of old, dense and tall *Calluna vulgaris.*

78 *Ammonium sulphamate 4·0 kg/10 litres water or 2,4,5-T 2·5 kg/100 litres water or oil for control of* Rhododendron ponticum, *applied to cut stump or regrowth less than 1·20 m high.*
The treatment in oil gives a better control of the stump and reduces regrowth more than when used in water. If water is used as a diluent, a minimum of 3 kg of 2,4,5-T per 100 litres should be used. With all treatments it is important for sprays to reach the surface of *Rhododendron* stumps and stems as well as the foliage. The above rates are dilution rates that should be sprayed to thoroughly wet the *Rhododendrons,* and cannot be related to any given size of treated area. The volumes required to treat a hectare of *Rhododendrons* are frequently in excess of 1700 litres.
An interval of at least 8 weeks should be left between the application of ammonium sulphamate and planting near treated stools (8.073).

Foliage spraying of woody weeds in conifer crops

79 **2,4,5-T** ester or **2,4-D + 2,4,5-T** ester at 2·2–3·5 kg/ha in suitable volumes of water or a special ultra low volume formulation of 2,4,5-T applied by means of hand-held rotary atomizers may be used. Selective application may be made to control woody weeds in young conifer crops, provided the conifer shoots have ceased elongation, the terminal buds have formed and hardened and the weeds to be controlled have not ceased to grow. Depending upon latitude this period should be between mid-August and mid-October.
Not all crop species tolerate such sprays, Scots pine, Corsican pine, Norway spruce, Sitka spruce, Douglas fir, *Abies grandis, Abies procera,* Western red cedar and Lawson cypress are relatively tolerant from about mid-August onwards. However, *Pinus radiata, Pinus pinaster,* Lodgepole pine, Western hemlock and larches, should not be sprayed whilst less than 3 m high and only then at the latter end of the recommended period.

80 Calluna vulgaris *(Heather) and* Erica spp. *(Heath) in young conifer plantations can be killed or severely checked by* **2,4-D-ester** *at 4·0–5·0 kg/ha in low or medium volumes of water or as an ultra low volume (ULV) application of 7–10 litres/ha of a special formulation of* **2,4-D** *low volatile ester by means of hand-held rotary atomizers.* Application should be made after the crop has hardened off and before the end of August. The following species appear to be resistant, Scots pine, Corsican pine, Norway spruce, Sitka spruce, Douglas fir, Western red cedar and Lawson cypress. If Sitka spruce is in check to the heather and is an average height of 1 m or more it may be sprayed from mid July onwards. If Sitka spruce is planted in mixture with other species care should be taken to ensure that all the species to be treated have ceased elongation and have hardened off before a July application is undertaken.

An improved control of *Calluna* and *Erica* spp. will result if the area receives a dressing of fertilizer in the spring prior to application.

8.081 *Rhododendron* regrowth is best treated by foliage spray of **2,4,5-T** as in 8.076 while the crop is dormant. This will kill the regrowth, kill or severely damage the stool and reduce subsequent regrowth. Sprays applied in the growing season are effective against the *Rhododendron* but drift of the herbicide used in the concentration recommended may cause damage to the foliage and occasionally also the shoots of the adjoining crop trees. Any spray falling directly on to crop trees may cause serious damage. (8.083.)

Ammonium sulphamate should not be used against *Rhododendron* in young plantations.

8.082 [**For information.**] *Rhododendron,* established plants and regrowth, has been successfully controlled by an application of 11·0 kg/ha 2,4,5-T oil-soluble amine as an invert emulsion through a bifluid system (8.071). This method has enabled *rhododendron* to be successfully treated in young crops without damage to the crop. ULV applications of a special 2,4,5-T formulation (8.069) have shown promise in controlling *Rhododendron*.

8.083 [**For information.**] *Rhododendron* has been successfully controlled in plantations of mature Scots pine and Sitka spruce (over 10 m in height) by an application of 2,4,5-T emulsifiable concentrate applied in water. The dilution rate should be 33·0 kg a.e. 2,4,5-T in 1400 litres of water, this mixture applied to the point of 'run off' to the foliage of the *Rhododendron* at a minimum rate of 17 kg/ha 2,4,5-T in 700 litres/ha of water has given a successful control when applied in July. Care should be taken to ensure that none of the mixture comes into contact with the needles of the trees, the lower branches of which should have been brashed. Any hard wood species such as *Fagus* (Beech) *Quercus* (Oak) etc. will be severely damaged or killed if the spray should come into contact with the foliage. Great care should be taken to avoid drift onto other susceptible crops.

8.084 **Paraquat** *1·0–2·0 kg/ha directed to avoid foliage and stems of crop trees to control* Calluna vulgaris *and* Erica *spp. (Heather) and grasses.*

Spraying of dormant shoots of deciduous woody weeds

8.085 **2,4,5-T-ester** *1·5–2·0 kg/100 litres oil for species shown in paragraph 8.074 as susceptible or moderately susceptible sprayed overall when weeds are dormant.*

The volume of spray used should be sufficient to wet all surfaces to the point of run-off. This technique requires less spray solution than foliage spraying, because leaves are not present, but must not be used in crops unless the sprays can be placed to miss crop trees.

Water is unsuitable as a diluent for this treatment.

This technique has been practised on a small scale on seedling woody weeds such as birch for several years.

Basal-bark sprays, pre- and post-planting

8.086   **2,4,5-T-ester** *1·5–2·0 kg/100 litres oil for species listed in paragraph 8.074. For species resistant to* **2,4,5-T, ammonium sulphamate** *solution at a 0·4 kg/litre of water.*

This technique and girdling or notching are complementary. Basal-bark sprays are best applied to trees up to 100- to 150-mm diameter, while larger stems are best girdled or notched.

In basal-bark treatment, a solution of **2,4,5-T** or **2,4-D** + **2,4,5-T** in oil is sprayed or painted on to the bark of each stem to be treated. The solution should be applied to saturate the bark to the point of run-off over the full circumference of the stem from a height of 300–450 mm to ground level. The main target is the bark at and immediately above ground level, and spraying should ensure run-down and thorough wetting of this region. Oil solutions are necessary to ensure adequate penetration of the bark.

The volume of spray required for a given area to ensure thorough wetting of the treated region varies greatly with size and density of growth but will usually be between 200 and 700 litres/ha. As a guide, the volumes required will be about 30 ml spray per 25 mm of stem diameter.

Basal-bark treatments may be made at any season but they are most effective between January and March, and least effective in the autumn. At all times, care must be taken to avoid spraying crop trees in the vicinity. During the crops growing season, especially at the beginning, it is safe to use a very low volatile ester of 2,4,5-T.

Stems should be dry at the time of spraying. Moss-covered stems require nearly twice as much spray solution as stems without moss and if possible should be girdled rather than given a basal-bark spray.

Basal-bark applications of 2,4,5-T have been very widely used since 1956.

Frill-girdling, notching and tree injection ('cut-bark') treatments of standing trees

8.087   **2,4,5-T-ester** *or* **ammonium sulphamate** *in frills and notches at similar concentrations to those for basal-bark sprays (*8.086*).*

A 'frill' girdle should be prepared as near ground level as possible by making a series of downward-sloping and overlapping cuts with a light axe or billhook. The herbicide solution should then be poured or sprayed into the fresh cuts to flood the whole length of the frill. The volume applied must be sufficient to wet the full circumference of the girdle, and it may be easier to spray the bark at the top edge of the girdle, allowing the solution to run down into the cuts. As a general rule about 5 ml per cent solution will be required per 25 mm of stem diameter. If ammonium sulphamate crystals are used, about 15 g/25 mm of stem diameter is required.

'Notches' may be cut with a small axe near the ground level, each notch being made by two slanting strokes of the axe to produce an inward-sloping notch penetrating at least to the cambium, and preferably into the outer sap-wood. Notches should be spaced not wider than 100 mm apart, edge to edge. The notches should be treated with the herbicide solution, using 5- to 10-ml solution or 15 g ammonium sulphamate crystals per notch. Notching is the cheapest and easiest method but frilling usually gives the most consistently good control.

2,4,5-T has been very widely used in frill-girdles for over 10 years; notching is less widely practised. Ammonium sulphamate is used in frills and notches on a much smaller scale than 2,4,5-T, but should be preferred for species resistant or moderately resistant to 2,4,5-T (paragraph **8.065**).

8.088   **2,4,5-T-ester** *(1 kg/litre unformulated) diluted with an equal volume of oil, or neat emulsifiable* **2,4,5-T-ester** *(0·5 kg/litre) injected in 1·0 ml doses at 7·5 cm centres round the circumference of species susceptible or moderately susceptible to* **2,4,5-T** *(8.074).*

Injections may be made at any convenient level above the ground, depending on the design of the injector. Injectors aim at making incisions which penetrate into the cambium and outer sapwood, into which the herbicide is injected automatically (a pump being actuated by the blade striking the tree) or by manually operating a pump mechanism.

8.089   [**For information.**] Injection of 1·0 ml of 2,4,-D-ester (0·5 kg acid/litre) at 7·5 cm centres round the circumference of species susceptible or moderately susceptible to 2,4,5-T has also given good results.

If this herbicide is shown to be reliable for tree injection, it should also be suitable for frills and notches.

Treatment of cut stumps

8.090   **2,4,5-T** *in oil or* **ammonium sulphamate** *in water at the same concentrations as for basal-bark sprays (see 8.086 and 8.074).*

8.091   **Ammonium sulphamate** *crystals at 15 g/25 mm of stem diameter as an alternative to spraying.*

In this technique, herbicides are best applied to the exposed wood of the stump of newly cut trees and to the surface of the bark between the cut and the soil. It is especially important that the bark near soil level is thoroughly wetted with herbicide. Ideally, stumps should be treated within 24 h of cutting. The herbicide should wet all surfaces to the point of run-off. Sprays should not be applied when stumps are wet with rain or dew. Retention of ammonium sulphamate crystals will be improved if stumps are cut to produce a level or 'V'-shaped surface. Crystals should not be applied if heavy rain is expected within a few hours of application.

8.092 Treatment, whether by spray or crystals, can be applied effectively at any season, January to March being the best period for winter treatment. Stumps which have resprouted producing coppice shoots can also be killed.

Section III Scrub control

8.093 Scrub is here defined as woody growth of no economic value. There are numerous situations in which control or removal of such woody growth is desirable (e.g. agricultural or horticultural land, roadsides, ditches, railway embankments, etc.). Some of these are discussed in Chapter 7. Suitable recommendations for most forest situations are given earlier in this chapter, paragraphs 8.074–8.078, it may however be of value to describe recommendations for scrub control in land that is not scheduled for afforestation.

Scrub, mainly in the form of *Ulex* spp. (Gorse) *Sarothamnus scoparius* (Broom) tends to invade and colonize hill grazing land, while *Rubus* and *Rosa* spp. are troublesome weeds of hedges.

Gorse and broom can be controlled by continuous cutting either mechanically or manually, or can be physically removed by mechanical means but with rising labour costs this is now uneconomic. Short-term control can be achieved by burning, but, as in most instances the gorse or broom will have been dropping seed over a period of many years, the burning merely induces germination of seeds that have been lying dormant beneath the mature bushes.

Effective control can be achieved by the use of 2,4,5-T or 2,4-D/2,4,5-T proprietary mixtures, at $2 \cdot 50$–$4 \cdot 50$ kg/ha applied in water from May to July; in a mixture of water and oil (diesel, paraffin, gas oil or vaporizing oil), in April or in August/September in the ratio of $9:1$ water to oil, (the higher rate of $4 \cdot 50$ kg/ha is required in October); or throughout the remainder of the year using oil alone as the diluent.

Management after application is an all-important part of the process of removing gorse/broom from hill grazing land; approximately 6 months after application the scrub will be brittle and will very easily burn, this should for the reasons stated be avoided, the bushes can, when in this brittle state, be easily broken down by machinery, this should be coupled with applications of lime/fertilizer and the breaking down process completed by increased stocking by cattle, the treated areas soon become colonized by grass and revert to valuable grazing land.

Briars and brambles can be controlled by an application of 2,4,5-T or 2,4-D/2,4,5-T mixtures at 1·1–2·2 kg/ha from May to August in sufficient water to ensure a complete cover of the foliage. Where briars or brambles are growing in a hedge of a species resistant to 2,4,5-T or 2,4-D/2,4,5-T, for example *Crataegus* spp. (Hawthorn) a selective control may be obtained, provided that only water is used as the diluent.

In all applications of 2,4,5-T or 2,4-D/2,4,5-T mixtures great care should be taken to ensure that there is no possibility of drift onto susceptible crops, this applies particularly to drift of the winter oil applications onto adjacent trees, great care should also be taken to ensure that there is no contamination of water courses, rivers, reservoirs etc. See Chapter 10.

Section IV Special forestry situations

Control of vegetation in fire breaks

8.094   **Paraquat,** *to which a wetter has been added, 0·5–1·0 kg/ha in medium volume in July or August to desiccate grasses and other weeds growing in firebreaks.*

The vegetation will be suitable for burning within a few days. Burning should take place while the surrounding vegetation is still green. This technique is used mainly in areas dominated by *Molinia caerulea* (Purple Moor-grass).

Commercial willow beds

8.095   Commercial basket willows are grown in soils high in alluvium and organic matter. In the year of establishment, simazine 3·4–4·5 kg/ha in high volume in spring soon after cutting insertion will control annual weeds and shallow-rooting perennial weeds. Thereafter an annual application of 1·7–2·2 kg/ha will suffice.

8.096   Beds that have been grassed down after their second year are often grazed in late April. An application of dalapon-sodium at 2·2–3·4 kg/ha in medium volume will then check grass growth and obviate the need for hand-sickling. Higher doses are to be avoided lest, by killing the grasses, they encourage the spread of more noxious weeds, especially *Urtica* *dioica* (Common Nettle) and *Cirsium arvense* (Creeping Thistle). Paraquat at 0·7 kg/ha in medium volume is an alternative to dalapon.

8.097 Where *Urtica dioica* (Common Nettle) is troublesome, repeated annual applications of aminotriazole at 4·5 kg/ha in high volume in late March before willow bud-break will reduce infestation to a level that may then be easily controlled by hand-cutting or by spot treatments of MCPA at 1·7 kg/ha in high volume. Basket willow shoots are acutely sensitive to growth-regulator herbicides and sodium and potassium salt formulations MCPA are to be preferred to the amine and ester formulations.

For recommendations for weed control in willows grown in the nursery, see paragraphs 8.023–8.029.

Poplar plantations

8.098 Poplars in the first 2–3 years of growth following planting can be seriously checked by weed competition. The best means of overcoming this is to lay a mulch of cut vegetation in a 0·6 to 0·9 m radius around each plant. Such mulches not only control weeds but also provide a source of nutrients. Black polythene sheet has been used but is difficult to fix down securely. Straw may also be used but is costly.

8.099 **Paraquat** at 1·0 kg/ha in medium volume is an alternative to a mulch but poplar growth is not quite so good on sprayed plots as on those mulched with cut vegetation. Sprays should be repeated as required.

Chapter 9
Recommendations for total weed control on non-agricultural land

9.001 The recommendations are intended for areas where the usual objective is to maintain ground free of all growth for a protracted period. If the need is only temporary, as when clearing ground before cultivation or grass establishment, there must be no carry over of effects, such as herbicide residues, beyond the required period. Herbicides are the usual means employed but in some situations, as in forest fire breaks, growth may be kept down by repeated cultivations.

With herbicides the first objective is to kill established vegetation and thereafter there is a need for preventive treatments to maintain ground free of weeds. It is important that both above- and below-ground parts of established weeds are completely killed before resorting to 'maintenance' rates of application. If not, resistant weeds can quickly increase. Additional spot treatments at high rate or a herbicide with a different mode of action than the overall maintenance treatment, can be used to kill such resistant weeds before they become widespread.

Performance of root-acting herbicides will be affected by ground conditions which can vary enormously in this type of weed control. Higher rates than usual are normally required on adsorptive surfaces such as clay soils, ashes, peat or sawdust, whereas lower rates may suffice on easily penetrated surfaces such as sandy soils, gravel or stone ballast. On such surfaces however it is necessary to re-treat regularly. Treatment of weeds on slopes or growing on paved surfaces requires special precautions to avoid leaching or run-off towards wanted vegetation.

9.002 Generally, the need is to control grasses and herbaceous weeds. Woody growth and scrub will normally require separate herbicide treatment (see 9.024). Other techniques for maintaining stable vegetation conditions over indefinite periods will be found in Chapter 3 for weed control in shrubberies, in Chapter 7 for grass growth-retarding, and in Chapter 8 for detailed recommendations on scrub control.

Before deciding on the treatment to use for a particular weed problem, reference can be made to paragraph 9.029 which lists the susceptibilities of weeds to the main herbicides. When using paragraph 9.029 select the herbicide dose capable of controlling the most resistant weeds present.

9.003 Herbicides recommended for total weed control

Herbicides	Effect on top growth		Effect in preventing survival or regeneration of perennials		Persistence of initial doses in soil and effect in prevention of seedling establishment of susceptible species
	Perennial grasses	Broad-leaved weeds	Perennial grasses	Broad-leaved weeds	
Root-absorbed residual herbicides					
Atrazine, bromacil, diuron, monuron, simazine	×	×	× ×	×	A season or longer
Borates, dichlobenil and chlorthiamid	×	×	×	× ×	A season
Foliage- and root-absorbed residual herbicides					
Picloram		×		× ×	A season or longer
Sodium chlorate	×	× ×	×	× ×	Three months to a season
2,3,6-TBA		×		×	A season or longer
Foliage-absorbed herbicides					
Aminotriazole	×	×	×	×	One or 2 months
Dalapon	×		×		Three to 4 months
Diquat	×	× ×			None
Glyphosate	× ×	× ×	× ×	×	None
MCPA, 2,4-D 2,4,5-T		×		×	A few weeks
Paraquat	× ×	×			None

× = generally effective on many species at recommended doses.
× × = particularly effective on many species at recommended doses.

Residual herbicides

Root-absorbed residual herbicides

9.004 Herbicides in this group are normally taken up by the plant via the roots although with some there is also absorption by the foliage. Consequently their action is slow and they are largely dependent on adequate soil moisture. Best results are obtained from application carried out before weeds start to grow. Higher doses are usually required on heavy or organic substrates and also when applied to established vegetation. Root-absorbed herbicides at the recommended doses will normally provide satisfactory weed control for at least one season. Lateral movement is negligible when used on level ground except under very wet conditions with sodium chlorate. For practical use these herbicides are formulated as wettable powders or granules.

The majority of root-absorbed herbicides are available as mixtures with one or more herbicides. These mixtures are generally designed for application during the growing season or to control weeds which are moderately resistant. These mixtures are discribed fully in paragraph 9.021.

9.005 **Atrazine** *wettable powder suspension concentrates and granules and* **simazine** *wettable powder at 20 kg/ha to control established vegetation including deep-rooted perennials—10 kg/ha for established vegetation including annuals and shallow-rooted perennials—2·5 to 5·5 kg/ha for maintenance to prevent seedling reinfestation for a season.*

The optimum time for application of both herbicides to established vegetation is February to April. Simazine may also be applied from October to January but may then become ineffective a little earlier than with spring applications. Atrazine is also absorbed through the foliage, thus application during the growing season will normally give satisfactory results. In addition atrazine gives a better control of certain perennials (9.029) and is more suitable for initial treatments where these type of weeds are predominant. Maintenance treatments may be applied at any time of the year, usually before growth recommences.

Atrazine at doses over 5·6 kg/ha may damage trees and shrubs with roots underlying the treated area. Simazine is preferred in such situations because it does not penetrate to a level where most trees and shrubs have their root zones, and is therefore safe on most established species.

9.006 **Boron** *compounds applied dry at 1250 kg B$_2$O$_3$/ha to prevent growth on ground cleared of weeds.*

9.007 **Bromacil,** *both wettable powder and granular formulations at 11·0 kg/ha to control established vegetation, including deep-rooted* *perennials—6·0 kg/ha for established vegetation, including annuals and shallow-rooted perennials—2·0 kg/ha for maintenance to prevent seedling reinfestation for a season.*

The optimum time for application on established vegetation is February to April.

Bromacil will generally damage trees and shrubs with roots underlying the treated area.

9.008 **Dichlobenil** *and* **chlorthiamid** *applied as granules at 17·0–18·0 kg/ha to control established vegetation.*

The optimum time for application to established vegetation is February to April. Warm moist soil conditions may increase the volatility of these compounds and reduce performance.

Dichlobenil and chlorthiamid do not penetrate deeply into soil but at the doses advised care should be taken when treating areas adjacent to susceptible trees and shrubs.

9.009 **Monuron** *and* **diuron** *at 22·0 kg/ha to control established vegetation including deep-rooted perennials—13·00 kg/ha for established vegetation including annuals and shallow-rooted perennials— 3·0–5·5 kg/ha for maintenance to prevent seedling reinfestation for a season.*

The optimum time for application to established vegetation is February to April. Monuron is preferred for initial treatments on heavy or organic soils where the annual rainfall is low, whereas diuron is more suitable on lighter soils particularly in areas of higher rainfall. Monuron is more suitable than diuron for later applications because it acts more quickly through the soil.

Monuron may damage trees and shrubs with roots underlying the treated area. Diuron is safer from this point of view because it penetrates less deeply into the soil.

Foliage- and root-absorbed herbicides

9.010 The three herbicides in this group are effective when applied either to the soil or as a foliage spray. Usually higher doses are required for soil treatments, particularly if growth is to be prevented for a season. Foliage sprays are most effective in killing deep-rooted perennials when applied in late summer. Picloram and 2,3,6-TBA are relatively persistent herbicides in the soil and residues may remain for 2 to 3 years, preventing the growth of susceptible species. Downward movement of these herbicides may damage trees and other vegetation with roots underlying the treated area as will drift when spraying. Sodium chlorate is much less persistent in soil than the others but it may also move laterally in the soil to affect adjacent vegetation.

These herbicides are commonly used in mixtures with root-absorbed residual herbicides to widen the spectrum of susceptible weeds or to extend the period of control.

9.011   **Picloram** *0·6−2·0 kg/ha as a spray application in early spring to control established herbaceous broad-leaved weeds.* **Picloram + 2,4-D** *0·6−2·2 kg/ha applied as a foliage spray from May to September to control herbaceous broad-leaved species.*

Picloram has little or no effect on established grasses at the above doses.

9.012   **2,3,6-TBA** *3·4−5·6 kg/ha as a foliar spray during the summer months to control many deep-rooted broad-leaved perennials.*

A mixture with 2·2 kg/ha of MCPA or 2,4-D increases the speed of action.

9.013   **Sodium chlorate** *at 220−450 kg/ha during the growing season to control established vegetation. For maintenance 170 kg/ha to prevent seedling reinfestation for about 3 months.*

Sodium chlorate gives a rapid kill on established vegetation. Dry sodium chlorate in contact with organic matter is easily ignited by friction and may give rise to fire or explosion risk, but this can be greatly reduced in liquid and dry powdered formulations containing fire retardants. It is recommended that only formulations containing a fire retardant are used.

Foliage-absorbed herbicides

9.014   Herbicides in this group are taken up by the plant primarily through the foliage, although with some there is also a lesser degree of root uptake. They may be either 'contact' or 'translocated' in action but both types require adequate leaf area to be available for maximum effectiveness. For this reason applications are normally made to emerged plants, and later in the growing season than is customary for root-absorbed herbicides. Short term persistence in the soil is a characteristic of the group.

These herbicides are formulated as liquids or soluble powders for spray application only.

Foliage-absorbed herbicides possessing particular selectivities are often combined to broaden the spectrum of weed species controlled. Either singly or in combination they are used as additives to residual root-absorbed herbicides to improve foliar activity and to give greater persistancy.

9.015   **Aminotriazole** *9·0 kg/ha for established perennial grasses and broad-leaved weeds; 4·5 kg/ha for seedlings and annuals.*

Application of aminotriazole is made from late spring onwards (mid-

May—August). Mixtures with root-absorbed herbicides are particularly useful for control of many established perennial weeds during the late spring and summer. Paragraph 9.029 indicates the species for which this complementary effect improves control. Late summer applications of 9·0 kg/ha give substantial kill of *Aegopodium podagraria* (Ground-elder) and partial kill of *Equisetum* spp. (Horsetails). A mixture of aminotriazole at 4·5 kg/ha with 2,4,5-T at 2·2 kg/ha applied in late summer gives useful control of *Aegopodium podagraria* (Ground-elder).

The activity of aminotriazole is enhanced by the addition of ammonium thiocyanate, and mixture formulations are commercially available. Aminotriazole may damage young trees and shrubs with roots underlying the treated area.

9.016 **Dalapon-sodium** *at 22·0–34·0 kg/ha for the control of grasses like* Agropyron repens *(Common Couch).*

Dalapon is most effective when applied to actively growing foliage in the spring.

It will prevent the regrowth from any surviving parts of grasses and a few broad-leaved species for about 3 months. As the activity of Dalapon is mainly against grasses the addition of a broad-leaved weedkiller is usually necessary for total weed control situations.

The foliar absorption of dalapon is improved by the addition of a suitable wetting agent.

9.017 **Paraquat** *at 1·1 kg/ha on established vegetation; 1·7–2·2 kg/ha on dense stands of tussocky perennial grasses; 0·5 kg/ha on seedling weeds and grasses.*

A fast top kill is obtained on all species of weeds and grasses but regrowth of some established perennials usually follows applications. As herbicidal activity is destroyed on contact with soil there is no residual effect. Paraquat can be safely used in the vicinity of shrubs and trees, providing all spray is kept away from the foliage and that there is no spray drift.

9.018 **MCPA-salt** *or* **2,4-D-salt** *or* **-amine** *for spot treatment or in mixtures at 2·2 kg/ha to control broad-leaved weeds—5·6 kg/ha on certain deep-rooted perennials as described in the section in Roadside Verges (see Chapter 7). A mixture of* **2,4-D** *2·8 kg/ha with* **2,4,5-T** *1·4 kg/ha in an ester formulation as a foliage spray during the summer months for controlling herbaceous broad-leaved and some woody species including* Rubus *species (Brambles).*

These herbicides which are most effective when applied to foliage during the growing season are generally used in mixtures with residual herbicides though they may also be used for spot treatment and to control specific broad-leaved weeds or woody species. They have negligible effect on grasses. Where a specific weed presents a problem reference should first be made to the index to this volume and then to recommendations which may be made in other sections or in the general tables. However, it is worth noting that in the absence of crop competition or cultivation higher doses are likely to be required in non-crop situations.

Many ester formulations of 2,4-D and 2,4,5-T are volatile and damage to surrounding vegetation may be caused by vapour drift for some time after application. When spraying near to crops or gardens only low volatile esters should be used.

9.019 **Glyphosate** *at 1·4—2·2 kg/ha in medium volume for spot or overall treatment of established annual and perennial grass and broad-leaved weeds.*

Weeds must have adequate leaf area at the time of application and if possible be near maturity. Provided there is sufficient leaf area glyphosate is active at all times of the year. It is readily translocated into all parts of the plant and gives good kill of underground parts of the plant. Grasses are more susceptible than broad-leaved weeds at equivalent doses but the higher rates will give control of perennial broad-leaved weeds.

Glyphosate is inactivated in the soil and leaves no residues. It should not be applied with any other herbicide as it is inactivated by them and results will be poor. All buds and green plant parts are susceptible to glyphosate and great care should be taken to avoid drift onto desirable plants.

9.020 [**For information.**] Dicamba applied in May or June at 0·56—1·1 kg/ha in combination with 2,4-D or MCPA at 2·2 kg/ha has provided control of *Rumex obtusifolius* and *Rumex crispus* (Docks).

Mixtures

9.021 Mixtures of herbicides are commonly used to control a wider range of weed species, to give a quicker kill and to reduce cost, a relatively cheap herbicide partly replacing a more expensive one without any considerable loss in performance. Since growth usually has to be prevented through a season, the residual herbicides atrazine, bromacil, diuron, monuron and simazine, are the primary components in most mixtures and, for initial applications they are in general interchangeable when used at around the minimum dose for application on established weeds as recommended in previous paragraphs. The other components in such mixtures normally have a foliar action, and are used at about half the highest recommended rate. It is not practicable to list all the mixtures of this kind which might be used but the following can be recommended. In practice, the doses can be varied according to the time of application, species present and degree of weed control required. With most of these mixtures the optimum time of application is during the spring months, though a reason for using certain mixtures is to extend the period over which a useful effect can be obtained.

Recommended mixtures for total weed control

9.022

Atrazine + aminotriazole + 2,4-D	Wettable powder
Atrazine + 2,4-D	Wettable powder
Atrazine + sodium chlorate	Granule
Atrazine + 2,3,6-TBA + MCPA	Wettable powder
Bromacil + borate	Granule
Bromacil + 2,4-D	Granule
Bromacil + diuron + aminotriazole	Granule
Bromacil + picloram	Granule
Diuron + aminotriazole + 2,4-D	Wettable powder
Diuron + aminotriazole + dichlorprop + MCPA	Wettable powder
Diuron + dalapon + MCPA	Wettable powder
Diuron + paraquat	Colloidal suspension
Diuron + paraquat + picloram	Colloidal suspension
Monuron + sodium + chlorate	Dry dusting powder
Monuron + sodium chlorate + 2,4-D	Wettable powder and granule
Monuron + 2,4-D	Wettable powder
Simazine + aminotriazole	Wettable powder

9.023 In considering the use of spray tank mixtures which are not commercially formulated, it is necessary to ensure that an effective mixture can be prepared and used *in situ*. All mixtures should be made at or near spray dilution. With wettable powders it is essential to maintain a good suspension during application. It is also advisable to carry out preliminary tests to ensure that there is no physical incompatibility such as may be encountered between oil-in-water formulations of selective herbicides and wettable powders. In using mixtures of herbicides the weather at the time of application must be considered in relation to the conditions desirable for all the chemicals present and any precautions required should be followed. Mixtures containing growth regulator herbicides should not be sprayed in windy weather.

Scrub control

9.024   *Special problems and situations.*

The recommendations for overall treatment of herbaceous weeds often give little or no control of established bramble, elder, hawthorn and other woody species that often grow in the absence of regular cutting or grazing. The increased range of top growth and root growth of woody species, plus differing susceptibilities, require special herbicides and application methods. Consequently, surviving scrub is normally controlled by local applications in late summer or even in the winter months. Most of the chemicals, doses and application techniques are described in Chapter 8. Additionally, on industrial sites picloram + 2,4-D at 0·6–2·2 kg/ha can be used for control of birch, bramble, hawthorn, etc., or at higher rates for control of hard-to-kill species such as oak and ash. Glyphosate at 2·2 kg/ha has also shown promise as a foliar applied herbicide on bramble, elder, hawthorn and other woody weeds.

Railway tracks

9.025   Clean stone ballast does not support heavy weed growth and allows easy penetration of herbicides. Consequently the lowest doses of root-absorbed residual herbicides given earlier in this chapter will usually maintain control for one or sometimes two seasons. When stone becomes fouled with soil and rubbish, as occurs on most sidings, or on ash ballast or cesses, weeds are more prevalent and more difficult to control, so that the normal recommendations may apply.

Access to railway track for sprayers mounted on road vehicles is often difficult or impossible. For running lines complete trains are employed, made up of spraying unit, living coach and water tankers, and capable of spraying different doses across the width of track and cess, according to weed growth and type of surface. Root-absorbed residuals, in combination with other herbicides such as sodium chlorate or aminotriazole when necessary, are sprayed at around 50 to 65 km.p.h.

Because of more restricted access, spraying in yards and sidings is often confined to barrow or knapsack units of special design, but when water supply is a further limiting factor granular herbicides are generally used.

Presurfacing applications of herbicides

9.026   Where asphalt is put down on a relatively shallow foundation, subsequent weed growth, particularly from deep-rooted perennials, may break up the surface and herbicides are commonly applied during construction as a preventive measure. Herbicides are also applied to the formation level of footpaths, paved areas, electrical installations and other similar sites. Boron compounds are recommended for dry application at 1800 kg B_2O_3/ha, to be watered in thoroughly after application. Atrazine wettable powder or granules at 16·0 kg/ha, and monuron or diuron at 34·0 kg/ha are also recommended as are dichlobenil and chlorthiamid at 17·0 kg/ha. For established weeds glyphosate can be used at 2·2 kg/ha but application should be followed by a residual herbicide.

Temporary total weed control

9.027 Where ground may be required for growing crops, ornamentals or grass in the following season, paraquat at 1·1–2·2 kg/ha, mixtures of dalapon 26·0 kg/ha plus 2,4-D 2·2 kg/ha or of aminotriazole 4·5–6·7 kg/ha plus 2,4-D 2·2 kg/ha, are all useful for giving temporary total weed control without leaving long-lasting harmful residual effects in the soil.

Moss control on hard tennis courts and other asphalt, tiled or paved surfaces

9.028 Boron compounds at 4·0 kg B_2O_3/100 m², atrazine, diuron, monuron or simazine at 11·0 kg/ha are recommended for controlling moss in such situations for 3–6 months.

9.029   The susceptibility of some established weeds to herbicides used for total weed control

NOTES

	Usual percentage control 5 months after application
S—Complete, or almost complete kill	At least 90
MS—Partial kill; effectively suppressed	About 70
MR—Temporary suppression only	About 50
R—No useful effect	Less than 40
— No information	—

Additives to the low dose of residual herbicide required to increase the response

1	4·5 kg aminotriazole	= S
2	4·5 kg aminotriazole + 11·2 kg 2,4-D	= S
3	4·5 kg aminotriazole + 11·2 kg 2,4-D	= MS
4	1·7 kg dicamba	= S
5	3·4 kg dicamba	= MS
6	1·1 kg paraquat	= MS
7	0·3 kg picloram + 1·1 kg 2,4-D	= S
8	0·6 kg picloram + 2·2 kg 2,4-D	= S
9	0·8 kg picloram + 3·4 kg 2,4-D post em.	= S
10	160 kg sodium chlorate	= S
11	5·6 kg TBA	= S

Chemical (dose in kg/ha)

	Simazine			Atrazine			Bromacil			Monuron or diuron			Glyphosate		
	11·0	17·0	22·0	11·0	17·0	22·0	5·6	9·0	12·0	13·0	18·0	27·0	1·0	1·4	2·2
Agropyron repens (Common Couch)	MS (1)	MS	S	S	S	S	S	S	S	—	S	S	MS	S	S
Agrostis stolonifera (Creeping Bent)	MS (1)	S	S	MS (1)	S	S	S	S	S	MS (6)	S	S	S	S	S
Arrhenatharum elatius (False Oat-grass)	MS	S	S	MS	S	S	S	S	S	MR (6)	S	S	S	S	S

Species															
Dactylis glomerata (Cock's-foot)	S	S	MS	S	S	MR (6)	S	S	S	S	S	MS	MS	MR	MR (1)
Deschampsia caespitosa (Tussock Hair-grass)	S	MS	MR	S	MS	MR (6)	S	S	MS (6)	S	MS	MS (1)	MR	R	R (1)
Festuca rubra (Red Fescue)		S	S	MR	S	S (6)	MS	S	S	S	S	SZS	S	S	MS
Holcus lanatus (Yorkshire-fog)	S	S	S	S	S	MS (6)	S	S	S	S	S	S	S	S	MS
Holcus mollis (Creeping Soft-grass)	S	MS	MS	S	S	—	S	S	S	S	S	S	S	S	MS
Lolium perenne (Perennial Rye-grass)	S	S	S	S	S	MS (6)	S	S	S	S	S	S	S	S	MS (1)
Poa annua (Annual Meadow-grass)	S	S	S	S	S	S	S	S	S	S	S	S	S	S	S
Poa pratensis (Smooth Meadow-grass)	S	S	S	S	S	MS (6)	S	S	S	S	S	MS	S	S	MS
Achillea millefolium (Yarrow)	S	MS	MR	S	S	MS (8)	S	S	S	S	S	S	S	S	S
Aegopodium podagraria (Ground-elder)	S	MS	MR	R	R	R	MS	MR	MR	MS	R	R (1)	MR	R	R (1)
Arctium lappa (Great Burdock)	S	MS	MR	R	R	R	S	MS	MR	R	R	R (8)	R	R	R (8)
Artemisia vulgaris (Mugwort)	S	S	MS	S	MS	MR (10)	S	S	S	S	S	MS (12)	MS	MS	MR (1)
Calystegia sepium (Hedge Bindweed)	MS	MR	MR	S	MS	MR	MS	MR	MR	S	S	MS (1, 2)	MR	R	R (2)
Cardaria draba (Hoary Cress)	S	S	MS	R	R	R	S	MS	MR	S	S	MR (2)	S	MR	R
Chamaenerion angustifolium (Rosebay Willowherb)	S	S	MS	S	MR	MR (10, 7)	S	S	MS	S	S	MS (1, 2, 7, 10)	S	MS	MR (2,7)

315

	Simazine			Atrazine			Bromacil			Monuron or diuron			Glyphosate		
Chemical (dose in kg/ha)	11·0	17·0	22·0	11·0	17·0	22·0	5·6	9·0	12·0	13·0	18·0	27·0	1·0	1·5	2·0
Cirsium arvense (Creeping Thistle)	MR (1, 3)	MR	MS	MS (1, 8, 10)	S	S	MS (8, 10)	MS	S	MR (8, 10)	MS	S	MS	MS	S
Convolvulus arvensis (Field Bindweed)	R (1)	R	R	MR (2, 4, 11)	MR	MS	R	R	MR	R (8, 10)	R	R	MR	MS	MS
Equisetum arvense (Field Horsetail)	R (3)	R	R	R (1, 2, 8, 10)	R	MR	MS (10)	MS	S	R (10)	R	R	MR	MS	MS
Glechoma hederacea (Ground-ivy)	MS (1)	S	S	MS (10)	S	S	MS (10)	S	S	MR (10)	MS	S	MR	MS	S
Heracleum sphondylium (Hogweed)	R	R	MR	MR (1, 2, 7, 10)	MS	MS	MR (8, 10)	MS	S	R (8, 10)	R	R	MS	S	S
Hypericum perforatum (Perforate St John's-wort)	R (7)	MS	S	MR (7)	MS	S	MS (8, 10)	S	S	MR (8, 10)	MR	S	MR	MS	S
Linaria vulgaris (Common Toadflax)	R (1)	MR	MS	R	MR	MS	MR (10)	MR	S	MS (10)	S	S	MS	S	S
Plantago species (Plantains)	S	S	S	S	S	S	S	S	S	R (1, 8)	R	R	MR	S	S

316

Weed															
Potentilla reptans (Creeping Cinquefoil)	R	MS	R (2, 7, 10)	MS	S	R (8, 10)	R	R	R (8, 10)	R	R	R	R	MS	S
Polygonum cuspidatum (Japanese Knotweed)	R	R	R (4)	R	R	MR	S	MS	MR	S	R	R	R	MS	S
Pteridium aquilinum (Bracken) R (5)	R	R	R (5)	R	R	R	R	R	R	R	R	R	R	S	S
Ranunculus repens (Creeping Buttercup) MR	MS	S	MS (2)	S	S	R (8, 10)	MS	MR	R (8, 10)	S	S	S	MS	S	S
Rumex obtusifolius (Broad-leaved Dock) R (1, 4)	MR	MS	MR (1, 4)	S	S	MS (7, 10)	S	S	R	R	S	R	MS	S	S
Senecio jacobaea (Common Ragwort) MS	MS	S	MS (2)	S	S	S	S	S	R	R	S	R	MS	S	S
Sonchus arvensis (Perennial Sow-thistle) MS	MS	S	MS (2)	S	MS	S	S	S	MS	S	S	R	MR	MS	S
Taraxacum officinale (Dandelion) R	MR	MS	R (1, 2, 6, 10)	MS	MS	R (6, 8, 10)	S	S	R (1, 8, 10)	S	S	MS	MS	S	S
Urtica dioica (Common Nettle) R	MR	MS	MS (1)	MS	S	S	S	S	S	S	S	S	MR	MS	S
Tussilago farfara (Colt's-foot) R	R	MR	R (8)	MR	MS	MS (8, 10)	S	S	MS (8, 10)	S	S	MS (8, 10)	MR	MS	S

Species	Chemical (dose in kg/ha)								
	Sodium chlorate			Dichlobenil			Picloram		
	220	340	450	7·5	11·0	17·0	0·56	1·4	2·2
Agropyron repens (Common Couch)	MS	MS	S	MR	MS	S	R	R	R
Agrostis stolonifera (Creeping Bent)	—	S	S	MS	S	S	R	R	R
Arrhenatharum elatius (False Oat-grass)	—	S	S	—	—	S	R	R	R
Dactylis glomerata (Cock's-foot)	—	MS	S	MR	MS	S	R	R	R
Deschampsia caespitosa (Tufted Hair-grass)	MS	MS	S	—	—	S	R	R	R
Festuca rubra (Red Fescue)	R	MS	S	—	—	S	R	R	R
Holcus lanatus (Yorkshire-fog)	—	S	S	MS	S	S	R	R	R
Holcus mollis (Creeping Soft-grass)	—	S	S	MS	S	S	R	R	R
Lolium perenne (Perennial Rye-grass)	—	S	S	MR	MS	S	R	R	R
Poa annua (Annual Meadow-grass)	S	S	S	S	S	S	R	R	R
Poa pratensis (Smooth Meadow-grass)	—	S	S	S	S	S	R	R	R
Achillea millefolium (Yarrow)	S	S	S	MR	MS	S	S	S	S

Species									
Aegopodium podagraria (Ground-elder)	S	—	—	S	S	MS	S	—	—
Arctium lappa (Greater Burdock)	S	S	S	S	—	—	S	S	MS
Artemisia vulgaris (Mugwort)	S	S	S	S	—	—	S	S	S
Calystegia sepium (Hedge Bendweed)	S	S	—	MS	MR	R	S	MS	S
Cardaria draba (Hoary Cress)	S	—	—	S	MS	MR	S	S	—
Chamaenerion angustifolium (Rosebay Willow-herb)	S	S	—	S	S	MS	S	MS	MS
Cirsium arvense (Creeping Thistle)	S	S	S	S	S	MS	S	S	S
Convolvulus arvensis (Field Bindweed)	S	S	S	MS	MR	R	S	S	S
Equisetum arvense (Field Horsetail)	S	S	—	S	S	S	S	S	S
Glechoma hederacea (Ground-ivy)	S	S	—	MS	R	R	S	S	—
Heracleum sphondylium (Hogweed)	S	S	—	MS	R	R	S	S	S
Hypericum perforatum (St John's Wort)	S	S	—	S	—	—	S	S	S
Linaria vulgaris (Common Toadflax)	R	R	R	—	—	—	S	S	—
Plantago species (Plantains)	S	S	S	S	S	S	S	S	MS
Potentilla reptans (Creeping Cinquefoil)	S	S	S	MR	R	R	S	S	MS

| | Chemical (dose in kg/ha) | | | | | | | | |
| | Sodium chlorate | | | Dichlobenil | | | Picloram | | |
	220	340	460	7·5	11·0	17·0	0·56	1·4	2·2
Polygonum cuspidatum (Japanese Knotweed)	R	R	R	—	—	—	— (9)	S Pre-	S em
Pteridium aquilinum (Bracken)	MR	MS	S	MS	S	S	—	S	S
Ranunculus repens (Creeping Buttercup)	S	S	S	R	R	MR	—	S	S
Rumex obtusifolius (Broad-leaved Dock)	MR	S	S	MS	S	S	—	S	S
Senecio jacobaea (Common Ragwort)	S	S	S	—	—	S	S	S	S
Sonchus arvensis (Perennial Sow-thistle)	S	S	S	S	S	S	—	S	S
Taraxacum officinale (Dandelion)	MS	S	S	S	S	S	S	S	S
Urtica dioica (Common Nettle)	S	S	S	MR	MS	S	S	S	S
Tussilago farfara (Colt's-foot)	S	S	S	S	S	S	—	S	S

Chapter 10
Recommendations for the
control of aquatic weeds

10.001 An account is given of mechanical and chemical methods of aquatic weed control. The use of herbicides is increasing and recommendations are given for those which have been cleared under the Pesticide Safety Precautions Scheme for safe use in or near water.

It is necessary to identify the most troublesome weeds before deciding on a method of control. The following publications will be found useful.

(1) Clapham, A. R., Tutin, T. G. and Warburg, E. F. *Flora of the British Isles. Illustrations.* 4 vols. Cambridge University Press.

(2) Ross-Craig, Stella. *Drawings of British Plants.* Parts 1–18. London. G. Bell & Sons Ltd.

(3) Keble Martin, W. *The Concise British Flora in Colour.* London. Ebury Press and Michael Joseph.

(4) Haslam, S. M., Sinker, C. A. and Wolseley, P. A. *British Water Plants.* Field Studies Council.

(5) Bursche, Eva M. *A Handbook of Water Plants.* London Fredrick Warner & Co. Ltd.

(6) Engelhardt. W. *Pond Life* (Young Specialist Series). London. Burke,

Classification of aquatic weeds

Aquatic weeds may be placed in 5 groups:

Emergent

10.002 Those with aerial stems and leaves protruding above the water surface and growing in situations where the water level ranges from just below ground to about half the maximum height of the plant.

Floating

10.003 Those with leaves that float on the water surface. The plants may be free-floating, e.g. *Lemna minor* (Common Duckweed) or rooted to the bed, e.g. *Callitriche* spp. (Water Starwort). They occur in a wide range of situations and are found intermingled with submerged and emergent plants.

Submerged

10.004   Those with all leaves below the water surface. Most are rooted to the bed, e.g. *Elodea canadensis* (Canadian Pondweed) whilst others are not, e.g. *Lemna trisulca* (Ivy-leaved Duckweed).

Algae

10.005   There are many forms of aquatic algae but those that cause most trouble are the filamentous forms known as 'blanket weeds', 'cott' or 'hair weed'. Although they can occur in running water they are usually only troublesome in situations where flow is very slow or the water is stationary.

Waterside plants

10.006   In addition to the control of aquatic weeds those responsible for the maintenance of waterways and lakes are also concerned with the control of vegetation on the banks. This aspect is dealt with here and also in Chapter 9.

Methods of control

Cutting

Hand-cutting

10.007   Where labour is still plentiful or where there is no alternative method available, hand-cutting using scythes, hooks and chain-scythes is often the only or the most economic choice. It is slow and as weed regrowth in the channel is rapid, it is usually a continuous operation throughout the summer.

Mechanical cutting

10.008   In channels that are wide and deep enough it is usual to use a boat designed for cutting both submerged plants and emergent weeds standing in the water.

There are now a number of boats available. Those most recently developed have fibre-glass hulls, hydraulically driven paddles and recoprocating cutter bars. They are lighter, more manoeuvrable in weedy conditions and much more versatile than their predecessors. A selection of different knives are available, which enables them to trim the banks as well as the channel. Steel boats with V-shaped cutting knives are still used and one with a steel hull, but with reciprocating cutting blades, has been imported from France.

10.009   Another introduction from Europe is a weed-cutting bucket for use on the jib of an excavator. It has an hydraulically operated reciprocating knife on its leading edge and the 'bucket' is designed to allow the water to escape while retaining the cut weed. Similar buckets are now produced in this country and can be up to 3·7 m in width. An essential requirement for the use of this implement is an hydraulically controlled jib and this limits its use to the smaller channels whose further bank is within reach of the excavator.

10.010   Few machines are capable of cutting weeds and grass on the sloping banks of drainage channels and ditches. Those with a flail-type cutting mechanism used for the maintenance of road verges are the most suitable but only if access for a tractor is possible along the bank and if the arm supporting the cutter mechanism is long enough to reach down the required distance.

   Small self-propelled mowers either with reciprocating blades or with horizontal rotary cutters are frequently used on all but the steepest banks.

10.011   It is necessary to remove all cut material from the water to prevent it blocking pump intakes, etc., and deoxygenating the water as it decomposes (Volume I, Chapter 17). Most plants float to the surface when cut and booms are placed across the channel at suitable places to hold the cut material until it can be removed either by a hand-rake attached to ropes or by draglines.

   Where access is possible draglines are used to remove filamentous algae, but where this is not possible raking by hand is still sometimes necessary.

Herbicides

10.012   **Attention is drawn to the recommendation sheets issued by the Pesticides Branch of the Ministry of Agriculture, Fisheries and Food for each herbicide cleared for use in aquatic situations and also to the official Code of Practice for the use of herbicides in water which appears as an Appendix to this chapter (10.026).** Reference should also be made to the section in Volume I, Chapter 17 that refers to the functions of the regional Water Authorities.

   It must be remembered that clearance under the Pesticides Safety Precautions Scheme is granted to a herbicide only in accordance with the instructions for use embodied in its label. **The recommendations in this chapter refer only to those commercial formulations with labels** specifically mentioning their use in or near water. No other formulations should be used.

Certain chemicals are currently being tested for safe use in or near water. These chemicals should not be used until cleared for such use under the Pesticides Safety Precautions Scheme.

Emergent weeds and waterside plants

10.013   The herbicide is sprayed on to the foliage of emergent weeds. When they are growing in the water some may be controlled by the treatment used for submerged weeds.

Information on spraying and spraying techniques may be found in Volume I, Chapter 5.

10.014   **Dalapon-sodium** *19·0–48·0 kg/ha in 700 litres/ha or more to foliage from May to September, for certain monocotyledonous weeds* (10.025).

Dalapon is a general grass-killer and careless or injudicious use could result in the total destruction of grass swards on the banks.

Fine weather and good growing conditions are necessary for the best results. The addition of a safe wetting agent will improve uptake of the herbicide and permit a reduction in dose of about 15 per cent. A commercial formulation incorporating a wetting agent is available. With many species late treatment in the summer gives a longer control of regrowth from the rhizome. 2,4-D may be added to dalapon for the control of broad-leaved weeds.

In aerial applications lower volumes (300–550 litres/ha) and lower doses (13·0 kg/ha dalapon-sodium) give satisfactory results but special spray equipment or invert emulsions must be used to avoid drift.

The treated plants should not be cut until 5 weeks after spraying, otherwise the effect of the treatment on regrowth may be impaired.

Water from water-bodies sprayed with dalapon should not be used for irrigation within 5 weeks of treatment or until the concentration in the water has dropped below 0·3 ppm.

10.015   **Dalapon-sodium** *19·0 kg/ha* + **paraquat** *0·5 kg/ha in 900 litres water in July or August for the control of* Phragmites communis *(Common Reed) and subsequent collapse of the dead reed.*

Only paraquat specifically formulated for aquatic use should be used. It is essential for the best results to add a non-ionic wetting agent which is non-toxic to fish.

When paraquat is added to dalapon in the tank, the mixture gives a more rapid desiccation of foliage and stem. *Phragmites communis* (Common Reed) disintegrates to a greater degree than when dalapon is used alone. Thus the need for cutting which is usually required after spraying with dalapon, is largely removed.

Similar effects have been observed on *Sparganium erectum* (Branched Bur-reed) and *Schoenoplectus lacustris* (Clubrush).

When the mixture is applied in July there is little regrowth of *Phragmites* (Common Reed) the following year.

Typha spp. (Bulrush) do not always disintegrate and regrowth is not controlled.

The mixture has shown promise on *Carex riparia* (Greater Pondsedge) and some other plants, but further information is required on which to base a recommendation.

10.016 **2,4-D-amine** *2·2–4·5 kg/ha in one or more applications in 200–700 or more litres/ha to foliage from May to September.*

Only amine formulations have been cleared under Pesticides Safety Precautions Scheme.

Do not use esters and oil-based formulations. Fish can tolerate concentrations of up to 50 ppm 2,4-D-amine but can be killed by concentrations of less than 1 ppm of some emulsions and ester formulations.

Undesirable taints and odours can be caused by 2,4-D and care must be taken to avoid contaminating domestic water supplies.

Dalapon may be added to 2,4-D to control a mixed population of monocotyledonous and dicotyledonous weeds.

Many broad-leaved plants on the banks or emerging from the water are susceptible. *Sparganium erectum* (Branched Bur-reed) is susceptible but regrowth occurs in the following season.

Water from water bodies sprayed with 2,4-D should not be used for irrigation within 3 weeks of treatment or until the concentration in the water has dropped below 0·05 ppm.

10.017 **Maleic hydrazide** *5·6 kg/ha in 450–900 litres/ha to waterside grasses actively growing but only 75–150 mm high between March and early May to retard growth for 12 weeks or more.*

If rain falls within 12 h of the application the effect may be reduced. A 'rain-fast' formulation is available which if applied to dry foliage and allowed time to dry reduces the adverse effects of rain.

Regular treatment over several years can change the sward composition by eliminating coarser grass species such as *Arrhenatherum elatius* (False Oat-grass) and *Dactylis glomerata* (Cock's-foot) and encouraging the finer grasses, e.g. *Poa pratensis* (Smooth Meadow-grass) and *Festuca rubra* (Red Fescue). Its effect on *Phragmites communis* (Common Reed) and other emergent aquatic weeds is variable. Maleic hydrazide may be combined with 2,4-D to control broad-leaved weeds (see also Chapter 7.035).

Water below banks treated with maleic hydrazide should not be used for irrigation within 3 weeks of treatment or until the concentration in the water has dropped below 0·02 ppm.

Floating weeds, submerged weeds and algae

10.018   When treating submerged water weeds the herbicide has to be introduced into the water to form a dilute solution. Its effectiveness depends upon the concentration of the solution and in these recommendations the dose is given in terms of milligrams of herbicide a.i. per litre of water (mg/litre) (this is a concentration of 1 part per million—ppm), e.g. 1 g in 1000 litres = 1 mg/litres (= 1 ppm) or 1 kg in 1 000 000 litres = 1 mg/litres (= 1 ppm).

To determine the amount of herbicide to add to water to obtain the required concentration the volume of water should first be calculated as follows:

$$\text{Area in m}^2 \times \text{average depth in m} = \text{volume in m}^3.$$

Because there are 1000 litres in 1 m³, 1000 mg (or 1 g) added to each m³ will give a concentration of 1 mg/litres i.e. 1 ppm. The amount of herbicide required is therefore determined by:

Herbicide a.i. in grams = concentration ppm × volume of water in m³ (1 ac × 1 ft deep = 1200 m³).

The recommendations that follow *apply only to still or sluggishly moving water,* i.e. where the water flow does not exceed approximately 1·5 m/min. (5 ft/min.).

10.019   **Diquat** *at a concentration of 0·5–1 ppm for the control of submerged, some floating and some emergent weeds when the plants are actively growing.*

It may be applied either by surface spraying or by injecting appropriate doses of the concentrate below the surface from a boat or in a drainage channel at 5 m intervals. Where there are floating and submerged weeds present it is necessary to apply the solution as a combination of injections and surface spray. Surface spraying at 0·56–1·12 kg/ha is recommended for free-floating plants, e.g. *Lemna minor* (Common Duckweed).

Diquat causes rapid top kills of a wide range of submerged and floating plants and control usually lasts for the rest of the year if the treatment is done when the weed is well grown. If the treatment is carried out too early, regrowth may occur the same summer. The water lilies *Nymphaea* spp. and *Nuphar lutea* are resistant, although they may be temporarily defoliated.

When in still or confined water, fish are present and the weed is thick treat only $\frac{1}{4}$ of the water-body at any one time to avoid deoxygenation.

Water treated with diquat should not be used for overhead irrigation within 10 days of treatment or until the concentration in the water is below 0·02 ppm.

10.020   **Dichlobenil** *at a concentration of 1 ppm in the water shortly before or* *soon after weed growth begins, to control submerged, some floating and some emergent vascular plants.*

Only granular formulations are available. For good results it is desirable to obtain an even distribution over the area treated, although small areas may be treated by hand, for larger areas the use of a granular applicator is recommended. When used at the recommended time deoxygenation should not occur.

Water treated with dichlobenil should not be used for irrigation within 4 weeks of treatment or until the concentration is below 0·3 ppm.

10.021   **Chlorthiamid** *at a concentration of 1 ppm in the water shortly before or soon after weed growth begins, to control some submerged and floating vascular plants.*

Only granular formulations are available.

For good results it is desirable to obtain an even distribution over the area treated. Although small areas may be treated by hand, for larger areas the use of a granule applicator is recommended.

Water treated with chlorthiamid should not be used for irrigation within 4 weeks of treatment or until the concentration is below 0·3 ppm.

10.022   **2,4-D-amine** (10.016) at 4·5 kg/ha with a suitable wetting agent applied to the floating and aerial leaves of water lilies (*Nuphar* and *Nymphaea*). This does not give complete control and repeat applications are necessary.

10.023   **Terbutryne** *at a concentration of 0·05—0·1 ppm soon after weed growth begins, to control many algae, submerged vascular weeds and some floating vascular weeds.*

Only the granular formulation should be used.

To obtain the best results the granules should be evenly distributed over the water surface using a suitable granule applicator.

Where fish are present and the weed growth is expected to be dense treatment should be made early in the season to reduce the risk of deoxygenation.

Water treated with terbutryne should not be used for irrigation within 7 days of treatment.

10.024   **Glyphosate** *at 1·8—2·2 kg/ha 220—670 l/ha of water for the control of* Nymphaea alba *(White Water-lily),* Nuphar lutea *(Yellow Water-lily) and emergent grass weeds.*

It is readily translocated to underground parts of treated plants and effects are rapidly seen in both *Nymphaea alba* and *Nuphar lutea.* Treatment should only be made to fully-expanded leaves in the July—August period. The effect on grass weeds such as *Phragmites communis* (Common Reed), *Glyceria maxima* (Reed Sweet-grass) and *Phalaris arunduracea* (Reed Canary-grass) takes longer to appear.

Treatment should be made to actively growing plants in the August–September period.

The maximum permitted concentration in water is 0·2 ppm and there is no interval required between treatment of water and its use for irrigation purposes.

10.025 The susceptibility of aquatic weeds to herbicides

S = Susceptible — Complete or almost complete kill in the year of treatment.
MS = Moderately susceptible — Partial kill and effective suppression in the year of treatment.
MR = Moderately resistant — Temporary suppression. Regrowth occuring during year of treatment.
R = Resistant — No useful effect.
— Insufficient information or Not applicable.

Key to type of weed
Sub Submerged
Em   Emergent
Fl   Floating
Alg Algae.

Chemical and dose

Weed	Type	Dalapon 22.0 kg/ha	Dalapon 34.0 kg/ha	Dalapon/Paraquat 9.0 kg/ha	Paraquat 0.5 kg/ha	2,4-D-amine 2.2 kg/ha	2,4-D-amine 4.5 kg/ha	Glyphosate 1.8–2.2 kg/ha	Dichlobenil 1 ppm	Chlorthiamid 1 ppm	Diquat 1 ppm	Diquat 1.1 kg/ha	Terbutryne 0.05 ppm
Alisma plantago-aquatica (Water Plantain)	Em	R	R	MR		S	S	—	S	—	S	MS	—
Apium nodiflorum (Fool's Watercress)	Em	R	R	MR		R	R	—	—	—	—	MS	—
Azolla filiculoides (Water Fern)	Fl	—	—	—		—	—	—	—	—	—	MS	—
Berula erecta (Lesser Water-parsnip)	Em	R	R	MR		—	—	—	MS	—	—	—	—
Callitriche spp. (Water Starwort)	Fl/ Sub	—	—	—		—	—	—	S MS	MS	S	—	S
Caltha palustris (Marsh-marigold)	Em	R	R	—		—	—	—	R	—	—	—	—

329

Weed	Habit	Dalapon 22.0 kg/ha	Dalapon 34.0 kg/ha	Dalapon/Paraquat 9.0 kg/ha	Dalapon/Paraquat 0.5 kg/ha	2,4-D-amine 2.2 kg/ha	2,4-D-amine 4.5 kg/ha	Glyphosate 1.8–2.2 kg/ha	Dichlobenil 1 ppm	Chlorthiamid 1 ppm	Diquat 1 ppm	Diquat 1.1 kg/ha	Terbutryne 0.05 ppm
Carex riparia (Greater Pond-sedge)	Em	S	—	MS	—	R	R	S	R	R	R	MR	—
Carex spp. (Sedges)	Em	MS	MS	MR	—	R	R	S	R	R	—	MR	S
Ceratophyllum demersum (Rigid Hornwort)	Sub	—	—	—	—	—	—	R	S	S	MR	—	S
Chara spp.	Alg	—	—	—	—	—	—	—	MS	MS	R	MR	S
Cladophora spp.	Alg	—	—	—	—	—	—	R	R	R	S	—	S
Elodea canadensis (Canadian Water-weed)	Sub	—	—	—	—	—	—	R	S	S	S	—	S
Enteromorpha intestinalis	Alg	—	—	—	—	—	MS	R	R	R	R	—	S
Epilobium hirsutum (Great Willow-herb)	Em	R	R	MR	—	MS	MS	—	MS	—	—	—	—
Equisetum fluviatile (Water Horsetail)	Em	R	R	—	—	—	MR	—	S	S	MR	MR	R
Fontinalis spp. (Willow-moss)	Sub	—	—	—	—	—	—	—	S	—	R	—	—
Glyceria fluitans (Floating Sweet-grass)	Em	MR	MR	—	—	R	R	S	S	MS	R	MR	—
Glyceria maxima (Reed Sweet-grass)	Em	MR	MR	MR	—	R	R	S	MR	MR	R	MR	—
Hippuris vulgaris (Marestail)	Sub	—	—	—	—	—	—	—	S	—	MR	—	S
Hottonia palustris (Water Violet)	Sub	—	—	—	—	—	—	S	S	S	MS	—	S
Hydrocharis morsus-ranae (Frog-bit)	Fl	—	—	—	—	—	—	—	MS	MS	MS	—	—
Hydrodictyon	Alg	—	—	—	—	—	—	—	—	—	S	MR	S
Iris pseudacorus (Yellow Iris)	Em	R	MR	—	—	—	—	—	MR	MS	—	MR	—

Species	Type	1	2	3	4	5	6	7	8	9	10	11
Juncus effuses (Soft Rush)	Em	MR	MR	MS	—	S	S	R	R	—	S	—
Juncus inflexus (Hard Rush)	Em	MR	MR	—	R	R	S	R	R	—	—	—
Lagarosyphon major	Sub	—	—	—	—	—	—	MS / R	—	R	—	S
Lemna spp. (Duckweeds)	Fl	—	—	—	—	—	S	R	R	S	S	—
Lemna trisulca (Ivy-leaved Duckweed)	Sub	—	—	—	—	—	R	—	—	S	—	—
Lythrum salicaria (Purple-loosestrife)	Em	R	R	—	R	MR	—	—	—	—	—	—
Mentha aquatica (Water Mint)	Em	R	R	—	S	S	—	—	—	—	—	S
Myriophyllum spicatum (Spiked Water-milfoil)	Sub	—	—	—	—	—	R	S	MS	S 0·5 ppm	S	S
Myriophyllum verticillatum (Whorled Water-milfoil)	Sub	—	—	—	—	—	R	S	MS	S 0·5 ppm	—	S
Nuphar lutea (Yellow Water-lily)	Fl	R	R	R	R	MS see text	S	MR	MR	MR	MR	R
Nymphaea alba (White Water-lily)	Fl	R	R	R	R	MS see text	S	MR	MR	MR	MR	R
Nymphoides peltata (Fringed Water-lily)	Fl	R	R	R	R	MS	—	MR	MR	—	MR	—
Oenanthe aquatica (Fine-leaved Water-dropwort)	Em	—	—	—	—	MR	—	MS	MS	—	—	—
Oenanthe crocata (Hemlock Water-dropwort)	Em	—	—	—	—	MR	—	MS	MS	—	—	—
Phalaris arundinacea (Reed Canary-grass)	Em	S	S	—	R	R	S	R	R	—	—	—
Phragmites communis (Common Reed)	Em	S	S	S	R	R	S	R	R	R	MR	—
Polygonum amphibium (Amphibious Bistort)	Em	R	R	—	—	MR	—	MR	MR	MR	MR	R

Chemical and dose

Weed		Dalapon 22.0 kg/ha	Dalapon 34.0 kg/ha	Dalapon/Paraquat 9.0 0.5 kg/ha	2,4-D-amine 2.2 kg/ha	2,4-D-amine 4.5 kg/ha	Glyphosate 1.8–2.2 kg/ha	Dichlobenil 1 ppm	Chlorthiamid 1 ppm	Diquat 1 ppm	Diquat 1.1 kg/ha	Terbutryne 0.05 ppm
Potamogeton berchtoldii (Small Pondweed)	Sub	—	—	—	—	—		—	—	S	—	—
P. crispus (Curled Pondweed)	Sub	—	—	—	—	—	R	S	MS	S 0.5 ppm	—	S
P. lucens (Shining Pondweed)	Sub	—	—	—	—	—	—	MS	MS	S	—	—
P. natans (Broad-leaved Pondweed)	Fl/Sub	—	—	—	—	—	R	MS	MS	S	—	MR
P. pectinatus (Fennel Pondweed)	Sub	—	—	—	—	—	—	MS	MS	S	—	S
P. praelongus (Long-stalked Pondweed)	Sub	—	—	—	—	—	—	—	—	S	—	—
P. pusillus (Lesser Pondweed)	Sub	—	—	—	—	—	—	—	—	S	—	—
Ranunculus aquatilis (Common Water Crowfoot)	Sub	—	—	—	—	—	—	S	MS	S 0.5 ppm	—	—
R. acutiformis	Sub	—	—	—	—	—	—	S	MS	S 0.5 ppm	—	—

Species	Type										
Ranunculus spp. (Water Crowfoot)	Sub	—	—	—	—	—	S	MS	S	—	S
Rhizoclonium spp.	Alg	R	—	—	—	R	R	R	S 0·5 ppm	—	S
Rorippa nasturtium-aquaticum (Water-cress)	Em	—	—	—	S	S	MS	MS	MR	—	—
Rumex hydrolapathum (Water Dock)	Em	R	—	—	—	—	MS	—	—	—	—
Sagittaria sagittifolia (Arrowhead)	Em	MR	MS	R	MR	—	S	MS	S	—	—
Schoenoplectus lacustris (Common Clubrush)	Em	R	S	R	R	—	R	R	—	—	—
Scirpus maritimus (Sea Club-rush)	Em	MR	MR	R	R	—	R	R	—	—	—
Sparganium emersum (Unbranched Bur-reed)	Sub	—	—	—	—	—	MR	MR	S	—	—
Sparganium erectum (Branched Bur-reed)	Em	MS	S	—	MS	—	MR	MR	S	MS	S
Spirogyra spp.	Alg	—	—	—	—	R	R	R	MR	MR	—
Stratiotes aloides (Water Soldier)	Sub	S	—	—	—	—	S	—	—	MR	—
Typha angustifolia (Lesser Bulrush)	Em	S	—	R	R	—	R	R	R	MR	—
Typha latifolia (Bulrush)	Em	S	MS	R	R	S	R	R	R	MR	—
Vaucheria dichotoma	Alg	—	—	—	—	R	R	MR	R	R	MR
Zannichellia palustris (Horned Pondweed)	Sub	—	—	—	—	R	MS	MR	—	—	S

English names based on 'English names of wild flowers' by the Botanical Society of the British Isles Butterworth Press 1974.

Code of practice for the use of herbicides on weeds in watercourses and lakes

Published by Pesticides Branch, Ministry of Agriculture, Fisheries and Food, Great Westminster House, Horseferry Road, London, SW1 2AE.

Introduction

10.026   Herbicides are chemical compounds which are used to kill or to reduce the growth of plants. Some of them are total weed killers and act on all plants while others are selective and only affect certain species leaving others unharmed.

There are very many different herbicides on the market for selective use in agriculture and horticulture and for non-selective use on waste areas, industrial sites, etc; and many more are in various stages of testing and development. A number have been tested and found useful in drainage channels against plants growing in water, while others have been shown to be suitable for use on emergent weeds, (i.e. those with 'emergent' or aerial leaves) near and on banks.

10.027   Herbicides can be placed in two classes according to how they act on a plant.

(a) Contact herbicides. These are chemicals that kill the part of the plant with which they come in contact.

(b) Translocated herbicides. These chemicals enter living plant tissue from where they are moved, to a greater or lesser extent, to other parts of the root or shoot. Their effect is to upset some physiological process. The way in which many of these substances work is not clearly understood and is being intensively studied. Some translocated herbicides enter the plant through its leaves, others through its root and others through both root and shoot.

The way in which a herbicide is applied is determined by the properties it possesses. A contact herbicide must be applied to those parts that have to be destroyed to achieve the desired results. This is usually the foliage. To be most effective it must come in contact with as much of the plant as possible and the commonest way of achieving this is by spraying it on the leaves and shoots. A wetting agent is sometimes added to encourage its spread over the plant's surface.

10.028   It is normally not essential to apply translocated herbicides so evenly over the plant, although in most cases this will increase the amount taken up and thus its effectiveness. It is, however, necessary to apply the chemical to the part of the plant that will absorb it and, as susceptibility can vary with the age of a plant, at a stage in growth when it will be most effective. Again wetting agents may increase efficiency.

In the case of water weeds, those with emergent leaves can be sprayed in the same way as an ordinary land plant but weeds with submerged foliage can only be reached by introducing the herbicide into the water.

10.029 The introduction of a herbicide into water by injection or as a result of spraying emergent weeds, may create hazards not encountered when the same chemical is used in agriculture or other situations. There may be some potential risk to people using the water for domestic, recreational or agricultural purposes or to fish and other forms of life living in the water. The degree of risk will depend upon the properties of the herbicide and the amount of chemical reaching the water.

10.030 A certain amount of herbicide sprayed on to the leaves of emergent plants may find its way into the water and in the absence of adequate data, the proportion of a high volume spray application that should, for safety purposes, be considered to have done so, should be estimated as:

(a) 100 per cent where the foliage of the sprayed plants emerges from or overhangs the water,

(b) 50 per cent where the plants are growing at the water's edge, and

(c) 10 per cent where the treated plants are on the bank and the chemical can only reach the water indirectly.

The risks, if any, will then be assessed after the concentration of herbicide in the water has been calculated and the dilution factor taken into account.

10.031 Because the herbicide formulations (solutions or powders) supplied in concentrated form by different manufacturers often differ from each other in the amount of herbicide they contain, it is necessary, when making general recommendation to refer only to the quantity of actual herbicide or 'active ingredient' (a.i.) present. Information on the amount of active ingredient contained in a product, if not stated on the label or instruction leaflet, should be obtained from the supplier.

10.032 The amount of herbicide formulation required for the control of weeds is derived from one of the following formulae. The volume of water to be treated is determined from the average depth and surface area. If the formula for imperial terms is adopted then the units in brackets should be used.

Metric terms	Imperial terms
$$Wf = \frac{V \times C \times 100}{Wa}$$	$$Wf = \frac{V \times C}{Wa \times 160}$$

Where Wf = weight of formulation required in grams (pounds)

Wa = weight of active ingredient in grams per 100 grams of formulation (pounds per 100 pounds)

V = water volume in cubic metres (cubic feet)

C = concentration of active ingredient required in milligrams per litre or grams per cubic metre (= parts per million)

Conversely to determine the concentration of active ingredient present in a body of water containing a known amount of formulation the following formulae may be used.

Metric terms	Imperial terms
$$C = \frac{Wf \times Wa}{V \times 100}$$	$$C = \frac{Wf \times Wa \times 160}{V}$$

When determining the concentration of herbicide in flowing water, any possible dissipation through difference in rate of flow across the channel should be disregarded but any dilution through inflows below the point of treatment should be taken into account.

10.033 Because treated water may remain in backwaters, or amongst weeds, restrictions applicable to the use of treated stationary water should be applied between the point of treatment and the point downstream at which the concentration of herbicide in the water reaches a non-herbicidal level.

Two points must be considered when selecting a herbicide for use on water weeds,

(a) whether the treatment will control the troublesome plants,

(b) whether there are likely to be any adverse side-effects to water users, e.g. toxicity to animals, irrigated crops, fish and water supply.

Information on the first of these would normally have to be available before a chemical was considered at all and would include the dose, method of application and time of treatment.

10.034 The second point is not always straightforward and obvious and it is the purpose of the code of practice to help those considering the use of herbicides to recognize the conditions where each can be used with safety and with no unwanted and harmful results.

10.035 Aerial application should be carried out only with the permission of Civil Aviation Authority, and only formulations specifically cleared under the Pesticides Safety Precautions Scheme for use in aerial spraying should be so applied. Full details, together with the conditions under which permission can be granted and retained, are set out in the CAA manual *'The Aerial Application Permission—Requirements and Information'* obtainable from the Civil Aviation Authority, Printing and Publications Services, Grenville House, 37 Gratton Road, Cheltenham, Gloucestershire GL50 2NB (price £1.50).

336

10.036   The risk of harmful side-effects is governed by:

(a) the property of the herbicide, i.e.

(i) its toxicity to man, animals and plants at the concentration reached in the water,

(ii) its persistence or that of its breakdown products, in a toxic form in water, weed and mud,

(iii) its other properties such as taste, colour, smell and corrosiveness.

(b) the condition and situation of the lake or watercourse to be treated,

(i) the use made of the water,

(ii) whether the water is flowing or stationary,

(iii) the importance of wildlife, fishing, land drainage and other interests in relation to each other,

(iv) the adjacent crops and their susceptibility to spray drift, seepage, etc.

Precautions

10.037   Only those herbicides that have been cleared under the Pesticides Safety Precautions Scheme for use in water should be used on aquatic weeds and this Code of Practice should be read in conjunction with the Government's recommendations for the safe use of the particular active ingredient of the herbicide. These are obtainable free from the address given in paragraph 12.

10.038   Water authorities are legally responsible for the control of pollution in watercourses and lakes and before a herbicide is used the appropriate water authority should be consulted in case there is a possibility of the treatment resulting in pollution. A person causing pollution is liable to a heavy fine or imprisonment.

10.039   The method of application and the rate at which the herbicide is applied are included in the directions for the use on the label or accompanying instructions. These directions and any additional requirements of the water authority should be followed strictly.

10.040   Great care should be taken to avoid accidental spillage of the concentrate into the watercourse. To reduce the risk of accident, the recharging of application equipment should be done as far away from the water as is practicable.

10.041   When spraying flowing water the operator should always proceed upstream to avoid any build-up of concentration of herbicide in the water.

Protection of operators

10.042   The appropriate precautions to be taken when handling and applying the herbicide are contained in the official Recommendations Sheets which also indicate whether the active ingredient of the herbicide is included in the Agriculture (Poisonous Substances) Regulations. The precautions are also incorporated in the directions for use supplied with the herbicide. These directions should be followed strictly.

Protection of the Public

10.043   Great care should be taken in disposing of empty containers, surplus spray mixture, washings from machines and unwanted concentrate remainders. Follow the detailed advice given in the Ministry's Code of Practice for the Disposal of Unwanted Pesticides and Containers on Farms and Holdings.

Protection of water users

10.044   *Public and private water supplies*
   Herbicides should not be used in watercourses, lakes or reservoirs from which water is eventually to be used as a source of public or private supply unless the appropriate water authority has been consulted who will wish to ensure that:

   (i) there will be no toxic hazard to humans, livestock and pet animals, (see appropriate Recommendations Sheet),
   (ii) there is no toxic hazard to cultivated plants (see appropriate Recommendations Sheet),
   (iii) no undesirable taste, odour or colour will develop in the water either on abstraction or after treatment by the methods used at a water undertaking (e.g. chlorination by a water authority could result in an unpleasant taste developing if phenolic materials were present in the water).

RECREATIONAL PURPOSES

10.045   In enclosed waters swimming should be prohibited after treatment for any period stated on the label. In flowing water where bathing is known to occur downstream, herbicides should not be applied unless it is shown that by the time the treated water reaches the length used by swimmers, the concentration will have been reduced by dilution or otherwise to a level at which there is no toxicity risk.

Protection of farm animals

10.046   Farmers whose animals have access to a watercourse or lake that is being considered for treatment with a herbicide should be notified of the type of any intended treatment and the precautions, if any, that may be necessary to protect their livestock.
   Under conditions of flowing water, this applies not only to those

farming the land adjacent to the treated length of watercourse, but also to those downstream and within the length between the lowest point of treatment and the point where concentration of herbicide in the water drops to a level considered safe for livestock. The latter point is calculated as explained in the Introduction, from the original concentration, the rate of flow, and the rate of dilution through increases in the volume of water.

Protection of crops and other plants of value

10.047 When the herbicide is applied in the form of a spray care should be taken to avoid accidentally directing it on to adjacent crops. Equipment and particularly the spray booms and nozzles should be selected to give a spray pattern to fit the target.

To avoid herbicide drifting on to susceptible beneficial plants so as to cause damage, application should only be made:

(i) at a time when wind speed is not above force 3 on the Beaufort scale, i.e. a gentle breeze, 7–10 knots, leaves and small twigs in constant motion and the wind extends a light flag.

(ii) as a coarse, well-directed spray with a minimum of fine droplets and a well-defined swath, i.e. using a high volume/low pressure equipment or a formulation containing an additive to increase viscosity, e.g. an invert emulsion,

(iii) through suitable and undamaged nozzles.

Where highly-susceptible plants are growing on adjacent land, the treatment should be postponed until they reach a stage of growth at which they are no longer susceptible. Alternatively, another method of aquatic weed control should be used.

The Code of Practice for Ground Spraying, obtainable free from Divisional Offices of the Ministry of Agriculture, Fisheries and Food, should be read in conjunction with this section.

10.048 When a herbicide is applied as a granular formulation, care should be taken to achieve an even distribution over the area of water or land to be treated. Whenever possible, a reliable mechanical granule spreader should be used.

10.049 Before a herbicide is introduced into the water, either directly to control submerged weeds or through foliar applications on emergent weeds, the eventual concentration of chemical in the water should be calculated as indicated in the Introduction.

(i) Herbicides should not be used in flowing water where aquatic crops, e.g. watercress, are being grown downstream unless it is ensured that the concentration of chemical will drop, between the treated stretch of watercourse and the crops, to a level at which there is no risk of damage and no risk to consumers of edible crops.

(ii) Water that is used for the irrigation of crops should not be treated with herbicide unless it is ascertained that the crops are not susceptible or that irrigation can be avoided for the period after treatment required for the toxicity to reach a safe level.

(iii) Herbicides that enter the roots of plants should not be used in situations where the roots of trees or shrubs it is wished to preserve, grow out into the water or mud of the watercourse or lake.

Protection of fish and wildlife

DIRECT TOXICITY

10.050   Herbicides can be toxic to fish and should not be used in water containing fish at concentrations in excess of the maximum stated in the official recommendations for the particular herbicide. Because some wetting agents and other additives are toxic to fish, only those commercial herbicides specifically recommended for use in or near water should be used. The rates and methods of application given on the product label or instructions leaflet should be strictly followed. No additives should be used.

10.051   *Indirect effects*
Submerged weeds killed by herbicide treatment usually decay *in situ* and cannot be removed from the water. Where weed growth has been heavy, the oxygen taken up from the water in the process of decay can be sufficient to reduce the dissolved oxygen content of the water to an extent lethal to fish. The same effect can result from dead emergent weeds falling into shallow water.

To avoid this, herbicides should be applied:

(i) before weed growth reaches serious proportions, or

(ii) to parts of the watercourse or lake at different times and not simultaneously over the whole area, so that fish have an opportunity to move to untreated areas should the dissolved oxygen content drop seriously. In a lake, not more than a quarter of the area should be treated at one time.

Some herbicides diffuse so rapidly in the water that it is not always possible to use this method. In narrow watercourse and particularly in standing or sluggish water, only short lengths of up to approximately $\frac{1}{4}$ mile should be treated and they should be separated from each other by an equal length of untreated water.

10.052   Before a herbicide is used on a watercourse or a lake, enquiries should be made to ensure that no Nature Reserve or Site of Special Scientific Interest is likely to be adversely affected by the treatment.

The exact location of any Nature Reserve, Site of Special Scientific Interest or similar wildlife sanctuary should be ascertained from the landowners, country or district planning officers, water authority or Nature Conservancy Council.

A herbicide should not be used within a Nature Reserve, Site of Special Scientific Interest or similar wildlife sanctuary, nor in water which flows into them, unless the Nature Conservancy Council or other authority responsible for their maintenance is satisfied that:

(i) there will be no significant hazard to the animals and plants of importance in the areas concerned, and

(ii) there will be no serious disruption of the habitat which will adversely affect the continued existence of important animal and plant communities.

Publications

10.053 The following publications are relevant to this Code of Practice and should be read in conjunction with it:

Code of Practice for Ground Spraying.
Code of Practice for the Disposal of Unwanted Pesticides and Containers on Farms and Holdings (Vol. 1., Appendix III).
The Safe Use of Chemicals on the Farm (APS/1).

These are available from Divisional Offices of the Ministry of Agriculture, Fisheries and Food, or from the adress given below:

Publications,
Ministry of Agriculture, Fisheries and Food,
Tolcarne Drive,
Pinner,
Middlesex HA5 2DT.

Department of Agriculture and Fisheries for Scotland,
Chesser House,
500 Gorgie Road,
Edinburgh EH11 3AW.

Chapter 11
Recommendations for the control of weeds in the garden by the amateur

11.001   The amateur or private gardener, whilst encountering many of the weed problems experienced by the professional grower or nurseryman, in seeking advice or information may often be handicapped by the fact that he is unaware of the identity of the weed or weeds troubling him. In seeking identification and advice, weed specimens collected by the amateur gardener should show sufficient of the weeds' characteristics for satisfactory identification to be made.

11.002   In other chapters in this volume are to be found detailed recommendations for the control of specific weed species in different crops. Those advising the amateur on weed control should therefore:

(a) Write or advise at a level which can be understood by the amateur.

(b) Include, where applicable, recommendations for cultural control and/or measures to encourage more competitive crop growth to minimize recurrence of the problem.

(c) Be aware of the limitations of the range of herbicide products marketed for amateur gardener use and avoid recommending preparations other than those readily available to the amateur.

(d) Always take into account that the kind of situation in which a weed is encountered in the garden dictates the control measures which can be safely practised or the type of herbicide which can be safely used.

(e) Always emphasize strict adherence to manufacturers recommendations for handling the product, timing of application, rates of usage and crop/situation limitations.

11.003   Herbicides available for the amateur user differ markedly from those available to the professional user. The clearance for safe use, granted for all pesticides differs between the amateur and the professional field. Many promising herbicides will never be available to the amateur because of their toxicity, formulation and potentially small sales. The manufacturer therefore produces specialist products for the amateur market which are formulated to safeguard the amateur user. As a result the manufacturer only produces products for the amateur market that are safe to handle, convenient to apply and have a large use in the amateur field. This restricts the number of herbicides available to the amateur as against the professional user.

Lawns

Newly-sown lawns

11.004 **Ioxynil** *1·1 kg/ha applied by watering can to seedling grass from the 2 leaf stage for the control of seedling broad-leaved weeds.*
Most seedling weeds will be killed or checked. Complete control is generally achieved by competition from the grass and the initial mowings. Established grass can be treated but weed control will generally be unacceptable.

Established lawns

Cultural control

11.005 Weeds rapidly invade and become established in neglected lawns. Vigorous actively growing lawn grass will help to suppress established weeds. Correct fertilizers, scarifying, spiking and mowing will control established weeds and prevent the growth of seedling weeds.

11.006 **2,4-D amine** *1·1–2·2 kg/ha applied by watering can to established lawns for the control of broad-leaved weeds.*
Many common broad-leaved weeds are adequately controlled by 2,4-D, such as *Taraxacum officinale* (Dandelion), *Leontodon* spp. (Hawkbits), and *Bellis perennis* (Daisy).

11.007 **Dichlorprop** *at 2·2 kg/ha with* **2,4-D** *at 0·8–1·7 kg/ha applied by watering can to established lawns for the control of broad-leaved weeds.*
Dichlorprop is useful against *Trifolium repens* (White Clover), *Sagina procumbens* (Procumbent Pearlwort) *and Cerastium holosteoides* (Common Mouse-ear), which are not adequately controlled by 2,4-D alone.

11.008 **Fenoprop** *at 1·1–2·2 kg/ha with* **2,4-D** *at 0·8–1·7 kg/ha applied by watering can to established lawns for the control of many broad-leaved weeds.*

11.009 **Ioxynil** *0·6 kg/ha with* **mecoprop** *1·9 kg/ha applied by watering can to control* Veronica filiformis *(Slender Speedwell) on closely-mown established lawns.*
Application should be made in the early spring before the flower heads have formed. This mixture also controls *Aphanes arvensis* (Parsley-piert), *Sagina procumbens* (Procumbent Pearlwort) and *Trifolium repens* (White Clover).

11.010   **Mecoprop-salt** *2·2–3·4 kg/ha applied by watering can to control the common leguminous weeds in established lawns.*

Lotus corniculatus (Common Bird's-foot-trefoil) and *Trifolium repens* (White Clover) can be adequately controlled by a single treatment per season, although some regrowth may occur in the following season, especially if the lawn has not been treated with a nitrogenous fertilizer. *Trifolium dubium* (Lesser Trefoil) however, may only be partially controlled by a single treatment as they can re-establish at any time from seed in the ground. At the higher rate of application there may be some temporary damage to the turf.

11.011   **Mecoprop-salt** *1·7–3·4 kg/ha with* **2,4-D** *at 0·8–1·7 kg/ha applied by watering can to control many broad-leaved weeds in established lawns.*

11.012   [**For information.**] Mecoprop with 2,4-D and bromofenoxim has shown promise when applied to lawns by watering can to control many broad-leaved weeds.

Herbicide/fertilizer mixtures for lawns

11.013   Several products are available for the combined application of herbicides with fertilizers either as liquid or granular formulations. These consist of fertilizer plus: dicamba/2,4-D, fenoprop/2,4-D, fenoprop, mecoprop, 2,4-D, mecoprop/2,4-D and dicamba/MCPA. While benefiting from the competition provided by the boost to the grass growth the fertilizer does not affect the efficiency of the herbicide and rates of herbicide similar to those listed above are used.

Moss control in lawns

Cultural control

11.014   Moss invades lawns as a result of deterioration in health and vigour of the turf due to such factors as drainage, drought, close mowing, nutrient starvation, heavy shade, disease, pest damage, or very acid soil conditions.

Where such conditions can be identified the appropriate curative measures should be followed to encourage the grass to grow and compete with the moss present.

11.015   **Lawn sand** *140 g/m² on a dewy morning when the soil is moist and the weather fine and warm, at any time during the growing season but preferably in the early spring using a granular applicator.*

If rain does not fall within 2 days, water thoroughly.

A suitable lawn sand mixture consists of:

3 parts ammonium sulphate

1 part calcined ferrous sulphate

10 parts carrier (sharp sand)

This treatment will control moss but only temporarily. It must be followed by vigorous scarifying about 2 weeks after application to remove dead moss.

Formulations of balanced compound turf fertilizers with ferrous sulphate are available. These enable application of ferrous sulphate to be made overall and so avoid any 'patchy' effect of greening that might otherwise occur if the compound is used alone for spot treatment.

11.016 **Mercurous chloride** *(Calomel) at 7–12 g/10 m², or up to 22 g/10 m² for very heavy infestations at any time of the year, but preferably in early autumn.*

Mercurous chloride will give more lasting control of moss than ordinary lawn sand, by persisting over several months and preventing re-establishment from spores. It can therefore be effectively applied throughout the year.

11.017 **[For information.]** Chloroxuron has shown promise when applied by watering can to control moss in established lawns.

11.018 **[For information.]** Dichlorophen has shown promise when applied by watering can for the control of moss in established lawns.

11.019 **[For information.]** Phenols have shown promise when applied by watering can for the control of moss in established lawns.

Paths and other hard surfaces

11.020 Perennial weeds and germinating annual weeds are always a problem in paths and other hard surfaces, as these areas are never dug or disturbed. Whilst annual weeds may be removed by hoeing, there is little that can be done to effectively remove perennial weeds except by herbicides. To this end herbicides are the only practical solution to weed problems in these areas.

11.021 **Dalapon-sodium** *22·0–34·0 kg/ha applied by watering can for the control of* Agropyron repens *(Common Couch) and other deep rooted grass weeds in garden paths.*

Dalapon is most effective when applied to actively growing foliage.

11.022 **Dichlobenil** *17·0–18·0 kg/ha applied by a granular applicator for the control of annual and perennial weeds in paths.*

The optimum time for application to established vegetation is February to April. Warm dry conditions may increase the volatility of the compound and reduce performance.

11.023   **Paraquat** *0.75 kg/ha with* **diquat** *0.75 kg/ha applied by watering can for the control of annual weeds in garden paths.*

11.024   **Simazine** *2.8–5.6 kg/ha applied by watering can or granule applicator to maintain paths free from germinating weeds.*
Application should be made in early spring or late autumn when the soil is moist. Areas to be treated should be as free from weeds as possible at the time of application. If weeds are present excessive top growth should be removed to allow the spray to penetrate to the roots through which it acts.

11.025   **Simazine** *3.4 kg/ha with* **aminotriazole** *1.7 kg/ha applied by watering can in the spring to control germinated annual or perennial weeds and prevent weed germination for the whole season.*
Simazine alone will not give control of germinated weeds except at higher rates than are normally recommended for path weed control and, for this reason simazine is mixed with other chemicals.

11.026   **Sodium chlorate** *60–500 kg/ha applied by watering can to control many established perennials on neglected paths.*

11.027   [**For information.**] Simazine with aminotriazole and MCPA has shown promise for the control of annual and perennial weeds on paths and other hard surfaces.

11.028   [**For information.**] Simazine with paraquat and diquat has shown promise for the control of annual and perennial weeds on paths and other hard surfaces.

Moss control on paths and other hard surfaces

11.029   **Chloroxuron** *11 kg/ha applied by watering can to control moss on hard surfaces.*

11.030   [**For information.**] Dichlorophen has shown promise when applied by watering can for the control of moss on hard surfaces.

11.031   [**For information.**] Phenols have shown promise when applied by watering can for the control of moss on hard surfaces.

Ornamental trees and shrubs

11.032 Once established ornamental trees and shrubs are readily accessible for mechanical or hand weeding as well as chemical weed control. Where they are underplanted with herbaceous flowering plants weed control becomes determined by the underplanted species. Annual weeds can be readily controlled and the greatest problem is with perennial weeds such as *Agropyron repens* (Common Couch) and *Aegopodium podagraria* (Ground Elder). They are difficult to dig out due to the surface feeding roots of the shrubs and trees and need therefore to be controlled by repeated removal of weed foliage or by the use of a selective weed-killer.

One difficulty in dealing with weedkillers is safety to the many species encountered. Manufacturers recommendations should be followed although some guidance is given in Chapter 3.

11.033 **Chloroxuron** *4·5−5·6 kg/ha applied by watering can to weed-free soil around trees and shrubs in early spring to control germinating weeds.*

11.034 **Dichlobenil** *5·9−9·2 kg/ha applied by a granular applicator for control of annual and some perennial weeds on tolerant trees and shrubs.*

Applications should be made before growth begins in the spring to trees and shrubs at least two years old. Since ornamental trees and shrubs do vary in their resistance, dichlobenil should not be used on small stock or on very light sandy soils. Do not use if herbaceous species are also present.

11.035 **Paraquat** *0·75 kg/ha with* **diquat** *0·75 kg/ha applied by watering can during the dormant season to control annual grasses, broad-leaved annuals and* Ranunculus repens *(Creeping Buttercup).*

There is no risk of damage to trees and shrubs due to root uptake but care must be taken to avoid wetting green tissue. Only the green parts of the weed are killed and regrowth usually occurs from established perennials.

11.036 **Propachlor** *4·5 kg/ha applied by granular applicator to weed-free soil for the control of germinating annual weeds in ornamental shrubs.*

11.037 **Simazine** *1·1−1·7 kg/ha applied by watering can or granular applicator to weed-free soil for control of germinating weeds amongst a wide range of trees, shrubs and conifers.*

Applications should be made in early spring. Since ornamental trees and shrubs vary in their resistance simazine should not be used on newly planted or small stock or on very light sandy soils. Do not use if herbaceous species are also present.

11.038 **Simazine** *0·5−1·0 kg/ha with* **2,4-Des,** *3·0−6·0 kg/ha in medium volume or by watering can for the control of annual weeds.*

This mixture can be used at any time of the year, the higher rates being used in the autumn and winter. 2,4-Des is only effective in warm conditions with moist soil.

11.039   [**For information.**] Chloramben has shown promise when applied by a granular applicator on weed-free soil to control germinating weeds around trees and shrubs. If no rain falls within 3 or 4 days the area should be watered to activate the chemical.

Tree, bush and cane fruit

11.040   Although tree fruit species tolerate weeds their growth can be severely retarded by high weed infestations in the years after planting. Bush fruits are more susceptible to weed competition. They are low growing and it is not uncommon for weeds to completely swamp the bushes.

Weed control is always difficult especially where perennial weeds such as *Heracleum sphondylium* (Hog Weed) and *Convolvulus arvensis* (Field Bindweed) have become established. In these circumstances herbicides provide a convenient means of controlling such weeds.

11.041   **Dalapon-sodium** *4·5–9·0 kg/ha applied by watering can for the control of* Agropyron repens *(Common Couch) and other deep-rooted grass weeds in apples, pears, blackcurrants and gooseberries.*

Applications should be made only during the dormant season. Apples and pears must be established for at least four years. Blackcurrants must be established for at least three years and gooseberries must be sprayed not later than the end of December. It is important to ensure that the applied dalapon is retained as much as possible by the weed foliage thereby minimizing contact with the soil. Best results are obtained when the grass weeds have plenty of actively growing foliage. Repeated applications in successive years will usually be necessary to eradicate *Agropyron repens* (Common Couch).

11.042   **Dichlobenil** *5·9–11·0 kg/ha applied by a granular applicator to control many existing perennial weeds and to give residual control of germinating annuals among apples, pears, raspberries, blackcurrants, redcurrants and gooseberries.*

Applications should not be made to any crop which has been planted within two years. The treatment should be applied in March or early April except in established raspberries when applications are best made in late winter before new cane emergence. For control of *Agropyron repens* (Common Couch) an application in November is recommended.

11.043   **Paraquat** *0·75 kg/ha with* **diquat** *0·75 kg/ha applied by watering can to control annual weeds and* Ranunculus repens *(Creeping Buttercup) around tree and bush fruit.*

Avoid wetting tree foliage or bark of fruit trees less than two years old. Immature bark of older trees may be damaged. Avoid dormant buds and leaves of blackcurrants otherwise damage will result. Young shoots of cane fruit are also susceptible to spray damage. Only the green parts of the weeds are killed and regrowth usually occurs from established perennials.

11.044 **Simazine** *1·1 kg/ha in medium volume or by watering can for the control of germinating annual weeds.*
Apply in winter months to moist soil free of weed growth.

11.045 **Simazine** *0·5–1·0 kg/ha with* **2,4-Des** *3·0–6·0 kg/ha in medium volume or by watering can for the control of annual weeds in fruit.*
This mixture can be used all the year round provided soil is moist. 2,4-Des is effective under warm conditions but not under cold conditions.

Rose beds

11.046 Apart from lawns roses are the largest single area in the amateur garden sphere. These are generally placed in a prominent position and as such are generally weeded regularly by hoe. Herbicides are extensively used in rose beds particularly since rose rootstocks tolerate herbicides well.

11.047 **Chloroxuron** *4·5–5·6 kg/ha applied by watering can to weed-free soil in early spring to control germinating weeds in roses.*

11.048 **Dichlobenil** *4·2–9·2 kg/ha applied by a granular applicator before bud burst in spring, for control of some perennial and most annual weeds.*
The dose will depend on weeds present with the higher dose being required for perennial weed control. Apply only where roses have been established for at least two years.

11.049 **Paraquat** *0·75 kg/ha with* **diquat,** *0·75 kg/ha applied by watering can between bush rows at any time of the year for the control of emerged weeds.*

11.050 **Propachlor** *4·5 kg/ha applied by granular applicator to weed-free soil for the control of germinating annual weeds in roses.*

11.051 **Simazine** *up to 1·7 kg/ha applied in medium volume or by watering can for the control of germinating annual weeds.*
Apply to moist soil free of weed growth.

11.052 [**For information.**] Chloramben has shown promise when applied by a granular applicator on weed-free soil to control germinating weeds around roses. If no rain falls within 3 or 4 days the area should be watered to activate the chemical.

11.053   **Simazine** *0·5–1·0 kg/ha with* **2,4-Des** *3·0–6·0 kg/ha in medium volume or by watering can for the control of annual weeds.*

This mixture can be used at any time of the year, the higher rates being used in the autumn and winter. 2,4-Des is only effective in warm conditions with moist soil.

Herbaceous annual and perennial borders

11.054   Perennial weeds should not be a problem in herbaceous plants as they can be moved at certain times of the year and the offending weeds dug up. Annual weeds can be controlled by regular hoeing. Herbicides are used mainly to prevent weed seed growth. They have little effect once weed seedlings have emerged.

11.055   **Chloroxuron** *at 4·5 kg/ha in medium volume or by watering can for the control of many germinating weeds.*

It should be applied to moist weed-free soil, preferably just after planting out.

11.056   **Paraquat** *0·75 kg/ha with* **diquat** *0·75 kg/ha applied by watering can to control annual weeds and* Ranunculus repens *(Creeping Buttercup) around herbaceous annual and perennial plants.*

Extreme care must be taken to avoid any spray getting onto plant leaves or green parts.

11.057   **Propham** *2·4 kg/ha,* **chlorpropham** *0·55 kg/ha and* **diuron** *0·27 kg/ha for the control of germinating annual weeds in herbaceous plants.*

Soil should be moist and weed-free at the time of application. All herbaceous plants, including bulbs can be treated.

11.058   **Propachlor** *4·5 kg/ha applied by granular applicator for the control of many germinating annual weeds.*

It should be applied to moist weed-free soil, preferably just after planting out.

Vegetables

11.059   The main weed problem in vegetables is that of annual weeds. Perennial weeds are troublesome when they occur but as most vegetables remain in the ground for only short periods perennial weeds can be removed by digging or spraying when the ground is empty. Annual weeds are generally removed by hand although residual herbicides are available to prevent weed growth in most crops.

11.060 **Chloroxuron** *at 4·5 kg/ha in medium volume or by watering can for the control of many germinating weeds.*
It should be applied to moist weed-free soil shortly after drilling or planting out.

11.061 **Paraquat** *0·75 kg/ha with* **diquat** *0·75 kg/ha applied by watering can to control annual weeds.*
Extreme care must be taken to ensure that no spray gets onto the leaves or green parts of the vegetable plants. Successful weed control can be obtained by applying a spray immediately before the vegetable seed germinates.

11.062 **Propham** *2·4 kg/ha,* **chlorpropham** *0·55 kg/ha and* **diuron** *0·27 kg/ha for the control of germinating annual weeds in vegetables.*
The soil should be moist and weed-free at the time of application. All vegetables can be treated.

11.063 **Propachlor** *4·5 kg/ha applied by granular applicator for the control of many germinating annual weeds.*
It should be applied to moist weed-free soil, just after drilling or transplanting or after cleaning the soil of weeds. Peas and runner beans may sometimes be checked by the treatment but rapidly outgrow any symptoms.

Weed control in neglected ground

11.064 The problem of cleaning up neglected ground in existing and new gardens is largely one of removing the high amount of perennial weeds that will have become established. Almost any species can be found in such land and in some cases land in gardens has been abandoned because of incurable perennial weed problems such as *Equisetum arvense* (Field Horsetail) and *Aegopodium podagraria* (Ground-elder).
Control of perennial weeds in neglected ground can be effectively carried out by digging or the use of herbicides. Whatever method is used control should be exercised for at least one year to completely remove the perennial weeds before planting with any plant material. Where herbicides have been used there may also be an interval specified on the label which must elapse in order to avoid harmful herbicide residues remaining in the soil.

11.065 **Ammonium sulphamate** *at 50–100 g/sqr.m. in 0·5 litres applied by watering can or sprayer for the control of annual and perennial weeds.*

Most weeds are controlled by ammonium sulphamate. Treatment should be made when the weeds are actively growing. In normal conditions 4 weeks should elapse between treatment and planting any crop.

Where woody weeds, such as *Rumex* spp. (Brambles), *Sambucus nigra* (Elder) and *Crataegus monogyna* (Hawthorn) occur a solution of 200 g/litre can be applied to the foliage or neat ammonium sulphamate crystals applied directly to the cut stumps.

11.066   **Aminotriazole** *1·7 kg/ha with* **simazine** *3·4 kg/ha for the control of annual weeds and shallow-rooted perennial weeds.*

Application should be made when weeds are actively growing. Do not plant in treated soil for twelve months after application.

11.067   **Aminotriazole** *0·3 kg/ha with* **simazine** *4·2 kg/ha and* **MCPA** *1·5 kg/ha applied by watering can for the control of annual weeds and shallow rooted perennial weeds.*

Application is best made in the spring to actively growing weeds. Do not plant in treated soil for eighteen months after application.

11.068   **Dalapon-sodium** *at 21·0 kg/ha applied by watering can or sprayer for the control of annual and perennial grasses.*

Application should be made to the foliage of grass when it is actively growing. Two weeks after treatment treated land should be dug and not disturbed for a further four weeks.

11.069   **Dichlobenil** *5·9–9·2 kg/ha applied by granular applicator for the control of annual and many perennial weeds.*

Application should be made in early spring as plant growth commences. Treated land should be left for at least twelve months and dug before being planted.

11.070   **Paraquat** *0·75 kg/ha with* **diquat** *0·75 kg/ha applied by watering can for the control of annual weeds and the aerial parts of perennial weeds.*

11.071   **Sodium chlorate** *130–550 kg/ha applied by watering can for the control of annual weeds and most perennial weeds.*

Proprietary formulations are available containing fire depressants. These are to be preferred for amateur use. Apply when soil conditions are moist and the weeds actively growing. Do not plant treated land for at least one year.

11.072   **2,4,5-T-ester** *2·2–4·5 kg/ha applied by watering can or sprayer for the control of* Urtica dioica *(Common Nettle),* Rumex *spp. (Docks),* Rubus *spp. (Bramble) and woody weeds.*

Care must be taken to avoid drift getting onto other crops as 2,4,5-T can be taken up through the bark of plants as well as the foliage. Watering cans and sprayers must be thoroughly cleaned after use. Do not plant treated land for at least six months.

Chapter 12
Notes on the control of some individual weeds

Introduction

12.001 This chapter deals with some especially serious weeds and with some which are less common but which create difficult management or advisory problems where they occur. Where the problems are also covered wholly or partly by other chapters, reference is made to these chapters.

Recommendations may be made in this chapter which are not specific to any crop situation. In cropped land, it is essential to ensure the proposed use is cleared by the Pesticide Safety Precautions Scheme.

Localized treatment of individual plants or patches

12.002 It is important to clear land thoroughly of these difficult weeds before planting crops, especially high value crops or those likely to remain in the ground for a long period, e.g. perennial horticultural crops. In cropped land, it is equally important to control invading plants (or plants re-establishing after treatment) *before* the population reaches problem levels.

Many populations of these weeds do start as a few isolated plants or patches and control by spot-weeding is cheap in terms of chemical costs. The labour cost has to be considered more carefully but usually proves cheaper than allowing a problem to develop.

There are three basic techniques of localized treatment; pulling or spudding; spot applications of herbicides to individual plants or isolated clumps; spraying herbicides to larger discrete patches of weed growth.

12.003 Pulling or spudding need little explanation save only that in most cases the whole plant must be removed to prevent regeneration.

With weeds that are most conspicuous during a relatively short period, e.g. wild-oats in cereals, wild annual beet in sugar beet, timing may be critical. If too early, a subsequent emergence of plants may reduce the efficiency of the operation. If too late some plants may shed viable seed before they are removed.

12.004 Spot treatment with herbicides is a practice that deserves more attention than has been the case. Selective materials may be used, or localized applications can be made in such a way as to avoid the foliage and/or root system of crops which may be damaged. Alternatively the crop may be damaged by what is essentially a non-selective treatment but has the power to recolonize the small areas left by removal of the weed. (Permanent pasture is a good example of this.)

Possibilities include the following:

1   Spot applications of solid formulations using a simple shaker-pot, or even a teaspoon. Candidate herbicides are sodium chlorate, dichlobenil, chlorthiamid which are active against many of the species listed in this chapter.

2   Spot application of liquid formulations using a water can or knapsack sprayer. With the latter, pressure may need to be reduced to minimize drift on to crop plants. Less than 5 ml of spray solution should be needed to wet the foliage of most large perennial weeds so that large areas can be covered without refilling the sprayer.

A wide range of candidate herbicides is possible for applications of this type. Translocated foliar materials are to be preferred, notably dalapon, aminotriazole and glyphosate. Care must be taken to direct the spray only onto the unwanted vegetation and, of course, only herbicides cleared by the PSPS should be used.

3   Spot application of liquid formulations by means of the herbicide glove. This equipment feeds a herbicide solution to the palm of a glove which is used to lightly grasp the foliage of a target plant. The technique is very economical of material; less than 0·5 ml are needed to treat a wild-oat panicle. Results have been promising where the foliage of crop and weed are in close proximity, as with roguing wild-oats in cereal crops.

12.005   Patch spraying of larger areas of weed by means of a conventional tractor mounted sprayer can also lead to considerable savings. The patches must be marked with some care or the tractor driver's task can be very difficult.

12.006   Glyphosate is a non-selective herbicide translocated with great efficiency into the rootstocks and rhizomes of perennial plants. A dose of 1·3 kg/ha is recommended for the control of perennial grasses and all of the species listed in this chapter are susceptible to doses up to 2·0 kg/ha. The only conditions for successful use appear to be:

1   Six hours freedom from rain after application.
2   Adequate foliage to receive the spray.
3   The target plant must be at a suitable stage of growth for efficient translocation into the propagative organs.

The last point is the most difficult to define, indeed it has not been systematically studied for all of the species listed here. With *Agropyron repens* (Common Couch) and some of the other rhizomatous perennials, downward translocation, and formation of new rhizome, appears to occur relatively early, as soon as the aerial shoots have started to tiller.

Applications at this stage, are likely to be satisfactory.

However, weeds such as *Phragmites communis* (Common Reed) and some of the broad-leaved perennials are slower in development and applications may best be made at very advanced stages of growth, up to flowering, although good results can be obtained from earlier applications.

Glyphosate is a relatively new compound and the number of uses cleared under the Pesticide Safety Precautions Scheme is likely to increase during the life of this Handbook.

At the time of going to press the following uses were cleared.

1   On non-cropped land and on land planted to non-edible crops (including herbage seed crops).

2   On land to be used for growing cereals (including undersown cereals) maize, sugar beet, mangels, red beet and fodder beet.

3   On grassland, as a preliminary for pasture renovation.

4   As a spot treatment for wild-oats in cereals, annual beet in sugar beet, and on weeds in fruit crops—only when applied using the Herbicide Glove (12.004).

Aegopodium podagraria (Ground-elder)

12.007   *A. podagraria* is one of the most persistent and troublesome weeds of the garden. It spreads quickly by means of brittle rhizomes which break into fragments with cultivation and rapidly produce vigorous new aerial shoots. Eradication can generally only be achieved by removing any valued plants and then repeatedly forking over the ground, removing as many pieces of rhizome as possible. Eradication in beds of established perennial plants or shrubs, or when the weed is growing in a hedge is difficult, but repeated hoeing between the plants accompanied by hand removal of all *A. podagraria* leaves as soon as they appear above the ground will do much to keep the weed under control. Only really persistent weeding will have a useful effect. Where hoeing or weeding is not possible *A. podagraria* can be controlled by repeated desiccation using paraquat at 1·1 kg/ha.

12.008   *A. podagraria* is resistant to MCPA and 2,4-D, but good control has been obtained with 2,4,5-T-amine and -ester at 1·1 to 2·2 kg/ha.

12.009   Good control can be obtained in certain fruit crops with chlorthiamid or dichlobenil at 7·8 to 11 kg/ha, formulated as granules, (see Chapter 3). Useful suppression of *A. podagraria* has been obtained in established ornamentals and roses with dichlobenil at 6·3 kg/ha, formulated as granules.

12.010   Aminotriazole at 4·0 kg/ha a.i., activated with ammonium thiocyanate will give good control, applied in late May or early June.

12.011   [**For information.**] A mixture of 3·7 kg/ha of simazine with 1·8 kg/ha of activated aminotriazole has given, in trials, good selective control of *A. podagraria* growing in Floribunda roses.

12.012   Glyphosate at 1·5–2·0 kg/ha shows promises either for directed applications in ornamental shrubs or to clean up an old border prior to replanting (12.006).

Agropyron repens (Common Couch), *Agrostis* spp. (Bent Grasses)

12.013   *Agropyron repens* can be distinguished from the rhizomatous species of *Agrostis* with which it is sometimes confused by the presence of auricles (small pointed projections at the base of the leaf blade) which often clasp the stem, by hairs on the upper side of the leaves and by the distinctive flowering head. The latter resembles that of perennial ryegrass except that the spikelets are set with the flat face opposite the stem; it is quite unlike the much-branched, diffuse flowering head of *Agrostis* spp. The species of *Agrostis* which are particularly troublesome as weeds are *A. gigantea,* which has underground creeping stems, and *A. stolonifera* which has surface creeping stems. *A. canina* and *A. tenuis,* which may have short rhizomes, are less important. The methods of control for all these grasses in arable land are similar (see also MAFF Advisory Leaflet No. 89).

As a general rule it is relatively easy to achieve a control of these weeds but extremely difficult to achieve complete eradication. Clearly, different standards of both cost and effectiveness must be applied to treatments intended for these two very different purposes. Whatever method is employed, at least some consideration should be given to the possible need to follow up with less intensive treatments in subsequent years.

Control by cultivation

Summer fallowing. Full fallowing

12.014   With a summer or full fallow the land is uncropped for a whole season with the aim of obtaining a very high degree of control or eradication. A cover crop such as mustard could be planted in August if the fallow has been very successful.

Since the whole summer is available a choice of eradication techniques is available utilizing two basic principles. The first is to desiccate the rhizomes using the plough and heavy cultivator. The land must be cultivated deeply and kept in as cloddy a state as possible to allow maximum desiccation. This was the traditional fallowing technique and has advantages other than those of weed control, especially on heavy land.

Control by desiccation can be extremely effective in dry summers but more reliable results have been obtained utilizing the second principle based on rhizome fragmentation. The aim is to break up the rhizomes and then to kill the resulting fragments by a process of exhaustion of their food reserves and the buds from which regrowth can take place. The key to success is in the first cultivation; this should be thorough enough to ensure efficient fragmentation. The rotary cultivator is ideal for this although other implements could be used. For subsequent operations the ratio between rotor speed and forward speed can be adjusted to give a coarse chop or other forms of cultivation could be used. Food reserves are at their lowest when the regrowth is at around the 1–2 leaf stage and further cultivation should normally be undertaken at about this time. Retreatment should be undertaken before the aerial shoots start to tiller as new rhizome may be produced after this stage is reached.

This technique is very effective in wet weather although soil conditions may limit the amount of recultivation.

Bastard fallowing. Half fallowing

12.015   With this technique an early crop is taken, namely, arable silage, vining peas or 'sheep keep' and cultivations are started in June or July. If the early crop is a very suppressive one such as arable silage, results from this technique can be just as successful as those from a full fallow. Less time is available and as there is less probability of a dry period, control systems based on fragmentation are most likely to be successful.

Cultivation after cereal harvest

12.016   This is the most common situation and in many ways the most challenging. Relatively little time is available and man- and tractor-power are all in great demand. Systems depending on desiccation are not likely to be reliable, indeed working the land into too cloddy a state could result in a situation that is too dry to allow regrowth but not dry enough for a fatal degree of desiccation.

In many cases rotary cultivation may be considered too expensive although it is likely to give most consistent results. Tine cultivators may be used with great success but the aim should be to move all the rhizome in the top 75–100 mm and produce a rough tilth condition.

If work is started as soon as possible after cereal harvest control of a very high order may be attained but eradication is not a realistic goal. Because of the shortage of labour for this autumn work it is commonly advisable to integrate the use of cultivations with application of herbicides. At the very least, a farmer should be aware of the properties of herbicides which are available to improve control of these weeds or, at least, to improve reliability in wet seasons.

The role of mouldboard ploughing

12.017   During the course of a programme of control, by cultivations and some herbicides, the rhizome is best left in the upper layers of the soil. At the completion of a treatment programme, however, regrowth can, in many cases, be minimized by deep burial of the surviving rhizome by ploughing. Ploughing should be deep, with the use of skim coulters to ensure efficient burial. Cultivations after ploughing should be shallow to avoid bringing rhizomes back towards the surface.

Where the depth of ploughing is restricted by soil depth and the degree of soil inversion is poor, commonly where the width of the furrow slice is great in relation to the depth, then mouldboard ploughing may have little or no advantage over much cheaper forms of cultivation.

Chemical control

12.018   For the control of *Agropyron repens* in arable land, sodium chlorate can be used as an early autumn application at 120–250 kg/ha. Oats, vetches, peas, potatoes and cabbage are relatively tolerant and may be sown in the spring following an autumn treatment; but barley, mangolds, beet and turnips are more sensitive and should not be sown until at least 12 months after treatment. Sodium chlorate is still used in Scotland, but elsewhere it has been superseded by other herbicides.

12.019   TCA can be used in the autumn or spring. Summer and autumn treatments can be followed by normal cropping in the following spring except on some fen soils and soils high in humus content, where only crops resistant to TCA should be sown. Wheat, oats, barley and rye are susceptible and should not be sown as winter crops following autumn treatment nor as spring crops following spring treatment. Winter cereals may generally be planted safely in land treated in the spring, provided at least 4 months have elapsed between the last application of the chemical and the sowing of the crop. The persistence of TCA in the soil is, however, influenced by rainfall and soil type and may be prolonged in soils of high humus content. Rape, kale, turnips and linseed appear to be the crops most resistant to TCA: potatoes, peas, sugar beet and beans also show considerable resistance, but should not be sown sooner than 2 months after treatment at 33·0 kg/ha.

Weed control is dependent on the weed being in active growth and the chemical being available in the soil moisture in the rooting zone. Cultivation is therefore desirable to break up the rhizomes and induce bud growth (12.014). Cultivation may also be desirable to mix the herbicide with the soil, bringing it into proximity with the developing buds. However, in a wet time this downward movement may be achieved naturally, by leaching, and best results may be obtained by spraying after cultivation not before.

There are therefore a number of techniques for the application of TCA:

1   Preceded by cultivation.
2   Followed by cultivation.
3   Preceded and followed by cultivation.
4   Applied by means of a special sprayer fitted to a rotary cultivator so as to spray the soil as it leaves the blades.

All techniques have been shown to be successful in practice; techniques involving herbicide incorporation have a greater chance of success in a dry time, but some soil moisture is required for activity.

The dose used in the autumn is most commonly 33·0 kg/ha.

In spring, lower doses of 17·0–22·0 kg/ha are commonly used. These have the advantage of a greater degree of safety to the following crop. Activity has also appeared to be greater when applied in good growing conditions in spring, so that the lower dose is adequate.

12.020   Dalapon and aminotriazole, in contrast to TCA, should be applied to the *foliage* of actively growing couch grass, where rain is not expected for at least 12 h. The dose of either chemical required to ensure a complete kill of the weed under all conditions is generally uneconomic for agricultural purposes, lower doses are therefore recommended which give a high degree of control but are unlikely to eradicate the weed completely unless careful attention is paid to timing of the application and to associated cultivations and cropping. Doses of 9·5–16·0 kg/ha dalapon-sodium or 4·5 kg/ha aminotriazole or half these rates in a mixture of the two compounds are generally recommended for the control of couch in arable land. Cultivation before treatment may assist by breaking up the rhizomes and stimulating dormant buds to grow. Sufficient time should elapse between cultivation and spraying to allow a good cover of foliage to develop. Ploughing (see paragraph *12.017*) and subsequent cropping with vigorous competitive crops should minimize the weeds recovery.

Dalapon and aminotriazole can be applied at any time between mid-March and the end of October provided the couch is growing actively. After couch grass has been sprayed with dalapon or aminotriazole and a crop is to be planted, it is important that any residue of the herbicides in the soil is sufficiently small not to damage the crop. It should be remembered that both herbicides tend to persist longer when the soil is exceptionally cold or dry and that the time between spraying and sowing or planting may have to be increased. When in doubt advice should be obtained from the suppliers.

12.021   *Autumn use.* Applications of 13·0–16·0 kg/ha dalapon-sodium or

4·5 kg/ha aminotriazole made in the autumn can be followed by normal cropping the following spring. Autumn treatment is more practical in the south than the north as there is more time between harvest and the onset of frosts to allow application of the herbicide onto actively growing foliage. When an autumn treatment is contemplated, particularly where cultivations are to be carried out before spraying, it is best to plan an early maturing crop such as winter barley or a spring sown feeding barley so that spraying is not carried out too late in the year to be effective. Conditions should remain suitable for the growth of couch for 1 or 2 weeks after spraying. In the case of dalapon, a minimum interval of 4 months should elapse between spraying and sowing if spring cereals are to be grown. If ploughing after treatment is delayed a minimum interval of 40 days should elapse between ploughing and sowing even if 4 months elapsed between spraying and ploughing. Following treatment with aminotriazole sowing can be done after 3 weeks have elapsed although on sandy soils this period should be increased to 6 weeks. Winter wheat or oats, but not barley, can therefore occasionally be sown following an early autumn treatment with aminotriazole but never following a dalapon treatment.

12.022 *Spring use.* Dalapon can be used in the spring but spring cereals cannot safely be sown afterwards. Certain other crops, e.g. carrots, kale, beet, potatoes can follow treatment provided some 6 to 7 weeks elapse between application of 10·0 to 13·0 kg/ha dalapon-sodium and sowing. Ploughing should take place 2 weeks after spraying and sowing various crops vary for the different products available. Aminotriazole may be applied in spring at 4·5 kg/ha before sowing wheat, oats, potatoes or maize. Three weeks should elapse between spraying and ploughing. The crop may then be sown as soon as the cultivations are complete. In sandy soils the interval between spraying and sowing or ploughing should be increased to 6 weeks. Both dalapon and aminotriazole can be used on headlands and verges to prevent couch grass spreading into the field. Where cultivations and cropping as indicated cannot be carried out, the dose applied should be increased to around 26·0 kg/ha dalapon-sodium and 6·7 kg/ha aminotriazole.

12.023 Paraquat as a desiccant at 0·2 kg/ha may be incorporated into a programme of work aiming to destroy the couch by defoliation and exhaustion of the rhizomes. In such a system cereal stubble would be broken up immediately after harvesting the grain and at 3-week intervals the land would be cultivated if dry or sprayed with paraquat if wet. These operations would continue until the onset of winter and the cessation of growth. This system of couch control is easier to apply to light or medium soils than to heavy soils.

12.024 Glyphosate at 1·3 kg/ha is also applied to the foliage of actively growing perennial grasses. This compound is translocated to the rhizomes extremely efficiently and very good kill, sometimes complete, can be obtained.

No special cultural operations are necessary. Indeed cultivation before spraying may be disadvantageous if some shoots have started into growth but do not have a sufficient area of green leaf at the time of spraying.

Poor results may be obtained if rain follows within 6 h of application.

Glyphosate is an extremely effective total herbicide so great care must be exercised to avoid application or drift on to crops, ornamental plants or areas of botanical interest or importance to wild life.

Soil persistence is low so that crops (12.006) can be sown very soon after spraying.

Control in crops other than cereals

12.025   Herbicide   Crop. Paragraph reference in brackets

Aminotriazole Apple, Pear (3.049)

Atrazine Maize, Sweet Corn (2.213)

Bromacil Blackberry, Loganberry (3.096), Raspberry (3.115)

Chlorthiamid Raspberry (3.117), Blackcurrant (3.064), Gooseberry (3.078)

Dalapon Agricultural Legumes (2.016), Asparagus (3.016), Carrot (2.131), Rhubarb (3.033), Apple, Pear (3.054), Raspberry (3.121), Currants (3.071), Gooseberry (3.083)

Dichlobenil Apple, Pear (3.043), Raspberry (3.118), Rose (3.213), Currants (3.065), Gooseberry (3.079)

Diuron Asparagus (3.008). Ornamental Trees and Shrubs (3.229)

EPTC Potatoes (2.305)

Propyzamide Agricultural Brassicae (2.235), Apple (3.045), Pear (3.045), Plum, Cherry (3.106), Blackberry, Loganberry (3.100), Raspberry (3.119), Currants (3.067), Gooseberry (3.081), Strawberry (3.137), Rose (215), Ornamental Trees and Shrubs (3.227)

TCA Agricultural Brassicae (2.082), Legumes (2.284), Carrot (2.123), Rhubarb (3.031)

Terbacil Asparagus (3.014), Apples (3.047)

Allium spp. (Onions)

12.026   *Allium vineale* (Wild Onion) and *A. ursinum* (Ramsons) are the 2 species most commonly occurring as weeds. *A. ursinum* has broad leaves and a triangular stem and prefers wooded or shady places, unlike *A. vineale*

which has rounded leaves and stem and is found in more open situations. *A. vineale* which causes tainted milk and flour, is an extremely persistent weed, and is particularly troublesome on heavy land.

Cultural control is possible by preventing the formation of the 3 types of bulb structure (main bulbs, hard offsets and aerial bulbils) which are responsible for the persistence and spread of the plant. All 3 structures sprout in autumn and grow until the following July when the plants die down. At this time a proportion produce a head of bulbils on the aerial shoots. Usually this is in place of the inflorescence, though sometimes flowers are carried on it together with the bulbils, which, after shedding, may lie on or in the soil for a considerable period before sprouting. At the base of the mature plant is a bulb, together with a number of offsets which can also persist for a long time in the soil. One successful programme of cultural control, described in MAFF Advisory Leaflet No. 313, is based on a succession of spring-sown crops, preceded each year by a late autumn ploughing. The object of this is to disturb the weed, thereby reducing main bulb and hard offset formation, and at the same time to destroy young plants developing from bulbils. Autumn-sown wheat, beans and short leys should be avoided whilst bare fallows serve only to spread the weed. If wild onion occurs on wet, heavy land, it is not worth attempting to eradicate it until the land has been drained.

12.027 Spraying with MCPA or 2,4-D in cereal crops may reduce the height of wild onion so that the bulbils are formed below the cutter-bar of the combine; otherwise herbicides used selectively are of little value.

12.028 *Allium ursinum* is only important because it can cause tainting of milk. Aminotriazole at 6·7 kg/ha, applied before flowering, has given good control. This treatment kills grasses. Livestock must be excluded from the treated area for the remainder of the growing season.

Alopecurus myosuroides (Black-grass)

See also MAFF Advisory Leaflet 522.

12.029 *In Arable Crops* this annual grass is frequently a troublesome weed, particularly on heavy soils. It is of greatest importance in autumn sown crops as most seed germinates in the autumn of the year in which it is shed. Some seed is more persistent and can survive for a year or so. Water-logging may induce dormancy in the seeds and lead to an increased proportion germinating in the spring or in subsequent seasons. *A. myosuroides* is commonly associated with water-logged patches or fields. This may be due to the seed persistence referred to earlier or to the importance of competition from vigorous crops in suppressing this weed. A check to crop growth by water-logging or any other cause encourages weed growth.

12.030   Possibilities for cultural 'control are mostly based on encouraging germination before the crop is sown. Late sowing of winter crops or, preferably, a succession of spring-sown crops where seedbeds are prepared thoroughly will greatly reduce an infestation. Unfortunately, on the type of land on which *A. myosuroides* is often most troublesome, this may not be practicable. A very heavily infested cereal crop may be cut for silage to prevent seed shedding. In some areas *A. myosuroides* can be severely checked by harrowing crops before the weed has tillered.

12.031   *In Herbage seed crops A. myosuroides* presents an especially serious problem. It is competitive and its seed is difficult and expensive to separate from cultivated grass and clover seed. The seed is most difficult to separate from seed of fescues, particularly meadow fescue (*Festuca pratensis*), ryegrasses and cocksfoot. It is much less of a problem in timothy and the clovers where it can generally be removed satisfactorily.

12.032   For herbage seed crops, every opportunity should be taken to eliminate *A. myosuroides* before sowing and during the seedling stage of the crop by the following methods:

In the year before sowing

  (a) Field beans or cereals can be grown, using herbicides to reduce *A. myosuroides* before sowing herbage seed crops either direct-sown or in undersown cereals (see Chapters 1 and 2).

In the autumn before sowing

  (b) Stubble cultivation (perhaps with contact herbicide) and late ploughing to ensure maximum germination of seed; complete inversion in ploughing to ensure a thorough kill.

In spring of sowing year

  (c) Destruction of plants surviving at the time of seedbed preparation.
  (d) In direct-sown herbage seed crops the possible use of the 'stale seedbed' technique and a contact herbicide before emergence of crop grass.

Later in the year

  (e) Topping of direct-sown crop as frequently as necessary to prevent seed being shed from any plants growing with the crop.
  (f) Inter-row cultivations, and if necessary (and possible) hand-weeding.

Ethofumesate and methabenzthiazuron may be used in seed crops of some species (see Chapter 4).

By this means it should be possible to prevent seed being formed and shed during the year of sowing in a crop sown direct in spring. This in turn will avoid the growth in autumn or afterwards of new plants whose seed would contaminate the crop seed. For an undersown crop, however, or one sown in autumn after a crop in which *A. myosuroides* was present and able to shed seed, such a contamination is likely. Inter-row cultivations, if possible, should be made to destroy the seedlings and young plants.

If the seed crop, in the summer of the first harvest year, shows a level of contamination likely to cause serious difficulty in cleaning, it is advisable to sacrifice the seed harvest and take hay or silage from the crop to prevent the weed from shedding seed. Subsequent topping is then advisable from time to time to deal with the recovering *A. myosuroides*.

12.033   Herbicides for the control of *A. myosuroides*

Paragraph references in brackets.

Pre-sowing	*Wheat and barley*	Beans	Oilseed rape
Contact	←———————— Paraquat ————————→		
Residual	Tri-allate (1.071)	Tri-allate (2.006)	Di-allate (2.224) TCA (2.225)
Post-sowing			
Pre-emergence	Tri-allate granular (1.073) Terbutryne (1.070) Methabenzthiazuron* (1.065) Chlortoluron† (1.059) Iso-proturon (1.063)	Simazine (2.012)	
Post-sowing			
Contact	Barban† (1.055)	Barban (2.015)	Barban (2.231) Dalapon (2.234)
Residual	Methabenzthiazuron* (1.065) Chlortoluron† (1.059) Iso-proturon (1.063) Metoxuron† (1.067) Metoxuron/simazine† (1.068)	Carbetamide (2.017) Propyzamide (2.011)	Carbetamide (2.233) Propyzamide (2.235)

* Can be used on oats. † With varietal restrictions.

Amsinckia intermedia (Fiddleneck, also Tarweed or Yellow Borage)

12.034   The genus Amsinckia is an American one, of the family Boraginaceae. A number of species have become established in Europe but *A. intermedia* is the most common as a weed, being introduced as a contaminant in crop seeds. It is a fast growing annual, coarsely hairy with long lax cymes of very small orange yellow flowers. It has adapted well to sandy soils in certain localized areas, notably along the East Anglian coast.

12.035   In cereals, Amsinckia is virtually resistant to growth regulator herbicides but good control can be obtained with the contact herbicide bromoxynil ester at 0·28—0·42 kg/ha.

Arrhenatherum elatius (Onion Couch, False Oat-grass)

12.036   This species, familiar as a weed of roadside verges and waste ground, has a form which produces strings of 'bulbs' at the stem bases. This form is occasionally a serious weed of arable land. Seed is produced prolifically but does not all 'breed true'; only about a third of the seedlings exhibit the extreme bulbous habit and many intermediate forms occur. The seeds have little dormancy and germinate soon after harvest so seedlings are most likely to establish in early-sown winter wheat.

12.037   Methods of control are similar to those for *Agropyron repens* (Common Couch) but autumn treatments generally seem less effective on this species.

Avena spp. (Wild-oats)

12.038   Two species of wild-oat occur in the United Kingdom: *Avena fatua* and *Avena ludoviciana*. *A. fatua* has a widespread distribution and germinates principally in the spring between March and May. Germination also occurs during the autumn from September onwards and emergence of seedlings can occur (during mild weather) at any time throughout the winter. *A. ludoviciana* is less widespread and germination only occurs between September and March. Thus *A. fatua* is found in both winter and spring sown crops while *A. ludoviciana* is largely restricted to winter sown crops. Recommendations for chemical control and some cultural control methods are similar for both species. MAFF Advisory leaflet 452 gives a guide to identification and much useful advice on the wild-oat problem.

CULTURAL CONTROL

12.039   On clean land, care must be taken to avoid contamination. The main sources of infestation are seed, straw and manure, and combine harvesters. Clean fields should be inspected regularly each summer to detect any invasion by wild-oats. When wild-oats appear for the first time in small numbers it is essential to remove them to avoid the build up of a serious problem. They should either be uprooted by hand, while still green, collected and burnt, or rogued chemically using a herbicide glove to apply a solution of dalapon or glyphosate to each panicle.

12.040 Heavy infestations, where yields are at risk require action to prevent new seeding and to encourage loss of existing seeds on the stubble surface and in the soil. Herbicides will normally be necessary but cultural techniques may improve the control achieved. Of special importance; crops should be managed to ensure vigorous growth and suppression of the weed. Where weakly competitive row crops are grown maximum use should be made of opportunities for chemical control and/or interrow cultivation in such crops. There are relatively few break crops, in the purest sense, where control can be obtained without any herbicide use. Seeding is, however, prevented by a ley, cut or grazed frequently in the first year. Crops grown for arable silage are also excellent break crops, completely eliminating seeding of this and other weeds.

In many crops, the wild-oat seedlings which appear before crop emergence are more competitive and may be more resistant to herbicides than those emerging later. These should be destroyed before sowing, as far as possible, by seedbed cultivations. In wet soil conditions they may be transplanted and survive and spraying with paraquat is likely to be more effective. Late sown crops will allow time for a flush of young plants to be encouraged by the preparation of a seedbeed: these can then be killed with the final preparations for sowing the crop. Unfortunately such control measures may be poor husbandry: yields of cereals are reduced by late planting and, with winter wheat, the opportunity to plant the crop at all may be lost if bad weather supervenes.

12.041 Losses of seeds from the stubble can be encouraged if straw is burnt, both by killing seeds and, indirectly, by reducing dormancy of the survivors. Burning soon after harvest will be most effective; delay allows seeds to work their way into the surface trash and soil where they are protected from the heat.

Seed losses can also be encouraged by leaving the stubble uncultivated until December. Seeds exposed on the surface can be eaten by birds and mice or die naturally as a result of the fluctuations of temperature and moisture. Conversely early cultivation of stubbles protects the seeds from these factors and allows maximum survivial.

Wild oat seeds can remain dormant in the soil for at least three years, more under some conditions (e.g. a ley), but large losses occur each year. Seeds may rot or they may germinate unsuccessfully. This unsuccessful germination will occur to a greater extent after ploughing than after tine cultivation where the seeds are retained near the surface, enabling more seedlings to establish successfully.

CHEMICAL CONTROL OF *AVENA* spp.

12.042   For cereal crops, refer to chapter 1.

Herbicide	Crop, other than cereals. Paragraph reference in brackets
Barban	Broad beans (2.015), field beans (2.015), peas (2.292), sugar beet (2.064).
Carbetamide	Overwintering brassicae (2.109), red and white clover (5.043), winter beans (2.015), lucerne, sainfoin (5.043).
Cycloate	Sugar beet, red beet, fodder beet, mangels (2.048).
Dalapon	Sugar beet (2.065), carrots (2.131), oilseed rape (2.234).
Di-allate	Brassicae (2.081), red beet (2.072), sugar beet (2.049).
EPTC	Potatoes (2.305).
Paraquat	Pre-sowing or pre-emergence of all crops.
Propham	Peas (2.283), sugar beet (2.051)
Propyzamide	Strawberries (3.137), lettuce (2.204), apples, pears (3.045), blackcurrants (3.067), raspberries (3.119), gooseberries (3.081), field beans (2.011), winter oilseed rape (2.235).
TCA	Kale (2.169), peas (2.284), rape (2.225), sugar beet (2.054), Brussels sprouts, cabbages (2.082).
Tri-allate	Beans (2.006), carrots (2.224), peas (2.285).
Trifluralin	Brassicae (2.083), sugar beet (2.069).

Cardaria draba (Hoary Cress)

12.043   *C. draba* is generally found on roadsides and waste places but it is a serious weed of arable land in several districts, particularly in Kent, Essex and Hertfordshire, where it has been a major problem for many years. It grows on a wide range of soil types. It is a perennial possessing an extensive system of vertical roots, which may penetrate downwards into the soil for 1–2 m and horizontal roots which may spread over a wide area. Flowering takes place from May to July and abundant seed is formed. The weed can be spread by introducing either seed or pieces of root into clean ground. Once established, *C. draba* is very difficult to control by normal methods of tillage but sowing the field to a long term ley will give good results. Fallowing alone, unless really deep ploughing is carried out, is seldom completely effective. Winter cereal favours the early growth of the weed in the following season and thoroughly cultivated root crops will help to reduce infestations.

12.044   The chemical control of *C. draba* has proved very successful and is based on a spraying programme carried out in cereal crops over 2–3 years. The weed cannot be eradicated by a simple treatment with MCPA or 2,4-D, but well over 90 per cent control can be obtained by treatment in a winter cereal in 2 successive seasons. If this is done, MCPA and 2,4-D are

368

equally effective and should be applied at 0·8 to 1·0 kg/ha during the period after the shoots are 25–150 mm high up to the flowering stage. To ensure eradication of the weed after 2 years' spraying, it is advisable to plant a spring cereal or other crop resistant to MCPA and 2,4-D in the third year so that a spray treatment can again be made, if a few remaining shoots appear. If only a single year's treatment can be made, the dose should be increased to the maximum permissible on the crop, and MCPA used in preference to 2,4-D if treatment is made shortly after the shoots have emerged. If the weed is treated at the flowering stage, MCPA and 2,4-D are equally effective. Where tolerant crops are grown (Chapter 3) dichlobenil at 9·2 to 11·0 kg/ha will give good control.

Cirsium arvense (Creeping Thistle)

12.045 Creeping thistle is one of the most persistent and troublesome perennial weeds of grassland and arable land. It spreads rapidly by means of brittle roots which readily produce new shoots or may remain dormant for many years if deeply buried under a vigorous sward. Seeds are not regarded as an important means of propagation because they are rarely, if ever, shed from the flowering head, and fertile seeds are not carried by the thistle-down which blows about in great abundance. The seeds remain in the flowering head and are released when the head falls to the ground and rots; seedlings of this thistle are uncommon, spread of the weed being principally by vegetative means. Control by cultivation must aim to destroy the root system by frost or drying, otherwise it will only serve to increase the infestation. Really deep ploughing is very effective. In cereal crops, spraying should be postponed as long as possible if the main object is to control creeping thistle. Spraying will kill any shoots that have emerged, but if carried out too early may be followed by considerable regrowth. Recommended doses for MCPA and 2,4-D are 1·1–1·7 kg/ha. MCPB and 2,4-DB should be applied at 1·7 to 2·2 kg/ha and dichlorprop and mecoprop at 2·8 kg/ha. The maximum safe dose of herbicide which may be applied to cereals is given in paragraph 1.018.

12.046 Chlorthiamid and dichlobenil is recommended at 7·7–11·0 kg/ha, formulated as granules, in certain fruit crops (see Chapter 3).

12.047 [**For information.**] Promising results have been obtained with bromacil and terbacil at 2·2–3·4 kg/ha in certain fruit crops (see Chapter 3).
      See paragraph 5.065 regarding *Cirsium arvense* in grassland. See also MAFF Advisory Leaflet No. 57.

Convolvulus arvensis (Field Bindweed)

12.048 *Convolvulus arvensis* is an important weed of fruit and other perennial horticultural crops and in some localities it is also important in annual cropping systems. It can be distinguished from the larger bindweeds (*Calystegia* spp.), which are mainly horticultural and garden weeds, by its smaller leaves and flowers, the latter being up to 30 mm across as compared with 40 mm or more for the larger bindweeds. *C. arvensis* sets abundant viable seed although this is not an important source of new infestations in Britain. Established plants have extensive and deep roots, which are difficult to eliminate. Cultivation produces root fragments and although these may start to produce new shoots, they usually perish. Regrowth after cultivation comes from buds on the roots beneath the depth of cultivation. The main period of shoot growth is from June to September and cultural control is usually impracticable.

12.049 Shoots of *C. arvensis* are readily killed by MCPA, MCPB, 2,4-D, mecoprop, dichlorprop, 2,4,5-T and mixtures containing dicamba. In cereal crops, the weed generally emerges too late to be much affected by these herbicides. In other crops too, the choice of herbicide, timing and dose is often restricted by their tolerance to the herbicide.

In order to obtain the maximum effect in the year after treatment spraying should be delayed until the *C. arvensis* shoots are well developed. Applying the maximum recommended dose also improves the effect in the year after treatment. At the maximum recommended doses MCPA, MCPB and 2,4-D give better long term control than mecoprop, dichlorprop, 2,4,5-T and dicamba. Promising results have been obtained by spraying *C. arvensis* in cereal stubble 2 to 3 weeks after harvesting when new growth has been made; the field should not be ploughed for at least 2 weeks after spraying.

Recommended doses are MCPA-salt $1 \cdot 1 - 2 \cdot 2$ kg/ha, MCPB $2 \cdot 2 - 3 \cdot 4$ kg/ha, 2,4-D amine $1 \cdot 1 - 2 \cdot 2$ kg/ha, 2,4-D-ester $1 \cdot 1 - 2 \cdot 2$ kg/ha, 2,4,5-T-ester $1 \cdot 1 - 2 \cdot 2$ kg/ha, mecoprop and dichlorprop $2 \cdot 2 - 2 \cdot 8$ kg/ha, dicamba up to $0 \cdot 14$ kg/ha.

12.050 *C. arvensis* can be suppressed with chlorthiamid and dichlobenil at the maximum doses recommended for selective use in woody crops. The manufacturers make only modest claims, but with accurate application and favourable conditions growth may be prevented until July. There is evidence that these treatments do not reduce the *C. arvensis* root as much as the translocated herbicides such as MCPA. Nevertheless they can provide worthwhile control in some soft fruit crops. There should be a follow-up application of translocated weedkiller such as MCPA or MCPB in the summer or early autumn.

12.051 *C. arvensis* can be controlled with the above herbicides in crops for which they are recommended (see appropriate crops).

12.052 [**For information.**] Promising results have been obtained using glyphosate. This would be very costly but it may be justified where only small areas need to be treated in land to be planted to high value crops. (See paragraph 12.006).

Crops as weeds

12.053   A number of crops may survive to become weeds in subsequent years of a rotation. They may cause direct weed problems, through competition, interference with harvesting, or by contaminating the harvested produce. In many cases, however, the indirect effect on pests or diseases may be more important. Thus volunteer cereal plants may be important in the epidemiology of mildew *Erisyphe graminis* and Rusts *Puccinia graminis*, *P. Striiformis*, whilst groundkeeper potatoes can have a marked influence on populations of potato cyst eelworms, *Heterodera rostochiensis, H. pallida.*

Efficient harvesting can reduce the occurrence of some of these problems. This is not a complete answer however; most potato harvesters, for example, are only designed to harvest tubers of seed or ware size so that smaller tubers are lost even at optimum efficiency. With grain crops, very high standards of efficiency are possible and are achieved in practice but, even when the losses before and during harvest are as low as 0·5 per cent, the potential number of volunteers cereal plants can be over $10/m^2$. With crops such as oilseed rape where pre-harvest losses can be much more severe potential 'volunteer' populations can be enormous.

12.054   Volunteer cereals and oilseed rape should be encouraged to germinate in the stubble by *shallow* cultivation; excessively deep working dries out the soil and may preserve some seeds among the clods so that they are able to germinate later in the presence of a crop. Seedlings can be destroyed by further cultivation or application of paraquat, *before* plants are too large. Cereal plants beyond the 3–4 leaf stage may be very difficult to control without ploughing.

12.055   Groundkeeper potatoes can be killed by the action of frost and may be eaten by rooks and other birds during the winter. Such mortality only occurs when the tubers are on or near the surface. For frost to be effective it has been estimated in the Netherlands that 50 'frost hours' at temperatures below $-2°C$ are necessary (i.e. approximately 24 h at $-2°C$ or 12 h at $-4°C$). Such conditions do not commonly occur at depths greater than 5–10 cm below the soil surface in the UK.

Potato growers are recommended to avoid mouldboard ploughing where possible and thus avoid placing tubers at greater, and safer, depths in the soil.

12.056   Carrot growers who have a problem with groundkeeper potatoes, which can be serious in this crop, may be advised to use a mixture of metoxuron and liquid linuron. Apart from being a valuable general purpose herbicide this mixture severely checks and may kill potatoes, although regrowth sometimes occurs.

12.057   Wild annual beet or 'annual bolters' are a serious problem of sugar beet crops in parts of Europe and have become established on a limited scale in the United Kingdom and Eire.

12.058   Most infestations are at very low populations and the weed should be eradicated at this stage by pulling or spudding (see paragraph 12.002) during the first two to three weeks in July. When pulling, the whole plant should be removed from the field to avoid the risk of seeds maturing and ripening: drawing on the reserves of food in the leaves and taproot. As an alternative the wild beet plants can be treated with glyphosate. using the herbicide glove (see paragraph 12.004).

12.059   At denser populations the flowering heads can be cut, exploiting the height difference between the bolters and the crop to avoid or minimize damage to the latter. Cutting in this way removes the physical obstruction to harvesting and very much reduces the weed population. However, small plants are missed and lateral branching may occur so that seeds are produced below the level of the crop. In some areas of Belgium beet can only be grown if the annual bolters are cut twice each year. Limited experience in the UK suggests that one cut is sufficient but the practical problem of choosing the critical time may indicate that two cuts, 3–4 weeks apart, are preferable.

Cutting should take place during the first 2–3 weeks in July. If too early, more plants may run up to seed after cutting; if too late the earliest plants may produce seed before they are cut. Mowers of the flail type have most commonly been used for this purpose. Whatever machine is used accurate control of the cutting height is essential.

Equisetum spp. (Horsetail)

12.060   *Equisetum arvense* (Field Horsetail) and *E. palustre* (Marsh Horsetail) can occur in arable land, although *E. arvense* is most frequently found because it can, once the rhizomes are established, survive under relatively dry conditions.

12.061   Recommended doses for control by MCPA, MCPB, 2,4-D and 2,4-DB can be found in paragraph 10.072. Generally the best results are obtained by spraying when the aerial shoots are well grown and about 30 cm high, but as the shoots emerge fairly late in spring this may not be feasible in cereals, and in practice the result is frequently only a short-term suppression of the foliage.

Aminotriazole at 4·5 kg/ha can give useful control with limited regrowth. For best results the chemical should be applied in late summer or early autumn but at least two weeks before natural die back of the foliage.

12.062 Good control is obtained with chlorthiamid and dichlobenil at 7·8 to 11·0 kg/ha, formulated as granules, in certain fruit crops (see Chapter 3). See paragraph 5.074 regarding *Equisetum* spp. in grassland.

Heracleum sphondylium (Hogweed)

12.063 Hogweed is a common roadside plant which has become an important weed of fruit crops in certain districts. Isolated plants are occasionally found in cereals, particularly those grown with reduced cultivation. Seedlings germinate from January onwards with the majority emerging in the spring. It is a biennial or perennial. The seed is dispersed over short distances and infestations usually start near the headland and spread slowly unless aided by cultural practices.

12.064 There is evidence that flowering shoots that are cut down before the florets of the primary umbels have been shed do not produce viable seed. Only the upper part of the root system is capable of regeneration. Even established plants can be killed by removing the top growth after cutting the roots 7–10 cm below the soil surface.

12.065 Established plants are resistant to most herbicides at the doses recommended in crops but they are controlled by atrazine, bromacil, sodium chlorate, dichlobenil and picloram at the doses used for total weed control (9.000).

Promising results for pre-emergence control of seedlings have been obtained with bromacil and terbacil at 0·5 kg/ha and chlorthiamid and dichlobenil at 10 kg/ha. Seedlings are resistant to the post-emergence treatments recommended for cereals but they are controlled by paraquat at 1 kg/ha.

Established plants have been controlled, but not eliminated, by aminotriazole 4·5 kg/ha plus 2,4-D-amine 2·2 kg/ha applied in April and May.

Spot-treatment of individual plants is often feasible when an infestation is starting. Promising results have been obtained with chlorthiamid and dichlobenil at 0·4 g (5 g of 7·5 per cent granules) applied to individual weeds. It is important that the granules are placed onto the crown of the plant and on the soil around the collar. Apply in March or April to prevent further seeding. Later application is effective but may not prevent seeding therefore the flower shoot should also be removed.

Juncus spp. (Rushes) (See Paragraph 5.077)

Mentha arvensis (Corn Mint)

12.066   *M. arvensis* is a rhizomatous perennial weed of arable land. The plant is downy, with whorls of small lilac flowers appearing in August to September. It has a characteristic smell. The normal use of MCPA, 2,4-D, mecoprop, dichlorprop and MCPA plus dicamba is generally ineffective in controlling this weed, but the latter mixture may suppress it if the weed has adequate foliage for uptake of the herbicide. This normally means spraying has to be delayed until as late as possible.

Good control has been reported following the use of 1·1–2·2 kg/ha simazine. It has also been observed that TCA-sodium at 22–33 kg/ha when used for couch control, has given a long term reduction of *M. arvensis*. Simazine or compounds based on boric oxide will give complete eradication of the weed in uncropped land (see Chapter 9).

Oxalis spp. (Oxalis)

12.067   There are 6 species of *Oxalis* that occur as weeds in the British Isles. The most important are the bulbous species: *O. corymbosa* D.C., *O. latifolia* H.B. and K., *O. pes-caprae* L. (*O. cernua* Thunb.) and *O. tetraphylla* Cav. to which these notes refer. All species are purely horticultural as opposed to agricultural weeds. *O. latifolia* and *O. pes-caprae* are by far the most serious although both are only half hardy and restricted to frost free areas. *O. pes-caprae* is restricted to the Isles of Scilly, *O. latifolia* is common in Devon, Cornwall and the Channel Isles and is very widespread as a weed of glasshouses throughout Southern England. *O. tetraphylla* is occasionally found in Jersey whilst *O. corymbosa* appears less common as a weed of commercial holdings although it is a serious, but occasional, problem of gardens throughout the southern and central counties of England.

The bulbils are easily detached from the root in late summer, and are spread through the soil by digging and cultivating. The bulbils are very persistent indeed and destruction of the foliage only stimulates the ripening of the bulbils, the food reserves in the taproot being called on for the purpose. Thus cultivating the soil may cause the plants to increase faster. The bulbils are carried over short distances by birds and probably in mud on machinery and men's boots. They are carried over greater distances in nurserymen's goods such as plant roots and compost, and fresh infestations are thereby started. Hygenic methods should be applied to prevent the spread of bulbils to new sites. Compost and peat should not be stacked on infested soil. In nurseries where *Oxalis* is prevalent such materials should be kept covered to keep birds out. Peat found to contain bulbils (looking like tiny hazel-nut kernels, about 6·5 mm long) should not be spread on clean soil. Individual plants, if dug up, should be burnt in an incinerator and under no circumstances put on a compost heap. Nursery plants grown in infested ground and lifted for despatch should be washed free of soil and examined for adhering bulbils. Buyers of nursery-grown stock must, of course, be vigilant to ensure that they do not acquire a new and especially obdurate problem.

Some growers have set young pigs to forage for the bulbs, with some success. It appears that bulbils will pass through full-grown pigs unharmed. A successful method of control is to choke out the plants by grassing-over infested land. The grass must be left down for at least 3 years to make sure that all bulbils are dead. Unfortunately few small growers can afford this. It is important to clean out all stray plants in paths, walls and odd corners that would otherwise be a source of reinfestation.

12.068   Fumigation of the soil with mixtures of dichloropropene and dichloropropane has shown some promise, but this treatment is too costly to use except where the ground is very valuable. Recent trials have shown that *Oxalis corymbosa* can be controlled by metham-sodium applied as a drench in autumn or summer at 674 litres/ha of the commercial product followed by heavy watering to provide a seal.

12.069   Good results have been obtained with trifluralin at 3·4 kg/ha. It should be applied to crop-free soil and, *within 30 minutes,* worked in with a rotary cultivator at high rotor speed but slow (4 kph) forward travel. Depth of working should be from 5 to 10 cm but this does not appear to be so critical as timing and conditions. Moist soil conditions improve control and 'sealing in' the vapour by rainfall or sprinkler may also improve results.

The best results are obtained with applications made in June and July, although, in the Isles of Scilly, May and June are to be preferred.

Most experience has been outdoors in the South West but excellent results have been obtained under glass, when the effective application period appears to be longer.

The following crops can be planted two days after spraying; daffodil, narcissus, tulip, iris, gladiolus, chrysanthemum, Tomato, strawberry and various well rooted hardwood cuttings.

Phragmites communis (Common Reed)

12.070   *P. communis* is a weed of drainage channels, ditches, shallow water swampy areas throughout the British Isles. When treating *P. communis* in ditches reference should be made to the chapter on aquatic weeds (Chapter 10) for details of the special problems involved.

12.071   *P. communis* can also be a serious problem of arable land, particularly in East Anglia and south eastern England, where the water table is suitable.

It can creep into fields from drainage ditches near their margins and may be introduced when spoil from ditch cleaning (containing rhizomes) is spread over the adjacent field.

The reed, which resembles a slim bamboo, spreads by means of stout far-creeping rhizomes. The leaves are flat with narrow long-tapering points and the ligule consists of a ring of hairs. The flower heads, which are borne as high as 2·5–3·0 m upon the stems, are nodding and a conspicuous dull purple in colour.

12.072   Because of the depth at which the rhizomes grow cultivations have little effect upon *P. communis* and indeed they may even help to spread the rhizomes that are cut up. However, *P. communis* can be controlled by dalapon-sodium at 19·0–25·0 kg/ha. It can be applied either as split doses for example 19·0 kg/ha soon after shoot emergence and a further 12·0 kg/ha later if necessary, or as a single dose of 19·0–25·0 kg/ha. The single dose should be applied either when shoots are 0·6–1·0 m tall and growing rapidly or, alternatively, in late summer or autumn to suit the crops. For maximum translocation into the rhizomes and control of regrowth the weed should be at flowering stage but this may be difficult to achieve without loss of a year's cropping.

Aminotriazole is also occasionally used at 4·5–9·0 kg/ha or even as an additive to dalapon to speed its action.

See also paragraph 12.006.

Polygonum cuspidatum (Japanese Knotweed)

Polygonum amphibium (Amphibious Bistort)

12.073   *Polygonum cuspidatum* is a tall rhizomatous perennial formerly planted as an ornamental curiosity in large gardens, ornamental woodlands etc. It has become a weed of gardens and waste places and is very resistant to most herbicides (see also 7.034).

Polygonum amphibium (Amphibious Bistort), although a plant of water and river banks, is also a weed of arable and horticultural land, commonly on lighter soils. It is a rhizomatous perennial, resistant to the soil herbicides used in horticulture and to most cereal sprays.

Both species are susceptible to glyphosate at 1·5–2·0 kg/ha (see 12.002, 12.006 and 9.029).

Pteridium aquilinum (Bracken) (5.079)

Ranunculus spp. (Buttercups) (5.084)

Rorippa sylvestris (Creeping Yellow-cress)

12.074   [**For information.**] This is a weed of nurseries which is difficult to control by cultivation. Continental information indicates that it is controlled with aminotriazole 4·5 kg/ha applied just before flowering. Details of following cropping can be found under *Agropyron repens*.

Rumex spp. (Docks)

12.075 The two most important species of *Rumex* occurring as weeds are *R. crispus* (curled dock) and *R. obtusifolius* (broad-leaved dock). Several other species can also be troublesome weeds, particularly *R. conglomeratus,* but as there are few records dealing with their control, these remarks will be confined to *R. crispus* and *R. obtusifolius*. The lower leaves of *R. crispus* usually have curled edges and the 3 corners of the perianth surrounding the seed do not have long prominent teeth. In contrast, *R. obtusifolius* has lower leaves with flat or slightly undulating margins and the 3 corners of the perianth surrounding the seed have up to 5 long, prominent teeth.

12.076 In the seedling stage, before a large taproot has formed, both species are readily killed by the commonly used growth-regulator herbicides (5.087). Established plants are much more difficult to kill and *R. obtusifolius*, particularly, may be almost completely resistant to these herbicides when well established in grassland. In cereal crops, the flowering shoots or docks arising from pieces of old root-stock may be severely checked or killed and seeding reduced or prevented by spraying with these chemicals. A method of control that has given good results is to plough and sow down to a 1-year ley of Italian ryegrass, followed by spraying as necessary during the summer to kill the docks, without loss of production. The ley is followed by a cereal, so that any surviving docks can be sprayed again.

12.077 [**For information.**] Rotary cultivation carried out in a manner similar to that described for the control of *Agropyron repens* (Common Couch) has given good control of *Rumex obtusifolius* (Broad-leaved Dock).

12.078   Herbicide recommendations for control of *Rumex* species.

Herbicide	Dose	Crop(s)	Refer to paragraph
MCPA-salt 2,4-D-amine	} *1·1–1·7 kg/ha*	*Cereals*	*12.086*
MCPB 2,4-DB	} *2·2–3·4 kg/ha*	*Cereals*	*12.086*
2,4-D-ester	*1·1 kg/ha*	*Cereals*	*12.086*
Mecoprop Dichlorprop	} *4·5 kg/ha*	*Cereals*	*12.086*
Asulam	*1·2 kg/ha*	*Grassland*	*5.090*
Asulam mixtures	*1·2 kg/ha*	*Grassland*	*5.091*
Mecoprop	*2·8 kg/ha*	*Grassland*	*5.092*
Dicamba mixtures		*Grassland*	*5.089, 5.093, 5.094*
Benazolin, MCPA and 2,4-D mixture		*Grassland*	*5.095*
Chlorthiamid	*9·2 kg/ha*	Fruits and ornamentals	*3.042*
Dichlobenil	*5·9–11·0 kg/ha*	Fruits and ornamentals	*3.043*
Bromacil	*2·2–3·0 kg/ha*	Fruits	*3.115*
Terbacil	*2·7 kg/ha*	Fruits	*3.047*

Silene alba (White Campion)

12.079   This is a weed of arable land, particularly where the soil is chalky. It can be an annual, biennial or short-lived perennial in behaviour. It is a scheduled weed under the herbage certification scheme for timothy and white clover. Its seed is a frequent contaminant of the seed of red and white clover, trefoil, kale, and broccoli. White campion is susceptible at the seedling stage to 2·8 kg/ha of mecoprop-salt which can be used on grass seed crops in which case seed production of the weed can be prevented. They cannot be used on clover.

Senecio jacobaea (Common Ragwort) (5.097)

Sonchus arvensis (Perennial Sow-thistle)

12.080   *Sonchus arvensis* differs from the two annual sow-thistles *S. asper* and *S. oleraceus* in being a perennial with creeping underground roots and in having conspicuous yellow glandular hairs on the flowering heads and on their stems. The annuals can easily be distinguished from each other by the nature of the auricles at the base of the leaf; the auricles of *S. asper* are rounded in outline and are pressed flat against the stem, whereas those of *S. oleraceus* are pointed and often project on the other side of the stem, but are not pressed flat against it. Control of *S. arvensis* can be achieved

378

by frequent cultivations, but they may not be successful unless the creeping rhizomes are fully exposed to dry or frosty conditions. The best results are obtained by combining cultural and chemical treatments.

12.081 The growth of aerial parts can be retarded and flowering completely suppressed if *Sonchus arvensis* is sprayed early, when growth is vigorous, with MCPA, MCPB, 2,4-D or 2,4-DB. This is unlikely to lead to permanent control with MCPA or 2,4-D; the long-term effects of MCPB and 2,4-DB are unknown.

Recommended doses for temporary suppression:

MCPA-salt and 2,4-D-amine 1·7 to 2·2 kg/ha; 2,4-D-ester 1·1 to 1·7 kg/ha; MCPB and 2,4-DB 2·2 to 3·3 kg/ha.

Mecoprop has given temporary control of aerial shoots at 2·8 kg/ha. The maximum safe dose of herbicide which may be applied to cereals is given in paragraph 1.047.

Tussilago farfara (Colt's-foot)

12.082 *T. farfara* is particularly troublesome on heavy soils but can occur in abundance on all soil types. It spreads rapidly by means of rhizomes, which often penetrate the soil to a considerable depth, making eradication difficult by normal cultivations. It flowers and sets seed long before the leaves appear. *T. farfara* is mainly a weed of arable land and waste places, and seeding an infested arable field down to a good ley can often be an effective means of eradication.

12.083 Spraying with MCPA or 2,4-D in a cereal crop does little more than kill the leaves. *T. farfara* is resistant to mecoprop but is reported to be severely checked by 2,4,5-T.

12.084 Sodium chlorate applied at 170–220 kg/ha to cereal stubble is effective against *T. farfara*. Spraying should be carried out as soon as possible, preferably at the end of July or early August (12.018).

12.085 *T. farfara* is susceptible to aminotriazole at doses used for couch control in cereal stubbles (see paragraphs 12.020 and 12.021).

12.086 Chlorthiamid and dichlobenil is recommended at 7·8–11·0 kg/ha, formulated as granules, in certain fruit crops (see Chapter 3).

12.087 [**For information.**] Promising results have been obtained with bromacil and terbacil at 2·2–3·4 kg/ha in certain fruit crops (see Chapter 3).

12.088 THE SUSCEPTIBILITY OF SOME HERBACEOUS WEEDS
TO GROWTH-REGULATOR HERBICIDES

Para 12.088 indicates the response of perennial and some annual weeds to individual herbicides at the doses shown at the head of each column. The response of the more common annual weeds, to the materials and to some additives can be found in para 1.054. Fenoprop is not included in the table as it is only available as a minor constituent with other growth regulator herbicides in proprietary mixtures. The table does not allow the user to predict accurately the effect of herbicides and the final choice must be made on the claims of the manufacturers and selection should, where possible, be confined to products approved under the Agricultural Chemicals Approval Scheme.

The categories below define the expected response of weeds to various herbicides when used according to the recommendations for appropriate crops.

Definition of categories

S   Susceptible

Annual and seedling biennials and perennials
Consistently good control at all stages of growth up to the beginning of flowering.

Established biennials and perennials
Consistently good control (both shoot and roots) when treated at the recommended time.

MS   Moderately susceptible

Good control in seedling stage (cotyledon to 2 or 3 leaves) and possibly a useful suppression at later growth stages.

Aerial growth usually killed and a useful measure of long-term control obtained under suitable conditions.

MR   Moderately resistant

Checked in seedling stage only (cotyledon to 3 or 4 leaves).

Variable effect on aerial growth – appreciable long-term control unlikely from a single application.

R   Resistant

No useful effect.

No useful effect.

The following abbreviations are used:
(A), (B), (P)—Annual, biennial, perennial respectively.
Sh—shoots. Sd—seedlings.
EP—established plants.
(a)—in arable land. (g)—in grassland.

* Total mecoprop or dichlorprop in terms of active and inactive isomers in ratio 50/50.

Weed	Chemical and dose in kg acid equivalent per ha						Paragraph reference
	MCPA-salt 1·7	2,4-D amine 1·4	MCPB-salt 2·2	2,4-DB-salt 2·2	Mecoprop-salt 2·8*	Dichlor-prop-salt 2·8*	
1. *Achillea millefolium* (P) (Yarrow)	MR	MR	R	R	MR	MR	
2. *Aegopodium podagraria* (P) (Ground-elder)	R	R	R	R	R	R	12·007 to 12·012
3. *Aethusa cynapium* (A) (Fool's Parsley)	MS	—	—	—	MR	—	
4. *Agrimonia eupatoria* (P) (Agrimony)	R	R	R	R	—	—	
5. *Agrostemma githago* (A) (Corncockle)	R	R	R	—	MR	—	
6. *Ajuga reptans* (P) (Bugle)	R	R	R	R	R	—	
7. *Allium ursinum* (P) (Ramsons)	R	R	R	R	—	—	
8. *Allium vineale* (P) (Wild Onion)	MR	MR	—	—	MR	—	12·026 to 10·23 12·028 12·034 & 12·035
9. *Amsinckia intermedia* (A) (Tarweed)	R	MR	—	—	MR	—	
10. *Anthriscus sylvestris* (P) (Cow Parsley)	MR	MR	R	R	MR	MR	
11. *Arctium lappa* (B) (Greater Burdock)	Mr	Mr	—	—	—	—	

12.088—*continued*

Weed	Chemical and dose in kg acid equivalent per ha						Paragraph reference
	MCPA-salt 1·7	2,4-D amine 1·4	MCPB-salt 2·2	2,4-DB-salt 2·2	Mecoprop-salt 2·8*	Dichlor-prop-salt 2·8*	
12. *Arctium minus* (B) (Lesser Burdock)	MS	MS	—	—	—	—	
13. *Arenaria serpyllifolia* (A or B) (Thyme-leaved Sandwort)	S	S	—	—	—	—	
14. *Armoracia rusticana* (P) (Horse-radish)	MS	MS	R	R	MS	—	
15. *Artemisia vulgaris* (P) (Mugwort)	MS	MS	R	R	MS	—	
16. *Bellis perennis* (P) (Daisy)	MS	MS	MR	MR	MS	MS	
17. *Brassica juncea* (A) (Indian Mustard)	S	S	—	—	—	—	
18. *Brassica napus* var. *arvensis* (A) (Rape)	S	S	—	MR	S	—	
19. *Calystegia sepium* (P) (Hedge Bellbine)	MS	MS	MS	MS	—	—	
20. *Cardaria draba* (P) (Hoary Cress)	MS	MS	—	—	—	MR	12·043 & 12·044
21. *Carduus nutans* (P) (Musk Thistle)	MS	MS	MS	—	—	—	

							Reference
22. *Carex* spp. (P) (Sedges)		R	R	R	—	—	—	
23. *Centaurea cyanus* (A) (Cornflower)		S	S	—	—	—	—	
24. *Centaurea nigra* (P) (Common Knapweed)		MS	MS	—	—	—	—	
25. *Centaurea scabiosa* (P) (Greater Knapweed)		MR	MR	—	—	—	—	
26. *Cerastium arvense* (P) (Field Mouse-ear)		R	R	R	R	MS	MR	
27. *Cerastium glomeratum* (A) (Sticky Mouse-ear)		MR	MS	R	—	MR	—	
28. *Chaenorrhinum minus* (A) (Small Toadflax)		—	—	—	—	MR	—	
29. *Chamaenerion angustifolium* (P) (Rosebay Willowherb)		R	MR	—	—	—	—	
30. *Chrysanthemum leucanthemum* (P) (Oxeye Daisy)		MR	MR	R	R	MR	MR	
31. *Chrysanthemum vulgare* (P) (Tansy)		MR	MR	—	—	—	—	
32. *Cichorium intybus* (P) (Chicory)		MS	MS	MR	MR	MS	MS	
33. *Cirsium acaule* (P) (Dwarf Thistle)		MR	MR	—	—	—	—	12·045 to 12·047
34. *Cirsium arvense* (P) (Creeping Thistle)	Sd, Sh	S	S	S	S	S	S	12·045 to 12·047
	EP (a)	S	S	S	S	S	S	
	EP (g)*	MS	MS	MS	MS	MS	MS	

* See introduction.

383

12.088—*continued*

Weed		MCPA-salt 1·7	2,4-D amine 1·4	MCPB-salt 2·2	2,4-DB-salt 2·2	Mecoprop-salt 2·8*	Dichlorprop-salt 2·8*	Paragraph reference
35. *Cirsium vulgare* (B) (Spear Thistle)	Sd	S	S	S	S	S	—	
	EP	MS	MS	MS	MS	MS	—	
36. *Colchicum autumnale* (P) (Meadow Saffron)		MR	MR	—	—	—	—	
37. *Conium maculatum* (B) (Hemlock)		MR	Mr	R	—	—	—	
38. *Conopodium majus* (P) (Pignut)		R	R	R	R	—	—	
39. *Convolvulus arvensis* (P) (Field Bindweed)	Sh	S	S	S	S	R	MS	12·048 to 12·059
	EP	MR	MR	MR	MR	R	MR	
40. *Conyza canadensis* (A) (Canadian Fleabane)		S	S	—	—	—	—	
41. *Coronopus didymus* (A) (Lesser Swine-cress)		S	S	MS	S	MS	MS	
42. *Coronopus squamatus* (A or B) (Swine-cress)		MR	MR	MR	MR	S	MS	
43. *Crepis biennis* (B) (Rough Hawk's-beard)		S	S	—	MS	MS	—	
44. *Crepis capillaris* (A) (Smooth Hawk's-beard)		—	MS	—	—	MS	—	

Chemical and dose in kg acid equivalent per ha

12·060 to 12·062

No. Species							
45. *Cuscuta epithymum* (A) (Dodder)		R	R	—	—	R	—
46. *Datura stramonium* (A) (Thorn-apple)		MS	MS	MR	MS	—	—
47. *Daucus carota* (B) (Wild Carrot)		MR	MR	R	MR	MR	MR
48. *Descurainia sophia* (A) (Flixweed)		S	S	—	—	—	—
49. *Epilobium* spp. (P) (Willowherb)		MR	MR	R	R	—	—
50. *Equisetum arvense* (P) (Field Horsetail)	Sh	S	S	S	S	S	S
	EP	MR	MR	MR	MR	R	R
51. *Equisetum palustre* (P) (Marsh Horsetail)	Sh	S	S	S	S	—	—
	EP	MR	MR	MR	MR	—	—
52. *Erodium cicutarium* (A) (Common Stork's-bill)		MR	MR	—	—	—	—
53. *Euphorbia exigua* (A) (Dwarf Spurge)		R	R	—	—	—	—
54. *Euphorbia peplus* (A) (Petty Spurge)		MR	R	—	—	—	—
55. *Filipendula ulmaria* (P) (Meadowsweet)		MR	MR	R	R	—	—
56. *Galeopsis speciosa* (A) (Large-flowered Hempnettle)		S	MS	MS	—	—	MS
57. *Galinsoga parviflora* (A) (Gallant Soldier)		S	S	MR	MR	S	—
58. *Galium saxatile* (P) (Heath Bedstraw)		MR	MR	—	—	MR	—

* See introduction.

12.088—*continued*

Weed	Chemical and dose in kg acid equivalent per ha						Paragraph reference
	MCPA-salt 1·7	2,4-D amine 1·4	MCPB-salt 2·2	2,4-DB-salt 2·2	Mecoprop-salt 2·8*	Dichlor-prop-salt 2·8*	
59. *Galium mollugo* (P) (Hedge Bedstraw)	—	—	—	—	MS	MS	
60. *Galium verrum* (P) (Ladies' Bedstraw)	R	R	R	R	—	—	
61. *Geranium dissectum* (A) (Cut-leaved Crane's-bill)	MR	MR	—	—	MR	—	
62. *Geranium pratense* (P) (Meadow Crane's-bill)	MR	MR	—	—	—	—	
63. *Gnaphalium uliginosum* (A) (Marsh Cudweed)	R	R	R	R	—	—	
64. *Heracleum sphondylium* (P) (Hogweed)	MR	MR	—	—	—	—	12·063 to 12·065
65. *Hieraceum pilosella* (P) (Mouse-ear Hawkweed)	MS	MS	—	—	—	—	
66. *Hyoscyamus niger* (A or B) (Henbane)	MR	MR	—	—	—	—	
67. *Hypericum perforatum* (P) (Common St John's-wort)	MR	MR	—	—	—	—	
68. *Hypochaeris radicata* (P) (Cat's-ear)	MS	MS	—	—	MS	MS	

69. *Iris pseudocorus* (P) (Yellow Iris)	—	—	R	R	MR	MR
70. *Juncus articulatus* (P) (Jointed Rush)	—	—	R	R	R	R
71. *Juncus conglomeratus* (P)	—	—	MS	MS	—	MS
72. *Juncus effusus* (P) (Soft Rush) — Sd, Sh / EP	MS / MR	MS / MR	MS / MR	S / MR	S / MS	S / MS
73. *Juncus inflexus* (P) (Hard Rush)	—	—	R	R	R	MR
74. *Juncus maritimus* (P) (Sea Rush)	—	—	—	—	MR	MR
75. *Juncus squarrosus* (P) (Heath Rush)	—	—	R	R	R	R
76. *Knautia arvensis* (P) (Field Scabious)	MS	MR	—	—	MS	MS
77. *Lamium album* (P) (White Dead-nettle)	—	R	—	R	R	R
78. *Lamium amplexicaule* (A) (Henbit Dead-nettle)	—	R	R	R	MR	MS
79. *Lamium purpureum* (A) (Red Dead-nettle)	R	R	R	R	MR	MR
80. *Legousia hybrida* (A) (Venus's-looking-glass)	—	—	—	—	MR	MS
81. *Leontodon autumnalis* (P) (Autumn Hawkbit)	—	MS	S	MS	S	MS
82. *Leontodon hispidus* (P) (Rough Hawkbit)	—	MR	—	—	MS	MR

* See introduction.

387

12.088—*continued*

Weed	Chemical and dose in kg acid equivalent per ha						Paragraph reference
	MCPA-salt 1·7	2,4-D amine 1·4	MCPB-salt 2·2	2,4-DB-salt 2·2	Mecoprop-salt 2·8*	Dichlorprop-salt 2·8*	
83. *Linaria vulgaris* (P) (Common Toadflax)	R	R	—	—	—	—	
84. *Lotus corniculatus* (P) (Common Birds-foot-trefoil)	MR	MR	—	—	MS	MR	
85. *Luzula campestris* (P) (Field Wood-rush)	R	R	R	R	MR	—	
86. *Lythrum salicaria* (P) (Purple-loosestrife)	—	MS	—	—	—	—	
87. *Medicago lupulina* (A or P) (Black Medick)	MR	MR	R	—	MR	—	
88. *Mentha arvensis* (P) (Corn Mint)	MR	MR	R	R	MR	MR	12-066
89. *Montia perfoliata* (A)	—	—	—	—	—	—	
90. *Odontites verna* (A) (Red Bartsia)	MS	MS	R	—	—	—	
91. *Oenanthe crocata* (P) (Hemlock Water-dropwort)	MS	—	—	—	—	—	
92. *Ononis repens* (P) (Common Restharrow)	R	R	R	R	R	—	
93. *Oxalis* spp. (P)	R	R	R	R	—	—	12-067 to 12-069

12-073

94. *Papaver argemone* (A) (Prickly Poppy)	—	—	—	—	MS	—
95. *Papaver dubium* (A) (Long-headed Poppy)	—	—	—	—	MS	—
96. *Petasites hybridus* (P) (Butterbur)	R	MR	R	R	R	—
97. *Picris echioides* (A or B) (Bristly Oxtongue)	—	MS	—	—	—	—
98. *Plantago coronopus* (A, B or P) (Buck's-horn Plantain)	MS	MS	—	—	MS	MS
99. *Plantago lanceolata* (P) (Ribwort Plantain)	S	S	S	S	S	S
100. *Plantago major* (P) (Greater Plantain)	S	S	S	S	S	S
101. *Plantago media* (P) (Hoary Plantain)	S	S	S	S	S	S
102. *Polygonum amphibium* (P) (Amphibious Bistort)	MR	MR	—	—	—	—
103. *Polygonum bistorta* (P) (Common Bistort)	R	R	R	R	R	MR
104. *Potentilla anserina* (P) (Silverweed)	MR	MR	R	—	MR	—
105. *Potentilla reptans* (P) (Creeping Cinquefoil)	R	R	R	—	R	—
106. *Prunella vulgaris* (P) (Selfheal)	MS	MS	—	—	—	—
107. *Pteridium aquilinum* (P) (Bracken)	R	R	R	R	R	R

* See introduction.

389

12.088—*continued*

Weed		MCPA-salt 1·7	2,4-D amine 1·4	MCPB-salt 2·2	2,4-DB-salt 2·2	Mecoprop-salt 2·8*	Dichlor-prop-salt 2·8*	Paragraph reference
		Chemical and dose in kg acid equivalent per ha						
108. *Pulicaria dysenterica* (P) (Common Fleabane)		MS	MS	—	—	—	—	
109. *Ranunculus acris* (P) (Meadow Buttercup)		MS	MS	MS	MS	MS	—	
110. *Ranunculus bulbosus* (P) (Bulbous Buttercup)	Sd, Sh EP	S MR	S MR	S MR	S MR	S MR	— —	
111. *Ranunculus repens* (P) (Creeping Buttercup)		S	S	S	S	S	S	
112. *Ranunculus sardous* (A) (Hairy Buttercup)		S	S	S	—	—	—	
113. *Rhinanthus minor* (A) (Yellow Rattle)		MR	MR	—	—	—	—	
114. *Rumex acetosa* (P) (Common Sorrel)	Sh EP	MS MR	MS MR	— —	— —	— R	— —	
115. *Rumex acetosella* (P) (Sheep's Sorrel)	Sh EP	MS MR	MS MR	— —	MS MR	— R	— —	
116. *Rumex conglomeratus* (B or P) (Clustered Dock)		MS	MS	—	—	—	—	
117. *Rumex crispus* (P) (Curled Dock)	Sd, Sh EP (a) Ep (g)*	S S MS	S S MS	S MS MS	S MS MS	S MS MR	S S MS	12-075 to 12-078

In each cell the three stacked values correspond to the growth stages **Sd, Sh / EP (a) / EP (g)***. A dash (—) indicates no data.

No. Species	Sd, Sh / EP (a) / EP (g)*					Reference
118. *Rumex obtusifolius* (P) (Broad-leaved Dock)	S / MS / R	S / S / MR	S / MR / R	S / MR / R	S / MS / MR · MS	12·075 to 12·078
119. *Scleranthus annuus* (A or B) (Annual Knawel)	MS	MS	—	—	MS	
120. *Senecio aquaticus* (B) (Marsh Ragwort)	MS	MS	—	—	MS	
121. *Senecio jacobaea* (B or P) (Common Ragwort)	MS	MS	R	R	MS	
122. *Sherardia arvensis* (A) (Field Madder)	—	—	R	R	—	
123. *Silene alba* (A, B or P) (White Campion)	R	R	R	R	MS	12·079
124. *Silene dioica* (B or P) (Red Campion)	R	R	—	MS	MS	
125. *Silene noctiflora* (A) (Night-flowering Campion)	R	R	—	—	—	
126. *Silene vulgaris* (P) (Bladder Campion)	R	R	R	MS	R	
127. *Sisymbrium officinale* (A) (Hedge Mustard)	S	S	—	—	—	
128. *Solanum dulcamara* (P) (Bitter-sweet)	MR	MR	—	MR	MR	
129. *Sonchus arvensis* (P) (Perennial Sow-thistle)	MS / MR	MS / MR	MS / —	MS / —	MR / —	12·080 & 12·081
130. *Stellaria media* (A) (Common Chickweed)	MR	MR	R	R	S	S

* See introduction.

391

12,088—*continued*

Weed		MCPA-salt 1·7	2,4-D amine 1·4	MCPB-salt 2·2	2,4-DB-salt 2·2	Mecoprop-salt 2·8*	Dichlor-prop-salt 2·8*	Paragraph reference
		Chemical and dose in kg acid equivalent per ha						
131. *Symphytum officinale* (P) (Common Comfrey)		MR	MR	R	R	—	—	
132. *Taraxacum officinale*(P) (Dandelion)	Sd, Sh	MS	S	R	MR	MR	MR	
	EP	MR	MS	R	MR	MR	—	
133. *Tragopogon pratensis* (A, B or P) (Goat's-beard)		MS	MS	—	—	—	—	
134. *Tripleurospermum maritimum* ssp. *inodorum* (A) (Scentless Mayweed)		MR	MR	R	R	MS	MR	
135. *Tussilago farfara* (P) (Colt's-foot)	Sh	MR	MR	R	R	MR	MR	12.082 to 12.087
	EP	R	MR	R	R	R	R	
136. *Urtica dioica* (P) (Common Nettle)	Sd, Sh	S	S	S	S	S	S	
	EP	MS	MS	MS	MS	MS	—	
137. *Veronica chamaedrys* (P) (Germander Speedwell)		MR	MR	—	—	MR	—	
138. *Veronica serpyllifolia* (P) (Thyme-leaved Speedwell)		MR	MR	—	—	—	—	
139. *Vicia cracca* (P) (Tufted Vetch)		MS	MS	—	—	—	—	
140. *Vicia sativa* (A) (Common Vetch)		MS	MS	—	—	S	S	

141. *Viola arvensis* (A) (Field Pansy)	MR	MR	MR	MR	MR	R	R
142. *Viola tricolor* (A) (Wild Pansy)	MR	MR	MR	MR	MR	R	R
143. *Xanthium spinosum* (Spiny Cocklebur)	S	S	S	S	S	—	—

Chapter 13
Recommendations for the use of growth regulators in agriculture and horticulture

13.001   This chapter aims mainly to provide practical recommendations for the use of plant growth regulators as aids in the production of agricultural and horticultural crops. The use of such chemicals is increasing and recommendations are given for those which have been cleared under the Pesticides Safety Precautions Scheme. Some other promising uses which have received provisional clearance have also been included for information. The control of weeds by hormonal-type herbicides is dealt with elsewhere in the handbook.

Cereals

Decreasing stem length to prevent lodging

Wheat

13.002   **Chlormequat** *at 1·7 kg/ha to winter wheat and 0·8 kg/ha to spring wheat at the start of jointing.*
    For optimum effects on the shortening and strengthening of the lower internodes, chlormequat should be applied to both winter and spring wheat at the commencement of jointing when the crop is making active growth. Applications at earlier stages of growth may be reduced in effectiveness particularly if a period of slow growth follows the treatment. Applications later than the commencement of jointing will shorten and strengthen the upper internodes only. In practice most applications are made between the 5-leaf stage and jointing, particularly if chlormequat is applied in mixture with a herbicide. Chlormequat is compatible with most herbicides except the dinitro compounds. The treatment with chlormequat of crops being grown for seed is subject to a code of practice issued under the British Cereal Seed Scheme. This should be consulted before application is made.

Oats

13.003   **Chlormequat** *at 1·7 kg/ha to winter and spring oats at the emergence of the second joint.*

For optimum effects on the shortening and strengthening of oat stems chlormequat should be applied at the emergence of the second joint when the crop is making active growth. A wetting agent should be added to the spray mixture.

As the stage of growth for application is after the commencement of jointing the mixture of chlormequat with herbicides is not recommended on oats.

The treatment with chlormequat of crops being grown for seed is subject to a code of practice issued under the British Cereal Seed Scheme. This should be consulted before application is made.

Rye

13.004   [**For information**] Chlormequat is recommended for use on rye in Sweden at 2·2 kg/ha alone or at 1·1 kg/ha with the addition of a wetting agent. In trials in Britain some shortening of stems was recorded following treatment with chlormequat but lodging was not prevented.

Barley

13.005   [**For information**] Chlormequat is poorly translocated in barley and only occasionally is any benefit seen in terms of shortening and strengthening of the stems. No clearance has been obtained for the use of chlormequat on barley and this crop should not be treated.

Vegetable and root crops

Celery

INCREASED YIELD AND STEM LENGTH

13.006   [**For information**] Gibberellic acid at 15 g/ha in low volume can increase plant height and subsequent yield of self-blanching celery. A single treatment only is necessary, and may be applied without the use of a wetting agent. Harvesting should take place within four weeks of application or there will be a risk of premature seeding and root-splitting.

Carrot

CONTROL OF ROOT SIZE AND SPLITTING

13.007   **Dimexan** *at 11 to 19 kg, according to the foliage density and variety, in 225–237 litres water/ha to check the growth of large roots and reduce root-splitting.*

Application of dimexan to carrot foliage reduces the productive leaf area but does not desiccate the crop completely. The lower fronds continue to grow but the growth rate, particularly of the larger carrots, is reduced. Total yield may be decreased but the yield of small carrots is increased. Associated with the treatment is a reduction in the amount of split carrots, giving a subsequent reduction in the amount of wastage and an increase in total saleable crop. If the carrots are likely to be too large at the time of harvest, application should be made when most of the roots by weight are in the required size range. To reduce splitting, application should be made when splitting is expected or has commenced. Carrots of the Amsterdam type should be treated with the lower doses, but higher rates should be used on crops with dense foliage. Rain within 2 h of application will reduce the effect of the material, which should only be applied to dry foliage under drying weather conditions.

Onion

SPROUT SUPPRESSION

13.008   Maleic hydrazide *at 3 to 4 kg in 560 to 675 litres/ha just prior to leaf senescence to reduce sprouting in store.*

For best results apply at high pressure around 5 bars. Application should be made to healthy crops when the leaves are dry. The chemical is best absorbed when the foliage is still erect, probably during the first two weeks of August. Rain within 24 h of application will reduce the effectiveness of the treatment unless a weatherproof formulation is used. An interval of four days is necessary before lifting. The lower dose rate should be used for onions stored up to December and the higher rate for those stored to March. Onions normally break dormancy in about March and successful sprout inhibiting may lead to browning of the growing point within the bulb from this time onwards.

DESICCATION

13.009   Dimexan *at 19 to 28 kg/ha in low to medium volume for preharvest desiccation of ware and pickling onions.*

Dimexan may be used to desiccate the leaves when the crop is maturing either to facilitate harvesting at the normal time or to bring forward the time of harvest.

Parsnip, turnip, red beet

CONTROL OF ROOT SIZE

13.010   [For information] Dimexan has given promising results when applied to parsnips (11 to 15 kg/ha), turnips (11 kg/ha) and red beet (15 kg/ha).

396

Root growth is inhibited so that a high proportion of prepacking grade produce is obtained at harvest. Further information is required before a firm recommendation can be made.

Potato

SPROUT SUPPRESSION

13.011 **Tecnazene** *at 0·14 kg/ton of potatoes at the time of lifting to prevent sprouting in store.*

Treatment is effective for 8–12 weeks after which it can be repeated if required. Treated potatoes should be clamped or stored in the normal manner.

13.012 **Chlorpropham** *at 0·28 kg or* **chlorpropham** *0·23 kg plus* **propham** *0·028 kg/20 tons of ware potatoes, to prevent sprouting in store.*

Up to three treatments can be applied with an interval of 100 days. The first treatment is applied after the potatoes have cured. Application is made by fogging the chemical and blowing it through the ventilation ducts. Do not use on seed potatoes. The effect is reduced by high temperatures in the store. The optimum is between 7–9°C. Treated potatoes should not be consumed for three weeks following treatment.

Ware potatoes stored in wooden boxes should be treated with a granular formulation. This reduces the amount of chemical absorbed by the wood and also avoids the loss that fogged formulations encounter due to air flow round the boxes.

13.013 **Nonanol** *at 2·6 litres/100 tons of stored ware potatoes per day of treatment to prevent sprout growth.*

Application is made with a suitable fumigator when the curing period is complete. Fumigate for 14 days and then change to an 'on-off' system. Fumigation can be one day with one day off or seven days with seven days off. Treated potatoes should be ventilated either naturally or by fan for 48 h before marketing.

Rhubarb

DORMANCY-BREAKING AND YIELD INCREASE

13.014 **Gibberellic acid** *at 25 mg in 0·25 to 0·5 litres water/plant, immediately after filling the forcing shed, to break crown dormancy in some varieties and to increase stick yield from plants emerging from dormancy in all varieties.*

This treatment is recommended for breaking dormancy and increasing subsequent marketable yields in responsive early varieties such as Timperley Early. Other varieties also give increased yields following treatment, provided they have received sufficient chilling to break dormancy before transfer into the forcing shed. The response to gibberellic acid will vary according to the amount of cold received by the crowns before lifting, but the proportion of top quality sticks is usually increased. Harvesting may be advanced by from a few days to several weeks depending on the depth of dormancy of the lifted crowns. The solution of gibberellic acid should be applied within 24 h of mixing as one dose at low pressure, e.g. from a watering can or under gravity.

Tobacco

CONTROLLING SUCKERS

13.015   [**For information.**] Fatty alcohols (C_8–C_{12}) as a 33 per cent spray to control primary and secondary suckers, or 2·2 per cent if to be followed by maleic hydrazide. Application is best done at early button stage of flowering before topping, but it can be applied after topping if required. Repeat applications may be made to control further suckering. Best control of suckers is obtained if fatty alcohols are followed after ten days by maleic hydrazide at 6·7 kg/ha. Application should be with coarse droplets at low pressure, directing the spray towards the centre of the plant.

Tomato (glasshouse)

INCREASING FRUIT SET

13.016   *Either* α-**(2-chlorophenoxy) propionic acid** *at 0·0025 to 0·0040 per cent;* **4-CPA acid** *at 0·003 to 0·004 per cent;* α-**naphthaleneacetic acid** *at 0·004 to 0·006 per cent; or* β-**naphthoxyacetic acid** *at 0·004 to 0·006 per cent with suitable wetter as a spray applied to the flower trusses to increase fruit set.*

The lower trusses of tomato plants tend to produce few fruit, particularly when the days are short and night temperatures and light intensities are low. Treatment of the flowers and large buds with any of the above growth regulators results in the production of seedless fruits in the absence of pollination.

FRUIT RIPENING

13.017   **Ethephon** *at 0·048 per cent in high volume for end of season ripening.*

Application should be made as an overall spray of 1000 litres/ha approximately 17 days before the final house clearance date. If necessary, foliage may be stripped to ensure wetting of the fruit. The glasshouse should be maintained at a maximum night temperature of 15·5°C.

Ethephon may also be used at the same rate applied as a directed spray for ripening lower trusses of tomato.

Watercress

INCREASING STEM LENGTH

13.018   [**For information**] During the winter months when natural growth of the watercress plant is considerably retarded it is difficult to harvest and market a root-free product. Application of gibberellic acid at 0·01 per cent as an overall spray about five days before harvest gives the desired increase in stem length.

Fruit

Apple

ROOTING OF CUTTINGS

13.019   **Indolyl-3-butyric acid** *at 0·25 to 0·5 per cent in 50 per cent alcohol as a dip for hardwood cuttings.*
          Methylated spirits can replace the alcohol. The basal end of the cutting is dipped as shallowly as possible for about five sec. The higher concentration is required for difficult varieties. Optimum dosage is achieved by standardizing concentration, duration of treatment, cutting dryness (suction) and depth of dipping.

INCREASING FEATHERING

13.020   **Methyl esters of fatty acids (C$_6$–C$_{12}$)** *at 2 to 3 per cent as a spray to terminal buds on maiden trees to stimulate the production of lateral branches (feathering).*
          Application is made in June or early July and has the effect of killing or temporarily checking the growth of the shoot tip. This treatment is preferable to hand-pinching as it produces side branches with a greater angle to the main stem. The treatment can be used on a range of cultivars including Worcester Pearmain, Tydeman's Early, Bramley and Discovery. Some variation in effectiveness from year to year has been evident.

13.021   [**For information**] On cultivar Bramley, young trees first planted in the orchard can be sprayed with methyl esters of fatty acids (13.020) when growth is 20 cm long; this can replace hand-pruning and if carried out every year for the first four years there will be an increase in yield in the fifth (first cropping) year.

13.022   **α-Naphthaleneacetic acid or α-naphthaleneacetic acid ethyl ester** *at 1 per cent as a paint or coarse spray to inhibit water shoot development.*

In mature trees, containment pruning often results in excessive production of water shoots. This growth can be controlled by application of NAA or its ethyl ester to the pruning cuts. Although 1 per cent is very effective (proprietary asphalt based paint) appre iable control may also be obtained with lower concentrations.

ADVANCING CROPPING

13.023   **Daminozide** *at 0·17 to 0·34 per cent up to 7–10 weeks before harvest on most cultivars to induce cropping in young trees.*

Application should be carried out in June before normal bud initiation has begun. This results in the formation of fruit buds. Treatment can also increase fruit set and for this use a post-harvest spray can also be effective. It can also promote fruit colour formation. In addition to young trees it is beneficial in bringing top worked trees into cropping by encouraging fruit bud formation and checking excessive growth.

Daminozide is not recommended on mature trees as it may reduce fruit size. On young trees it delays fruit maturity and may increase the incidence of core-flush and breakdown, especially in the cultivars Fortune and Cox. This can be avoided by not storing the fruit later than November and December respectively.

13.024   [**For information**] Chlormequat at 1·1–2·2 kg in 1120 litres/ha applied at post-petal fall to young unproductive trees can stimulate fruit-bud initiation in the year following application. Application can be made either once at 2 kg in 1000 litres/ha 2 weeks after petal fall or twice at 1 kg in 1000 litres/ha at two and five weeks after petal fall. These treatments have a minimal effect on shoot growth but normally increase fruit bud for the following year by between two and three times.

FRUIT THINNING

13.025   **Carbaryl** *at 0·075 per cent applied to run off for the thinning of fruit, from seven to ten days after 80 per cent petal fall.*

The degree of thinning with carbaryl usually declines from a maximum at petal fall to zero about four weeks later. Variation in effect occurs from season to season due mainly to weather conditions in the immediate post-bloom period. The response from individual cultivars differs but it is widely used on cultivars Golden Delicious, James Grieve, Grenadier, Tydeman's Early and Worcester Pearmain. Cox and Bramley do not readily respond to treatment at the concentrations recommended for the other cultivars.

FRUIT RETENTION

13.026   **α-Naphthaleneacetic acid** *at 0·001 per cent in high volume to prevent premature fruit drop.*

Application should be made in dry weather from 6 to 14 days before the usual pre-harvest dropping of fruit commences. Efficiency is greater under warm conditions. Treatment enables some cultivars to be picked at a later than normal date and fruit colour is generally promoted by the increased exposure which is allowed. The chemical is effective on a wide range of cultivars but individual cultivars differ in their response.

13.027   **Daminozide** *at 0·17 to 0·34 per cent up to seven to ten weeks before harvest on most cultivars to assist fruit retention* (13.023).

13.028   **(±)2-(2,4,5-trichlorophenoxy)-propionic acid** *at 0·001 to 0·0015 per cent to prevent pre-harvest fruit drop.*

This treatment is widely used on Worcester and other early cultivars especially where ethephon has been used to enhance maturity (13.029).

FRUIT COLOURING

13.029   **Ethephon** *at 0·048 per cent as an overall spray 7 to 14 days before expected harvest to hasten maturity.*

The treatment accelerates fruit ripening, improves the colour and allows earlier picking. It is normally used in conjunction with an auxin, e.g. 2,4,5-TP, to minimize pre-harvest drop (13.028).

FRUIT STORAGE

13.030   **Ethoxyquin** *at 0·7 to 1 kg in 400 litres water as a dip to prevent scald developing on cultivar Bramley during storage.*

The rate of use depends on the daily throughput of fruit. The prime requirement is that all fruits are wetted with the solution before storage. This is normally achieved with a dip treatment but drenches or sprays may be employed.

Pear

INCREASING FEATHERING

13.031   **Methyl esters of fatty acids (C_6–C_{12})** *at 2 to 3 per cent as a spray to the root tips of maiden trees to stimulate the production of lateral branches (feathering).*

May be used on William's pear (13.020).

WATER SHOOT SUPPRESSION

13.032   α-**Naphthaleneacetic acid ethyl ester** *at 1 per cent as a paint or coarse spray to inhibit water shoot development* (13.022).

ADVANCE TREE CROPPING

13.033   [**For information**] Chlormequat applied at 1 kg in 1000 litres/ha two weeks after petal fall or twice at 0·5 kg in 1000 litres/ha two and five weeks after petal fall to young non-bearing trees has stimulated fruit bud initiation in the year following application. At these rates there was little effect on shoot elongation.

PARTHENOCARPIC FRUIT

13.034   **Gibberellic acid** *at 0·002 to 0·005 per cent spray for stimulating fruit set.*
   This use is most helpful in a year of severe frost when applied at full blossom. It produces parthenocarpic fruit and should only be used when it is clear that little blossom will survive. It can be used on the cultivars Conference and Triomphe de Vienne. It should not be used in the absence of frost damage as there is great risk of excess fruit set. It reduces fruit bud formation for the following year. When used regularly on cv. Triomphe de Vienne the trees are subsequently treated with chlormequat chloride to counteract its effect on fruit bud formation.

FRUIT RETENTION

13.035   α-**Naphthaleneacetic acid** *at 0·001 per cent in high volume to prevent premature fruit drop in cultivar Conference* (13.026).

Plum

ROOTINGS OF CUTTINGS

13.036   **Indolyl-3-butyric acid** *at 0·25 to 0·5 per cent in 50 per cent alcohol as a dip for hardwood cuttings* (13.019).

INCREASING FEATHERING

13.037   **Methyl esters of fatty acids (C_6–C_{12})** *at 2 to 3 per cent as a spray to the terminal buds on maiden trees to stimulate the production of lateral branches (feathering).*
   Successful use is reported for cultivar Marjorie's Seedling and Laxton Cropper.

Blackcurrant

ENHANCING FRUIT-DROP

13.038   **Ethephon** *at 0·025 to 0·035 per cent in high volume five to seven days before expected harvest date to loosen the fruit.*

The rate of use is increased as indicated for machine-picking or hand-picking and shaking respectively. Treatment results in earlier and easier separation of fruit from the bush and also ripens green berries at the end of the strig.

Gooseberry

ROOTING OF CUTTINGS

13.039   *A mixture of* **indolyl 3-butyric acid** *0·25 per cent and* α-**naphthaleneacetic acid** *0·25 per cent in 50 per cent alcohol as a dip for hardwood cuttings* (13.019).

Ornamentals and nurserystock

Nurserytock and herbaceous plants

13.040   [**For information**] Where the growth regulators chlormequat and chlorphonium chloride are added to peat or peat/sand composts as a drench or compost additive, the type of peat used in the compost can materially affect the response to any given dose of chemical. If the response with moss peat is taken as standard then sedge peat produces a much smaller response, and young peats such as Finnish peats produce a much greater response.

ROOTINGS OF CUTTINGS

13.041   **Indolyl-3-acetic acid, indolyl-3-butyric acid** *and* α-**naphthaleneacetic acid** *to promote callus and root formation in cuttings.*

Commercial rooting compounds contain these growth regulators in concentrations from 0·1 per cent to 1·5 per cent but strengths below and above these levels may be needed in special circumstances. The active ingredient can be formulated as a dip in suitable solvents, as a powder in talc or as a paste in lanolin. The effectiveness of the powder formulation is influenced by the wetting agent and the method of incorporating indolyl-3-butyric acid into the powder. The powder formulation is the one most commonly used. A fungicide (commonly captan) is sometimes incorporated to reduce the risk of fungal attack. Apart from the inconvenience a disadvantage of liquid formulations, especially low-strength water solutions where the base of the cutting is given a prolonged soak, is the risk of transferring virus and fungus diseases from an infected cutting to healthy cuttings sharing the same dip. A complete list of responsive species and cultivars cannot be given in the space available, but some experimental results with more difficult species are mentioned below. Many genera and species root freely without the use of growth regulators but their use can improve both the uniformity and rate of establishment.

Liquid preparations of 0·005 to 0·01 per cent indolyl-3-acetic acid in ethyl- or isopropyl-alcohol have been shown to improve rooting with *Chamaecyparis lawsoniana* cultivars *Erecta Viridis, Stewartii, Triomf van Boskoop.*

Indolyl-3-butyric acid (0·4 per cent) powder formulations improved rooting with *Chamaecyparis lawsoniana* (most cultivars except those listed under indolyl-3-acetic acid *C. obtusa, C. pisifera* and *Thuja.* This treatment also benefits *Chimonanthus, Cytisus, Deutzia, Diervillia, Euonymous, Forsythia, Hypericum, Magnolia, Prunus, Sarcococca, Senecio* and *Skimmia.*

Indolyl-3-butyric acid (0·8 per cent) powder formulations improve rooting with the following broad-leaved trees and shrubs: *Acer, Aesculus, Berberis, Berberidopsis, Betula, Carpinus, Ceanothus, Clematis, Coggygria, Cotoneaster, Eleagnus, Ilex, Mahonia, Potentilla, Pyracantha, Spiraea* and *Wisteria.* Conifers responding to this treatment include *Juniperus, Picea* (dwarf cultivars) and *Metasequoia.* Some cultivars of *Rhododendron* also respond well to 0·8 per cent indolyl-3-butyric acid powder (Gomer Waterer, Purple Splendour, Blue Peter, etc.), whilst others perform better with 0·4 per cent solution (Britannia, Scarlet Wonder, Royal Flush, etc.). Recent results suggest that many deciduous ornamental species will respond similarly (13.019).

Nurserystock (lined out hardwoods)

CONTROLLING PLANT SHAPE

13.042   **Methyl esters of fatty acids (C_6–C_{12})** *as a 10 per cent spray to the terminal buds as an alternative to hand pinching.*

The first pinch should be done by hand to start the shape and also the last pinch to finish the shape. Intermediate pinchings (for Azaleas this is three) may be done with methyl ester sprays. Treatment should be with fine droplets at low pressure (coarse droplets can cause phytotoxicity) and should be washed off with clean water after 30 minutes. A few plants should be treated first and observed for 15 to 20 minutes to assess effects and any small adjustments made to rate of use. Azalea, Cotoneaster, *Rhamnus, Taxus, Juniperus* and *Ligistrum* spp. may be treated.

SHOOT SUPPRESSION

13.043 [For information] Maleic hydrazide has given promising results when used for the suppression of shoot growth and bud development in lined-out hardwood nurserystock (13.075).

Azaleas

CHEMICAL PINCHING

13.044 [For information] Dikegulac-sodium at 0·4 per cent acts as a pinching agent on azaleas, increasing the number of breaks produced. It has similar effects, at varying concentrations, on other ornamentals.

Azaleas/Rhododendrons

CONTROLLING PLANT FORM AND FLOWERING

13.045 **Chlorphonium chloride** *may be used at 2·0 to 4·0 per cent as a soil drench after potting.*

It accelerates the time of flowering, increases flower bud numbers, inhibits shoot development during flowering and induces a more compact plant habit. Chlorphonium chloride is not an approved product.

Begonia and Bougainvillea

CONTROLLING FLOWER DROP

13.046 α-**Naphthalaneacetic acid** *at 0·00125 per cent when flower buds are just emerging from the foliage to reduce flower drop.*

Bromeliads

FLOWER INDUCTION AND IMPROVED BRACT COLOURING

13.047 [For information] Ethephon has been investigated on various species. In summary, desirable effects have been produced by overall sprays between 0·048 and 0·45 per cent according to species and age of plant (one to three years).

Carnation (cut flower crops)

SHORTENING AND STIFFENING FLOWER STEMS

13.048   [**For information**] Two or three spray applications of chlormequat chloride at 0·25 per cent with a wetter at 10–14 day intervals can shorten the internodes and stiffen the stems of flowering shoots. Variable results have been obtained with this treatment and sometimes crops have failed to respond. Only crops which have initiated the majority of buds in the flush should be sprayed. The first spray for illuminated crops can be applied as soon as the lights are turned off. Young crops and unlit crops initiate buds less uniformly and the precise timing of sprays is more difficult. Chlormequat chloride should only be applied between September and February and sprays applied at any other time may result in excessively short internodes.

Carnation (pot plants)

REDUCING PLANT HEIGHT

13.049   [**For information**] Cultivars Bailey's Apricot and Royalette have been successfully grown as pot plants, using two to four applications of 0·6 per cent or 0·9 per cent chlormequat chloride, applied as a soil drench. Monthly application after stopping resulted in increasing reductions in plant height correlated with increasing concentrations and number of applications. 'Sim' cultivars proved too vigorous and untidy in habit.

Celosià piumosa (as a pot plant)

REDUCING PLANT HEIGHT

13.050   [**For information**] Chlormequat as a 0·31 per cent soil drench shortened the plant height by half and suppressed the flower head side shoots. The compact conical flower head which resulted remained in marketable condition for several weeks, and may be suitable as a cheap pot plant.

Chrysanthemum (standard)

SHORTENING AND STIFFENING THE FLOWER STEM

13.051   **Daminozide** *at 0·5 per cent as a foliar spray a few days before disbudding to shorten and stiffen the stem (neck) just below the flower head.*

Cultivars American Beauty and Jane Ingamells show a typical 'weak-necked' habit which is improved by this treatment. The application can be split into two 0·25 per cent sprays, the first a few days before the most advanced stems are disbudded and the second seven to ten days later, where flower development is uneven.

Cultivar Fred Shoesmith and its sports, grown as a controlled crop, often benefit from one 0·06 per cent spray a few days before disbudding.

Chrysanthemum (spray)

SHORTENING AND STRENGTHENING THE FLOWER STEM

13.052   **Daminozide** *at 0·06 per cent as a spray 10 to 14 days before short-day treatment begins, to shorten and strengthen the stems of vigorous cultivars in winter to give improved market quality.*

More than one spray may be needed. The same treatment applied to weak cultivars can reduce rather than enhance market quality due to excessive internodal shortening.

SHORTENING FLOWER PEDICELS

13.053   [**For information**] *Daminozide at 0·06 per cent as a spray two weeks after short-day treatment begins to shorten the pedicels of the individual flowers forming the spray.*

With some cultivars the number of flowers developed is increased by this treatment.

LENGTHENING FLOWER PEDICELS

13.054   [**For information**] Gibberellic acid, 0·01 per cent has been used experimentally at disbudding to lengthen the pedicels of B.G.A. Fandango.

Chrysanthemum (pot plants)

DECREASING PLANT HEIGHT

13.055   **Daminozide** *at 0·25 per cent as an overall spray when the breaks following pinching (stopping) are 13–18 mm long to reduce internode length.*

Shortened internodes produce a plant of balanced market proportions. Earlier application can produce a more compact plant if this is required.

13.056   **Chlorphonium chloride** *as a compost additive at 4·5 to 34·5 g/m² of compost to shorten the stem internodes, improve leaf and flower colour and prolong flower life.*

Rate of use varies with the vigour of the cultivar being treated but thorough incorporation in the compost is essential for uniform results. Internodes are shortened to produce a well-balanced and proportioned plant in accordance with market requirements. Although this chemical has been marketed and widely used in the UK for many years, application has only recently been made for its approval.

13.057   **Chlorphonium chloride** *at 0·003 to 0·025 per cent as a soil drench after potting to shorten the stem internodes, improve leaf and flower colour and prolong flower life.*
Chlorphonium chloride is not an approved product.

13.058   **Chlorphonium chloride** *(dust) compost additive and (liquid) soil drench may be used in combination.*
Chlorphonium chloride dust can be incorporated in the compost to provide a base level treatment: cultivars with more vigour can then receive additional chlorphonium chloride in the form of a soil drench. Chlorphonium chloride is not an approved product.

Chrysanthemum (Stock/cutting production)

CONTROLLING PLANT FORM

13.059   **Chlorphonium chloride.** As a compost additive at 4·5 to 9·0 g/m² *of compost to increase wet/dry weight and leaf count in a given length of cutting.*
Leaf texture and colour are also improved and increased calibre and number of cuttings are obtained on certain cultivars. Increased resistance to Botrytis and drought tolerance have been observed following treatment. Chlorphonium chloride is not an approved product.

Lily (Asiatic hybrids)

CONTROLLING PLANT HEIGHT

13.060   **Chlormequat** *at 2·5 per cent as a soil drench of 60 ml/127 mm pot when shoots are 6 to 7 cm high to control plant height.*
Control of plant height for good market appearance is usually only necessary in winter and early spring. If height reduction is needed in late spring and early summer a 1·5 per cent solution is usually sufficient.

Narcissus (cut flower crop)

REDUCING STEM AND LEAF LENGTH

13.061   **Ethephon** *at 0·024 per cent as a soil drench of 4·4 litres/m² when the*

408

flower stem averages 15 cm (from neck of the bulb to base of the flower bud), to prevent excessive elongation of stem and leaves.

The treatment counteracts long, weak growth of bulbs housed from January onwards, following long periods of low temperature.

Narcissus (pot plants)

DECREASING PLANT HEIGHT

13.062   Ethephon *at 0·048 per cent as a soil drench of 57 ml/12·7 cm half-pot when flower stems average 15 cm (from neck of the bulb to base of the flower bud), to reduce stem and leaf elongation and so produce compact plants.*

For both cut flower (13.061) and pot plant production of *Narcissus*, the timing of ethephon application is important. Applications made before stem length averages 15 cm may lead to stunted growth and flower blindness; those made when stem length exceeds 19 cm are ineffective. Watering should be suspended for two to three days before and after application to avoid leaching of the chemical. The recommendations relate to culture in soil as distinct from peat substrates.

Zonal Pelargonium (Carefree strain, from seed)

CONTROLLING PLANT FORM AND FLOWERING

13.063   Chlormequat chloride *at 0·25 per cent as a soil drench when plants are established after potting to shorten stem internodes, promote laterals and hasten flowering.*

In some experiments two applications two weeks and six weeks after potting have been used.

Zonal Pelargonium (geranium—from cuttings)

CONTROLLING PLANT SHAPE

13.064   [**For information**] Ethephon, applied as a foliar spray at 0·048 per cent after cuttings have been potted, increases branching to give plants of compact habit and improved appearance. Responsive cultivars include Springtime, Treasure Chest, King of Denmark and Irene.

13.065   [**For information**] A chlormequat soil drench has produced compact, bushy plants, with increased breaks and darker foliage. Applications at 0·125 per cent were made as soon as plants were established after potting and repeated 21 days later when clay pots were used. In plastic pots one application at 0·25 per cent was more effective. The treatment could improve bedding plants and establish the use of geranium as a cheap pot plant.

Regal/Zonal Pelargonium (bedding and pot plants)

CONTROLLING PLANT SHAPE AND FLOWERING

13.066   Chlorphonium chloride *as a compost additive at 18 to 54 g/m³ of compost hastens.*

Increases flowering, improves leaf colour and texture, promotes uniform lateral development. Rate of use varies depending on cultivar, type of compost and time of year. Treatment produces a more compact, well balanced and proportioned plant for bedding and pot plants. Chlorphonium chloride may also be used in the propagation stage for earlier control and growth regulation. It is not an approved chemical.

Petunia

CONTROLLING PLANT HEIGHT

13.067   Chlorphonium chloride *as a compost additive at 9 to 18 g/m³ of compost can be used to shorten the stem internodes and promote uniform lateral shoot development.*

Rate of use varies with the vigour of the cultivar, time of year and type of compost. Chlorphonium chloride is not an approved product.

Poinsettia

REDUCING PLANT HEIGHT

13.068   Chlormequat *at 0·3 per cent as a soil drench, or at 0·15 per cent to 0·25 per cent as a foliar spray to shorten stem internodes and produce a plant of balanced market proportions.*

The number, strength and timing of the applications depends upon the cultivar treated, the time of potting, and whether the plant is pinched (stopped) or grown as a single stem. Too high a concentration of active ingredient in foliar sprays can cause a permanent chlorosis of the leaf margins, and the commercially acceptable rate usually lies between 0·2 per cent and 0·25 per cent. With lower concentrations, an increased number of applications are needed to produce the same retardant effect.

Roses

DEFOLIATION PRIOR TO LIFTING

13.069 **Ethephon** *at 270 g/ha plus hydriodic acid at 180 g/ha as a foliar spray for defoliation prior to lifting on a number of cultivars.*

Some yellow cultivars are sensitive to the treatment and may be damaged. Ease of defoliation varies with different cultivars. Defoliated roses must be lifted and stored under cool conditions with high humidity; if left in the soil regrowth will occur.

Roses (glasshouse)

BASAL SHOOT STIMULATION

13.070 **Ethephon** *at 0·5 per cent (14 ml/plant) applied to the basal 15 cm of stem to stimulate development of basal shoots.*

Unpruned plants can be treated at any time but pruned plants should be treated about seven weeks after beginning of heating. Buds which have already broken may be scorched, but these normally recover or are compensated for by new shoot development.

Other uses

Grasses

SUPPRESSION OF GROWTH

13.071 **Maleic hydrazide** *at 5·6 kg/ha in high volume between March and early May to retard the growth of grasses for up to 12 weeks.*

This treatment can be used in combination with 2,4-D on coarse grass.

Grasses and broad-leaved weeds

SUPPRESSION OF GROWTH

13.072 [**For information**] Chlorflurecol-methyl at 1·1 to 1·7 kg/ha plus maleic hydrazide at 2·8 to 3·3 kg/ha in high volume between March and May has been shown to retard the growth of grasses and broad-leaved species for 10 to 14 weeks.

While most broad-leaved species are suppressed but not damaged by the treatment, good control of *Anthriscus sylvestris* (cow parsley) and *Heracleum sphondylium* (hogweed) is obtained. Best results are achieved when application is made during a period of active growth before grasses head or, if this is not possible, after cutting and allowing 75–100 mm of regrowth. Rain following the application will reduce the effectiveness of the treatment.

Hedges

GROWTH SUPPRESSION IN HAWTHORN *(Crataegus monogyna)* AND PRIVET *(Ligustrum ovalifolium)*

13.073   **Maleic hydrazide** *at 0·45 per cent for the suppression of growth in established hawthorn and privet hedges.*

Hawthorn should be treated when in full leaf. Privet should be treated six to seven days after clipping or shaping. Particular care should be taken to avoid drift on to adjacent plants. It is essential that the spray should penetrate to the inside of the hedge as well as covering all the leaf surfaces. Special rainfast formulations are available for this purpose.

GROWTH SUPPRESSION IN PRIVET *(Ligustrum* spp.*)*

13.074   [**For information**] Dikegulac-sodium at 0·1 to 0·2 per cent retards shoot elongation of privet for several months. It induces side-branching, produces dense foliage coverage and compact growth. Similar effects have been observed on other hedge species, at concentrations depending on the species.

Established trees

INHIBITION OF SUCKERS, SHOOTS AND BUDS

13.075   **Maleic hydrazide** *at 3·3 to 8·8 per cent as a coarse spray to pruned areas of street trees.*

On many ornamental trees in suburban areas problems arise due to shoot growth from the trunk and main branches and also to suckering from the base of the trunk. This is accentuated on trees that have been pollarded. Regrowth after pruning can be prevented by spraying the pruned area with special proprietary formulations of maleic hydrazide, or in the case of pollarded trees the entire trunk. Rates vary according to the time of year, being highest in April–May.

A repeat application at 5·5 per cent is required in the season following treatment to suppress new bud growth. Subsequent treatment to these areas eventually leads to a reversion to normal bark.

Maleic hydrazide, used in this manner, is recommended on acacia (*Robinia pseudo-acacia*), ash (*Fraxinus excelsior*), black and golden poplar (*Populus* spp.), crimson thorn (*Crataegus oxycantha*), elm (*Ulmus* spp.), European lime (*Tilia* spp.), London plane (*Platanus platinoides*), oak (*Quercus* spp.).

13.076   α-**Naphthalenaecetic acid ethyl ester** *at 1 per cent as a paint or coarse spray to pruned areas of ornamental trees (13.022).*

This treatment is recommended on ash (*Fraxinus excelsior*), aspen (*Populus tremula*), birch (*Betula* spp.), crab apple (*Malus sylvestris*), horse chestnut (*Aesculus hippocastanum*), European lime (*Tilia* spp.), pine (*Pinus* spp.), poplar (*Populus* spp.), Maple and Sycamore (*Acer* spp.), Oak (*Quercus* spp.), Walnut (*Juglans regia*) and willow (*Salix* spp.).

FRUIT INHIBITION IN HORSE CHESTNUT (*Aesculus hippocastanum*)

13.077   [**For information**] Tree injections of a proprietary formulation of 18 per cent maleic hydrazide has been successfully used to prevent fruiting in horse chestnut. The flowering of the trees appears to be normal. Application is carried out in March. The chemical is injected into holes drilled 100–125 mm apart in a spiral up the trunk.

Chapter 14
Statutory Regulation of Herbicides—
an outline of the acts and regulations
affecting their sale and use

Introduction

14.001 The sale of certain herbicides is regulated by the Pharmacy and Poisons Act (see 14.002).

The use of all herbicides involves obligations under the Health and Safety at Work etc. Act (see 14.003) and the use of certain of the more toxic of them is regulated in detail under the Health and Safety (Agriculture) (Poisonous Substances) Regulations (see 14.004).

The use of herbicides in or near water is regulated under the Rivers (Prevention of Pollution) Acts (see 14.005), to be superseded by the Control of Pollution Act (see 14.007).

The disposal of herbicides and herbicide containers must comply with the Deposit of Poisonous Waste Act (see 14.006), to be superseded by the provisions of the Control of Pollution Act (see 14.007).

The aerial application of herbicides is regulated by the Civil Aviation Authority under the Air Navigation Order (as amended) and Rules of the Air and Air Traffic Control Regulations (as amended) (see 14.008).

Users of herbicides are reminded that compliance with these Acts and Regulations alone does not reduce their civil liability for damages, e.g. if crops or ornamental plants are damaged, nor does it absolve them from a responsibility to ensure that wild plants and animals are not unnecessarily affected by herbicide use. General guidance on safeguards for the user, the public and wild life is given in Chapter 20 of Volume I.

The Pharmacy and Poisons Act

14.002 Pesticides can be considered at any time for inclusion in the regulations made under the *Pharmacy and Poisons Act 1933*. This is done automatically when a pesticide is recommended for scheduling in the Health and Safety (Agriculture) (Poisonous Substances) Regulations (14.004). Dinoseb, DNOC, endothal and paraquat—and also mercuric chloride—are included in Part II of the *Poisons List Order, 1972* (Statutory Instrument 1972 No. 1938) which means they may generally be sold only by a retail chemist or by 'a listed seller of poisons', that is, someone such as an ironmonger or corn merchant who is registered with the local authority for the purpose. The *Poisons Rules, 1972* (Statutory Instrument 1972 No. 1939) lay down the conditions under which listed poisons must be labelled, packed, transported and stored in the shop. They also specify the conditions under which the poisons may be purchased. For example, any of the herbicides mentioned above may normally be purchased only on production of a 'signed order' in a prescribed form and by attending the shop to sign the poisons book. However, there are exemptions from these Rules for certain chemicals when these are supplied in specified types of formulation containing only a low concentration of the listed poison. The pelleted formulation of paraquat sold for home garden use is exempted in this way.

The annual booklet *Approved Products for Farmers and Growers* (14.009) states which products approved under the Agricultural Chemicals Approval Scheme (Volume I, 20.027) are scheduled and labelled as poisons under the Pharmacy and Poisons Act.

The Health and Safety at Work etc. Act and the Health and Safety (Agriculture) (Poisonous Substances) Regulations

14.003   The *Health and Safety at Work etc. Act, 1974* places general obligations on:

  a. *employers* to ensure so far as reasonably practicable, the health, safety and welfare at work of their employees;
  b. the *self-employed* and *employees* to take reasonable care of their own health and safety at work;
  c. *employers*, the *self-employed* and *employees* not to put at risk, by their work activities, the health and safety of others.
  d. *manufacturers* and *suppliers* of articles and substances for use at work to ensure so far as is practicable that they are safe when properly used and that the purchaser is informed of any potential hazard which use of the articles or substances may present.

Under this Act, anyone who intentionally or recklessly interferes with or misuses anything provided under a requirement of law in the interests of health, safety or welfare is liable to prosecution.

The passing of this Act emphasizes the need to seek advice before using a herbicide (or any other pesticide) and to take proper care when using it. General guidance on safe use of pesticides is given in a leaflet, *Take Care When You Spray,* and in a booklet, *Code of Practice for Ground Spraying,* both available from the Ministry of Agriculture, Fisheries and Food (14.009). More specific information is provided on the labels and instruction leaflets of pesticide products, in accordance with the requirements of the Pesticides Safety Precautions Scheme (Volume I, 20.002). The use of certain of the more toxic pesticides, including some herbicides, is regulated under the Health and Safety

(Agriculture) (Poisonous Substances) Regulations (14.004, below), which prescribe the precautions to be taken for each operation. If a pesticide product cleared under the Pesticides Safety Precautions Scheme is suitably packaged and labelled in accordance with transport, poison law and Pesticides Safety Precaution Scheme requirements and the user then applies it in accordance with the specific advice given on the label, the Health and Safety (Agriculture) (Poisonous Substances) Regulations (if applicable) and the general guidance given in the leaflet and booklet mentioned above, there seems to be no reason to expect that the supplier or user would have any difficulties under the general provisions of the Health and Safety at Work etc. Act.

The local Safety Inspector should be consulted if there is any doubt or problem concerning the safety of any intended application of a herbicide or any other pesticide.

14.004   The *Health and Safety (Agriculture) (Poisonous Substances) Regulations, 1975* made under this Act supersede those made between 1966 and 1969 under the *Agriculture (Poisonous Substances) Act, 1952*. The Regulations, which cover users in England, Scotland and Wales, and similar Regulations* made under other Acts applying to Northern Ireland, the Channel Islands and the Isle of Man, are designed to protect operators from poisoning by the more dangerous chemicals. Users of such compounds listed in these Regulations are required by law to take certain precautions, including the wearing of the protective clothing prescribed for particular operations. Contravention of the Regulations may lead to prosecution and heavy fines.

The Regulations applying to England, Scotland and Wales are wider in scope than those previously made under the Agriculture (Poisonous Substances) Act, 1952. For example, they cover additional substances and operations; and they apply not only to employees and their employers (i.e. farmers, growers and contractors) but also, for the first time, to the self-employed. Inspectors are appointed to enforce the provisions of the Health and Safety at Work etc. Act and of regulations made under the Act (including the present Regulations). These inspectors have rights of entry to premises and can also conduct investigations, enforce the production of certain documents, take statements, and take samples of substances for independent analysis. These inspectors will also give advice and assistance in connection with the precautions to be observed under the Regulations, and may be able to give vital help if cases of poisoning or suspected poisoning are reported to them without delay.

The present Regulations in force under the Act (which, as explained above, have replaced all earlier ones made under the Agriculture (Poisonous Substances) Act, 1952) are the *Health and Safety (Agriculture) (Poisonous Substances) Regulations, 1975* (Statutory

---

* Intending users in these countries must consult the relevant Regulations in force.

Instrument 1975 No. 282) and the chemicals to which they apply are listed in Schedule 2. The herbicides included (all in Part II) are as follows:

potassium arsenite†; sodium arsenite†; dinoseb (DNBP) and its salts; dinoterb and its salts; DNOC (DNC) and its salts; endothal and its salts; medinoterb and its salts.

The Regulations are designed to take into account the fact that one method of using a chemical may be inherently more dangerous to the operator than another; thus, other factors being equal, soil or granular application is safer than ordinary spraying. It should be noted that in the Regulations, 'spraying' does not include 'soil-application' when pesticides are applied onto or into the soil in unbroken liquid form; nor does it include 'soil-injection' when pesticides are discharged or released in unbroken liquid form into the soil wholly below the surface in order to fumigate it; nor does it include 'granular placement' when pesticides in granular form are deposited on or in the soil or on plants.

The Regulations specify 26 scheduled operations and list the type of protective clothing which must be worn, according to the chemical being used, depending on its classification as a Part I, II, III or IV substance.

The Regulations impose obligations on the employer, who must provide the prescribed protective clothing, and make certain that the worker wears it, and on the employee who must wear the prescribed protective clothing. Similar obligations are imposed for the protection of the self-employed. Generally this means that farmers and growers will be required to take the same precautions for their own protection as employees when using specified substances. Various other matters covered in the Regulations include the maximum number of hours operators may carry out scheduled operations; the minimum age of operators working on operations covered by the Regulations; precautions when working in greenhouses and livestock houses; the provision and maintenance of protective clothing; the provision of washing facilities; the notification of sickness; the training and supervision of operators carrying out scheduled operations; the provision of drinking water and vessels; ensuring that tanks and containers for storing the substances are securely closed when not in use; and the keeping of a register containing details of all scheduled operations carried out.

Certificates of exemption may be granted from some or all the provisions of the Regulations if it can be established that operators can be adequately protected by other precautions or that the provisions are unnecessary under the proposed conditions of use. Any certificates granted may specify conditions binding upon the employer or self-employed person and/or worker. For further details of the procedure to

---

† The use of potassium arsenite and sodium arsenite as potato haulm destroyers and weed-killers is banned by voluntary agreement of all the national organizations concerned.

be followed in applying for such certificates, see MAFF leaflet APS/1 described in the next paragraph.

The Ministry of Agriculture, Fisheries and Food and the Department of Agriculture and Fisheries for Scotland, issue a leaflet APS/1 *The Safe Use of Poisonous Chemicals on the Farm,* which includes a valuable summary in non-legal terms of the main provisions of the Regulations, as well as much general advice on the safe use of pesticides in relation to people, livestock and wildlife; the cleansing and maintenance of respirators and dust-masks; notes on the symptoms of poisoning by various chemicals, and the necessity for constant medical supervision of workers. The leaflet also contains a list of regional and area safety inspectors appointed under the 1974 Act.

Chemicals included in the Health and Safety (Agriculture) (Poisonous Substances) Regulations are generally also subject to the provisions of the Pharmacy and Poisons Act, 1933, and Poisons Rules (14.002).

Rivers (Prevention of Pollution) Acts, 1951 and 1961

14.005   These Acts and the corresponding Scottish Acts of 1951 and 1965, which are administered by Regional Water Authorities (River Purification Boards in Scotland), make it an offence to cause poisonous, noxious or polluting matter to enter a stream. The water authorities have power under the Acts of 1951 to make bylaws to prohibit or regulate the putting into a stream of objectionable matter, whether polluting or not. 'Streams' include any river, stream or watercourse or inland water discharging into a stream.

Deposit of Poisonous Waste Act

14.006   The *Deposit of Poisonous Waste Act, 1972* makes it an offence punishable by heavy penalties to deposit on land any poisonous, noxious or polluting waste in circumstances in which it can give rise to an environmental hazard i.e. in circumstances in which it might cause danger to persons or animals or might pollute any water supply. The Act also introduces a notification procedure under which those concerned are required to give local authorities and Regional Water Authorities information about the nature and quantities of certain wastes arising or being deposited in their areas. Regulations made under the Act provide, in effect that farmers need not follow the notification procedures if they dispose of pesticides (and, by extension, used containers) in any safe manner on agricultural land. Full advice on notification procedures may be obtained from local authorities.

The Control of Pollution Act

14.007   The *Control of Pollution Act, 1974* has reached the statute book; and at the time of going to print the commencement date of the provisions of Part I mentioned below was expected to be April 1976, or soon after, but no commencement date had been announced for Part II (see below). Part I of the Act deals with 'Waste on Land' and will supersede the *Deposit of Poisonous Waste Act, 1972* (14.006); it will retain those provisions of the latter Act which make it an offence punishable by heavy penalties to deposit on land any poisonous, noxious or polluting waste in circumstances in which it can give rise to an environmental hazard (see above). Farm waste (including pesticides and used containers) is otherwise excluded from the controls of Part I by virtue of its exemption from the definition of 'controlled waste' with which that part of the Act is mainly concerned but provision has been made in the Act for farm waste to be brought under such control if this is considered necessary in the future.

Part II of the Act deals with 'Pollution of Water' and will largely supersede the *Rivers (Prevention of Pollution) Acts* (14.005); it will retain those provisions of the latter Acts which make it an offence to cause or knowingly permit any poisonous, noxious or polluting matter to enter any stream or controlled waters or any specified underground water; and it will make it an offence for any matter to enter a stream so as to tend (directly or in combination with other matter entering the stream) to impede the proper flow of the water in a manner leading or likely to lead to a substantial aggravation of pollution due to other causes or of the consequences of such pollution; or any solid waste matter to enter a stream or restricted water. However, a person will not be guilty of an offence if the entry is attributable to an act or omission in accordance with good agricultural practice (unless the act or omission is of a kind specified in a notice to desist issued under the Act). Provision has been made for the approval of codes of practice by the Minister of Agriculture, Fisheries and Food as constituting good agricultural practice for the purposes of the Act. Three of the proposed Codes of Practice will be of particular relevance to the use and disposal of pesticides and their containers—namely, *Ground Spraying, Disposal of Unwanted Pesticides and Containers on Farms and Holdings* and *Use of Herbicides on Weeds in Watercourses and Lakes*. All are available free of charge from the Ministry of Agriculture, Fisheries and Food (14.009). For details of the Code of Practice for Use of Herbicides on Weeds in Watercourses and Lakes see Chapter 10.

The Aerial Application Permission

14.008   The operators of aircraft may only apply pesticides from the air if they have been granted permission by the Civil Aviation Authority. Full details of the requirements for this are set out in a document *The Aerial Application Permission—Requirements and Information,* available from Civil Aviation Authority, Printing and Publication Services, Greville House, 37 Gratton Road, Cheltenham, Glos. GL50 2BN.

Those not directly concerned with the operation of aircraft who are, nevertheless, involved in the application of herbicides or other pesticides from the air should note that the only pesticides which may be applied from the air are those listed in an appendix of the above-mentioned document, together with such other products as have been granted a probationary clearance for aerial application under the Pesticides Safety Precautions Scheme.

The annual booklet *Approved Products for Farmers and Growers* (14.009) states which products approved under the Agricultural Chemicals Approval Scheme (Volume I, 20.027) are in the 'permitted list' for aerial application.

Official publications mentioned in this chapter

14.009   Copies of the Acts and Statutory Instruments mentioned, and any subsequent amending legislation can be obtained from Her Majesty's Stationery Office, either direct or through a bookseller.

Copies of all the following publications are available free of charge from the Ministry of Agriculture, Fisheries and Food (Publications), Tolcarne Drive, Pinner, Middlesex, HA5 2DT. They are also normally available at Divisional Offices of the Ministry of Agriculture, Fisheries and Food and the main offices of the Department of Agriculture and Fisheries for Scotland. The main offices of the Agricultural Departments in Northern Ireland, the Channel Islands and the Isle of Man can supply *Approved Products for Farmers and Growers* and leaflets explaining the relevant regulations applying to those countries.

Code of Practice for Ground Spraying—a booklet giving general guidance on use of sprayers, field procedure and avoidance of hazards to operators, consumers, neighbouring crops, gardens, livestock, wildlife, etc.

Take Care when you Spray—a leaflet summarizing the main requirements of the Health and Safety (Agriculture) (Poisonous Substances) Regulations and general advice on safe application of pesticides.

The Safe Use of Poisonous Chemicals on the Farm (Leaflet APS/1)—a detailed explanation of the requirements of the Health and Safety

(Agriculture) (Poisonous Substances) Regulations with advice on methods of working with poisonous chemicals to ensure their safe use. Includes addresses of Safety Inspectors.

Poisoning by Pesticides—First Aid Measures (Leaflet APS/3).

Code of Practice for the Use of Herbicides on Weeds in Watercourses and Lakes—also reproduced in full in Chapter 10.

Code of Practice for the Disposal of Unwanted Pesticides and Containers on Farms and Holdings—a detailed guide as to how such pesticides and containers can be disposed of without infringing the law or endangering people, domestic animals, water supplies, cultivated or wild plants or wildlife (Volume 1, Appendix III).

Approved Products for Farmers and Growers—basically an annual list of products approved under the Agricultural Chemicals Approval Scheme (Volume I, 20.027) but the introductory pages contain general guidance and include annually updated lists (relating to Approved products only) of chemicals subject to the Poisons Rules, and the Health and Safety (Agriculture) (Poisonous Substances) Regulations and of products on the 'permitted list' for aerial application.

Appendix I

The Decimal Growth Stage Key of J.C. Zadoks, T.T. Chang and C.F. Konzak with illustrations by H. Broad, edited by D.R. Tottman and R.J. Makepeace

15.001 The decimal growth stage of Zadoks, Chang and Konzak is discussed and compared to that of Feekes-Large and Keller-Bagglioni in *Weed Research* (1974) **Volume 14,** p. 415–421. This has been made possible as a result of international collaboration arising from the need for a growth stage key in cereals more in keeping with the needs of new cereal varieties, the needs of all specialists dealing with cereals and the necessity of having a key designed to fit in with data processing and computer storage and retrieval. The key can be applied to all cereals including rice and maize but is here confined to wheat, barley and oats. Having established the key there immediately arises the need to produce a set of appropriate illustrations. At the time of printing these are being drawn up at the ARC Weed Research Organization. In order to make the recommendations in this volume complete a set of preliminary illustrations have been produced.

15.002 In the use of the key it must be appreciated that a truly chronological development does not occur in cereals, especially at certain growth stages in winter wheat. Thus at one time a plant can be described by the number of fully expanded leaves, the number of tillers present and the number of nodes detectable. In practice due to the death of the first formed leaves it is unlikely that leaf number would be assessed with the number of nodes detectable. This system allows a very high level of precision to be used which may not be desirable in some circumstances. For very general descriptive use the principle growth stages can be used. These are as follows:

15.003 *Decimal code for the Principal Growth Stages of Cereals*
- 0 Germination
- 1 Seedling growth
- 2 Tillering
- 3 Stem elongation
- 4 Booting
- 5 Inflorescence emergence
- 6 Anthesis
- 7 Milk development
- 8 Dough development
- 9 Ripening

For more precise descriptions of a whole crop the secondary growth stages will be required and the population defined by either the commonest occurring growth stage or the limits between which the majority of plants occur. Where there are overlapping growth stages, especially that of leaf number and tiller number, it may be possible to omit one of the stages if the other is the important determinant under consideration.

15.004 The secondary growth stages are shown below. Considerable care has been taken in choosing the descriptive wording. One of the main principles in drawing up the key was the establishment of a set of accurate descriptive phrases, the code numbers being intended for recording and data processing. It is assumed that in all published work these phrases will be used and the code numbers only used in parenthesis.

The inclusion of the germination stage is new to cereal growth stage keys and will be of value in pre-drilling and pre-emergence herbicide work. In seedling growth a leaf is counted as being unfolded when the tip of the following leaf appears in its axil. The tillering stage is relatively easy to define in the field but care must be taken in recording the main stem as separate from the tillers. This becomes progressively more difficult with time. The stem elongation growth stage presents one of the most difficult growth stages. Pseudo-stem or leaf sheath erection only applies to cereals with a prostrate or semi-prostrate growth habit. It occurs in winter cereals and is a critical growth stage for several grass weed herbicides used in cereals. This is followed by the jointing stage which is normally the latest time broad-leaved weed herbicides can be used in cereals. The booting stage covers the period when the inflorescence can be detected swelling inside the leaf sheath. It is followed by the emergence of the inflorescence. Zadoks, Chang and Konzak make the distinction here that ear emergence within a crop is either all at the same stage, i.e. synchronous, or at various stages, i.e. non-synchronous. They further suggest that the odd digits be reserved for the synchronous crops and the even digits for the non-synchronous crops. For example, a wheat crop with half of each of the ears emerged would be described as stage 55 but for a non-synchronous crop of wheat with 50% of the stems in the crop with their ears 50% emerged they suggest using growth stage 54. Three stages cover caryopsis formation. These are anthesis, milk development and dough development. The anthesis stages are difficult to detect in barley whilst differences in the milk stages can also be difficult to define. The late milk stage can be detected by the increase in solids of the liquid endosperm, notable when crushing the caryopsis between the fingers. The soft dough stage can be detected by the finger nail impression not being held and the hard dough stage by the impression being held and the inflorescence losing colour. The ripening stages can be associated with harvesting in that 91 is considered to be the stage at which the crop is binder ripe and 92 as being the stage at which the crop is being ripe for combine harvesting.

15.005 Decimal code for the secondary growth stages of cereals

2-digit code	General description	2-digit code	General description
	Germination		*Inflorescence emergence*
00	Dry seed	50	} First spikelet of inflorescence just
01	Start of imbibition	51	} visible
02	—	52	}
03	Imbibition complete	53	} $\frac{1}{4}$ of inflorescence emerged
04	—	54	}
05	Radicle emerged from caryopsis	55	} $\frac{1}{2}$ of inflorescence emerged
06	—	56	}
07	Coleoptile emerged from caryopsis	57	} $\frac{3}{4}$ of inflorescence emerged
08	—	58	} Emergence of inflorescence com-
09	Leaf just at coleoptile tip	59	} pleted
	Seedling growth		*Anthesis*
10	First leaf through coleoptile	60	—
11	First leaf unfolded	61	} Beginning of anthesis
12	2 leaves unfolded	62	—
13	3 leaves unfolded	63	—
14	4 leaves unfolded	64	}
15	5 leaves unfolded	65	} Anthesis half-way
16	6 leaves unfolded	66	—
17	7 leaves unfolded	67	—
18	8 leaves unfolded	68	} Anthesis complete
19	9 or more leaves unfolded	69	}
	Tillering		*Milk development*
20	Main shoot only	70	—
21	Main shoot and 1 tiller	71	Caryopsis water ripe
22	Main shoot and 2 tillers	72	—
23	Main shoot and 3 tillers	73	Early milk
24	Main shoot and 4 tillers	74	—
25	Main shoot and 5 tillers	75	Medium milk
26	Main shoot and 6 tillers	76	—
27	Main shoot and 7 tillers	77	Late milk
28	Main shoot and 8 tillers	78	—
29	Main shoot and 9 or more tillers	79	—
	Stem elongation		*Dough development*
30	Pseudo stem erection	80	—
31	1st node detectable	81	—
32	2nd node detectable	82	—
33	3rd node detectable	83	Early dough
34	4th node detectable	84	—
35	5th node detectable	85	Soft dough
36	6th node detectable	86	—
37	Flag leaf just visible	87	Hard dough
38	—	88	—
39	Flag leaf ligule/collar just visible	89	—
	Booting		*Ripening*
40	—	90	—
41	Flag leaf sheath extending	91	Caryopsis hard (difficult to divide by thumb-nail)
42	—	92	Caryopsis hard (can no longer be dented by thumb-nail)
43	Boots just visibly swollen	93	Caryopsis loosening in daytime
44	—	94	Over-ripe, straw dead and collapsing
45	Boots swollen	95	Seed dormant
46	—	96	Viable seed giving 50% germination
47	Flat leaf sheath opening	97	Seed not dormant
48	—	98	Secondary dormancy induced
49	First awns visible	99	Secondary dormancy lost

15.006 Seedling growth and tillering. Growth stages: 10–30

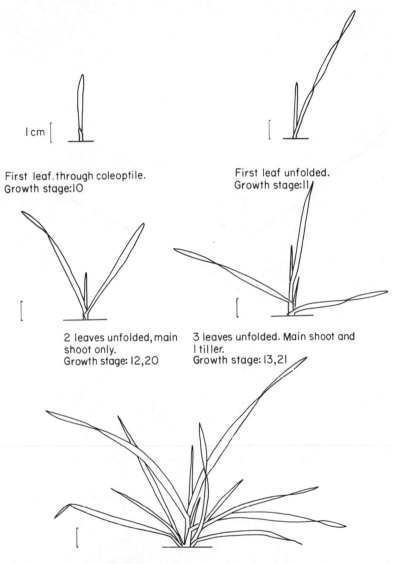

I cm

First leaf. through coleoptile.
Growth stage: 10

First leaf unfolded.
Growth stage: 11

2 leaves unfolded, main
shoot only.
Growth stage: 12,20

3 leaves unfolded. Main shoot and
1 tiller.
Growth stage: 13,21

5 leaves unfolded. Main shoot and 3 tillers.
Growth stage: 15,23 (leaf sheaths longer in barley)

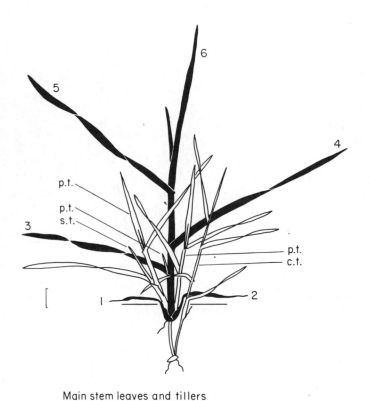

Main stem leaves and tillers
(latest leaf counted when next leaf appears in its axil)

6 leaves unfolded. Main shoot and 5 tillers.
Pseudostem erect.
Main stem leaves shaded and numbered. p.t., primary tiller; s.t., secondary tiller; c.t., coleoptile tiller
Growth stage:16,25,30.

15.007 Stem elongation. Growth stages: 30–39

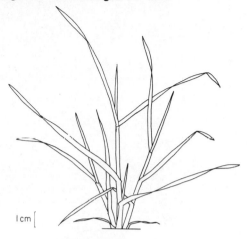

1 cm

6 leaves unfolded.
Main shoot and 3 tillers.
Pseudostem erect.
Growth stage: 16, 23, 30

1st node detectable.
Growth stage: 31

8 leaves unfolded.
Main shoot and 3 tillers.
2nd node detectable.
Growth stage: 18, 23, 32

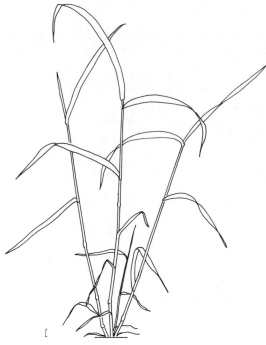

Main shoot and 3 tillers.
Flag leaf ligule visible.
Growth stage: 23, 39

15.008 Booting. Growth stages: 40–49

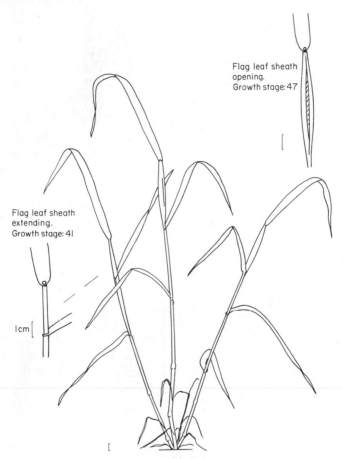

Flag leaf sheath
opening.
Growth stage: 47

Flag leaf sheath
extending.
Growth stage: 41

I cm [

[

Main shoot and 3 tillers (I infertile).
4 th node detectable. Boots swollen.
Growth stage: 23, 34, 45

15.009   Anthesis to ripening. Growth stage: 60–99

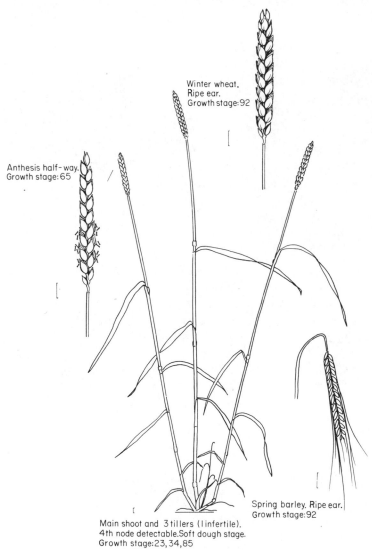

Winter wheat.
Ripe ear.
Growth stage: 92

Anthesis half-way.
Growth stage: 65

Spring barley. Ripe ear.
Growth stage: 92

Main shoot and 3 tillers (1 infertile).
4th node detectable. Soft dough stage.
Growth stage: 23, 34, 85

Appendix II
Glossary of technical terms

16.001 *Absorption*, uptake (e.g. of a herbicide by a plant)

Acid equivalent, the amount of active ingredient expressed in terms of the parent acid

Activator, a substance added to a herbicide to increase its phytotoxicity

Activated, formulated with an activator

Active ingredient, that part of a herbicide formulation from which the efficacy is obtained

Acute oral LD$_{50}$, in toxicological studies the dose required to kill 50 per cent of the test animals when given as a single dose by mouth. The dose is normally expressed as the weight of chemical per unit weight of animal

Adjuvant, a herbicidally inactive material which when added to a herbicide formulation enhances the efficacy of that formulation

Adsorbent (see *Adsorption*)

Adsorption, the taking up of one substance (the adsorbate) at the surface of another (the adsorbent)

Application

Band, when the herbicide is applied as a band, normally straddling the crop row (as opposed to *overall* application)

Directed, where the herbicide is directed towards the ground or weeds to avoid or minimize contact with the crop

Overall, where the spray is applied uniformly over the whole area, as opposed to *band* application

Overhead, where the spray is applied over the crop, as opposed to application *directed* specifically to weeds

Post-emergence, application of a herbicide after the crop has emerged from the soil. (Note: The term when qualified is often also used to denote treatment in perennial crops made after emergence of weeds, e.g. post-weed-emergence)

Pre-emergence, application of a herbicide where a crop is present but has not emerged from the soil. (Note: The term 'pre-emergence' is sometimes applied to weeds if suitably qualified, e.g. 'pre-weed-emergence')

Contact pre-emergence, pre-emergence application of a contact herbicide to weeds

Residual pre-emergence, pre-emergence application of a residual herbicide to the soil

Pre-planting (sowing), application of a herbicide before planting (sowing) a crop

Split, treatment in which the total dose of herbicide is divided between two or more times of application

Spot, application of a herbicide to individual, small patches or clumps of weeds

Sub-surface, application of a soil-acting herbicide under the soil surface by means of special equipment to provide a thin layer of herbicide-treated soil at a specified depth

Auxin, a generic name for compounds characterized by their capacity to induce elongation in cells of shoots. Auxins may, and generally do, affect processes other than elongation, but elongation is considered critical

16.002 *Basal bark treatment,* a treatment for killing trees and bushes where herbicide is applied (by sprayer or paint brush) to a band of bark encircling the basal 1 to 2 ft of the stem

Blow-off, the removal by high winds of a herbicide, such as DNOC, as solid particles, either from the foliage of treated plants or mixed with soil

B.O.V., brown oil of vitriol. A commercial grade of sulphuric acid containing about 77 per cent by volume of sulphuric acid

16.003 *Carrier,* the liquid or solid material added as a diluent to a chemical to facilitate its application

Chemical stopping (see *Stopping*)

Chlorosis, pathological condition of a plant due to a deficiency of chlorophyll shown by yellowing

Contact herbicide (see *Herbicide*)

Contact pre-emergence application (see *Application*)

Controlled drop application, the spraying of a herbicide as discrete drops of a pre-determined uniform size. At present this method of application is confined to spinning disc units spraying at very low volume

16.004 *Defoliant,* a chemical which, when applied to a plant, causes leaf fall

Desiccant, a compound which promotes loss of moisture from plant tissues

Direct-drilling, drilling seed into soil without any mechanical seed-bed preparation since the previous crop

Dose, amount (wt or vol) active agent per unit area, per plant, etc. (*Dosage, dose-rate,* and *rate* are often but incorrectly used as synonyms)

Dribble-bar, device fitted normally to watering cans to facilitate the uniform application of certain herbicides without drift, consisting of a tube perforated with a row of small holes along its axis

16.005 *Emulsifiable concentrate* (see *Formulation*)

Emulsifier, a surface-active agent which reduces interfacial tension and which can be used to facilitate formation of an emulsion of one liquid in another

Emulsion, a mixture in which very small droplets of one liquid are suspended in another liquid, e.g. oil in water. When the emulsion consists of droplets of water in oil, it is known as an 'invert' or 'mayonnaise' emulsion

432

Epinasty, the more rapid growth or elongation of the upper side of an organ, e.g. of a leaf, resulting in downward curling, but often incorrectly used in a more general sense to mean any curling or twisting of leaf blades, petioles, stems, etc. caused by uneven growth

16.006 *Feathering,* stimulation of the production of lateral branches in nursery stock

Formulation, (1) the process by which herbicidal compounds are prepared for practical use; (2) a preparation containing a herbicide in a form suitable for practical use

Activated, formulated with an *activator*

Emulsifiable concentrate, a concentrated solution of a herbicide and an emulsifier in an organic solvent, which will form an emulsion spontaneously when added to water with agitation

Granular, a type of formulation for dry application consisting of granules which serve as a carrier for the herbicide

Pelleted, a type of formulation for dry application consisting of pellets of active herbicide or of inert material containing a herbicide

Wettable powder, a type of formulation for spray application in which a herbicide is mixed with an inert carrier, the product being finely ground, with a surface-acting agent added, so that it will form a suspension when agitated with water

Frill-girdle, a series of overlapping cuts made downwards into the bark of a tree trunk to form a girdle to which a herbicide is applied

16.007 *Granular* (see *Formulation*)

Growth regulator, synthetic (see *Plant growth regulator*)

16.008 *Herbicide,* a chemical which can kill or suppress the growth of certain plants

Contact herbicide, a herbicide which affects only that part of the plant with which it comes into contact, as opposed to a translocated herbicide

Selective herbicide, a herbicide which if used appropriately will result in control of some plant species without injury to others

Translocated herbicide, a herbicide which, after uptake, is moved within the plant and can affect parts of the plant remote from the point of application

Residual herbicide, a herbicide applied to the soil where it remains active for at least several weeks

High volume spray (see *Volume rate*)

Hormones, chemical substances produced by the plant, which in low concentrations regulate plant physiological processes. Hormones usually move within the plant from a site of production to a site of action

16.009 *Industrial weed control,* control of all vegetation on industrial and similar sites including factories, special installations, railways, etc.

Injurious weed seeds (see *Weed seeds*)

Invert emulsion (see *Emulsion*)

16.010   *Liner shrubs* and *liners* (see *Transplant lines*)
Low volume spray (see *Volume rate*)

16.011   *Medium volume spray* (see *Volume rate*)
Minimum tillage, crop production whre soil cultivation is kept to the minimum necessary for crop establishment and growth, weed control where necessary being by use of herbicides

16.012   *Necrosis,* the death of plant tissue. Generally used in connection with localized death
Non-selective treatment (see *Total weed control*)
Nursery stock, hardwood ornamental and tree species being grown in a nursery for planting elsewhere

16.013   *Phytotoxic,* toxic to at least some plants
Pinching (see *Stopping*)
Plant growth regulator, synthetic, a synthetic organic compound, other than a nutrient, which in small amounts promotes, inhibits or otherwise modifies, growth
Pollarding, the cutting off of tree trunks at around 2–3 m to induce the formation of a crown of branches
Post-emergence (see *Application*)
Pre-emergence (see *Application*)
Pre-planting (see *Application*)
Pre-sowing (see *Application*)

16.014   *Residual pre-emergence* (see *Application*)
Ring-barking, a method of killing trees by removing a ring of bark down to and including the cambium near the bottom of the trunk
Roguing, removal of crop plants which do not conform to type

16.015   *Scheduled weeds* (see *Weeds, scheduled*)
Selective herbicide (see *Herbicide*)
Sod-seeding, sowing directly into a sward without previous cultivation
Soil incorporation, mixing herbicide with soil by mechanical means
Soil-sterilant, in the context of herbicides refers to volatile fumigants such as methyl bromide which are applied to the soil to kill insect pests, fungi and weed seeds. The treatment results in freedom from weeds for a considerable period
Split application (see *Application*)
Spot-treatment (see *Application*)
Spray boom, a length of tubing, usually horizontal, fitted with spray nozzles
Spray lance, a length of rigid tubing held and directed by the operator and fitted with a spray nozzle
Stale seed-bed, a seed-bed which is prepared and left untouched to encourage weed germination and into which the crop is later sown with a minimum of soil disturbance, before or after the weeds are killed with a herbicide. This enables pre-sowing and pre-emergence contact herbicide treatments to be used with maximum efficiency

Stopping, removal or suppression of apical buds in order to stimulate the production of lateral branches

Surface-active agents, also known as 'surfactants', substances, which when added to a liquid, affect the physical properties of the liquid surface. This enables them to be used for increasing the wetting properties of sprays and also for the formulation of emulsifiable liquids and wettable powders

Surfactant (see *Surface active agents*)

Suspension, particles (of herbicide) suspended in liquid

Synergism, the combined effect of two or more herbicides mixed together leading to a greater phytotoxic effect than would be predicted from the behaviour of each compound when applied singly

Synthetic plant growth regulator (see *Plant growth regulator*)

16.016 *Total weed control,* use of a herbicide to kill all vegetation on uncropped land in situations where selectivity is not required

Transplant lines, juvenile shrubs and trees planted in nurseries from seedlings or rooted cuttings in order to reach acceptable size for planting elsewhere

Translocated herbicide (see *Herbicide*)

16.017 *Volume rate,* amount of liquid applied per unit area. The following definitions refer only to herbicide use

High volume, spray application of more than 675 l/ha. In this handbook the term applies a maximum rate of about 1120 l/ha

Medium volume, spray application within the range of 225 –675 l/ha of liquid

Low volume, spray application within the range of 56–225 l/ha of liquid

Very low volume, spray application within the range of 11–56 l/ha of liquid

Ultra-low volume, spray application using unformulated compounds or concentrated oil-based formulations within the range 1·0–11·0 l/ha

16.018 *Weedkiller* (see *Herbicide*)

Weeds, scheduled, injurious weeds listed in the Weed Act, 1959

Weeds seeds, injurious, weed seeds subject to statutory regulations

Wettable powder (see *Formulations*)

Wetting agent, a surface-active agent which, when added to a liquid, increases its wetting properties

Appendix III
The crystal violet test

17.001 One of the problems encountered in peas is to decide whether the plants have sufficient leaf wax to enable post-emergence applications of herbicides to be made without damaging the crop. It is not always possible to know the previous weather conditions which might affect this issue and therefore a simple method for carrying out a test on the plants has been developed using a solution of crystal violet. Over many seasons it has proved to be an excellent method of determining leaf wax deposits. The method is described below.

Material

17.002 A 1 per cent w/v solution of crystal violet. The crystals can be purchased and dissolved in water or a made-up solution obtained.

    The crystal violet is best carried in a wide-necked jar, sealed with a strong screw top. A 1 kg Kilner jar is suitable.

Method

17.003 The plants to be tested must not be roughly handled and a large pair of forceps or tongs should be used to pull the plant by gripping the base near the soil. It is then completely immersed in the dye. The plant is removed quickly and the surplus dye shaken off. The areas of the plant retaining the dye are where the wax deposit is either deficient or has been damaged. Several plants should always be tested.

17.004 *A normal healthy pea plant* will retain a certain amount of dye on the stem, the midribs, the tendrils, the leaf margins and on the oldest leaves at the very bottom of the plant. There is very little retention on the upper leaf areas and on the unopened growing points. Any mechanically damaged areas will also show retention.

    There should be less than 5 per cent of the area of upper leaf surfaces showing retention and less than 10 per cent of lower leaf surfaces showing retention. Such a crop would be safe to spray.

17.005 *A plant with either insufficient or damaged wax deposit*

Depending upon either the amount of wax or the degree of damage the dye will be retained on a considerable proportion of the leaf area and indeed under certain conditions virtually all the surface may show retention. If more than 5 per cent of the upper leaf surface or more than 10 per cent of the lower leaf surface retains the dye spraying should be delayed until the plants when tested show a normal amount of dye retention. This will probably take at least 5–7 days.

436

With a little experience this test can rapidly indicate whether pea crops are safe to treat with herbicide, although knowledge of previous weather conditions will also be of value in helping to decide whether to spray or not.

Appendix IV
The definition of soil types

18.001 The soil texture may affect the performance of a soil applied pesticide. Many pesticides which are applied to the soil have to be taken up by plants before they can be effective. This uptake can be either by direct absorption by plant roots or by vapour entering the roots. In general, soils need to be moist for use of such pesticides to be successful but excessive moisture can leach pesticides downwards in the soil and lead to adverse results. Dry conditions will prevent both absorption and natural breakdown, which can lead to residues of a pesticide in the soil and these may prove hazardous to a succeeding crop.

18.002 Soils containing a high proportion of coarse sand will readily leach with the result that a chemical may be moved out of the correct soil position to where it is ineffective, phytotoxic or both. On the other hand soils containing a large fraction of clay, silt or organic matter will often adsorb a chemical and may render it completely unavailable or may require higher rates of use in order for it to be effective.

18.003 Since the terms light and heavy soils are relative they are not of themselves accurate enough for label recommendations to be made. The definition of soil types opposite has therefore been drawn up by government soil scientists in conjunction with the British Agrochemicals Association and will in future be used on all approved herbicide labels. For guidance on soil types present on individual farms and holdings the grower should consult his local Advisory Officer or a Spray chemicals specialist trained in the identification of soil types.

18.004

Textural class	Symbol	Textural group
Coarse sand	CS	
Sand	S	
Fine sand	FS	Sands
Very fine sand	VFS	
Loamy coarse sand	LCS	
Loamy sand	LS	
Loamy fine sand	LFS	Very light soils
Coarse sandy loam	CSL	
Loamy very fine sand	LVFS	
Sandy loam	SL	Light soils
Fine sandy loam	FSL	
Very fine sandy loam	VFSL	
Silty loam	ZyL	
Loam	L	Medium soils
Sandy clay loam	SCL	
Clay loam	CL	
Silt loam	ZL	Heavy soils
Silty clay loam	ZyCL	
Sandy clay	SC	
Clay	C	Very heavy soils
Silty clay	ZyC	

18.005 NOTES

1. Adsorptive capacity for pesticides increases with soil organic matter content.
2. Organic matter content tends to increase with clay content, 'heavy' soils generally contain $2 \cdot 8 - 4 \cdot 0$ per cent organic matter compared with $1 \cdot 0$ $1 \cdot 5$ per cent on 'very light' soils.
3. Within each textural group the organic matter content will be lowest under continuous arable cropping, particularly in the low rainfall areas of Southern England and highest in ley-arable systems in the high rainfall areas of the north and west. Thus optimum doses for a textural group may be slightly higher in the north and west than in the south and east of the country.
4. The prefix 'organic' is applied to the above mineral texture classes if organic matter levels are relatively high. The 'sands' and 'very light' soils however appear 'organic' when they only contain 5–6 per cent organic matter. Organic matter levels between 1 and 10 per cent cannot be detected by texture and must be determined by analysis.
5. The prefix 'peaty' is applied when organic matter levels are between 20 per cent and 35 per cent.
6. 'Peat' soils are those containing more than 35 per cent of organic matter.
7. The risk of herbicide leaching on very stony or gravelly soils is greater and textural grouping for such soils should be modified accordingly. Stones are particles greater than 2 mm. In 'stony' soils stone content is 5–15 per cent. In 'very stony' soils stone content is more than 15 per cent.
8. Shallow soils over chalk appear very silty in nature and may behave more like 'light' rather than 'medium' soils towards soil acting herbicides.

Appendix V
Conversion tables in British and metric units

19.001 Conversion Table 1
(kg/ha to oz/ac)

kg/ha	oz/ac	kg/ha	oz/ac	kg/ha	oz/ac	kg/ha	oz/ac
0·07	1	1·47	21	2·87	41	4·27	61
0·14	2	1·54	22	2·94	42	4·34	62
0·21	3	1·61	23	3·01	43	4·41	63
0·28	4	1·68	24	3·08	44	4·48	64
0·35	5	1·75	25	3·15	45	4·55	65
0·42	6	1·82	26	3·22	46	4·62	66
0·49	7	1·89	27	3·29	47	4·69	67
0·56	8	1·96	28	3·36	48	4·76	68
0·63	9	2·03	29	3·43	49	4·83	69
0·70	10	2·10	30	3·50	50	4·90	70
0·77	11	2·17	31	3·57	51	4·97	71
0·84	12	2·24	32	3·64	52	5·04	72
0·91	13	2·31	33	3·71	53	5·11	73
0·98	14	2·38	34	3·78	54	5·18	74
1·05	15	2·45	35	3·85	55	5·25	75
1·12	16	2·52	36	3·92	56	5·32	76
1·19	17	2·59	37	3·99	57	5·39	77
1·26	18	2·66	38	4·06	58	5·46	78
1·33	19	2·73	39	4·13	59	5·53	79
1·40	20	2·80	40	4·20	60	5·60	80

19.002 Conversion Table 2
(kg/ha to lb/ac; l/ha to gal/ac; bars to lb/in²)

kg/ha	lb/ac	kg/ha	lb/ac	l/ha	gal/ac	bar	lb/in²
1·12	1			11	1	0·1	1·45
2·24	2	11·2	10	22	2	0·2	2·90
3·36	3	22·4	20	34	3	0·3	4·35
4·48	4	33·6	30	45	4	0·4	5·80
5·6	5	44·8	40	56	5	0·5	7·25
6·7	6	56·0	50	67	6	0·6	8·70
7·8	7	67·2	60	79	7	0·7	10·2
9·0	8	78·4	70	90	8	0·8	11·6
10·1	9	89·6	80	101	9	0·9	13·1
11·2	10	101	90	112	10	1·0	14·5
12·3	11	112	100	225	20	2·0	29·0
13·4	12	224	200	337	30	3·0	43·5
14·6	13	336	300	450	40	4·0	58·0
15·7	14	448	400	562	50	5·0	72·5
16·8	15	560	500	674	60		
17·9	16	672	600	787	70		
19·0	17	784	700	899	80		
20·2	18	896	800	1012	90		
21·3	19	1008	900	1124	100		
22·4	20	1120	1000				

19.003 Conversion Table 3
British and metric conversion factors

Weight	BRITISH	METRIC		
1 ounce (oz)		=	28·3 grammes (g)	
1 pound (lb)	= 16·0 oz	= 454 grammes		
1 hundredweight (cwt)	= 112 lb	= 50·8 kilogrammes (kg)		
1 ton	=2240 lb	=1016 kilogrammes (kg)		

Conversion factors

ounces to grammes	×	28·3
zpounds to grammes × 454		
pounds to kilogrammes	×	0·454
hundredweights to kilogrammes	×	50·8

Volume

1 pint		=	0·568 litres (l)
1 gallon (gal) Imperial	= 8 pints	=	4·55 litres
1 fluid ounce	= 1·73 cu in (in³)		
	or 0·05 pints	=	28·4 millilitres
1 Imperial gallon	= 1·2 US gallons		

Conversion factors

pints to litres	×	0·568
gallons (Imp.) to litres	×	4·55
gallons (Imp.) to millilitres	×4546	

Length

1 inch (in)		=	2·54 centimetres (cm)
1 foot (ft)	= 12 in	=	30·5 centimetres
1 yard (yd)	= 3 ft	=	0·914 metres (m)
1 mile	=1760 yd	=	1·61 kilometres (km)

Conversion factors

inches to centimetres	×	2·54
feet to metres	×	0·305
yards to metres	×	0·914
miles to kilometres	×	1·61

Area

1 square inch (in²)		=	6·45 square cm (cm²)
1 square yard (yd²)		=	0·836 square metres (m²)
1 acre (ac)	=4840 square yards	=	0·405 hectares

Conversion factors

square feet to square metres	×	0·093
square yards to square metres	×	0·836
acres to hectares	×	0·405

Other conversions

1 lb per acre	=	1·12 kilogrammes per hectare *or* 1120 grammes per hectare
1 gallon per acre	=	11·2 litres per hectare
1 cwt per acre	=	1·25 quintals per hectare

Weight	METRIC	BRITISH		
100 grammes		= 3·53 ounces		
1 kilogramme	= 1000 g	= 2·20 pounds		
1 quintal	= 100 kg	= 220 pounds		
1 ton (metric)	= 1000 kg	= 2205 pounds		
	Conversion factors			
	grammes to ounces		×	0·0353
	grammes to pounds		×	0·00220
	kilogrammes to pounds		×	2·20
	kilogrammes to hundredweights		×	0·020
Volume				
100 millilitres (ml)		= 0·176 pints		
1 litre	= 1000 ml	= 1·76 pints		
1000 litres	= 1 kilolitre	= 220 gallons (Imp.)		
1 cubic centimetre	= 1·0 ml	= 0·00176 pints		
	Conversion factors			
	litres to pints		×	1·76
	litres to gallons (Imp.)		×	0·220
	millilitres to gallons (Imp.)		×	0·00022
Length				
1 millimetre (mm)		= 0·0394 inches		
1 centimetre	= 10 mm	= 0·394 inches		
1 metre	= 100 cm	= 39·4 inches *or*		
		3·28 feet		
1 kilometre	= 1000 m	= 1094 yards *or*		
		0·621 miles		
	Conversion factors			
	centimetres to inches		×	0·394
	metres to feet		×	3·28
	metres to yards		×	1·09
	kilometres to miles		×	0·621
Area				
1 square metre	= 10·8 square feet *or*			
	1·20 square yards			
1 hectare	= 2·47 acres			
	Conversion factors			
	square metres to square feet		×	10·8
	square metres to square yards		×	1·20
	hectares to acres		×	2·47

Other conversions

1 kilogramme per hectare	=	0·9 lb per acre *or* 14·2 oz per acre
1 litre per hectare	=	0·09 gallons per acre t2or 0·7 pints per acre
1 quintal per hectare	=	0·8 cwt per acre

Index

Index

References to tables are by paragraph number in italic

Index

Index

Reference to tables are by paragraph number in italic

Index

    References to tables are by paragraph number in italic

Index

Index

Reference to tables are by paragraph number in italic

Index

Index

Index

Index

bean (dwarf green) 2.036
  (dwarf, dried or navy) 2.028
  (runner) 2.044
cereals 1.011
Chrysanthemum segetum 1.011
+ dichlorprop 1.011
Galium aparine 1.011
+ MCPB, peas 2.293
+ MCPB, weed response *2.353*
oats 1.011
Polygonum spp. 1.011
Stellaria media 1.011
Tripleurospermum maritimum ssp.
    inodorum 1.011
weed response *2.353*
weed susceptibility *1.074*
winter and spring wheat 1.011
Benzoylprop-ethyl
Avena spp. 2.232
bean (broad and field) 2.016
grass crops 4.020
oil-seed rape 2.232
wheat 1.057
Berberis cv
dichlobenil *3.232*
lenacil *3.232*
simazine *3.232*
Bergenia cv
chloroxuron *3.217*
lenacil *3.217*
simazine *3.217*
Berula erecta, dalapon *10.025*
Betula cv
dichlobenil *3.232*
simazine *3.232*
Betula spp. (Birch)
ammonium sulphamate 8.074
2,4-D 8.034, 8.074
2,4-T 8.034, 8.074
mixtures 8.034
Biennial flowers, *see* Flowers, biennial
Bilberry, *see Vaccinium* spp.
Bindweed, Hedge, *see Calystegia sepium*
Birch, *see Betula* spp.
Bird's-foot-trefoil, Common, *see Lotus
    corniculatus*
Bistort, Amphibious, *see Polygonum
    amphibium*
Bistort, Common, *see Polygonum bistorta*
Bittercress, Hairy, *see Cardamine hirsuta*
Bittersweet, *see* Solanum duicamara
Black Bent, *see Agrostis gigantea*
Black-bindweed, *see Polygonum
    convolvulus*
Black-grass, *see Alopecurus myosuroides*
Black Medick, *see Medicago lupulina*
Black Mustard, *see Brassica nigra*
Blackberry
Agropyron repens 3.100
Atriplex patula 3.095, 3.099
bromacil 3.096
chlorpropham + fenuron 3.097
contact treatments 3.095–101

dalapon-sodium 3.102
dichlobenil 3.098
diuron 3.099
foliage-applied translocated treatments
    3.102–3
Galium aparine 3.100
MCPB-salt 3.103
paraquat 3.095
Polygonum aviculare 3.095, 3.099
propyzamide 3.100
Ranunculus repens 3.095
simazine 3.101
Blackcurrant
asulam 3.070
Atriplex patula 3.062, 3.066
Chenopodium album 3.062
chlorpropham 3.063
chlorpropham + fenuron 3.063
chlorthiamid 3.064
dalapon-sodium 3.071
dichlobenil 3.065
diuron 3.066
ethephon 13.038
foliage-applied translocated treatments
    3.070–2
Galium aparine 3.062, 3.067,
    3.068
lenacil 3.060, 3.069
MCPB-salt 3.072
paraquat 3.061
pentanochlor 3.062
Polygonum aviculare 3.062, 3.063,
    3.066, 3.069
Polygonum persicaria 3.062
propyzamide 3.067
Rumex spp. 3.070
simazine 3.059, 3.068
soil-applied residual treatments
    3.059–60, 3.063–9
Veronica spp. 3.068
Viola spp. 3.068
see also Fruit
Blackthorn, *see Prunus spinosa*
Bladder Campion, *see Silene vulgaris*
Booting, cereals 1.002, 15.004, 15.008
Borage, Yellow, *see Amsinckia intermedia*
Borates
total weed control, non-agricultural
    land *9.003*
mixture 9.022
Boron
total weed control, non-agricultural
    land 9.006
moss on hard surfaces 9.028
pre-surfacing 9.026
Botrytis 13.059
Bougainvillea, α-naphthaleneacetic acid
    13.046
Box, *see Buxus sempervirens*
Bracken, *see Pteridium aquilinum*
Brassica juncea (Indian Mustard)
2,4-D-amine *12.088*
MCPA-salt *12.088*

Index

Index

Broom, *see Sarothamnus scoparius*
Brussels sprout
  Agropyron repens 2.082, 2.093
  Alopecurus myosuroides 2.081, 2.092,
    2.101
  Avena spp. 2.081, 2.092, 2.101
  aziprotryne 2.088, 2.096
  desmetryne 2.089, 2.097
  di-allate 2.081, 2.092
  dinitramine 2.095
  nitrofen 2.085
  post-planting treatments 2.096−100
  pre-emergence contact treatments
    2.085−7
  pre-planting treatments 2.092−5
  pre-sowing treatments 2.081−3
  propachlor 2.086, 2.090, 2.098
  simazine 2.100
  sodium monochloroacetate 2.091
    2.099
  sulfallate + chlorpropham 2.087
  TCA 2.082, 2.093
  trifuralin 2.083, 2.094
Brussels sprout seed crops 4.049−51
  desmetryne 4.049
  paraquat 4.050
  simazine 4.051
Buckthorn, *see Rhamnus cartharticus*
Buddleia cv
  lenacil *3,232*
  simazine *3.232*
Bugle, *see Ajuga reptans*
Bugloss, *see Lycopsis arvensis*
Bulbils, *Oxalis,* spread and cultivation
  12.067
Bulbous crops 3.167−90
  see also specific bulbs and corms
Bulrush, *see Typha latifolia*
Bulrush, Lesser, *see Typha angustifolia*
Buphthalmum cv, simazine *3.217*
Burdock, Greater, *see Arctium lappa*
Burdock, Lesser, *see Arctium minus*
Bur-reed, Branched, *see Sparganium*
  erectum
Bur-reed, Unbranched, *see Sparganium*
  emersum
Burning of herbaceous vegetation
  7.011
Butterbur, *see Petasites hybridus*
Buttercup, bulbous, *see Ranunculus*
  bulbosus
Buttercup, Corn, *see Ranunculus arvensis*
Buttercup, Creeping, *see Ranunculus*
  repens
Buttercup, Hairy, *see Ranunculus sardous*
Buttercup, Meadow, *see Ranunculus acris*
Buxus cv
  lenacil *3.232*
  simazine *3.232*
Buxus sempervirens (Box)
  ammonium sulphamate *8.074*
  2,4-D *8.074*
  2,4,5-T *8.074*

Cabbage
  Agropyron repens 2.102, 2.114
  Alopecurus myosuroides 2.101
  Avena spp. 2.101, 2.109
  aziprotryne 2.108, 2.116, *2.122*
  carbetamide 2.109, 2.117
  desmetryne 2.110, 2.118, *2.122*
  di-allate 2.101, 2.113
  dinitramine *2.122*
  foliage-applied herbicides *2.122*
  nitrofen 2.105, *2.122*
  post-emergence treatments 2.108
  pre-emergence contact treatments
    2.104
  pre-emergence residual treatments
    2.105−7
  pre-planting treatments 2.113−5
  pre-sowing treatments 2.101−3
  propachlor 2.106, 2.111, 2.119, *2.122*
  simazine 2.121
  sodium monochloroacetate 2.112,
    2.120
  soil-applied herbicides *2.122*
  sulfallate + chlorpropham 2.107,
    2.122
  TCA 2.102, 2.114
  trifluraline 2.103, 2.115, *2.122*
Cabbage seed crops 4.049−51
  desmetryne 4.049
  paraquat 4.050
  simazine 4.051
Calabrese, *see* Cauliflower
Calamagrostis epigejos (Wood Small-reed)
  atrazine *8.037*
  chlorthiamid *8.037*
  dalapon *8.037*
  dichlobenil *8.037*
  forest *8.037*
  paraquat *8.037*
Callicarpa cv
  simazine *3.232*
Callistemon cv
  simazine *3.232*
Callitriche spp. (Water Starwort)
  chlorthiamid *10.025*
  dichlobenil *10.025*
  diquat *10.025*
  terbutryne *10.025*
Calluna cv
  dichlobenil *3.232*
  lenacil *3.232*
  simazine *3.232*
Calluna vulgaris (Heather)
  2,4-D, 2,4,5-T and mixtures, aerial
    application 8.034
  2,4-D *8.074*
  2,4,5-T *8.074*
  forests *8.035*, 8.070, 8.077, 8.080,
    8.084, 8.070
Calomel (mercurous chloride)
  amateur use 11.016
  moss control 11.016
    sports turf and lawns 6.030

References to tables are by paragraph number in italic

Index

Index

Index

References to tables are by paragraph number in italic

Index

Index

Index

Index

Index

Index

Index

Index

References to tables are by paragraph number in italic

Index

Index

References to tables are by paragraph number in italic

Index

Index

References to tables are by paragraph number in italic

Index

Index

Index

Index

Index

Index

References to tables are by paragraph number in italic

Index

Index

References to tables are by paragraph number in italic

Index

Index

Index

Index

Index

Index

Index

Index

References to tables are by paragraph number in italic

legumes, newly-sown *5.027*
Mentha arvensis 12.066
mixtures, *Achillea millefolium* in turf
  6.020
  barley 1.056
  cereals 1.046, 1.051
  grass 5.048
  turf 6.018
non-agricultural land 7.025, 7.026,
  7.029
oats 1.047–9
pear 3.056
Rumex spp. 5.089, 5.092, 5.093,
  5.094
Sagina procumbens in turf 6.023
Senecio jacobaea 5.100
Silene alba 12.079
Sonchus arvensis 12.081
Stellaria media 1.048
susceptibility in turf and lawns *6.016*
Tripleurospermum maritimum ssp.
  inodorum 1.049
turf 6.017, 6.018
  newly-sown 6.008
Urtica dioica 5.107, 7.029
wheat 1.047–9
windbreaks 3.154
Medicago lupulina (Black Medick)
  atrazine *3.156*
  chloroxuron *3.156*
  chlorpropham *2.139*
  chlorthiamid *3.156*
  2,4-D *6.016, 12.088*
  2,4-D + mecoprop, fenoprop,
    dichlorprop, or dicamba *6.016*
  dichlobenil *3.156*
  dinoseb *2.336*
  diuron *3.156*
  ioxynil 6.010
  ioxynil + mecoprop *6.016*
  linuron *2.139*
  linuron + monolinuron *2.336*
  MCPA *6.016, 12.088*
  MCPB *12.088*
  mecoprop *6.016, 12.088*
  pentanochlor *2.139*
  propyzamide *3.156*
  simazine *3.156*
  trifluralin *2.122*
  turf 6.010, *6.016*
Medicago sativa (Lucerne)
  bromacil *3.156*
  chlorthiamid *3.156*
  dalapon *5.010*
  dichlobenil *3.156*
  glyphosate *5.010*
  paraquat *5.010*
  terbacil *3.156*
Medick, Black, *see Medicago lupulina*
Melandrium album (White Campion)
  cycloate + lenacil *2.080*
Mentha cv
  lenacil *3.217*

trifluralin *3.217*
Mentha spp. (Mint)
  Agropyron repens 3.024
  chloroxuron 3.021
  contact treatment 3.020
  lenacil 3.022
  paraquat 3.020
  Poa annua 3.024
  simazine 3.023
  soil-applied residual treatments
    3.021–5
  terbacil 3.024, 3.025
Mentha aquatica (Water Mint)
  2,4-D-amine *10.025*
  dalapon *10.025*
Mentha arvensis (Corn Mint) 12.066
  2,4-D 12.066, *12.088*
  2,4-DB *12.088*
  dicamba 12.066
  dichlorprop 12.066, *12.088*
  MCPA 12.066, *12.088*
  MCPB *12.088*
  mecoprop 12.066, 12.088
  simazine 12.066
  TCA-sodium 12.066
Mentha spicata and *M. piperita, see*
  Mint
Mercurialis annua (Annual Mercury)
  chlorthiamid *3.156*
  dichlobenil *3.156*
Mercurous chloride, *see* Calomel
Mespiulus cv
  simazine *3.232*
Metamitron
  weed response *2.353*
Metasequoia cv
  simazine *3.232*
Methabenzthiazuron
  Alopecurus myosuroides 1.065
  barley 1.050, 1.064–5
  cereals 1.050, 1.064–5
  grass 5.052
  grass weeds 5.025
  grasses, seedbed 5.014
  herbage seed crops 4.011
  Matricaria spp. 1.050
  oats 1.050, 1.064–5
  Poa spp. 1.050
  Poa annua 1.064
  Poa trivialis 1.064
  Stellaria media 1.050
  susceptibility of annual weeds to, when
    applied for annual grass weeds
    1.074
  wheat 1.050, 1.064, 1.065
Methazole
  leek 2.189, 2.197
  onion 2.248, 2.260
  weed response *2.353*
Methoprotryne
  + simazine, *Alopecurus myosuroides*
    1.066
  + simazine, wheat 1.066

Methoprotryne—*cont.*
  susceptibility of annual weeds to, when
      applied for annual grass weeds
      1.074
Methyl bromide
  lawns and sports turf 6.005
Methyl esters of fatty acids
  apple 13.020–1
  azaleas 13.042
  nurserystock 13.042
  pear 13.031
  plum 13.037
Metobromuron
  potato 2.311, *2.336*
Metoxuron
  Alopecurus myosuroides 1.067
  Avena spp. 1.067
  barley 1.067
  bulbous crops 3.176
  carrot 2.133
  cereals 1.067
  Poa spp. 1.067
  + simazine, *Alopecurus myosuroides*
      1.068
  + simazine, barley 1.068
  Solium spp. 1.067
  susceptibility of annual weeds to, when
      applied for annual grass weeds
      1.074
  wheat 1.067
Metribuzin
  Polygonum convolvulus 2.328
  potato 2.319, 2.328, *2.336*
Mignonette, wild, *see Reseda lutea*
Milk development, cereals 1.002
Mind-your-own-business, *see Soleirolia*
      soleirolii
Mineral oils
  carrot 2.137, *2.139*
  celery 2.157
  coriander 2.165
  parsley 2.267
  parsnip 2.278
  umbelliferous crops *2.139*
Mint, *see Mentha* spp.
Mint nest *(Puccinia menthae)*
  paraquat 3.020
Mint, Water, *see Mentha aquatica*
Molinia caerulea (Purple Moor-grass)
  atrazine *8.037*
  chlorthiamid *8.037*
  dalapon *8.037*
  dichlobenil *8.037*
  forests *8.037*
  paraquat *8.037*
Monada cv
  lenacil *3.217*
  simazine *3.217*
Monolinuron
  bean (dwarf, dried or navy) 2.027
  bean (dwarf green) 2.034, 2.035
  leek 2.190, 2.198
  peas 2.287

  potato 2.314, 2.318, 2.320, 2.321,
      2.336
Monuron, total weed control, non-
      agricultural land *9.003,* 9.009
  mixtures 9.022
  moss on hard surfaces 9.028
  pre-surfacing 9.026
  susceptibility *9.029*
  total weed control, susceptibility,
      9.029
Moor-grass, Purple, *see Molinia caerulea*
Morfamquat, turf, newly-sown 6.010
Morus cv
  simazine *3.232*
Moss control
  cultural, amateur 11.014
  hard tennis court, asphalt, tiled or
      paved surfaces 9.028
  lawns, amateur 11.014–9
    calomel 11.016
    chloroxuron 11.017
    dichlorophen 11.018
    lawn sand 11.015
    phenols 11.019
  paths and hard surfaces 11.029–31
    chloroxuron 11.029
    dichlorphen 11.030
    phenols 11.031
  sports turf and lawns 6.027, 6.028
Mouldboard ploughing, role 12.017–8
Mountain Pine, *see Pinus mugo*
Mouse-ear, Common, *see Cerastium*
      holosteroides
Mouse-ear, Field, *see Cerastium arvense*
Mouse-ear Hawkweed, *see Hieracium*
      pilosella
Mouse-ear, Sticky, *see Cerastium*
      glomeratum
Mowing of herbaceous vegetation 7.011–3
Mugwort, *see Artemisia vulgaris*
Mulching, poplar plantations 8.098
Muscari
  chlorpropham 3.185
    + diuron 3.185
  linuron 3.186
    + chlorpropham 3.186
    + lenacil 3.186
  pyrazone 3.187
    + chlorbufam 3.187
Musk Thistle, *see Carduus nutans*
Mustard, Black, *see Brassica nigra*
Mustard, Hedge, *see Sisymbrium officinale*
Mustard, Indian, *see Brassica juncea*
Mustard, Treacle, *see Erysium*
      cheiranthoides
Mustard, White, *see Sinapis alba*
Myosotis arvensis (Field Forget-me-not)
  atrazine *3.156*
  bentazone *1.054, 2.353*
  bentazone + MCPB *2.353*
  bromoxynil + ioxynil *1.054*
  chlorbromuron *2.139*
  cyanazine *2.353*

Index

Index

References to tables are by paragraph number in italic

Index

Index

Pelargonium—*cont.*
  zonal, chlormequat chloride 13.063,
    13.065
  ethepon 13.064
Pennisetum cv
  simazine *3.217*
Pennycress, Field, *see Thlaspi arvense*
Pennywort, Marsh, *see Hydrocotyle*
  vulgaris
Penstemon cv, *3.217*
Pentachlorophenol
  lucerne seed crop 4.043
  red clover seed crop 4.043
  white clover seed crop 4.043
Pentanochlor
  Atriplex patula 3.062, 3.105
  blackcurrant 3.062
  carrot 2.134, *2.139*
  celery 2.154
  Chenopodium album 3.062
  cherry 3.105
  + chlorpropham, carrot 2.135
    celery 2.155
    parsley 2.269
    parsnip 2.270
  chrysanthemum 3.191, 3.241
  Fumaria officinalis 3.062, 3.105
  Galium aparine 3.062, 3.105
  gooseberry 3.076
  parsley 2.268
  parsnip 2.279
  plum 3.105
  Polygonum aviculare 3.062, 3.105
  Polygonum persicaria 3.062, 3.105
  redcurrant 3.126
  tomato 3.240
  umbelliferous crops *2.139*
Perennial flowers, *see* Flowers, perennial,
  and specific names
Perennial herbaceous plants, *see*
  Herbaceous plants
Perforate St. John's-wort, *see Hypericum*
  perforatum
Pernettya cv
  lenacil *3.232*
  simazine *3.232*
Perowskia cv
  simazine *3.232*
Persicaria, pale, *see Polygonum*
  lapathifolium
Petasitus hybridus (Butterbur)
  2,4-D-amine *12.088*
  2,4-DB-salt *12.088*
  MCPA-salt *12.088*
  MCPB-salt *12.088*
  mecoprop *12.088*
Petroleum distillate, forest seedbeds 8.010,
  8.012
Petunia
  chlorphonium chloride 13.067
Phalaris arundinacea (Reed Canary-grass)
  chlorthiamid *10.025*
  2,4-D-amine *10.025*

dalapon *10.025*
dichlobenil *10.025*
glyphosate 10.024, *10.025*
Pharmacy and Poisons Act 14.001, 14.002
Phenmedipham
  Avena fatua 4.063
  + barban, beet (fodder and sugar)
    2.066
  + barban, red beet 2.078
  beet/annual weeds *2.080*
  beet (fodder and sugar) 2.066, 2.067,
    2.070
  + lenacil, red beet 2.079
  Polygonum spp. 2.066, 4.063
  red beet 2.078
  Stellaria media 4.067
  strawberry 3.142, 3.143
  sugar beet seed crop 4.062–4, 4.067
  transplanted seed crops 4.075–6
  Tripleurospermum maritimum ssp.
    inodorum 4.063
Phenols
  amateur use 11.019, 11.031
  moss control 11.019
  paths and other hard surfaces 11.031
Philadelphus cv
  dichlobenil *3.232*
  lenacil *3.232*
  simazine *3.232*
Phillyrea cv
  simazine *3.232*
Phleum pratense (Timothy)
  asulam *5.010*
  dalapon 5.010
  glyphosate 5.010
  herbage seed crop 4.015
  linuron 4.026
  spraying *4.024*
  paraquat *5.010*
Phlox cv
  lenacil *3.217*
  simazine *3.217*
Photinia cv
  simazine *3.232*
Phragmites communis (Common Reed)
  12.070–2
  aminotriazole 12.072
  chlorthiamid *3.156, 10.025*
  2,4-D-amine *10.025*
  dalapon *10.025*
  dalapon-sodium 12.072
  dalapon-sodium + paraquat 10.015
  dichlobenil *3.156, 10.025*
  diquat *10.025*
  glyphosate 10.024, *10.025*
  maleic hydrazide 10.017
  paraquat *10.025*
Phyllocladus cv
  simazine *3.232*
Physocarpus cv
  simazine *3.232*
Picea cv
  dichlobenil *3.232*

Index

Index

References to tables are by paragraph number in italic

Index

Index

Index

Index

Index

References to tables are by paragraph number in italic

Index

Index

References to tables are by paragraph number in italic

Index

Index

References to tables are by paragraph number in italic

Index

Index

Index

References to text are by paragraph number in roman

Index

References to tables are by paragraph number in italic

Index

Index

Index

Index

Swards, established, grass only
  broad-leaved weeds 5.045, 5.065–110
  2,4-D-amine 5.047
  2,4-D-ester 5.047
  dalapon-sodium 5.050, 5.051
  dicamba 5.048
  ethofumesate 5.053
  grass weeds 5.050–53
  linuron 5.053
  management factors 5.044
  MCPA 5.048
  mecoprop 5.048
  methabenzthiazuron 5.042
  poisonous weeds 5.046
Swards, grass/legumes 5.054–9
  benazolin 5.056
  carbetamide 5.059
  2,4-D-amine 5.055
  2,4-D-ester 5.055
  2,4-DB 5.054, 5.055, 5.056
  dalapon-sodium 5.058
  dinoseb 5.054
  MCPA mixtures 5.055, 5.056
  MCPB 5.054, 5.055
Swards, *see also* Grass, Grassland
Swede
  Agropyron repens 2.342
  alachlor 2.351
  aminotriazole 2.342
  Cirsium spp. 2.342
  dinitramine 2.344
  nitrofen 2.349, 2.352
  post-emergence treatment 2.352
  pre-drilling treatments 2.347
  pre-emergence contact treatments
    2.348
  pre-emergence residual treatments
    2.349–51
  pre-sowing treatments 2.342–6
  propachlor 2.350
  Rumex spp. 2.342
  seed crop 4.052
  simazine 4.052
  TCA 2.345, 2.346
  trifluralin 2.347
Sweet corn
  atrazine 2.213, 2.216, 2.219, 2.221
  cyanazine 2.222
  2,4-D-amine 2.220
  2,4-D-amine + atrazine 2.221
  EPTC 2.214
  post-emergence treatments 2.219–22
  pre-emergence contact treatments 2.215
  pre-emergence residual treatments
    2.216
  pre-sowing treatments 2.213–4
  propachlor 2.217
  simazine 2.218
Sweet-grass, Floating, *see Glyceria fluitans*
Sweet-grass, Reed, *see Glyceria maxima*
Swine-cress, *see Coronopus squamatus*
Swine-cress, Lesser, *see Coronopus
    didymus*

Sycamore, *see Acer pseudoplatanus*
Sycopsis cv
  simazine *3.232*
Symphoricarpus cv
  lenacil *3.232*
  simazine *3.232*
Symphytum officinale (Common Comfrey)
  2,4-D-amine *12.088*
  2,4-DB-salt *12.088*
  MCPA-salt *12.088*
  MCPB-salt *12.088*
Syringa cv
  lenacil *3.232*
  simazine *3.232*

2,4,5-T
  Aegopodium podagraria 12.008
  apple 3.057
  Convolvulus arvensis 12.049
  forests 8.085, 8.086, 8.087–9
    application 8.034, *8.035*, 8.069
    conifer crops 8.079–83
    cut stumps 8.090
    tree injection 8.087–9
  neglected ground 11.072
  pear 3.057
  Rumex spp. 5.094
  total weed control, non-agricultural
    land *9.003*, 9.018
  Tussilago farfara 12.083
  Urtica dioica 5.107, 5.108, 5.109,
    7.029
  windbreaks 3.154
Tables, conversion 19.001–3
Take care when you spray 14.009
Tamarix cv
  dichlobenil *3.232*
Tanacetum vulgare (Tansy)
  2,4-D-amine *12.088*
  MCPA-salt *12.088*
Taraxacum officinale (Dandelion)
  asulam *5.111*
  atrazine *3.156, 9.029*
  bromacil *3.156, 9.029*
  chloroxuron *3.156*
  chlorpropham + fenuron *3.156*
  chlorthiamid *3.156*
  2,4-D *5.111*, 6.012, *6.016*, 11.006,
    12.088
  2,4-D mixtures 6.012, *6.016*
  2,4-DB-salt *12.088*
  2,4-DES *3.156*
  dicamba 6.012, *6.016*
  dichlobenil *3.156, 9.029*
  dichlorprop 6.012, *6.016, 12.088*
  diuron *3.156, 9.029*
  fenoprop 6.012, *6.016*
  glyphosate *9.029*
  ioxynil 6.012, *6.016*
  lawns, amateur control 11.006
  lenacil *3.156*
  MCPA *5.111*, 6.012, *6.016, 12.088*

References to tables are by paragraph number in italic

Index

Index

References to tables are by paragraph number in italic

Index

Index

References to tables are by paragraph number in italic

Index

Index

References to tables are by paragraph number in italic

Index

Index

References to tables are by paragraph number in italic

Index

Index

References to tables are by paragraph number in italic

Index